Social Movements
and American
Political Institutions

People, Passions, and Power: Social Movements, Interest Organizations and the Political Process
John C. Green, Series Editor

This series explores the people, activities, and institutions that animate the political process. The series emphasizes recent changes in that process—new actors, new movements, new strategies, new successes (or failures) to enter the political mainstream or influence everyday politics—and places these changes in context with the past and the future. Books in the series combine high quality scholarship with accessibility so that they may be used as core or supplementary texts in upper division political science, sociology, and communication studies courses. The series is consciously interdisciplinary and encourages cross-discipline collaboration and research.

Titles in the Series

The State of the Parties: The Changing Role of Contemporary American Politics, Second Edition, edited by John C. Green and Daniel M. Shea

After the Boom: The Politics of Generation X, edited by Stephen C. Craig and Stephen Earl Bennett

Multiparty Politics in America, edited by Paul S. Herrnson and John C. Green

The Social Movement Society: Contentious Politics for a New Century, edited by David S. Meyer and Sidney Tarrow

Social Movements and American Political Institutions, edited by Anne N. Costain and Andrew S. McFarland

Cyberpolitics: Citizen Activism in the Age of the Internet, Kevin A. Hill and John E. Hughes

Forthcoming

Social Movements Since the Sixties, edited by Jo Freeman and Victoria Johnson

The Changing Role of Labor Unions in American Politics, Herbert B. Asher, Randall B. Ripley, Karen Snyder, and Eric Heberlig

Social Movements and American Political Institutions

edited by
ANNE N. COSTAIN
and
ANDREW S. McFARLAND

ROWMAN & LITTLEFIELD PUBLISHERS, INC.
Lanham • Boulder • New York • Oxford

ROWMAN & LITTLEFIELD PUBLISHERS, INC.

Published in the United States of America
by Rowman & Littlefield Publishers, Inc.
4720 Boston Way, Lanham, Maryland 20706

12 Hid's Copse Road
Cumnor Hill, Oxford OX2 9JJ, England

British Library Cataloguing in Publication Information Available

Library of Congress Cataloging-in-Publication Data

Social movements and American political institutions / edited by Anne
   N. Costain and Andrew S. McFarland.
       p.   cm. — (People, passions, and power)
   Includes bibliographical references and index.
       ISBN 0-8476-8357-5 (cloth : alk. paper). — ISBN 0-8476-8358-3
 (pbk.: alk. paper)
       1. Lobbying—United States.   2. Social movements—Political
   aspects—United States.   3. United States—Politics and government.
   I. Costain, Anne N., 1948–   .   II. McFarland, Andrew S., 1940–   .
   III. Series.
   JK1118.S685   1998
   324'.4'0973—dc21   98-13239
                                                                  CIP

ISBN 0-8476-8357-5 (cloth : alk. paper)
ISBN 0-8476-8358-3 (pbk. : alk. paper)

Printed in the United States of America

♾ ™ The paper used in this publication meets the minimum requirements of American
National Standard for Information Sciences—Permanence of Paper for Printed Library
Materials, ANSI Z39.48-1984.

Anne Costain dedicates this book to Doug and Lynne Costain.

*Andrew McFarland dedicates this book to the memory of
Susan Mary Sawyer.*

Contents

Introduction

Anne N. Costain and Andrew S. McFarland

Social movements—such as those for civil rights, women, the environment, Protestant fundamentalism—are a great force in American politics. Social movements clearly bring about major change in our country. As such, they should be an important area of study for political scientists interested in American politics.

Political institutions shape social movements, and these movements sometimes, in turn, shape the institutions. Most political scientists are generally familiar with how the paradigmatic American social movement, civil rights, was molded by actions of national, state, and local governments, by presidential decrees, by congressional legislation, and by federal court decisions. After a bit of consideration, one also sees that the civil rights movement had a profound impact on political institutions, as in the increased assumption of authority by the federal courts, the altered filibuster rules of the Senate, changes in support for the political parties, and the use of executive power by the president. For a better understanding of politics and political institutions in America, students need to generalize from this and other examples about the role of social movements.

Unfortunately for such an understanding, the relationship between social movements and political institutions has been split between two disciplines. Sociologists study the origin and development of social movements. Political scientists study the eventual effects of movements on politics, such as the passage of legislation or the issuance of judicial decisions. The sociologist rarely looks to see the impact movements have on lobbying, elections, and other political events. The political scientist infrequently generalizes about the relationships between political events and institutional change or how the development of social movements affects such events. The result is a truncated view of the world, a distortion in our understanding of American politics.

Within the last twenty years, the study of social movements has been hugely transformed. Researchers in the social movement field are confident that they are making great advances. Their field is a booming area of research, as evidenced by the long list of references in this volume. Yet, most students of American politics and political institutions know little of this new scholarship, even though it might be usefully applied to American political data.

The purpose of this book is to help correct this problem. We want to bring together the study of social movements with the study of American political institutions. Analyzing the relationships between movements and American political institutions enhances our understanding of politics. In this volume, we have collected a number of essays to demonstrate how this can be done. The authors all participate in the theoretical discourse of applying social movement theory to American politics, although they may emphasize different aspects of these recent theoretical developments. Our purpose is not to endorse one particular theoretical package. Scholars of American politics can deal with such questions later. At this time, we want to demonstrate how social movement theory challenges existing perspectives on the study of American institutions by adding new questions and alternative assumptions to the field.

The chapters in the book are organized to move from examining broad questions about how theoretical understandings of American institutions might be transformed by including movements, to more focused applications of current social movement theory to studies of particular institutions. The first section of the book opens as McFarland (chap. 1) traces the decades-long dialog over the adequacy of pluralism as a theory of American democracy, arguing that incorporation of social movements enriches the debate by recasting some of its key questions. Sidney Tarrow (chap. 2) reaches back into the early period of American state building to offer a reinterpretation of Alexis de Tocqueville's classic book, *Democracy in America*. Tarrow suggests that Tocqueville misjudged the primary character of American politics because he did not recognize that political institutions in the United States were fostering a kind of contentious politics that would frequently result in powerful social movements incubated by the state. Finally, in this section sociologist Paul Burstein (chap. 3), after reviewing the different terminology and questions applied to the study of social movements, interest groups, and political parties by political scientists and sociologists, challenges both groups to admit that much of the behavior they are studying overlaps, that their terms are imprecise and blur more than illuminate differences, and that a common set of questions spanning all three groups may be more productive than the current course of scholarship.

The second section of the book considers how American social movements form and emerge. Claude Dufour (chap. 4) examines the gay rights movement in the competitive contexts of Chicago city and Illinois state politics. He demonstrates how activists used elections and the American federal structure to force recognition from a generally unsympathetic political establishment. In chapter 5, sociologists Daniel Cress and David Snow take one of the groups that would seem least likely to be able to organize effectively, the homeless. They show that although the standard types of resources accepted as increasing political influence (e.g., money, strong organization, etc.) were significantly related to a group's success, a wide range of other resources can also facilitate mobilization and make success more likely. Last, Lee Ann Banaszak (chap. 6) compares the development of the woman suffrage movements in Switzerland and the United States. She finds that even with similar institutional and tactical opportunities for movements to gain political influence, these may not be sufficient, if activists and leaders fail to perceive circumstances as providing genuine opportunities for success.

In the book's third section, political parties and electoral politics are analyzed as institutionalized parts of American politics that both shape and constrain movement activity. John Green, James Guth, and Clyde Wilcox (chap. 7) use the case of the Christian Right's bid to broaden its influence within state Republican parties to argue how complex and subtle the interaction is between party and movement. Applying a variety of sociological theories of movement development and testing them empirically, they conclude that each reveals part of the experience of the Christian Right but that none adequately models the strengths and limitations that inhere in the political role of movements. Jeffrey Berry and Deborah Schildkraut (chap. 8) trace the electoral activity of citizen movements. Although they use the language of social movement research less than many of the other authors, they describe a relatively successful effort to organize the general public to influence politics. They find that as political opportunities expand, features of the political landscape change in response, with this change producing additional alterations in the institutions of politics.

The presidency and Congress are the focus of Part 4. Douglas Imig (chap. 9) examines another group that is unlikely in conventional political science scholarship to wield much clout: the poor. He shows how, over time, poor peoples' movements interacted with presidential administrations, both seizing and losing initiative, depending on the levels of political opportunity available to them in different periods. The dynamics of social movement activism are such, as Imig reveals them, that both conventionally supportive and hostile executive actions may expand the clout of movement-linked interests. Anne Costain (chap. 10) notes the historic correlation between the appearance of mobilized women's movements in America and national legislation changing public policy toward women. She provides empirical evidence that the level of mobilization of a women's lobby is linked to legislative success and that it is possible to sustain influence even following a fall in movement activity. This suggests that the intensity of social movement politics may provide the wedge to claim a place on the national legislative agenda. Douglas Costain and James Lester (chap. 11) trace the evolution of environmentalism over the past century, focusing on the interactions the movement has with Congress. Environmentalism has emphasized both conventional lobbying tactics and grassroots mobilization, depending upon congressional receptiveness to each set of tactics across time.

Part 5 shifts the focus to the courts. Michael McCann's chapter 12 makes the point that clear victories in court are not necessary for effective legal mobilization to occur. Drawing on evidence from movements ranging from civil rights, women, and wage equity to animal rights, he argues that the power of law to increase a group's leverage can shake existing hierarchies, providing greater opportunity for maneuver by challenging groups. Oneida Meranto in "Litigation as Rebellion" (chap. 13) picks up this theme, examining how courts were used by American Indians after other means of acquiring political power, including violent protest, failed. Tribes have fought to increase their legal sovereignty as a way to protect their interests from state and national intrusion. Laura Woliver (chap. 14) has looked at the amicus curiae (or friend of the court) briefs filed by movement groups favoring legalized abortion and those opposing it. She demonstrates that the language used to influence the court by each side is intended to frame the broad issues at stake in ways compatible with each side's preferences. Because legal language rings so strongly with entitlement to rights and protections, it becomes a logical battlefield for groups struggling to have their understandings of abortion policy prevail.

The concluding section raises several broad implications of integrating social movements into theories of American politics. Doug McAdam (chap. 15) observes that successful social movements jump national boundaries easily. He argues that integrating movements into the study of American politics creates a natural opening to incorporate international interests into this research. Mark Lichbach (chap. 16) groups most current theories into two camps, one offering a more structural and the other a more individualized view of political change. Using the widely studied case of the American civil rights movement, he demonstrates how each side has contributed to understanding this movement. Finally, as a conclusion, we draw together the work presented here and summarize its implications for the integration of research on social movements with study of American political institutions.

Part 1

Theories of American Politics and Social Movements

1

Social Movements and Theories of American Politics

Andrew S. McFarland

The theory of social movements and the study of American politics and political institutions have come together as a recent development in a forty-year-long theoretical dialog, referred to as pluralism. This is the discussion, beginning with the rejection of C. Wright Mills's power elite theory by Dahl and his students in the late 1950s, that has continued in two further stages (Mills 1956; Dahl 1958; Polsby 1963). After the first stage, called simply pluralism, came a second stage, called here multiple-elite pluralism, which itself has been followed by a third stage of discussion, which I call post-pluralism. The study of social movements has become closely tied to the theory of post-pluralism. Here let us review the first two stages of the pluralism discussion to understand this development.

Mills (1956) surprised the academic world with his eloquent statement that America is actually ruled by a power elite, consisting of a few hundred individuals at the top of the national security decision-making apparatus, plus corporate and Pentagon elements referred to by others as "the military-industrial complex." Because these few hundred persons made the life-and-death decisions during a Cold War era, and because they made decisions regarding the potential expansion of American power as a new form of impe-rialism, they had power over the issues mattering most. A parallel argument was made by Floyd Hunter (1953), who argued that Atlanta was ruled by a corporate elite, and, by implication, so were most other American cities.

Robert Dahl and his students objected that Mills and Hunter had based their observations on analytical criteria extraneous to the political process and that they themselves had not conducted empirical studies of the working of political institutions on important issues (Wolfinger 1960; Dahl 1961; Polsby 1963). Accordingly, Dahl (1961) conducted a study of power in New Haven, Connecticut (published as *Who Governs?*), and found that power on important issues was not controlled by an elite but was instead dispersed, under the control of many persons. Dahl's students conducted similar deci-sion-making studies of other cities and of national political institutions, such as the U.S. Congress, and came to similar conclusions (Polsby 1963). Dahl's pluralism became something like a paradigm in the study of American politics and political institutions during the 1960s, although some political scientists studying American politics disagreed with this formulation.

However, this paradigm did not last long, and it was overthrown for at least two major theoretical reasons. First, it was almost immediately pointed out that Dahl's studies may have dealt with power on issues on the political agenda, but pluralism did not have a good theoretical approach to explaining why some issues were on the agenda and others were not. To understand power in American politics, the critics Peter Bachrach and Morton Baratz (1962) argued, one needed to understand the politics of agenda formation. (Social movement theory obviously does this, but that comes later.)

The other cause for the overthrow of Dahl's paradigm was Mancur Olson's (1965) theory of "the logic of collective action." He observed that public policies offer collective benefits, so that if one person or organization in a collectivity gets a benefit, all such persons or units must do so. If the state provides national security, it benefits all citizens. If the state provides a special benefit by establishing import quotas for sugar, thereby raising the price of sugar, this policy benefits all sugar producers, not just those who may have contributed to a sugar lobby. In other words, it is irrational for a person or an organization to contribute to a lobby, if such persons/organizations will receive the collective benefit from it anyway, even if they do not contribute. It follows that, if one assumes rational self-interest motivation, many lobbies representing widely shared interests will not be organized, because citizens and organizations will prefer the course of being "free riders," benefiting from a collective good without contributing to the interest group lobbying for that good.

But even worse from the standpoint of Dahl's pluralism, small groups of oligopolistic corporations or other units can be expected to organize, because it would be in the rational self-interest of a single unit to contribute, because the cost of the contribution would be offset by the probability of gaining the collective benefit. Further, in the case of a small number of units, the contributors are normally able to pressure a noncontributor to prevent free riding. Olson's theory states, then, that the few, well organized politically, will frequently defeat the many, not well organized politically. The "many," of course, is a synonym for the consumers, or the taxpayers, or the general public.

Making assumptions similar to those of Olson's, writers such as Lowi (1969) or Schattschneider (1960) observed that while power was dispersed in America, Mills hence being incorrect, such dispersed power was not widely shared, as Dahl had argued. Instead, as this new theory of pluralism assumed center stage during the 1970s, it argued that power in America was dispersed into the hands of multiple separate elites, each tending to control a particular area of public policy, ruling it as a subgovernment, sometimes called an "iron triangle," or referred to as "capturing" a single policy area. In other words, there was a *pluralism of multiple elites*.

Such a particular elite often consisted of a coalition of oligopolistic corporations, a few members of Congress on a key committee, and a governmental agency or regulatory commission. It was not difficult to organize and maintain such a coalition in the pursuit of its own interest, normally contradictory to the purposes of consumers or the general public, which remained largely unorganized as Olson's theory described. Multiple-elite pluralists assumed that such policy areas as trucking, airline commerce, nuclear power generation, banking interest rates, regulation of grazing on government land, the distribution of federal land-conservation funds, the protection of prices of sugar, peanuts, oranges, and other agricultural products, and the acquisition of airplanes and other expensive hardware for the military were each under the control of a separate mini-elite in the overall system of multiple-elite pluralism. Each mini-elite pursued its own self-interest, while the interests of consumers, taxpayers, or the general public were not represented in such systems, known as subgovernments (McFarland 1987; McFarland 1992).

This multiple-elite pluralism was an attractive theory. It postulated a dispersal of power in a fragmented political system, yet it was critical of that system, arguing that major reforms are necessary in the interests of widespread publics. It seemed predictive of outcomes in many areas of the policy-making process. But this theory of pluralism, too, did not hold center stage for a long time, for by 1980 it started to be replaced by observations constituting post-pluralism.

The major problem for multiple-elite pluralism was that indication of subgovernments or iron triangles seemed to be more frequent in the 1950s than in the 1970s (Wilson 1980; Walker 1991; Heinz et al. 1993). Deregulation swept away the iron triangle coalitions in such areas as trucking, airline commerce, and nuclear power policy. In such agricultural areas as tobacco and smoking policy, powerful forces appeared challenging the formerly ruling coalition. And, in such areas as sugar import quotas, in which the quota was abolished and then reinstated, it appeared as if the ruling mini-elite might wax and wane over time, thereby necessitating a theoretical development to account for such fluctuations.

Further, in some new areas of public policy, such as environmental regulation, the multiple-elite hypothesis did not work, for rather than being taken over by an issue-area elite, dominated by corporations, environmental policy has been characterized by continuing battles among businesses and coalitions of environmental and health groups. A typical situation is the regulation of pesticides: scores of interest groups have formed a coalition to oppose the business point of view (Bosso 1987).

First-stage pluralism had sometimes used the term *countervailing power* to refer to the organization of groups to oppose the interests of oligopolistic corporations (Galbraith 1952). The second-stage pluralists had posited rule by numerous separate mini-elites, each controlling its own policy area. But empirical research after 1980 showed that such mini-elites are frequently opposed by well-organized interest groups and political coalitions, providing a type of countervailing power to the subgovernments or iron triangles. Earlier pluralists had sometimes mistakenly implied that countervailing power was organized almost automatically and would almost automatically balance the excessive power of oligopolistic organization. However, no one after Olson's work believes in an automatic quality in the organization of groups. Where, then, is this countervailing power coming from?

The third stage of the forty-year pluralism discussion, post-pluralism, has four answers to this question. The description and analysis of such countervailing power is something that separates post-pluralism from its predecessor. Three sources of countervailing power are standard stock in political science; the fourth is, of course, social movements.

A first source of countervailing power is part of the early pluralist theory: well-organized economic elites often take opposing sides and check one another (Galbraith 1952). For instance, sugar growers lobby for an import quota, but Coca-Cola and candy makers lobby on the other side.

Hugh Heclo (1978) proposed a second source of countervailing power: issue networks. These may be seen as communications networks among numerous and various persons concerned with some area of public policy. For instance, on the issue of tobacco policy, the issue network contains not only growers and manufacturers but scientists, public health specialists, trial lawyers, politicians, and journalists. In such an expansive issue network, no mini-elite can control how the public issues are framed and where and when such issues become part of the political process.

A third source of countervailing power is patronage. As a reply to Olson's theory of the logic of collective action, Jack Walker (1991) observed that many groups have a patron, which pays for the costs of organizing and some of the costs of maintaining the group. Research indicates that the most important patron is actually the U.S. federal government, which has often started groups through organizing conferences and advisory boards. The federal government subsequently has supported groups through grants and subsidies. Other patrons include foundations, preexisting organizations spinning off new groups, and wealthy individuals.

But social movements are certainly a very important source of countervailing power to the mini-elites of the second-stage theory. Such groups as environmental interest groups, African-American interest groups, women's groups, and Christian fundamentalist groups are important actors in the political process and capable of challenging the influence of established subgovernmental coalitions. The existence of such groups, originally developing from social movements, is a fundamental point in the post-pluralist stage of this theoretical dialog. Hence, the scholar of American politics and political institutions must ask questions such as these: How did social movements develop these interest groups? (See chap. 2–6.) Did the political process itself provide political opportunities for these groups to develop, and then to affect politics in a sort of feedback mechanism? (Social movement scholar Doug McAdam, as in chap. 15, is well known for addressing this question in his political process theory of movements.) What role did cultural definitions of personal identity play in creating movements and these interest groups, and can we use concepts of rational self-interest in analyzing this? (See chap. 16.) How do the countervailing power lobbies, based on a social movement, relate to the more radical sectors of the movement? Do these two enhance one another or work at cross-purposes?

To address these questions, one must resort to social movement theory. But such a theory cannot simply focus on the more radical and antiinstitutional facets of movements. Social movement theory useful to the student of American political institutions must consider how a movement enters the political, legal, and public policy processes. Happily, over the last twenty years, social movement scholars have developed such a theory, although various scholars may emphasize different concepts within it. Sociologists John McCarthy and Meyer Zald (1977) stress the importance of analyzing how movements mobilize resources—how movements deal with the problems of the logic of collective action. Other sociologists such as Charles Tilly (1978) and Doug McAdam (1982) emphasize that the political process itself might have much to do with the genesis of social movements, as the political process might be analyzed as providing varying *political opportunities* for movements to develop. Finally, the political process may encourage or discourage the definition of new personal identifications, as, for instance, the federal system may enhance the development of "rights" movements or religious movements, through providing them with local victories and power bases (see chaps. 2, 4, 6, and 7). This last point can be discussed in light of movement theory's concepts of resource mobilization and of political opportunities for movement development.

Social movement theory also joins post-pluralist theory in providing a systematic treatment of how many issues become part of the political agenda. As noted, the lack of a theory of the agenda was a major reason for the decline of Dahl's pluralist paradigm. And while the second-stage theorists had much to add in observing the problems of collective action and the existence of subgovernments, they had little to add to a theory of the political agenda. One might say, however, that the concepts of issue networks and patronage, dealing with the question of how interest groups form, are also useful in understanding how new issues get on the political agenda: from issue networks or sponsorship by patrons.

The major answer to the agenda question in postpluralism is Kingdon's (1984) events-process theory. Following Cohen, March, and Olsen's (1972) garbage-can theory of complex organization, Kingdon describes issues as appearing on the agenda when events streams defining social problems are joined by politicians to other streams defining social solutions, during times when politicians are forced by circumstances to act on new questions. This concept is similar to the political process theory of social movements, in which we might say that movement leaders have defined a social problem, have linked it with proposed social solutions, and are looking for an opportunity to get the state to implement their proposed policies.

We can say then that a second important link between the theory of social movements and the study of political institutions is in providing a treatment of which issues are subject to decision making by these institutions. The theory of post-pluralism, whether called neopluralism or not identified with a label, is the inheritor to the forty years of discussion called pluralism. As such, it is a major perspective for political scientists in understanding the workings of American politics and political institutions. Post-pluralism rejects elite theory but accepts collective action theory and its positing of the difficulty of organizing political groups on an equal basis. As such, post-pluralism acknowledges that the appearance of subgovernments or iron triangles is an inherent problem in American politics. But this problem is mitigated by the appearance of countervailing power to the mini-elites. Such power appears in a fragmented way, within separate areas of political action, as a result of opposing interests of economic groups, the existence of issue networks, and the actions of patrons. But social movements also are an important source of countervailing power to subgovernments. Furthermore, social movements greatly add to our understanding of which issues get onto the political agenda. Consequently, the theory of social movements is becoming a basic, integral part of how political scientists, specializing in American politics, understand the workings of American political institutions.

Structural Theories and Social Movement Theory

The pluralism discussion, at the center of the study of American political institutions for forty years, might be called a theory of the political process. It originated in distinction to elite theories that concentrated on identifying elites without studying specific examples of political decision making. The pluralists, on the other hand, insist that one should examine cases of political action, involving individual politicians, elections, lobbying, legislation, pol-

icy formulation and implementation by the executive branch, and the interactions of political actors with the judicial system.

Studies of the political process and its effects on institutions may constitute the greater part of the research of political scientists studying American
institutions. Sometimes, however, political scientists publish research having
a long-run cultural and social perspective and emphasize the effects of such
general structural factors on the more immediate political process (see, e.g.,
chaps. 2 and 15). Such theories might be called structural theories.

Structural theories may be cyclical, or they may point to historical constraints that do not operate in cycles. A well-known cyclical theory of American politics is the theory of Arthur Schlesinger, Sr., and Arthur Schlesinger,
Jr., that American politics is characterized by alternating cycles of reform
and conservatism. Another theory, by Stephen Skowronek (1993), emphasizes cycles of presidential leadership in forming new political coalitions
that weaken as decades pass (discussed later). Finally, Louis Hartz (1955)
put forth a theory that a relatively stable political culture structures the
American political process (McFarland 1991; Schlesinger, 1986).

The Schlesingers' political cycles theory regards American political history as cycling between periods of political/social reform and periods of
conservatism, at least during the twentieth century and perhaps back to the
American Revolution (Schlesinger, 1986). My own version of this outlook
is found in Table 1.1, in which the conservative or traditional pole is referred
to as "business," meaning a time when business interests regain power over
reformers (McFarland 1991: 269).

If this structural theory is, on the whole, accurate, then it can be fruitfully joined to theories of social movements. For instance, during the reform
periods, we can hypothesize that political process variables (political opportunities) will encourage "rights" movements and "identity" movements.
During the more traditional, business-dominated eras, political process variables will encourage the appearance of traditional nationalistic and religious
movements, as well as countermovements opposing the legacy of previous
rights and identity movements. This can be a predictive theory, in that we
can predict movements appearing in a previous historical period will reap-
pear during the next appropriate cycle, although the content of movement
ideology may change. (For instance, nativist movements differ in specific
ideology and targets.)

Social movements with political cycles provide a theory of the political
agenda, which is thus useful to political scientists of the school called here
recent political process theorists. Currently it seems that traditionalist religious movements, nativist groups (militias), and countermovement ideology
is having a major effect on the political agenda, hence on issue networks,
and on Kingdon's problem and solution streams (chap. 7). Charles E. Lindblom's (1977) argument about the dominance of business over the political

Table 1.1
American Political Cycles

Reform	Transitional	Business
CV, AA higher		*CV, AA* lower
		1890s National corporations Issue area laissez-faire Monopolies Jim Crowism
1901–14 Progressive Era Professional groups "Public interest" Muckrakers Antitrust, etc. Regulatory commissions	**1915–18** World War I	**1919–33** Red Scare 1918–19 "Normalcy" "The dollar decade" Cooptation of progressive government agencies Klan revival
1933–39 New Deal Unions (Wagner Act) Leftist social movements New federal agencies	**1940–48** World War II and aftermath	**1949–61** McCarthyism Tocquevillean consensus Korean War Eisenhower Heyday of business capture (see Stigler, McConnell, Lowi, etc.) "What's good for General Motors . . ."
1961–74 The sixties (may begin ca. 1963) Civil rights Public interest groups Feminism Vietnam controversy Issue networks more powerful New regulation Environmentalism Warren court	**1974–80** Presidents Ford and Carter Deregulation begins Business regroups (see Vogel) Traditionalist movements begin Burger court	**1980–Present** Reagan-Bush presidencies Business power, but more checks from *CV, AA* Deregulation Markets and entrepreneurs Antiabortion Fundamentalists Rehnquist court Clinton centrism

CV = countervailing power groups; *AA* = autonomous agencies of government.

Source: Andrew S. McFarland, "Interest Groups and Political Time: Cycles in America," *British Journal of Political Science* 21 (July 1991), p. 269.

agenda seems much stronger during the time periods referred to as "business."

Political cycles theory does not imply that reform is wiped out during business periods, nor, obviously, is business wiped out during reform periods. Apparently, the surge of citizen groups organizing that began in the 1960s has the effect of providing a greater degree of countervailing power to the countermovements during the succeeding reform era. For instance, environmentalist lobbies checked President Reagan's attempts to deregulate in the environmental field and are likely to have a similar effect in opposing current deregulation efforts. But the reverse is also true—the countermobilization of business lobbies and traditionalist lobbies will brake the effects of many future liberal reform measures.

Social movements may provide a mechanism to explain the political cycles. During the last few years of the business period, a number of political/social policies may strike potential movement activists as extreme. When they act to change the situation, probably abetted by the minority faction of politicians of the time, they find that their platform is favorably regarded by the mainstream, middle-class voter. The civil rights movement disrupted the 1950s business era, and populism disrupted the 1890s era of business dominance, and so forth. On the other hand, traditionalist religious movements disrupted the recent liberal reform era, influencing millions to vote Republican.

The Schlesingers themselves refer to the reform eras as times of public participation, while the conservative eras are characterized by a return to private activity, such as economic activity (Schlesinger, 1986). This description is intended to depict both the general activity of government and politics and the incentives of single individuals. One should remember, however, that traditionalist movements too represent a turning from private to public activity by millions of persons, such as evangelical Protestants. Yet, the general tone of government and politics during such periods is indeed private in that the marketplace is preferred to the activities of government. The contradiction of such periods, which is likely to cause the end of the present business era, is that traditionalist religious groups often prefer to expand the scope of government to enforce policies enforcing public morality. Such policies are not well regarded by political forces representing the business community.

Skowronek's Political Cycles

Stephen Skowronek's (1993) *The Politics Presidents Make* is now considered the leading book about the presidency, but it is also a theory of American politics in general. Skowronek observes that five presidents—

Jefferson, Jackson, Lincoln, Franklin Roosevelt, and Reagan—were master politicians who created and led new political coalitions, setting the general tone for the American presidency and national politics for at least a subsequent generation. However, after the presidential administration of these master politicians, their supporting political coalitions were rent with conflict, and this governing coalition became less and less effective. Presidents following the original coalition builder are less effective and have less historical reputation than he, until the final president in the coalition cycle finds himself in a very weak position due to the disintegration of the governing coalition (J. Q. Adams, Buchanan, Hoover, Carter). Then, a new master politician appears, who creates a new governing coalition, and the presidential cycle of coalition decay begins again (Skowronek 1993).

Aside from the recency of publication of *The Politics Presidents Make*, this theory is currently interesting since it implies that Clinton's administration is not the start of a new reform era but is, in Skowronek's terms, comparable to the Cleveland and Eisenhower presidencies. In these presidencies, the out-party captures the presidency, yet its president does not make important new policy departures but compromises with the ethos of the governing coalition.

Skowronek's book, in general, discusses the interaction of the president with congressional and party leaders and has little to say about social movements. But one connection seems important. Social movements had a major role in the decline of the New Deal coalition, as the black civil rights and other "rights" movements created conflict within the Democratic party. Similarly, within the Reagan coalition, Christian fundamentalism is creating conflicts that are difficult to resolve and might prove to be the most important factor in the inevitable break-up of this coalition (see chap. 7).

But, in Skowronek's terms, social movements are not a direct cause of the formation of a new governing coalition. Instead, an especially talented political leader creates the new coalition, negotiating with other politicians and presenting a platform and perspective very appealing to a strong majority of voters. The new coalition is explained by directly political variables. Similarly, political factors brought down the long-lasting Lincoln/Republican coalition in 1932, and not a social movement. For the time being, let us leave open the questions of whether Jacksonian egalitarianism was a social movement bringing down the Jefferson coalition and how important abolitionism was in bringing down the Jacksonian coalition.

Still, the role of social movements in dividing the New Deal coalition, and possibly dividing the Reagan coalition, is a very intriguing question, since it yields a prediction of instability. Of further interest, the argument emerges that McAdam's political process variables (political opportunities) in one form destroy the very political process in which they originate, as middle-of-the-road voters come to reject social movements encouraged by a governing coalition. For instance, white working-class voters turned to Reagan's coalition, partly because of resentment against the rights movements. The parallel observation may apply to the Reagan coalition, if conflict develops between religious fundamentalists and relatively secular advocates of business interests. The addition to Skowronek's theory, then, is that presidential governing coalitions contribute to their own destruction by encouraging social movements that eventually divide the coalition itself.

Hartz's Theory of the Liberal Consensus

The late political theorist Louis Hartz's (1955) *The Liberal Tradition in America* states a basic theory of American politics, which has been influential at Harvard and at the University of Chicago, among other places. The basic question Hartz tried to answer was, Why have socialism, communism, and organized fascism been less important in America than in Western Europe? Hartz's answer lay in the settlement of America. The eighteenth-century settlers were preponderantly egalitarian in values (as Tocqueville observed in 1830), while European institutions of aristocracy were not transplanted to America. This meant that America did not develop the social conflicts and types of class solidarity resulting from the efforts of the bourgeoisie to limit the nobility, subsequently feeding into tension between the new capitalist order and its workers. Americans, on the other hand, saw themselves as individuals, not in terms of class or group solidarity. Further, Americans subscribed to the classical values of Lockean liberalism: a strong adherence to political and social equality, but not to economic equality; a belief in limiting the power of government, especially a central government; and, in particular, an adherence to limiting the scope of activity of government. In short, liberal values implied more restrictions on the scope of public activity, and a greater latitude for private activity.

Hartz's notion of the strength and extent of liberal values (in the European sense) helps in understanding the goals of major American social movements in the twentieth century. Recently we have had many rights movements, social movements of those proclaiming their political and social equality to the others in the society. These movements assert that all individuals have basic human rights in society. While rights movements may develop ideas of group solidarity, such group-oriented norms seem to be part of the movement struggle for equality and then dissipate as the society acknowledges a new set of rights. For instance, the solidarity of the church-based movement under the Rev. Martin Luther King later gave way to interest group bargaining, electoral competition among individual candidates, and affirmative action for individual job applicants, construction companies, and so forth.

Hartz's concepts seem more relevant than ever because they also predict that important social movements will develop from individuals seeking to limit the power of government, especially the central government. After the Oklahoma City bombing, we all have come to recognize that a number of relatively small but significant social movements have formed as individuals, reflecting an extreme form of liberal values, strike out against a federal government they believe is destructive of the fundamental rights of the individual.

Hartz predicted a period of great intellectual, cultural, and political change as the island of American liberalism increasingly dealt with other values and cultures in the process of "globalization" (see chap. 15). However, this would not occur during the time of the Cold War with the Soviet Union, because the threat of solidaristic communism, an ideology quite opposite to American values, would act to maintain American adherence to liberal individualism. But the Cold War is now ended, so Hartz (1955) seemed to imply a period in which some Americans would consider solidaristic values, thereby provoking a social clash with traditional individualists (Brzezinski and Huntington 1963).

Such a cultural turmoil is now retarded by the fact that most countries are moving toward liberal, individualist values and away from solidaristic or Marxist values, at least in their governmental policies. In the last few years, Americans have not experienced a basic challenge to liberal values as the world impinges on us in the post-Soviet era. No social movement has emerged among American workers, for example, for the adoption of European medical, vacation, and unemployment compensation systems.

Unexpectedly, the major challenge to individualist values has come from the environmental movement, which in its first stage has been domestic, although recently it has moved to an international focus (see chap. 11). Environmentalism is based on such ideas as the tragedy of the commons, individuals pursuing their own self-interest destroying the greater good of all. Some environmentalists regard nature in terms similar to "natural law," it seeming to be a sin for economic development to disrupt the natural environment, even though the economic interests of many individuals may be attained. Environmentalism sometimes has a solidaristic aspect, as symbolized by the implication of the Earth photographed from a satellite that "from a distance" "we are all in this together" on a rather small, resource-limited planet.

Environmentalism presents a new definition of public action—we are all on this planet together and we must accordingly guide our actions. Normally, environmentalists call for government regulation to enhance the environment, although in general they are not opposed to individual volunteerism, such as in local recycling campaigns. But environmentalism tends to minimize the scope of purely private behavior.

Christian fundamentalism is ambivalent about individualistic liberalism.

Its political leaders adamantly support the limited and local government of market liberalism. At the same time, however, the fundamentalists apparently aspire to an America in which communities 90, or 95, or 99 percent Christian can, as communities, express their solidarity in terms of Christian symbolism. Further, the fundamentalists want to expand the scope of government over publicly defined morality, by supporting increased state action in such realms as opposing abortion or pornography, however defined.

Apparently Hartz was correct in expecting a period of conflict about individualism after the Cold War. But rather than social movements adopting solidaristic ideas—such as socialism, communism, or forms of nationalism—from Europe, the major challenges to the liberal consensus come from home-grown environmentalism and Christian fundamentalism.

Conclusion

An overall theory of American political institutions might attempt to link a structural theory with a theory of the political process, such as post-pluralism. I would suggest that some variant of post-pluralism is an excellent theory of American political institutions. Post-pluralist theory is useful in showing us what to expect in politics and political decision making. Post-pluralism as a process theory can be combined with a number of structural theories, such as those by the Schlesingers, Skowronek, and Hartz.

Here I do not want to single out one structural theory as the best for understanding American politics. However, it seems clear that social movement theory is inextricably linked with both process theories and structural theories of American political institutions. Our understanding of American politics will be greatly enhanced as we pursue this question further, as we do in subsequent chapters in this book.

2

"The Very Excess of Democracy":
State Building and Contentious Politics in America

Sidney Tarrow

During Alexis de Tocqueville's travels through the American South in 1831, he and his friend Beaumont met a candidate who had just competed in Baltimore's congressional elections. Tocqueville asks him:

> Q. But do you see nothing to fear in such disorderly and tumultuous assemblies?
>
> A. (Mr. Finley): For my part I think the hustings system detestable. But it does not present the dangers you imagine. Our people is accustomed to that type of election. They know just how far they can go, and how much time they can devote to this sort of ancient saturnalia. . . . *[T]he very excess of democracy partly saves us from the dangers of democracy.* (emphasis added)

Finley then told of how, during the campaign, the boos of the opposing party drowned out his and his opponent's voices; how several limbs had been broken at the hustings; but he went on to tell how, the very next day, he and his adversary went off to tour the different parts of the county, riding in the same carriage, eating at the same table, and lodging at the same inns (1960:3).

How different from Tocqueville's own recent experience of contentious politics! Distressed by the bloodletting, the collapse of legitimacy, and the "dangers of democracy" he had seen in France's 1830 revolution, the French traveler confided to the American candidate that such a scene as had just been described would have led to widespread bloodshed in France. "You argue," he said, "as a man who has never seen a people stirred by *real* and *profound* political passions. Everything with you up to now has been on the surface. There have been no large substantial interests at hazard" (83, emphasis in the original).

America not "stirred by real and profound political passions"? Everything "on the surface"? "No large substantial interests at hazard"? What was Tocqueville thinking of? What of the anti-Stamp Tax agitation of the 1760s and the wave of revolts that produced the American Revolution a decade later (Maier 1972)? Of the revival movements that swept across the country during the Second Great Awakening (Cross 1982)? Of the anti-Catholic violence that was about to break out?[1] Or the conflict over slavery that was gathering force as he wrote? Tocqueville was one of the world's first and great comparativists whose work has become a mantra for students of American state building.[2] Where did he go wrong?

Beginning with Tocqueville will serve more than a corrective purpose. It will help us see American social movements through a prism that silhouettes both their special and universal characters: a special character that relates to the particular patterns of state building in America, and a universal character that links them with contentious politics in the modern world. I will argue that in the short and medium run, America's contentious politics was very different than that of Europe's; but in the longer run, it was marked by an imbrication of social movements with conventional politics that was not so much exceptional as precocious.

In its most general sense, the term *contentious politics* is used to include all situations in which actors make collective claims on other actors, claims that, if realized, would affect the actors' interests, when some government is somehow party to the claims. In these terms, wars, revolutions, rebellions, (most) social movements, industrial conflict, feuds, riots, banditry, shaming ceremonies, and many more forms of collective struggle usually qualify as contentious politics.[3] While some of these forms clearly escape the rules of the polity, others cross the boundary between institutional and noninstitutional politics. From very early on, I will argue, the American pattern of state building gave social movements this dualistic capacity (Dryzek 1996).

In the first part of this chapter, I will argue that, although Tocqueville well understood the effect of American institutions on *formal* democracy, he failed to see how they would shape contentious politics and the role that social movements would play within them. Seeing movements through postrevolutionary French eyes, he failed to recognize that American movements would operate most effectively within the boundaries of the state—and not against it.

To some degree, to tax Tocqueville with failing to understand contentious politics in America may demand too much of him, for the most volatile American movements arose only after the 1830s.[4] But even in Tocqueville's day, the impact of the American state on social movements was substantial. In the second part of this chapter, I will argue that America's institutions produced a complex intersection among religion, social movements, and politics;[5] and then I will show how they gave movements the possibility of operating at many levels of the state and, shifting their activities among them, lowered the boundary between institutional and noninstitutional forms of contention. I will close, tendentiously, by asking whether modern European movements are not following the example of contentious politics in America.

The French Connection

Tocqueville was the first theorist to write about the implications of the modern state for collective action—but not in America! In *The Old Regime and the French Revolution* (1955: pt. 2), he would argue that the old regime's centralization produced the catastrophic patterns of contention that culminated in the French Revolution and the Terror. His reasoning was complex: the French monarchy had aggrandized itself by destroying corporate and intermediate bodies, attacking local autonomy, and reducing the aristocracy to a parasitic caste. The process strangled civic participation, created a special (and dangerous) role for intellectual ideologues, and meant that, when serious contention broke out—as it did in 1789 and 1830 and again in 1848 (Tocqueville 1992)—no one was prepared, and the process would spiral out of control. In contrast, in weak states like the United States, local self-government filled the gap left by a void in central authority, local autonomy stimulated self-help and private association, and contention was based on pragmatic—and negotiable—personal interest. Local autonomy, private association, and the politics of interest allowed democracy to flourish without the dangers it posed for France (Tocqueville 1960: 55).

American scholars who have followed in Tocqueville's footsteps have emphasized the American side of his perceptions and forgotten where they came from—from the Terror, born of the "dangerous" democracy that arose out of the centralization of the French monarchy and decimated his own family (Schama 1989: chap. 19). For this reason, it is worth pointing out that both Tocqueville's image of France's *ancien régime* and of the regimes that followed were exaggerated or just plain wrong.

With respect to the old regime, it is now well known that Tocqueville grossly overrated both its strength and how thoroughly it had eviscerated society's intermediate bodies. On the one hand, on the eve of the Revolution, far from a parasitic caste reclining in petrified splendor at Versailles, the French aristocracy was full of men like Lafayette who had imbibed liberal ideas and were enraptured by the American experiment (Schama 1989: chap. 3). On the other hand, France was not nearly as centralized as Tocqueville would have had it: its provincial *parlements*, and especially the *Parlement* of Paris, resisted the designs of the monarchy in the 1780s, leading the bankrupt crown to take the fateful step of calling the Estates General.

If Tocqueville's views about the centralization of the old regime were exaggerated, his vision of the continuity between it and postrevolutionary state and society was just plain wrong. While it was certainly true that Napoleon built a strong territorial state, the old regime—with its patchwork of *pays d'état* and *pays d'élection*, its rickety and unproductive taxation system, and its stubbornly independent *parlements*—was far from resembling such a state. As for French society, far from disappearing beneath the steamroller of state centralization, the corporate spirit—if not the actual structure—of the prerevolutionary guilds and other intermediate bodies survived among craftspeople and workers long after the revolution had ended (Sewell 1980, 1986).

Why are Tocqueville's errors and exaggerations about France important for our subject? The most obvious reason is that his view of the centralization of the old regime and his horror of its consequences for the French Revolution and what followed strongly colored his causal reasoning about America. It was from these assumptions that he inferred that a state with no centralized bureaucracy, which had left local institutions and private associations to flourish, and that was based on the politics of personal interest would produce an orderly associational politics without suffering the "dangers of democracy."

A broader issue arises for social scientists in Tocqueville's misreading of French history and its mirror application to the United States: it produced an either-or model of the relationship between state strength and social movement activity that has flourished among Tocqueville's followers to this day. The contemporary model of state-movement relations reads something like this: Strong civil societies with weak states produce autonomous forms of participation and conventional collective action, whereas weak societies with strong states produce centralized forms of participation and ideological/violent forms of collective action.[6]

A serious problem with such an either-or model is that it leads to a focus on comparative statics and ignores the shifts in political opportunity structure that trigger specific cycles of social movement activity, as well as underspecifying the differences in capacity to use the state of well- and badly placed social actors.[7] But a more serious problem, common to both Tocqueville and his followers, is that such a model also underspecifies how state development *of all kinds* provides opportunities for collective action and has done so since the creation of consolidated national states. By providing targets and fulcrums for contention and standardized collective identities and opportunities for the aggregation of interests for groups of social actors,[8] states become the structuring principles of social movement development. This situation was no less true in decentralized America than in centralized France.

This is where the observations of Tocqueville's friend Finley become most relevant to our story: it was not the *absence* of an American national state but the specific forms of American democracy that produced the "excess of democracy" of which Finley shrewdly approved and that countered the "dangers of democracy" that frightened Tocqueville. It was also specific features of the American state, such as the free coinage of religious associations, federalism, and the court system, that gave a special character to social movement strategy and organization. This point takes us to the structure of contentious politics in the United States.

Coming to America

In both state and society, Jacksonian America showed Tocqueville a mirror image of the strong state and weak society that had dismayed him in his native land. A July 4 celebration in Albany during his journey to the West encapsulates this image:

> Perfect order that prevails. Silence. No police. Authority nowhere. Festival of the people. Marshall of the day without restrictive power. And obeyed. Free classification of industries, public prayer, presence of the flag and of old soldiers. Emotion real. (Tocqueville 1960: 128)

What Tocqueville (1960: 55) so admired in his travels across America was that no strong state had emerged to constrain local autonomy, a vigorous associational life, and a flourishing civil politics. To be sure, America had never had the traditional corporate bodies whose passage he regretted in France. But he thought there was a functional equivalent in the churches, interest groups, and town meetings that channeled participation and provided Americans with a buffer against state expansion (Tocqueville 1954: ch. 16). With these resources at hand, he argued, America could avoid the extremes of social egalitarianism and statist despotism that France suffered from 1789 onward.

Social Movements and Conventional Politics

But where did this leave social movements? It is striking that throughout his travel diaries, the only social movement to which Tocqueville gave any attention apart from temperance was the convention in South Carolina calling for nullification of the tariff. And he condemned it—not because of its potential usurpation of federal power but because it sidestepped the institutions of formal democracy (Tocqueville 1960). Tocqueville's obsession with the French experience not only warned him that extremism and violence were dangerous; it convinced him that all forms of participation that sidestepped the institutions of formal democracy should be avoided.

The result was that Tocqueville was insensitive to the tremendous amount of social activism that was gathering force in the United States, much of which was only a half-step removed from institutional politics. Had he been in America in the 1790s, he would have observed the role of Federalist politicians in launching the anti-Illuminati movement (Aho 1996) that helped lead to the first antiimmigrant panic and to passage of the Alien and Sedition act. Had he studied the Whiskey Rebellion, he would have seen not only shirt-tailed farmers waving muskets but provincial notables, well connected in the federal system, refusing to give the central government taxing power over America's favorite drink (Gould 1995). Had he studied the antimasonic movement, he would have seen it turn from an evangelical reform movement into a political party—one that invented the presidential nominating convention in 1831 (Moore 1994: 78). He would also have seen how the Know-Nothings turned anti-Catholicism and antiimmigrant feeling into an electoral platform. And had he been able to study the settlement of the prairies in the 1840s and 1850s, he would have seen that even that quintessentially individualist project was partly financed by eastern abolitionists trying to keep slavery out of the frontier.[9]

American electoral institutions were key factors in shaping contentious politics. The weakness of class-based movements in America—and thus the absence of socialism—is often blamed on the importance of ethnicity. But would ethnicity have turned out to be as important if not for the structure and early expansion of the franchise?[10] Far from cutting off formal democracy from contentious politics, elections were an umbrella under which some movements flourished and others failed to develop. Amy Bridges (1986) has argued that partisanship embraced many facets of public life, especially work and ethnicity, providing a public identity for many people.[11] For a later period, Ira Katznelson (1981) has argued that, although urban Americans had a strong sense of class in their workplaces, the separation of work from neighborhood and the organization of the latter through elections cut across the lines of class solidarity.

As it developed in antebellum America, contention was so closely linked to conventional politics that if one looked for the kind of social movements that had culminated in the Terror, it would be hard to find any movements at all. But the United States from the late eighteenth through the early nineteenth centuries was positively blooming with contentious politics: from the sabotaging of British rule in the 1760s to the raising of a popular army in the 1770s; from the Shay's and Whiskey rebellions that followed the American Revolution and required armed force for their suppression to the frontier mobilization that produced Jackson's presidency; from the religious elements in American revolutionary ideology to the religious fervor of the Second Great Awakening that was "burning over" wide swaths of newly settled territory in New York and Ohio (Cross 1982). These episodes escaped the neat institutional pluralism that Tocqueville saw in his travels.

The center of gravity of American contention was still local in 1832, and this context fit the Tocquevillian paradigm perfectly. But even before industrialization, in the cities of the Atlantic coast a lively workers' movement was empowered with a strong dose of Painite republicanism (Wilentz 1984; Bridges 1986). Already, interchurch coalitions in places like Rochester, New York, were forming to oppose drink and Sunday work (Johnson 1978). And most important, regionally based religious movements were laying the groundwork for abolitionism and for the sectional conflict that would culminate in the most cataclysmic episode of collective action in the nation's history (Walters 1976: chap. 3).

Great differences in state centralization, private association, and collective action were evident between France and the United States. But in both countries, the particular pattern of state building provided an opportunity structure for social movements. America was not as stateless (nor was France as centralized) as Tocqueville thought. He found in the United States what he thought France had lost—a flourishing associational life that he mistook for the equivalent of a lost corporate order. But because he understood contention in the savage forms it had taken in France, he missed the contentious implications of American democracy and the very different connections among movements, contentious politics, and state building in America.

Three characteristics in particular marked America's social movements: the great importance of religious movements, the capacity to mount and shift activism among different levels of the American state, and the intersection between social movements, association, and routine politics.

Religion and Contentious Politics in America[12]

In a conversation with Joel Roberts Poinsett during his swing through the South, Tocqueville (1960: 114) asked the former diplomat:

> Q. What do you think of the influence of religion on politics?
> A. I think that the state of religion in America is one of the things that most powerfully helps us to maintain our republican institutions. The religious spirit exercises a direct power over political passions, and also an indirect power by sustaining morals.

Poinsett was not the first, nor even the most important, American to say so. In his farewell address, Washington had seen religion as an indispensable support for political prosperity (Moore 1994: 71). But both regarded religion more as a form of social control and a source of moderation of the political passions than as a core of beliefs about sacred transcendence that might make demands on the polity to reflect the demands of religious conscience (Smith 1996: 5). Neither emphasized the noninstitutional side of religion or the frequency, in America, with which religion animates social movements and slides into political activism.[13]

Like most upper-class gentlemen of his time, Tocqueville was more than ready to accept Poinsett's dictum. Although he did notice the Temperance Societies that were already developing in reaction to a whiskey-sodden frontier (1960: 212), it was mainly the *institutional* forms of religion that interested him as he traveled across the country. As he journeyed across New York state, he missed seeing the buzzing, blooming, and enthusiastic revivals that were "burning over" the regions of central New York (Cross 1982), the sabbatarian movement that was trying to stamp out Sunday work (Johnson 1978: chap. 6), the antimasonic movement that grew both out of such efforts and also a recurring fear of secular humanism (Johnson: chap. 3; Aho 1996: 191), and the anti-Catholic Protestant crusade that was the dark side of American "republican" religion (Billington 1938).

Why did so sensitive an observer as Tocqueville fail to detect the importance of religious movements in America? One reason is that much of his information came from the upper-class gentlemen and clerics he interviewed in his travels, who were unlikely to be active in enthusiastic religious revivals.[14] Another, as I argued earlier, is that his image of social movements was colored by the great and dangerous principles that animated successive revolutions in France, in which the Catholic Church had figured mainly as a target (Tocqueville 1955). However, a third and fourth reason are more important to our story, since they are directly related to the pattern of American state building: Tocqueville understood and valued the importance of both interest and association in American politics, but he missed their intersection with moral purpose in the world of religion.

Marketing Religion for Religious Consumers[15]

Most observers of the role of religion in American politics have focused heavily on the Establishment Clause of the First Amendment, inferring from it that religion and politics are, and should be, two separate spheres.[16] But they have frequently failed to see the importance of the other half of the amendment, the one that permits the free coinage of religious denominations. In the context of an anarchic, expanding, and soon continent-wide capitalist society, the First Amendment guarantee of religious freedom helped to produce a proliferation of religious sects, of competition between them and of commodification (Moore 1994).

Even before the passage of the federal Constitution,[17] American clerics had understood that they would have to "make religion *popular*, able to compete in a morally neutral and voluntaristic marketplace environment alongside all the goods and services of this world," writes Harry Stout (1991: xvii). Already, they were "caught up in a 'consumer revolution' stimulated by vast increases in manufacturing, capital, and leisure time." The trend could be observed in England too, but it was only in America that a written constitution gave denominational proliferation a juridical basis. As R. Laurence Moore (1994: 7) writes, "The environment of competition among denominations created by the First Amendment's ban on religious establishment simply accelerated the market rationale." In a laissez-faire market economy where the establishment of religion was banned and free creation of new religious organizations was encouraged, it was but a short step to a marketlike competition for souls between independent religious entrepreneurs.[18]

In his study of religion in America, Moore details how religious congregations sought parishioners like businessmen seeking clients, through print, revival meetings, the media, in workplaces, and in leisure activities (chaps. 1, 2, 4–8).

> Without an established church, they [religious leaders] could not depend upon the high social status that had formerly belonged to many of them as quasi public officials. Churches and clerics held their own in American life, however much their relative authority in public life declined, but they had to drum up business both among wealthy and influential lay people and among the general population. (1994: 69)

If the Jim and Tammy Bakkers of our century have taken the profit motive to a new low of exploitation, they were working within a well-worn repertoire of religious entrepreneurship.[19]

"Drumming up business" could mean selling Bibles or subscriptions to religious publications, but it also led to mounting movement-like revival campaigns, especially on the part of younger clerics without their own parishes in New England. The sales-people of enthusiastic religion who swept across New York and Ohio in the 1830s were offering a new product to an already religion-surfeited society; to succeed, the product had to be different, and to the degree that it was different, it challenged existing denominations with radical forms of religious practice and doctrine.

These successive waves of enthusiastic religion resembled nothing so much as the competitive outbidding found in a cycle of protest.[20] Not only that: the techniques of the revival meeting as they developed in the 1830s were strikingly similar to those of the mass movement—for example, "large-scale efforts to try to control behavior by inventing new forms of publicity to stir people" (Moore 1994: 72). "In religious protest," writes Moore, Americans "flexed their muscles, cast off habits of deference, and felt the thrill of empowerment" (73).

At times, mainstream clerics would merely complain of the vulgarity and danger of revival meetings (Moore 1994: 48). Forced to feed and house the traveling sales-people of enthusiastic religion, they often grumbled at the chaos left behind when their guests moved on to the next town. We find here striking parallels to the complaints that twentieth-century party leaders would voice at the excessive behavior of their radical competitors. In both sets of complaints, there is a worry about "liminality"—a state in which people are in danger of losing the bearings of everyday life.

At times, however, revivalism led to a process of catching up in which mainstream clerics would adopt the most palatable aspects of the reformers' programs. At other times, it led to competitive outbidding and radicalization. Protestant preachers tried to outdo one another—and to wean people from participating in competing forms of activity, like going to the theater (Moore 1994: chap. 2; Stout 1991: chap. 6)—by adopting forms of proselytizing that would win them a larger share of the religious market.

It was inevitable that this stirring in the American religious mentality would lead to intersections with politics (Moore 1994: chap. 3). It was no accident that the great age of religious revivalism, the 1830s and 1840s, was also the period in which the modern American party system was born. The enthusiastic turn in religious life helped produce the demand that the state reflect the moral standards of Christianity. It was not long until many religious leaders began to insist on the moral duty of Christians to lobby politicians and demanded legislative changes on behalf of moral issues (Moore 1994: 75).[21]

The most portentous of these was the cause of antislavery. By the 1840s, liberal ministers in New England and elsewhere were using their churches as "movement halfway houses" (Morris 1984) or as "movement midwives" (Smith 1996: 16–17) in which to develop consensus around abolitionist programs and recruit what a later age would describe as a cadre of movement militants.[22] Many of these would form the core of the underground railway network that infiltrated escaped slaves out of the South and to Canada.

Religious Movements and Private Associations

The underground railway is a good example of a classical social movement. Animated by deep religious faith and moral concern at the plight of escaped slaves, it operated outside conventional politics, employed radical civil disobedience rather than institutional means, and involved its core activists in relatively high-risk activities. Though it seldom led to violence, Tocqueville would have recognized it as a species of early movement organization.

But the underground railway was only the radical prow of a vast mass movement that had its center in more conventional church-and-association-based activities that intersected at many points with conventional local, state, and national politics. Had antislavery depended only on the archipelago of convinced militants who ran the underground railway, abolition might have remained a marginal cause. The movement was built on Protestant ministers and their congregations, abolitionist societies—many of them staffed by women of good family—and the antislavery wing of the party system. These networks of activists, sympathizers, and political entrepreneurs used the civic and associational capacity that Tocqueville had praised to build a social movement closely interlarded with the political system. So closely did it become imbricated with politics that its challenge could ultimately be met only through the destruction of antebellum federalism.

But it was not only in antislavery that religious moralists used the habits of association that Tocqueville treasured in American civil society to build social movements. Throughout American history, the same habits of association, pressure tactics, and coalition formation successfully developed by business and civic associations were used by combinations of church militants for moral purposes. Consider the sabbatarian movement in Rochester in the 1830s studied by Johnson (1978: chap. 4); it was formed by a coalition of members of different churches who got together to put pressure on the city leaders to stop Sunday work and drink. Or the cooperation that has developed across denominational lines in the antiabortion movement today. And the use of bloc recruitment—the blocs in question being parish churches—used by the most successful urban community groups in American cities today.[23] In all three cases, the same forms of association used to advance humdrum economic interests and civic goals are the common glue that holds religious movements together.

More than perhaps any movement sector, religion in America illustrates the ease with which American social movements move in and out of conventional politics. The First Amendment saved Americans from a state-imposed official religion, but it also gave religious reformers the incentive and the freedom to organize their parishioners much as social movement entrepreneurs do. The separation of church and state and the free coinage of religious denominations in the presence of an expanding capitalist society not only produced a commodification of religion but created a durable religious movement sector in shifting relations with the political struggle.

Movements and Institutions

That struggle has changed its shape and its intensity so often that it would be foolish to attempt to set out a permanent map of how movements and institutions intersect within it. But one regularity we can point to is that, as a direct result of the structure of the American state, movements could survive negative changes in political opportunity, by using the institutions of the political system astutely and in a differentiated manner. This was, first, because federalism gave them the opportunity to shift between different levels of the system; and, second, because their tactics frequently combined the extrainstitutional forms of contention of classical social movements with the institutional tactics of private associations.

Multilevel Movements, Light-footed Movements

The American federal system was designed to govern territorial expansion, manage diversity, and split up potentially corrosive adversaries, and for sixty years it more or less achieved its aim. But as the events leading up to the Civil War showed, this multilevel system had a negative side: it could provide strong points for forms of territorial contention that could not be disassembled through the give-and-take of institutional politics. On the other hand, federalism also provided movements of a less exclusive cast than abolitionism and proslavery with a variety of levels in which to operate, allowing them to shift their bases of activity, combine local and higher-level activism, and take advantage of local power structures.

The history of late nineteenth-century temperance shows how this development could occur in the case of one recurring social movement. Like many movements, temperance described a cyclical trajectory of activism and quietism, responding to favorable opportunities with greater activism and to the pressure of broader issues by lying low (e.g., we seldom hear of temperance activity during the Civil War years).

Temperance activists could also shift between levels of the federal system. "As one of the primary goals of the temperance movement in the late nineteenth century," writes Ann-Marie Szymanski (1996: 2), "[state-level] constitutional prohibition captured much of the movement's idealism." Agitation at the local level was at first frowned upon, "for it was wrong for the state to surrender its sovereignty, evade its duty and divest itself of responsibility on a matter vitally affecting the welfare of the state."[24]

In search of a constitutional prohibition of drink, temperance advocates learned to "navigate the quagmires of the amendment process and the party system," successfully getting prohibition referenda onto the ballot in eighteen states (Szymanski 1996: 3). Unfortunately for the movement, this high level referendum strategy failed in most states and at the federal level as well.[25] Reacting to this failure, and facilitated by local home rule, first the Massachusetts Law and Order League and then the Anti-Saloon League turned to the local level.

Localism was an incremental but not necessarily a moderate strategy. In the short run, it allowed temperance advocates to nibble away at the illegalities and improprieties of local saloons; in the long run, it helped them mobilize consensus around the broader goals of the movement. As Szymanski (1996: 5–6) observes:

Instead of expecting its recruits to possess the "correct" beliefs about prohibition *prior* to their involvement in the movement, the Anti-Saloon League first sought to engage Americans in local prohibition skirmishes which barely dented the profits of the liquor industry, but which helped socialize them into the militancy of the broader movement.

Far from burying the movement in the meandering rivulets of private interest and local association (*pace* Tocqueville), localism exposed nascent supporters of prohibition to the obstinacy of the liquor industry and "unleashed the democratic potential of the decentralized American state" (Szymanski 1996: 6). Localism intersected with association to allow the movement to develop networks of supporters—often through local churches—which allowed them to gain tactical advantage where it was strong, engage its members in capillary activities where it was weak, and wait out the doldrums of unpromising political periods for new political alignments and opportunities to arise.

A contemporary example of the same strategy of shifting between levels of the polity can be found in the Christian Coalition's shift from national agitation to state-level organizing during the 1980s and 1990s (Moen 1996: 461–3). The coalition at first directed its support at voters through a barrage of media propaganda, and at the highest levels of the state, first by working closely with Ronald Reagan's administration and then through its support for Reagan's and Pat Robertson's candidacies for the Republican nomination. But although increasing proportions of the electorate declared themselves sympathetic to its programs, little was gained from either Reagan or Bush other than pious platitudes and an antiabortion plank in the Republican platform that was as disturbing for some as it was stirring for others.

By the early 1990s, under the skillful leadership of Ralph Reed, the Christian Coalition had shifted its attention to the local and state levels of the party, using both its internal machinery and local church-based groups to gain seats at state nominating conventions and win congressional nominations for candidates sympathetic to its cause. By some estimates, by the 1994 congressional elections, it had taken control of the nominating process in seventeen state organizations of the Republican party (Persinos 1994; Usher 1996).

As in the case of the Anti-Saloon League, the story of the Christian Coalition shows that the American state provides alternative access points for movements that are unable to achieve their goals at their chosen level of the political system. It also provides opportunities to shift from contention on the margins of the polity to participation within it and back again. And this point takes us to my final subject: the relationship between conventional politics and the politics of contention.

Convention and Contention

According to an old tradition in American sociology, social movements are part of a distinct universe called "collective behavior" which differs from "institutional behavior" in being, simply, noninstitutional (see the review in McAdam 1982: chap. 1). Though few scholars working in this tradition had the dread of movements of a Tocqueville, its advocates drew a clear distinction between uncontrolled, spontaneous, and emergent forms of collective action and those forms that are routine, operate within political institutions, and have clearly defined goals. In the former category we find social movements; in the latter are interest groups and parties.

The resource mobilization and political process schools that succeeded collective behavior as dominant paradigms in social movement sociology were more concerned than their predecessors with how movements are shaped by organizations, how they marshall resources, use opportunities and repertoires, and interact with political elites.[26] But in both of these traditions, movements continue to be defined in terms that take them "outside" institutions, and their relationship to institutional politics remains elusive. In the face of the fact that many of the most successful recent movements in recent American history, starting from the Civil Rights movement, have been skilled in the use of political and legal institutions, social movement theorists have not yet tackled in an integrated way their relationship to conventional politics.[27]

Trends in the politics of advanced capitalist democracies call for greater efforts in relating movements to institutional politics.[28] Three trends in particular deserve more attention. *First,* since the 1960s, it has been apparent to many observers of liberal democracies that the use of classical forms of contentious collective action like the sit-in, the march and demonstration, and the obstruction has expanded to broad sectors of the populations of these countries.[29] *Second,* police practice appears to have admitted many of these forms to the repertoire of legitimate—or, at least, tolerated—participation; in the United States and Western Europe, the police have adopted a largely managerial attitude to public protest (McCarthy, McPhail, and Smith 1996; della Porta 1995). *Third,* the decades since the 1960s have seen the appearance of hybrid forms of interest group/social movements like the public interest group and the franchised movement organization.

These trends have begun to blur the lines between conventional politics and social movements. Consider the activities of an organization such as Greenpeace; best known for its highly visible symbolic activities against environmental abuse, it also operates a major educational program (Wapner 1995). Greenpeace maintains only a skeletal cadre of activists who choose their targets carefully for their media and political impact, and it depends financially on a mainly passive periphery of members, a well-oiled publicity strategy, and high-tech access to the media. Given these properties, Greenpeace is as much part of the bureaucratic world of nongovernmental organizations and interest groups as it is that of the action-oriented world of classical social movements.

How do changes such as these affect the analytical distinction between social movements and institutional politics? If the forms of collective action formerly associated with social movements are also used by interest groups, civic associations, and, on occasion, elected politicians, what remains distinctive about social movements? Like Greenpeace, many movements in Western democracies combine the use of institutional forms of activity like legal claims, educational activities, and lobbying with more traditional confrontational forms like demonstrations, sit-ins, and strikes. How can we differentiate social movements from interest groups when both use the tools of computerized mailings, direct access to the media, lobbying, and legal action, and occasional confrontations with powerholders?

It is in this respect that the American political tradition may have a great deal to teach us about the recent evolution of social movements in Europe. Many of the characteristics that European scholars saw as "new" in European social movements have been germinating in this country since the early nineteenth century (see D'Anieri, Ernst, and Kier 1990). Consider the forms of activity used at one time or another by the temperance movement: from its origins in the 1830s to the passage of the Eighteenth Amendment, temperance used a broad repertoire of organizing and pressure tactics, ranging from educating and proselytizing efforts in the schools and churches, to invoking legal restraints on the sale of liquor, to supporting candidates and lobbying, to mounting public demonstrations, to employing confrontational tactics, like invading taverns and staging public breaking of whiskey bottles (Blocker 1989).

The same has been true of the civil rights movement. From the legal strategy of the early 1950s, to the church-based mobilizations and peaceful sit-ins of the late 1950s, to the mass demonstrations and marches of the early 1960s, to the occasional recourse to violence in parts of the movement in the late 1960s, the civil rights movement also ran the gamut of both institutional and noninstitutional contention. Part of its success was due to its leaders' ability to react strategically to elite responses to their strategy of nonviolent resistance (McAdam 1983), but a good part of it was also due to the availability of alternative and complementary sites for interaction with opponents and elites within the American state.

The same can be said for the American women's movement, which some scholars have sometimes interpreted as being either "new" (and therefore radical) or "old" (and therefore moderate). A more nuanced and more historicized account shows that both the old and the new wings of the movement have employed both institutional and noninstitutional tactics at various times and in different combinations. This is *not* simply a matter of old versus new, radical versus moderate wings of the movement: the women's organizations that we see testifying before congressional committees may be the same ones that march, demonstrate, sit in, and raise consciousness among their constituencies. What democratic theorist John Dryzek (1996: 485) calls a "dualistic" strategy is not the invention of the "new" social movements of the 1980s; it has been part of American contentious politics since the founding of the American state.

A Contentious View of Social Movements

Is it the "special" quality of American social movements—or of American democracy—that allows movements to shift their activities between different levels and arenas of politics, to use the same forms of private association as business and civic groups, and to traverse the frontiers between the conventional and confrontational repertoires? Or is it simply that, as the world's longest-running electoral democracy, the American political system showed earlier than others how contentious politics is shaped by democratic institutions?

We have seen how the First Amendment, together with a rampant market economy and models of civic organization available to all, led religious groups competing for believers to adopt new forms of organization and mobilization that made them closely akin to social movements and led them into politics. We have also seen how federalism—a particular though not unique American institution—could both foster hardened territorial movements like pro- and antislavery and provide movements like temperance with the institutional sites in which to operate at several layers of the political system. We have, finally, seen how social movements in America developed a repertoire of contention that could allow them to bridge contentious and interest group politics without permanently losing their insurgent character.[30]

What can we conclude from these regularities in the American experience?

First, it seems clear that the early and extensive expansion of the ballot produced an "excess of democracy" that, because it led much social activism into electoral forms, prevented the "dangers" of democracy that Tocqueville so feared.

Second, state formation was also a process of structuring movements, one that our great French interpreter missed because he defined states in European terms and only recognized movements when, in the French mold, they attacked institutions.

Third, because American movements have so easily shifted between institutional and noninstitutional modes of action, we will only successfully place American movements in a comparative framework when we cease to study social movements on their own and broaden our optic to include all forms of contentious politics.

This is not to say that the "American" properties of social movements sketched in this chapter have not existed elsewhere. Since the mid-1980s, a growing tradition of transatlantic comparative work has been turning up a number of parallels and intersections between European and American movements in the late twentieth century.[31] Even in France, the strike wave of 1995 led to a vigorous debate about whether a conflict in which the major actors were trade unions could still be regarded as a social movement (Mouriaux and Subileau 1996). By the 1990s, even the most exceptionalist European country may be no more exceptional than its equally exceptionalist cousin across the Atlantic.

But it is nevertheless intriguing that the United States, a country whose politics are so often compared with none other than its own, foreshadowed many of the practices of social movements that have emerged in other advanced capitalist democracies in recent decades. The joke is on Tocqueville. In its ability to avoid the "dangers of democracy," America was unique in his opinion. But the "excess of democracy" that he feared, and which Americans developed earlier than Europeans, ultimately showed Europeans how to build social movements into contentious politics.

Notes

I am grateful to a number of busy and talented people for comments on an earlier draft of this chapter: Glenn Alschuler, Richard Bensel, Stuart Blumin, Amy Bridges, Anne Costain, Allen Hertzke, Doug Imig, Ira Katznelson, Larry Moore, Nick Salvatori, Elizabeth Sanders, Steven Skowronek, Ann-Marie Szymanski, Doug Usher, and Megan Whelan. None are responsible for my errors or misunderstandings.

1. Nick Salvatori points out to me that the first major outbreak of anti-Catholic violence was in Boston and that Tocqueville could not have predicted it. However, Tocqueville's journal is full of references to the anti-Catholicism of American Protestants, and his Catholic respondents were at pains to point out how important it was for Catholics to avoid any hint of church involvement in politics.

2. Commenting on an earlier version of this chapter, Richard Bensel observed that "framed through European eyes, his [Tocqueville's] vision has become one of the most powerful justifications for the Euro-centric nature of comparative analysis of the United States. In the process, most other comparative possibilities are shunted aside as we focus narrowly on what Tocqueville saw as different and remarkable in the United States." The following paragraphs should be read in that spirit.

3. This definition, and the perspective it has led to, draws on my collaborative work with Doug McAdam and Charles Tilly, especially on McAdam, Tarrow, and Tilly (1996, 1997).

4. This argument has been made by some of the colleagues who read an earlier version of this chapter. I cannot do them justice here but will try to reply in a subsequent work.

5. I am guided in this assertion by Christian Smith (1996: 2), who writes that "religion's important contribution to social movements remains conspicuously under-explored—arguably virtually ignored—in the academic literature on social movements." In this book and two others (1991, 1996), Smith's work is going a long way to correct this lacuna.

6. Two excellent treatments of state centralization in regard to social movements are Kitschelt (1986) and Kriesi et al. (1995). Although only the former includes the United States in his study of "new" social movements, both scholars regard France as a strong state in which social movements are, as a result, volatile. The purest adoption of the strong/weak state dichotomy is that of Pierre Birnbaum, who focuses mainly on France but also gives some attention to the United States. Citing Kitschelt's work on antinuclear movements, Birnbaum (1993: 173) writes of the "violent confrontations that take place in France, during which large crowds confront the forces of order, while the action of lobbying and negotiation in the United States are revealed as much more efficacious than in France."

7. For this argument, see Tarrow (1994, 1996). The approach of Kriesi and his collaborators (1995) does include a dynamic element of political opportunity structure, but only with respect to shifting alliance structures between movements and allies (chap. 3) and cycles of protest (chap. 5).

8. By "targets" I refer to the well-known tendency of national states to stimulate contention through their campaigns to integrate the periphery, extract resources, and suppress parochial forms of organization; by "fulcrums" I refer to the less well-studied effects of national states in providing arenas in which contending groups struggle against one another in standard and modular forms. For the historical and theoretical justifications for this argument, see Tarrow (1994, 1996) and Tilly (1986, 1995).

9. I am grateful to my colleague, Richard Bensel, for pointing this out to me.

10. For example, Irish immigration to Liverpool and Manchester was as high in the 1820s and 1830s as it was to America, yet nothing like the Irish-run urban machines of New York or Boston developed there.

11. I am grateful to Professor Bridges for sharpening my understanding of her argument in her 1986 essay in a comment on an earlier version of this chapter.

12. Richard Bensel, an exceptionally sharp-eyed reader of an earlier draft of this chapter, has pointed out that at least two types of religious movements existed in America: revivalism and utopian separatism, the first fairly mainstream and the latter insurgent. I bow to his greater knowledge of American political development, but I would point out that at least some revival movements could be classified as "insurgent," in the sense that they challenged mainstream religious institutions.

13. One reader of an earlier version of this chapter challenged the initial language of this sentence ("the *ease* with which religion turns to political activism"). Of course, I cannot claim to know whether it was easy or difficult for religious activists to turn to politics. Nor do we have relative statistics on the frequency of such processes. But to me it seems at least impressionistically true that religion has persistently given rise to social and political movements in America. More than in other countries? The comparative research has not yet been done to demonstrate either this or the opposite.

14. It seems ironic that Americanists have largely accepted the judgment about their own democratic system of a European aristocrat who based many of his conclusions on the testimony of upper-class, Europe-oriented men like himself. Except for his trip to the western frontier, neither women nor Americans from the popular classes appear as interlocutors in Tocqueville's journal.

15. The following section leans heavily on the interpretations of my Cornell colleague R. Laurence Moore in his insightful *Selling God: American Religion in the Marketplace of Culture* (1994) and on his thoughtful comments on an earlier version of this chapter.

16. Tocqueville's (1959: 82) clerical interlocutors, probably frightened at the dangers

of militant anti-Catholicism in America, insisted over and over on the importance of the separation of church and state.

17. Note that many state constitutions, notably in New England, continued to allow the establishment of religion until well into the nineteenth century.

18. Nick Salvatori points out that the commodification argument probably had more power for Protestants than for either Catholics or Jews. This is linked to his broader criticism of the analysis in this section with which I concur: my argument has no discussion of the ethos or belief systems of religious groups that might induce them (apart from any social or political reality) to take up political roles. Christian Smith's (1996) introduction to his edited volume provides the beginning for such an understanding.

19. Far less notorious religious figures than the Bakkers are also touched by the profit motive. In commenting on an earlier version of this chapter, Elizabeth Sanders pointed to the growing number of "full-service churches" in America today.

20. On protest cycles, see Brand (1990), Koopmans (1993), and Tarrow (1989, 1994). For the geography and timing of the waves of revival in central New York, see Cross (1982).

21. I am grateful to both Doug Imig and Ann-Marie Syzmanski, who remind me that not all denominations or ministers were tempted by a political outlet for moral issues. Episcopalians and Congregationalists were less likely to agitate against slavery than were Quakers and Methodists—both of whom had been in the vanguard of antislavery in England.

22. The term *consensus mobilization* is from Klandermans (1997: chap. 2).

23. I refer here to the dissertation research of Heidi Swarts, who is comparing congregational- and individual-based recruitment into community action groups and who has taught me much about religious movements in America.

24. Quoted by Szymanski from D. Leigh Colvin, *Prohibition in the United States* (1926, 360–1). I am grateful to Ann-Marie Szymanski for permission to quote from her unpublished work.

25. Szymanski notes that the voters of twelve states rejected it outright; in four others prohibition won fleeting victories; and as of 1900, only Kansas, Maine, North Dakota, New Hampshire, and Vermont had either constitutional or statutory prohibition. See Szymanski (1996: 3) for details.

26. For representative sources, see Jenkins and Klandermans (1995); McAdam (1982: chaps. 2–3); McAdam, McCarthy, and Zald (1996); Oberschall (1973); Tarrow (1994); Tilly (1978, 1995).

27. But see the contributions of Burstein, McCann, and Woliver to this volume.

28. For some preliminary moves toward the definition and mapping of an integrated field of contentious politics, see McAdam et al. (1996, 1997). For a preliminary attempt to relate theories of social movements to theories of American politics, see Andrew McFarland's introduction to this volume.

29. For example, see Dalton (1996), Tarrow (1994: chap. 11), and the contributions to Meyer and Tarrow (1997).

30. I am aware that this list scarcely exhausts the relevant characteristics of American state building. As Ira Katznelson writes, in commenting on an earlier version of this chapter, "I think we need, but don't yet have a portrait of the American state that includes the elements of space and scale, which incorporates the problematic of empire and its characteristic issues of center and periphery, which makes sectionalism constitutive of stateness, and which finds a place for the military, communications, and the post office, internal improvements, and the incorporation of incredibly diverse populations at the heart of its treatment." My goal has been much narrower: to underscore some key aspects of state building that both impacted and helped generate social movements in this country.

31. See, for example, the work collected in Dalton and Kuechler (1990), Katzenstein and Mueller (1987), Klandermans, Kriesi, and Tarrow (1988), Mcadam, McCarthy, and Zald (1996), McAdam and Rucht (1993), and Rucht (1994).

3

Interest Organizations, Political Parties, and the Study of Democratic Politics

Paul Burstein

Anyone reading what social scientists have to say about democratic politics would conclude that there are three types of intermediary organizations linking citizens and governments: social movement organizations (SMOs), interest groups, and political parties (see, e.g., Greenberg and Page 1995; Walker 1991: 2–3). The three types are studied separately, for the most part, by different scholars in different disciplines (sociologists focus on social movement organizations, political scientists on interest groups and parties). Each type of organization has essentially a separate subdiscipline, with its own history and theories.

McAdam, Tarrow, and Tilly (1996) have recently argued against this division of intellectual labor. Political activity cannot be so neatly divided, they claim.[1] Groups that engage in street demonstrations one day may lobby legislators the next and nominate candidates for office the day after that. Each type of organization is affected by the others; SMOs compete for influence with interest groups, and both may be affected by how political parties respond to their demands. If we want to understand the political struggle as a whole, McAdam et al. contend, we have to break down the barriers between subdisciplines and study all the intermediary organizations together.

Their argument is convincing, as far as it goes, but it does not go far enough. McAdam et al. contend that SMOs and interest groups should be studied together because they are closely linked. I claim that we cannot avoid studying them together, because they are actually the *same thing;* in addition, the differences between them and political parties, while important, are few. The cost of intellectual specialization has been even greater than McAdam et al. surmise. Social scientists have not simply failed to see how different kinds of organizations affect each other; they have often thought they were studying different things when in fact they were studying the same thing under different labels.

This chapter has three parts. In the first, I examine how social scientists have defined "social movement organization," "interest group," and "political party" and contend that the conventional ways of distinguishing among them are unsatisfactory and should be abandoned. In the second, I propose that it would be more useful to think about intermediary organizations in terms of how they developed historically and what they do today. Finally, I consider the implications of this rethinking for theory and research on democratic politics.

Social Movement Organizations,
Interest Groups, Political Parties: Definitions

It is the rare work on democratic politics in which all three types of intermediary organizations—SMOs, interest groups, and political parties— are defined with care. Instead, the terms are defined in one of three ways.

The first, frequently used by authors who see themselves addressing readers interested in only one type, is to define that type carefully without distinguishing it from the others. Such definitions are often very broad—so broad, in fact, that they seem to encompass many organizations that scholars in other subdisciplines would characterize differently. For example, in a book targeted to scholars more interested in social movements than interest groups or political parties (the title is *Statemaking and Social Movements*) Tilly (1984: 306) defines SMOs as an essential part of any social movement; a social movement, in turn, is

> a sustained series of interactions between power holders and persons success-
> fully claiming to speak on behalf of a constituency lacking formal representa-
> tion, in the course of which those persons make publicly visible demands for
> changes in the distribution or exercise of power, and back those demands with
> public demonstrations of support.

How does this definition distinguish SMOs from interest groups and political parties? Experts in American politics would immediately note that in the United States formal representation is accorded only to geographical areas—at the federal level, to states and congressional districts. All other "constituencies" lack formal representation, so the definition would encompass all interest groups publicly and repeatedly demanding change in the distribution or exercise of power, and arguably the minority party as well— and what interest group or minority party does not want more power?

Alternatively, one type of organization may be contrasted with another in order to justify studying it separately, but in a way that seems almost pro forma. Thus, for example, in their pathbreaking article on social movements,

McCarthy and Zald (1977: 1218) could not help noting that SMOs resemble interest groups, actually asking, "Is a SMO an interest group?" Their answer is "No"; but the question is only in a footnote, and McCarthy and Zald themselves admit that they are "not fully satisfied" with the answer before dropping the issue completely.

Finally, there may be no theoretical definition at all. Heinz and his collaborators (1993: 24), for example, state that they are analyzing interest groups, but they define the term entirely operationally, identifying organizations active in politics without making any attempt to distinguish between interest groups and SMOs.

These approaches to definition are not very satisfactory. If there really are three types of important intermediary organizations, we ought to be able to define each clearly in a way that distinguishes it from the others. What happens when we try to do so?

Social Movement Organizations

I will try to define *social movement organization* first, because the nature of social movements has been very much at issue during the last couple of decades, and much effort has been devoted to defining the term. Those who study interest groups and political parties generally find it easy to define the objects of their interest; but because SMOs are often seen as being on the boundary between the organized and the unorganized, what they are as intermediary *organizations* is subject to dispute.

Attempts to define *social movement organization*, like attempts to define *interest group* and *political party*, probably began with careful observation of organizations that seemed both important in politics and different from other groups. It is mostly sociologists who study what they call SMOs, so it is they who have tried hardest to identify what distinguishes SMOs from other organizations.

By ideology and theoretical predilection, sociologists are inclined to study groups of "outsiders" who seem powerless and purportedly have to resort to desperate measures to win even recognition—much less substantive concessions—from the powerful. They suggest that SMOs differ from other organizations in (1) what they want, (2) whom they represent, and (3) what tactics they use. Unfortunately, these distinctions, while intuitively appealing, prove impossible to apply consistently in real life.

What do SMOs want? They want change. To quote two well-known definitions, they favor "changing some elements of the social structure and/ or reward distribution of society" (McCarthy and Zald 1977: 1217–8); they "make publicly visible demands for changes in the distribution or exercise of power" (Tilly 1984: 306).

But interest groups and political parties often want change too. Sometimes, of course, they do not, but that is also true of SMO-like organizations. McCarthy and Zald (1977: 1218) note that organizations often arise to oppose the changes demanded by SMOs (see McAdam 1982: 25). Because SMOs want change, by definition, such organizations cannot be called SMOs, so McCarthy and Zald find themselves forced to call such opposition a "countermovement" rather than a movement; but this terminological distinction does not seem helpful, any more than calling the Democrats a "political party" and the Republicans a "counterparty." Attempts to distinguish between SMOs and other intermediary organizations by focusing on goals are not successful.

Whom do social movement organizations represent? Those outside established political institutions (e.g., McCarthy and Zald 1977: 1217; Freeman 1975: 46–47; McAdam 1982: 25; Tilly 1984: 306). But this is not very useful, either. No one has defined very satisfactorily what it means to be an outsider. Gamson (1975: 16), for example, focuses on constituencies not previously mobilized to participate in politics; does this mean that the majority of adult American citizens who do not vote are outsiders? More importantly, the focus on outsider status places a huge stumbling block on the road to understanding politics. If SMOs represent outsiders, then once they begin to succeed, they seemingly cease to be SMOs, even if their goals, membership, and tactics do not change. Defining SMOs as representing outsiders requires that analysis cease once they start to succeed; one can analyze SMOs or the determinants of political change, but not both.

Perhaps social movement organizations are best defined in terms of tactics. This was McAdam's (1982: 25) focus at one time; he defined social movement organizations in terms of their use of "noninstitutional forms of political participation," meaning activities that are not part of the formal political process and are intended to be disruptive (whether legal or illegal). This seems more satisfactory, more essential to our notions of "social movement organization" than goals or the identity of participants. When people think of SMOs, they think of sit-ins, mass marches, boycotts, and similar tactics, while such tactics do not immediately come to mind when we think of political parties or interest groups. Indeed, I adopted McAdam's definition myself in a previous work (Burstein, Einwohner, and Hollander 1995).

Nevertheless, tactics are not a satisfactory basis for distinguishing between social movement organizations and other intermediary organizations. This point may best be seen by considering interest groups.

Interest Groups

Definitions of *interest group* tend to be broad and vague. Wilson's and Walker's are typical. Wilson (1980: 8) requires that interest groups be organizations "which have some autonomy from government or political parties and that . . . try to influence public policy," while Walker (1991: 4) focuses on organizations "that can reasonably be described as voluntary associations . . . seeking in one way or another to petition the government on behalf of some organized interest or cause." These are reasonable definitions of *interest group* but also seem to encompass SMOs.

Organizations wanting change of the sorts identified by McCarthy and Zald and Tilly fit these definitions, as would organizations of outsiders; and because the definitions say nothing about tactics, organizations using the tactics listed by McAdam could be considered interest groups as well.

Intuitively, McAdam's focus on tactics makes sense—people do think of interest groups as highly conventional and their members as averse to disruptive behavior, while social movement organizations bring a contrasting picture to mind. Nevertheless, attempts to distinguish between interest groups and SMOs on the basis of tactics do not work. The distinction cannot be based on whether tactics are disruptive: for example, business threats to reduce or shift investments certainly promise to disrupt the economy (Lindblom 1977), and American interest groups often prevent the implementation of laws and regulations for years through repeated court challenges. Thus, it must be the "noninstitutional" aspect of tactics that is crucial. But what does "noninstitutional" mean? It cannot mean "not regulated by law"; much political activity not thought of as "noninstitutional" is not regulated by law, such as letter-writing campaigns, visiting legislators' offices, and placing political advertisements in newspapers. Might it mean tactics that are somehow disorderly or unstructured? Tilly (1984) argues convincingly that the tactics used by those involved in social movements are typically chosen from a set of well-known and understood possibilities, sometimes planned and rehearsed. Thus, the tactics of "SMOs" often are orderly and predictable, while those of "interest groups" often are arguably noninstitutionalized and certainly intended to be disruptive.

The notion that interest groups are more "institutionalized" than SMOs, not just in terms of tactics but more broadly, is widely seen as a key difference between them. McCarthy and Zald (1977: 1218; their paraphrase) rely on Lowi's formulation: "a SMO which becomes highly institutionalized and routinizes stable ties with a governmental agency is an interest group." Similarly, Wilson (1990: 9) writes that "a social movement may or may not become an interest group depending on whether or not it develops the appropriate degree of institutionalization." Intuitively, again, this way of making the distinction matches people's sense that SMOs are somehow closer to the unorganized masses than interest groups are.

But how institutionalized does an organization have to be to qualify as an interest group? I am not aware of anyone having provided a theoretical rationale for dividing a continuum of institutionalization at one place— interest groups on one side, social movement organizations on the other—

rather than another. It would be very difficult to do so in any case, since *institutionalization* itself is not defined with any precision; indeed, often it is not defined at all.

Several researchers have used what could be considered implicit measures of institutionalization to identify interest groups. Heinz et al. (1993: 19) and Walker (1991: 203) draw much of their samples of what they call interest groups from lists of organizations identified by publishers as trying to influence federal policy. They then supplement the lists by screening media reports of organizational activity and by interviewing government officials, and they weight their samples by the size or prominence of the organizations in the public record. Thus, organizations entered their samples to the extent they were big or important enough to be noticed by publishers, reporters, or government officials. Such notice could be interpreted as evidence of institutionalization. Effectively, though, what Heinz et al. (1993) and Walker (1991) really do is to delegate decisions about what constitutes an interest group to other organizations (publishers and the like), which in turn rely on unreported (in Walker 1991 and Heinz et al. 1993) measures of organization or visibility. This approach does not seem very satisfactory from a theoretical perspective.

One aspect of the Heinz et al./Walker approach, however, is worthy of note in the present context: neither makes any distinction between "interest groups" and "SMOs"—that is, they distinguish among groups, including some but not others in their samples, solely on the basis of certain forms of visibility rather than goals, membership, or tactics. In effect, if an organization conventionally thought of as a social movement organization were included in one of the lists they relied on, it would be treated as an interest group—or, from the Heinz et al./Walker point of view, it would *be* an interest group.

Where does this kind of reasoning lead? As sociologists and political scientists think more deeply about the distinctions among types of political organizations, it becomes increasingly difficult to make a strong theoretical argument that the distinctions are real. McAdam, for example, seems to have abandoned his earlier contention that SMOs can be distinguished from other types of organizations by their tactics. He, Tarrow, and Tilly (1996: 27) have recently claimed that organizations choose what tactics to use by considering how best to use the resources they have to deal with the opportunities and constraints they face in any particular situation. "There are no inherently 'social-movement oriented' actors or groups," they write; "the same groups that pour into the streets and mount the barricades may be found in lobbies, newspaper offices, and political party branches . . . these various types of activities may be combined in the repertoire of the same group and may even be employed simultaneously." Indeed, they conclude, "there is *no fun-*

damental discontinuity between social movements and institutional politics" (emphasis added; see also Tarrow 1995).

If there is no "fundamental" discontinuity, what, then, is the difference? Here McAdam et al. (1996: 21) fall back on a version of Tilly's (1984) definition quoted earlier: "A social movement is a sustained interaction between mighty people and others lacking might: a continuing challenge to existing powerholders in the name of a population whose interlocutors declare it to be unjustly suffering harm or threatened with such harm." But this definition is, if anything, less satisfactory than the earlier one. If we accept the views of the "interlocutors," then many, perhaps most, interest groups would fit the definition of such a population. For example, tobacco companies see themselves unjustly suffering harm as the result of actions by the "mighty" state and federal governments. The Republican party would fit, too; the rhetoric of Republican officeholders and candidates is filled with claims that their basic values are under attack by a variety of powerful forces. Yet if we do not accept the interlocutors' views, we have to gauge objectively for ourselves who is "mighty" and who is not in every sustained political interaction. This has long been the task of those trying to define "power" satisfactorily—and they have never produced a definition that can be successfully operationalized (Wilson 1990: chap. 1).

The time has come to change our approach. Every serious attempt to distinguish between social movements and other forms of political action, and between SMOs and interest groups, fails.[2] And they fail not because our conceptualizations are not quite sophisticated enough—with a satisfactory formulation always "just around the corner"—but rather because there is "no fundamental discontinuity," indeed no discontinuity at all, between them. We should conclude that the distinction between "SMOs" and "interest groups," which seems so obvious initially, *does not exist*, in the sense that no one has developed a convincing basis—theoretical or empirical—for distinguishing consistently between the two. Rather than continue trying to make the distinction, therefore, we should simply say that a variety of non-party organizations try to influence political outcomes; the organizations vary in a variety of important ways (tactics, organization, number of members, resources, goals, etc.), but the simple dichotomy between "interest group" and "social movement organization" cannot stand up to scrutiny and should be abandoned.[3]

What should these nonparty organizations be called? One who dislikes neologisms has a dilemma; calling them "interest groups" will anger sociologists, while adopting the term "social movement organizations" will upset political scientists. Because political scientists define interest groups as a type of *organization*, and because sociologists would agree that the organizations are representing *interests*, I suggest the compromise term *interest organization*.

Now there are two types of intermediary organizations, rather than the three we started with: interest organizations and political parties. But do real differences exist between the remaining two?

Political Parties

Like *social movement organization, political party* has been defined in a variety of ways. Beck and Souraf (1992: 8) begin their textbook on political parties by listing six, and they argue that the definitions "reduce to three forms in essence": one defining parties in terms of commonly held ideas, the second focusing on organizational structure, and the third on what they do or what functions they perform. Aldrich (1995: 7–14), too, identifies three "basic views" of "major political parties": one sees parties as broad, encompassing organizations sharing similar values and seeking support from a majority of the public; the second is the normative, "responsible party" view; and the third "sees competition for office as the singular, defining characteristic of the major American political party" (12).

Those writing about parties note that many of these definitions are ambiguous; many interest organizations are held together by the shared views of their members, they may be organized in ways similar to parties, and so on. Indeed, Beck and Souraf describe similarities between interest groups and parties at length; their views are echoed by Yishai (1994) on parties and interest groups, and Aminzade (1995) and Maguire (1995) on similarities between parties and SMOs.

So are there any significant differences between parties and interest organizations, or might only one type of organization link citizens and government? Parties cannot be satisfactorily distinguished from interest organizations on the basis of ideas, organizational structure, or functions. They "occupy the same political space" as movements and interest groups, to use McAdam et al.'s (1996: 27) phrase, and trying to make such distinctions leads into the same morass as the attempt to distinguish between interest groups and SMOs. There is, however, one difference between political parties and interest organizations that truly distinguishes between them: their role in the competition for office. Perhaps Mayhew (1986: 18) puts it best: political parties are "organizations specific to the electoral sector and devoted to advancing a number of candidates for a number of offices (rather than a single candidate for one office)," in competition with other parties. Parties, unlike interest organizations, effectively control access to office (see Aldrich 1995: 273; Jenkins 1995: 21). Controlling access to office is essentially a matter of legal status. Even though Aldrich (1995: 19) describes parties as "fundamentally extralegal," meaning nongovernmental, their role as official nominators of candidates is regulated by law; all jurisdictions have laws regulating access to the ballot, and almost all make it very difficult to win election without having been nominated by a party.[4]

Because they control access to office, parties, unlike interest organizations, are an arena for struggle among those ambitious for office. The public nature of this competition, along with potential responsibility for forming a government, means that parties, again unlike interest organizations, can be called to account on all issues of public concern (Aldrich 1995). Even small parties with little chance of winning office have to be treated as such; by choosing to focus their energies on electoral competition, they subject themselves to the same regulations and constraints, and seek the same opportunities, as their larger competitors.

Thus, two types of intermediary organizations exist in democratic polities: interest organizations and political parties. Both link citizens and government and seek to influence public policy using a variety of means. The distinguishing feature of political parties is their control of access to office. To understand the role of both kinds of organizations in democratic politics, it is necessary to examine what they have done historically and what they do today.

What Political Parties and Interest Organizations Do

"The rise of the national social movement"—movements challenging those who run national states—writes Charles Tilly (1984: 304), "belongs to the same complex of changes which included two other profound transformations in the character of popular collective action—the growth of national electoral politics, and the proliferation of created associations as the vehicles of action." Modern forms of political organization arose, in other words, in response to the opportunities and challenges provided by the beginnings of democracy; their development was made possible by social, economic, and technological changes that made it easier to create large organizations for the pursuit of goals at the national level.

Political parties specifically have long been seen as arising to fulfill particular "needs" of national states, such as interest aggregation and articulation. This way of thinking proved unsatisfactory to many social scientists because it reified states and their "needs," and since the 1970s the analysis of parties and other political organizations has focused increasingly on how those involved in national politics create and alter organizations to serve specific needs of their own. Often, though not always, the analyses adopt a rational choice perspective.

The archetypical case in the new research is the United States, probably because it was "the first new nation" (Lipset 1979)—the first large and populous nation confronting the problems of democratic governance. This sketch is far too brief to even begin to do justice to the literature on American political development, but it seems fair to say that a coherent story is beginning to emerge.

In the beginning, the federal government was created by the current U.S. Constitution, and then, in response to the challenges of democratic governance, those charged with running the new government developed political parties. Aldrich (1995: chap. 3) argues that national leaders found themselves facing a difficult problem during the first several congresses: representatives' and senators' preferences were distributed in such a way that the outcomes of votes were unstable and unpredictable.[5] But stable, patterned outcomes were very important. Hamilton, Jefferson, Madison, and others not only wanted to win on specific issues but also wanted very much to establish a coherent *set* of policies to show the nation that the new government could be counted on. The development of a means to produce such a set of policies was neither easy nor inevitable, but Hamilton was able to organize those in Congress who favored his views into a rudimentary organization, with characteristics now associated with party activities in legislatures. The consequent series of victories for these Federalists led Jefferson and Madison to conclude that they had to organize their supporters in opposition and, in addition, to try to appeal to the voters.

Thus, parties began in Congress because it was there that individuals faced real problems and had strong incentives to solve them. But it was also true that parties could have begun nowhere else. The primitive state of communication and organizational capacity made it impossible to organize parties in the electorate at large, and the collective action problem would have proven insurmountable in any case.

Parties did gradually extend their reach beyond the capital, however, in a process taking decades and culminating, thanks to the organizational genius of Martin Van Buren and others, in the creation of the first mass-based political party, the Democrats, during and after the 1828 presidential campaign. According to Aldrich, there were immense obstacles to organizing a mass party, providing incentives for people to participate, and acquiring the resources necessary to sustain the organization. Once these obstacles were overcome, the Democratic Party was by far the most pervasive organization in the country.

Although the most obvious consequence of the rise of the Democratic party was its ability to mobilize voters, its activities were critical to the United States in another way as well: they held the nation together. Skowronek (1982: chap. 2) describes how the parties helped overcome the institutional conflicts and decentralization of power built into the Constitution. Using formal organization rather than personal ties among notables, they provided a way to organize government institutions and bring some coherence to national politics.

Thus, parties were developed in response to problems arising in the elected legislature; they spread into the electorate and were, for awhile, the only nongovernmental national organizations of consequence. Interest organizations, in turn, were created in response to the national government and the political parties.

Like many others, Aldrich (1995: 295) accepts the truism that the extension of democracy in the United States would almost surely have been impossible without parties, and many political scientists have claimed that parties are essential for democracy in general. Nevertheless, increasing numbers of social scientists are taking a decidedly unsentimental view of parties: they exist to solve problems faced by politicians; and if some other type of organization proves more useful, politicians will turn to them and abandon parties (Aldrich 1995; Hansen 1991).

Politicians will turn to interest organizations, Hansen (1991) writes, when they become convinced that interest organizations are better able than parties to provide information and assistance that will help them win election (or reelection).[6] Such organizations may be more useful than parties because parties are able to encompass only a limited range of views on any particular set of issues and may therefore lack the flexibility to respond to many specific demands. Thus, individuals sharing some political demand may find that the political parties are unable or unwilling to respond. Wanting to exert influence in some other way, they have to confront the problem of collective action: the fact that while all stand to gain if an attempt to influence government is successful, each person will be inclined to let others incur the costs involved. Costs and benefits are a crucial consideration.

The potential benefits of organizing will increase, in general, with the size of government. The federal government of 1790 had little to offer most citizens, but today's government can offer a great deal, providing great potential rewards to interest organizations.

When political parties exist, most people are likely to find it least costly to express their interests through the parties; only when the parties fail them are people likely to think about establishing alternative organizations. Then interest organizations would seem most likely to grow where the costs of organizing are especially low. One likely circumstance for such growth would be where political organization can be a byproduct of interactions already occurring among those potentially interested. Occupational communities seem a likely locale for the formation of interest organizations viewed this way, and, indeed, such communities were among the first to form interest organizations in their modern form; they remain central to the system of interest organizations in the United States (Walker 1991: chap. 2). The cost of organizing has also been reduced by government sponsorship; the government has often supported the formation of specific interest organizations, because those in power believed the organizations could provide otherwise unavailable information about specific sectors of the economy, because they wanted to encourage particular activities on a voluntary basis, and for other reasons. Organizing has also been made easier by technological advances that reduce the cost of finding and communicating with those potentially interested in an issue.

Interest organizations, thus, have arisen out of the same forces that led to the formation of mass political parties: electoral politics, the development of resources and organizational skills, and the felt needs of politicians and those trying to influence government. But their rise was also influenced by the parties themselves or, rather, by the perceived failings of political parties for the expression of some interests.[7]

What political parties do can be summarized in many ways, but recent work focuses increasingly on how they compete for office. To win office, they try to respond (or appear to respond) to the expressed desires of those likely to vote, to get voters to pay more attention to issues on which they are likely to agree with the candidates, and to reformulate issues in ways that will appeal to voters (see, e.g., Carmines and Stimson 1989; Erikson, Wright, and McIver 1993; Jones 1994; Riker 1986). To do so, they must acquire information about the electorate, communicate to the electorate, and acquire the resources necessary to do so, in an environment in which they are competing for voters and resources with other parties and interest organizations. Both in and out of office, parties try to influence what the government does.

Interest organizations are also in the business of influencing government and therefore do many of the same things parties do, except for nominating candidates and competing for office. Initially, they organized in response to perceived party failure, but now they are in many respects as important as parties and are often sources of innovation in policy proposals and political tactics. They, too, both reflect parts of the public and try to lead it; they, too, must be concerned about information, communication, and the acquisition of resources in a competitive environment.

Implications for Theory and Research

McAdam (1984: 24) writes that we need "several theories specifically tailored to particular categories of action," and, in particular, we need to distinguish between "change efforts generated by excluded groups and by established polity members." I claim the opposite. When trying to convince social scientists to rethink their views of social movements, Gamson (1990: 138) argues that "the old duality of extremist politics and pluralist politics" was based on a mistaken premise; instead, "there is simply politics." Similarly, I think that the old duality of SMOs and interest groups was based on a mistaken premise; instead, there are simply organizations—interest organizations and political parties—trying to influence government. The theories we need, therefore, are theories that unify different "categories of action." I cannot provide such a theory here but want to suggest what such theories should focus on.

The central focus must be democratic politics. Democracy represents, above all, an attempt to make government responsive to its citizens—if not perfectly, at least much more responsive than alternative forms of government. Most social scientists who study democratic politics are, ultimately, very much concerned about how responsive the government is and about the forces affecting such responsiveness.

A decision to focus on the role played by interest organizations and political parties in democratic politics has two broad implications. The first is theoretical: analyses of interest organizations and political parties must be pursued in the context of theories of democratic politics, particularly theories that show how democratic institutions link the government and the public (see, e.g., Carmines and Stimson 1989; Dahl 1989; Riker 1982). To the political scientists who study interest groups and political parties, this point will seem obvious; it is natural for them to think of interest groups and parties as intermediaries between the public and government, in a context in which elected officials are continually concerned about satisfying their constituents. To most sociologists who study SMOs, however, this point is not obvious at all; they seldom consider how SMO strategies or success might be affected by public opinion, electoral politics, or the concerns of legislators and rarely take seriously the work of major theorists of democratic politics.[8]

The second implication of the focus on democratic politics and government responsiveness is methodological. Much work on democratic politics is done by scholars who specialize in what they define as a particular type of organization: SMOs, interest groups, or political parties. Organizing scholarly research this way is fine for some purposes, but not for studying the determinants of government action. If government is affected by many factors (and we have every reason to believe that it is) then it makes little sense to conduct what amounts to a series of bivariate studies, examining the relationship between SMO activity and government action in one, interest group activity and government action in a second, party activity and government action in a third, public opinion in a fourth, and so on. The best research strategy will be directed at finding the best explanation for government action, whatever the influences on government might turn out to be and however they interact.

From these broad principles follow five more specific implications for theory and research on interest organizations and political parties.

First, the failure of interest organizations and parties to exert any action in a third, public opinion in direct, independent influence on government action will often be a sign that democracy is working well—that the government is responding to the preferences of the majority. According to what has been called the "theory of dynamic representation" (Stimson, MacKuen, and Erikson 1995), democratic governments respond first and foremost to public opinion, particularly on issues the public cares deeply about, because elected officials want so strongly to be reelected and believe that the way to win reelection is to do what their constituents want (see also Erikson et al. 1993; Jones 1994). Hypothetically, therefore, interest organizations or parties that represent a minority of the public should have no impact on the government when the majority is concerned enough about an issue to make its demands clear to elected officials. This hypothesis has seldom been rigorously tested, but enough logic and evidence for it exist that further work is surely warranted.[9]

Second, because it is probably very difficult for interest organizations or political parties to get the government to act against the wishes of an intensely concerned public, we may hypothesize that they influence government directly on an issue when the public is relatively indifferent and indirectly by altering the public's preferences. This leaves substantial room for influence, of course. Recent work by sociologists and political scientists is beginning to specify how the influence process works, but it also shows how difficult and uncertain the process is for those involved.

If interest organizations and political parties can directly influence government action on issues the public cares relatively little about, the opportunities for influence will be many, because the public has the capacity to be very concerned about only a small number of issues at any one time (Hilgartner and Bosk 1988; Jones 1994). Nevertheless, it has been argued, the influence of interest organizations and political parties will usually be limited; elected officials will be afraid to ignore their constituents' opinions entirely because they are afraid that their political opponents may find ways to make constituents concerned about issues on which their wishes are being ignored (Arnold 1990; Jones 1994; Krehbiel 1991).

If interest organizations and political parties wish to influence government action indirectly, by altering the public's preferences, they have three important avenues of attack. They can try to change the public's intensity of concern about an issue, the public's substantive preferences on an issue as currently framed, or how the issue is framed—that is, how people define the issue and what they see as the relevant policy alternatives. Influencing the intensity of public concern is probably the easiest (though not easy in any absolute sense), and it has certainly been a successful tactic but works to the advantage of an interest organization or political party only if the public is sympathetic to its goals in the first place (Burstein 1985; Jones 1994). Changing the public's preferences is arguably much more difficult; organizations trying to move the public one way are often opposed by organizations trying to move it the other, and attempts to influence public opinion even by well-known organizations sometimes have a negative effect, moving opinion away from what the organization wants (Page and Shapiro 1992). Changing how an issue is framed is probably most difficult of all, and also the most difficult to study; we know that organizations that succeed in reframing an issue can transform their own political fortunes but have very little understanding of why some attempts at reframing succeed while others fail (see, e.g., Carmines and Stimson 1989; Gamson 1993; Jones 1994; Riker 1986; Snow et al. 1986).

The third implication of studying interest organizations and political parties together in the context of theories of democratic politics is that more attention must be paid to the relationship between the tactics used to express political demands and how the demands are perceived by elected officials. Political scientists who study elected officials emphasize that they devote great effort to finding out what their constituents, campaign contributors, and others want them to do; accurate information is necessary if they are to satisfy the voters and win reelection (Arnold 1990; Hansen 1991; Krehbiel 1991). Organizations making demands on officials have two, somewhat contradictory goals: to provide information about their strength that is accurate, so that officials will find them reliable and turn to them regularly for advice; and to provide information that exaggerates their strength, so that officials will accede to their demands more than they would if they had better information (Hansen 1991; Lohmann 1993). In either case, their choice of tactics will be motivated in part by the desire to influence how officials perceive their power to sway election outcomes.[10]

Public officials realize, of course, that organizations are trying to manipulate their perceptions and try to discount organizational activities accordingly; the organizations, in turn, try to adjust their tactics to overcome political leaders' tendency to discount their actions, and so on. Thus, as Lohmann (1993) argues most cogently, the number and type of political actions necessary to produce policy change are endogenous. Even a small number of actions may be effective if the actors can convince elected officials that they represent the views of many nonparticipants. The likelihood of convincing them, however, depends on the history of political action in the particular society—the first public demonstrations of a particular type may be effective even if relatively few participate, but later ones may be less so even if more people take part, because the tactic has grown routine and the cost of participation has declined.

Unfortunately, those who do most of the empirical work on the effectiveness of various tactics (mostly sociologists) seldom take electoral concerns and elected officials' need for information into account; as a result, their work is much less useful than it might be. Gamson (1990: 50), for example, states that the number of members in an SMO "is not theoretically interesting in its own right." Not all the groups he studied were trying to influence government, and his statement may be correct for those, but within the context of theories of democracy, his statement is certainly incorrect for groups trying to influence government—the struggle for democracy is in large measure a struggle to see to it that those with the most votes have the most power. Similarly, when McAdam et al. claim (1996: 23) that the effectiveness of new tactics derives largely from their novelty and capacity to cause public disorder, they fail to consider why organizations adopt new tactics—not for the sake of novelty or to cause disorder, but to convince elected officials of their power. The union of empirical work on tactics with theoretical work on democracy will benefit both.

The fourth point also concerns tactics used to influence government. Those who study SMOs are much concerned about how particular tactics (especially violent ones) affect success. Yet if we acknowledge that SMOs operate in complex and competitive political environments, the focus on particular tactics may not be a very fruitful basis for research. Each successful tactic will be met by attempts to develop effective countertactics (McAdam 1983); each successful effort to exaggerate an organization's support in the population will lead eventually to elected officials' discounting similar efforts when they are repeated. No plausible tactic will be inherently more effective than any other.

Finally, we need to think carefully about what we are trying to explain when studying democratic politics. Gamson (1990) made a breakthrough of tremendous importance when he argued for examining a large random sample of SMOs rather than only a few unusually successful ones. Yet, if we are most concerned about particular outcomes (policy changes, e.g.), it makes more sense to sample a set of outcomes and then analyze their determinants than to sample a set of possible determinants and then see whether they matter. The activities of interest organizations and political parties are strongly influenced by the activities of other such organizations and of formal political institutions. As Beck and Sorauf (1992: 2) write, "the division of labor among political organizations is . . . neither clear nor permanent." Their activities always overlap; they compete with each other; and the nature of their activities changes over time, partly in response to what the others are doing (see also Burstein 1985; Haines 1988; McAdam et al. 1996). Sampling policy outcomes and then analyzing their determinants is a task even more daunting than the one Gamson set for himself, yet it seems essential if we are to understand the role of organizations in democratic politics.

Conclusion

Recent years have seen substantial progress in social scientists' ability to explain both the activities of intermediary political organizations and their consequences. Unfortunately, tradition, vocabulary, and perhaps assumptions about the nature of democratic politics have served to divide those who study political parties and interest groups (mostly political scientists) from those who study social movement organizations (mostly sociologists). As a result, they focus on seemingly different aspects of the political process, and their failure to unite their efforts hinders further progress.

The conventional response to this impasse is to urge members of both disciplines to combine their efforts (I participated in an interdisciplinary roundtable that reached this conclusion at the 1985 American Political Science Association meetings), with sociologists putting together one part of the puzzle and political scientists the other. I have concluded that this suggestion is misguided. It is not that sociologists and political scientists are studying different things that could usefully be combined; rather, they are studying the same thing without realizing it. The commonsense distinction between SMOs and interest groups cannot stand up to scrutiny and should be abandoned. In addition, political parties are so similar to the other intermediary organizations that they, too, should be studied in the same framework (keeping in mind the important differences between them and the others as well).

Those interested in interest groups and SMOs should, therefore, see synthesis as their next task, drawing together the concepts that seem most useful for analyzing intermediary organizations and using them uniformly to analyze the entire spectrum of such organizations. Perhaps in ten years there will be no more talk of "interest groups" or "social movement organizations" but only of interest organizations.

Notes

This chapter is a revision of a paper presented at a session on "Social Movement Theory," annual meeting of the American Political Science Association, Chicago, September 2, 1995. I would like to thank Anne Costain, Douglas Imig, Sidney Tarrow, and Mayer Zald for helpful advice and comments.

1. Their argument is actually a broader one about what they call "contentious politics," but it certainly applies to the organizations addressed here.

2. Even thoughtful scholars casually abandon the distinction when doing empirical work. For example, as a sociologist, Clemens (1993: 773) naturally claims to be addressing the literature on social movements in her analysis of the American "woman movement" of the late nineteenth and early twentieth centuries; yet she quickly slips into discussions of "interest-group bargaining" by a movement that relied on lobbying as a tactic. Similarly, political scientists Page and Shapiro (1992: 350–7) claim to be interested in the impact of "interest groups" on public opinion, but their examples include the nuclear freeze movement, the civil rights movement, and the anti-Vietnam War movement.

3. Tarrow (1995: 3) raises this question but arrives at a different conclusion: "If there is no essential difference between movements and interest groups, what justifies the specialization of large numbers of scholars on movements?" His claim seems to be that the existence

of a large group of specialists legitimates the object of study, and that if there are two groups of specialists (one for "movements," one for "interest groups"), there must be two objects of study. I would argue that it is the object of study that legitimates the group of specialists; and if two groups find themselves studying the same thing, the groups should merge.

4. This point is true of all federal offices; the major exception at the state level is Nebraska, where elections are officially nonpartisan; and a fair number of local governments also hold elections on a nonpartisan basis.

5. In modern parlance, there was no equilibrium in the distribution of preferences of members of Congress as they addressed many issues arrayed along multiple dimensions.

6. Hansen is writing about interest groups, not interest organizations more broadly, but the logic of his argument applies to the organizations customarily considered SMOs.

7. It should be noted that those writing about interest groups describe the conditions of their creation in ways similar to what others say about SMOs. Both emphasize the existence of unmet needs, the unresponsiveness of government and the political parties, and the obstacles to organizing; see Hansen (1991) and Gamson (1975).

8. They rarely cite the works of major theorists of democratic politics, and when they do, they often fail to address such work in a serious way. For example, both Gamson (1990) and McAdam (1982) refer to Dahl's writings on pluralism, but the book they cite is his undergraduate political science textbook rather than his much more nuanced scholarly publications. I am not suggesting that sociologists must agree with the major theories of democratic politics, only that they take such theories seriously.

9. See Burstein (1985), Lohmann (1993), and Neustadtl (1990: 553–4). Piven and Cloward (1977) are among the few specialists on social movements who both cite major theorists of democratic politics and give electoral concerns an important place in their analysis. But they do not quite get to the point of suggesting that poor people's movements may fail because they represent only a minority, nor do they ponder the implications for democracy were they, as a minority, to succeed.

10. Their choice of tactics will often be constrained by other factors; for example, the NAACP emphasized legal action for decades because blacks were denied the vote in most of the South, and tactics oriented to electoral politics were therefore useless. In addition, organizations sometimes adopt particular tactics to communicate with potential members (Walker 1991).

Part 2
Mobilization

4

Mobilizing Gay Activists

Claude Dufour

Social movements scholars have written extensively about the way political processes and political opportunity structures (POS) influence movements' emergence, development, and choice of strategies (Dufour 1994; Eisinger 1973; Gamson and Meyer 1995; Kitschelt 1986; Kriesi 1990; McAdam 1982; Tarrow 1996; Wilson 1990). There seems to be agreement that institutions and movements influence one another in multiple ways (della Porta 1996; Jenkins and Klandermans 1995; Offe 1985; Tarrow 1994). Since a goal of this volume is to examine how agendas, alternatives, and public policies, to use Kingdon's (1984) formulation, can be shaped by movements, the gay and lesbian rights movement (GLRM) serves as an interesting example.

Over the past thirty years, in the United States and around the world, gay men and lesbians have mobilized and their movement for civil rights has transformed the life of those sharing this collective identity (Taylor and Whittier 1992). Especially in the Western world, there has been an explosion of gay and lesbian organizations that have professionalized activism, and to some extent, institutionalized the movement. In some policy areas, gay and lesbian social movement organizations (SMOs) and gay interest groups have become significant "lobbies." Governments and political parties at various levels must now respond to or reckon with organized gay constituencies. But in what ways has this movement affected political processes and institutions? Are government responsiveness and policy reform the result of the movement's mobilization of individuals, articulation of grievances, and its accumulation of resources? Has this movement simply gained "a place at the table" of the pluralist American political system, or has it helped transform American institutions?

In this chapter, I focus on the utilitarian aspect or instrumental action of the movement. I use three civil rights law reforms—decriminalization of homosexual activity, statutory protection against discrimination, and hate crime laws—to examine the connection between changes in policy and the movement's influence. These cases illustrate how policy responsiveness is associated with specific changes in institutional behavior toward the movement, its SMOs, and the individuals benefiting from these reforms. In observing the movement's development and its relation to the state, I will suggest that this social movement was one of many facilitating forces in a law reform and/or "modernization" cycle. It sometimes acts as a traditional, self-interested political actor. Finally, in some cases, its influence is found in the creation of alternative institutions and the development of new social norms.[1]

The Context

Law reform and civil rights protection for gays and lesbians in the United States offer a very complex configuration of types of evidence, showing the movement's influence and government's policy responsiveness. The decentralized American system, with its fifty state jurisdictions, each with its own particular body of laws, creates a mosaic of legislation and statutes not easily described as a unit. Focusing on a specific and circumscribed environment rather than trying to account for this vast array of situations is a practical way to illustrate the movement's impact on public policy. Illinois and Chicago provide for an interesting case. Although located in the relatively conservative Midwest, Chicago has been a concentration point for many gays and lesbians. Unlike the usual suspects of San Francisco, New York, and Los Angeles, Chicago does not represent a lead actor in the gay rights movement or in gay politics. Yet, during the last thirty years, Chicago and Illinois gay activists have mobilized and gained significant influence within the (local) political process. Although no statewide, gay-inclusive, antidiscrimination law exists in Illinois, measures to protect gays from discrimination have been implemented in Chicago and other localities, and by various offices and agencies of the state of Illinois.

Early Mobilization and Sodomy Laws

Historians and gay scholars have recently documented the early development of a homosexual subculture in the United States. Chauncey (1994) focused on New York at the turn of the century, Russell (1993) observed the interwar period of 1918–1945, while Berube (1990) chronicled the emergence of gay and lesbian social and political networks following World War II. However, it was only during the 1950s and early 1960s that "political-activist" homosexual organizations were established throughout the United States (Adam 1979, 1987; Cruikshank 1992; D'Emilio 1983; Duberman et al. 1989; Faderman 1991; Katz 1992). The Mattachine Society, an organization created in 1951 in Los Angeles, and the Daughters of Bilitis (DOB), the lesbian organization created in 1955 in San Francisco, were the most significant early organizations of what became known as the "homophile" movement. During the late 1950s and early 1960s, local chapters of both organizations were created in larger cities across the United States, including Chicago's Mattachine Midwest.

Mattachine and DOB, as well as other homosexual groups formed during that period, evolved in the climate of social conformity in the early 1950s. Therefore, these organizations were largely occupied with portraying homosexuals as "normal," ordinary individuals. In expressing grievances and advocating for equal rights for homosexuals they used nonthreatening and nonconfrontational strategies such as letter writing, picketing, and, importantly, litigation. Although these SMOs had important social functions, their political agenda was largely limited to gaining First Amendment rights protections afforded to most citizens (i.e., freedom of expression, assembly, and speech).

Until 1961, "practicing" homosexuality was outlawed in all fifty states. Although homosexuality was never illegal per se, the legal conditions for gay people were rather precarious because of the variety of statutes, such as vagrancy laws, obscenity laws, and sodomy laws that were selectively used to target and criminalize homosexual behaviors and practices. The most interesting and widespread example of selective application of the law was sodomy laws. Historically, sodomy laws were formulated according to religious principles that proscribed sexual behavior that did not lead to procreation. Such laws usually included oral and anal sex between people of the same *or* opposite genders. Although these laws were not originally, specifically targeted toward homosexuals, they were often applied to control acts of homosexuality and rarely applied to heterosexuals. In other words, in applying the law, the state's coercive institutions selectively harassed and repressed a specific group that engaged in proscribed behavior.

During the 1960s, however, significant changes in the American legal system, at both the national and state levels, directly affected legal conditions for homosexuals. Some changes were influenced by homosexual individuals and groups challenging discriminatory practices through test court cases. As Cain (1993, 1579) documents in her legal history of lesbian and gay litigation:

> The Supreme Court's formulation of obscenity doctrine in the 1950s and 1960s ensured gay and lesbian publications of greater First Amendment protection. Court decisions pronouncing the rights of homosexuals to be served in bars provided safer social environments and federal employees challenged their dismissal for homosexuality with some degree of success.

In addition, as Harry and DeVall (1978, 153) suggest, the minor step of gaining legal access to the use of the federal mail was crucial in developing networks of communication among gays and their organizations and instrumental in creating a collective identity.

If some changes in institutional behavior (i.e., recognizing homosexuals' First Amendment freedoms) were the result of a stream of court cases by gay individuals and gay SMOs, other changes affecting homosexuals' legal status came from legislated "administrative" modernization of criminal codes. Beginning in the early 1960s, a number of state governments, influenced by a movement to modernize the system of criminal law, legislated reform of their entire system of criminal law by adopting a version of the Model Penal Code. As Rubenstein (1993: xvi) explains, "The Model Penal Code proposed decriminalizing private, consensual, adult sexual behavior, including homosexual sex. As state legislatures adopted the Code throughout the 1960s and 1970s, they did away with their sodomy laws."

In 1961, Illinois became the first state to adopt the Model Code position and to decriminalize homosexual sex in private and between consenting adults. While some states added new laws with "homosexual specification," banning only homosexual sodomy, most states during the 1970s and 1980s relaxed and even abandoned enforcement of their sodomy laws. Yet, the 1986 Supreme Court's ruling in the case of *Bowers* v. *Hardwick* upheld the constitutionality of Georgia's sodomy statute, outlawing sexual relations between consenting adults of the same sex.

How are we to interpret these changes in policy regarding sodomy statutes? How influential was the movement in states' abandoning their sodomy laws or their enforcement?[2] Gay organizations by themselves were not powerful enough to pressure legislators into abandoning their sodomy laws. In Illinois, only very few and mostly underground gay organizations operated in 1961, when sodomy laws were repealed.

If early mobilization efforts were crucial in initiating mass communication and political mobilization among homosexuals, their impact on sodomy law reform can only be understood as one of many forces partaking in a cyclical modernization of public thinking and public policy. Several scholars have discerned that these policy changes were the result of a general "relaxation of moral climate" in the West brought about by several social and economic factors, including long economic expansion, growing affluence, geographical and social mobility, increased urbanization, changes in family practices, and other technological advances (Abramson and Inglehart 1995; Dufour 1995; Inglehart 1990; Jeffery-Poulter 1991; Kriesi et al. 1995; Wotherspoon 1991). As a consequence of these broad social and economic changes, "more and more professionals, politicians, and clergymen began to doubt the effects of the criminalization and oppression of homosexuality and argued for a humanitarian attitude" (Kieisi et al. 1995: 170). Decriminalization of sexuality in general, and of homosexuality in particular, was not necessarily enlightened or benevolent action by legislators and the courts. The rapid change in social and economic conditions had accelerated the emergence of "new social movements" (e.g., women's, student, new left, gay and lesbian movements) and stimulated older social movements (e.g., labor, civil rights movements) (Freeman 1973, 1975, 1982; Jenkins and Eckert 1977; McAdam 1982). These movements challenged antiquated laws and mores regarding sexual issues such as age of consent, contraception, miscegenation, and abortion. The abandonment of sodomy laws, then, was the result of a general modernization of civil and criminal statutes brought about by important socioeconomic changes, the mobilization of new social movements (NSMs), including the gay and lesbian movement, and their challenge to codification of "traditional" moral values and practices into law.

Antidiscrimination Protection in the United States

The lack of federal legislation protecting citizens from discrimination based on sexual orientation has led several states, counties, and cities to experiment with extending civil-legal protection through legislation, ordinances, and executive orders. Protection from these laws include at least one, and in many cases several, of the following categories: public employment, public accommodations, employment, education, real estate/housing, credit, and union practices.

Wisconsin (1981) and Massachusetts (1990) were the first states to enact statewide antidiscrimination laws protecting lesbians and gays.[3] In 1996, nine states and the District of Columbia, and more than 150 counties and cities, including Los Angeles, San Francisco, Portland, Seattle, New York, and Chicago, had gay-inclusive antidiscrimination laws.[4] Overall, these state and local regulations offer protection to a relatively large segment of the American population—between one in eight (Hunter et al. 1993: 16) and one in five Americans (Button et al. 1994: 3).

How are these protective statutes produced? How do gay and lesbian activists gain influence and help shape such policies? The case of Chicago and Illinois is illustrative of the relative strength of the movement in influencing political actors to change institutional behavior regarding sexual orientation and discrimination.

Human Rights Ordinances: Chicago and Cook County

Since the mid-1960s, a concentration of gay and lesbian dwellers have located and gay-owned businesses have developed in a few districts of Chicago. This numerical concentration provides a base for political mobilization around issues affecting gays and lesbians. In recent years, Chicago's politics have largely been organized around two central axes: the Democratic party and race. It is no surprise, then, that as early as the 1970s, gay business leaders and gay political activists evolved within the Democratic party organization and formed organizations associated with it, such as the Chicago Gay Democrats. It is also no surprise that more favorable public policy toward gays and lesbians resulted from the evolution of "minority" politics and rise to power of minority politicians at Chicago's city hall.

As early as 1973, a bill to "bar discrimination based on sexual choice" was introduced in the Chicago city council. Similar measures were regularly introduced in the city council over the next ten years but got little or no support. Only during the early 1980s, with Jane Byrne as mayor, did the issue of gay rights pick up some support and make inroads at city hall. The attention given to gay and lesbian issues was prompted by several factors. On the one hand, by the late 1970s, a sophisticated communication network of activist groups, gay and lesbian newspapers, and organizational newsletters was mobilizing large numbers of individuals and helping coordinate lobbying and protest campaigns. Alternative media allowed groups to quickly plan and advertise demonstrations or campaigns to lobby Mayor Byrne. On the other hand, the previous death of Richard G. Daley, in 1976, had weakened the Democratic "machine" and produced leadership instability within the party and city government. Electorally, "nonmachine" and black politicians were challenging the old Democratic power holders. Struggling to maintain control of City Hall and intent on seizing the "gay vote," Mayor Byrne developed policies, during her tenure, that addressed some of the concerns of gays and lesbians, for example, by issuing an executive order banning discrimination based on sexual orientation in city hiring.

Meanwhile, gay restaurants, bars, and clubs and gay-owned businesses were proliferating, and they, as well as a growing number of gay and lesbian residents, were resettling in the Lakeview area, in the city's 44th Ward. Inner-city gay migration and the formation of a "gay ghetto" or "gay village" is a common trend in large urban centers of the United States. This phenomenon has a significant social, political, and economic impact on local governments, wards, and district constituencies (Castells 1983; Murray 1992). As in this case, elected officials eventually recognize the necessity of responding to such politically mobilized and articulate groups.

If Mayor Jane Byrne cracked open the door of city hall to gays, the election of African American Harold Washington as mayor was the turning point for minority politics in Chicago: it produced unprecedented grassroots mobilization. During his campaign and following his election in 1983, Washington helped develop coalitions of minority groups, including gays and lesbians. Minority groups had long been kept out of participation in city politics, and Washington knew he would need them to challenge the "old guard" of city hall. Once in office, Washington established the position of "mayor's liaison to the gay and lesbian community" and sanctioned the Mayor's Council on Gay and Lesbian Issues (COGLI). Washington's actions, the creation of new, although limited government agencies, changed the norm by officially recognizing gays and lesbians as "worthy" constituencies. These new official bodies were to increase opportunities of all sorts for gays and lesbians, including the gain of extended access to city hall and allowing gays some participation in local governance. The political mobilization of gay activists around the electoral process had helped legitimize the movement's role in city politics and would be repeated for further gains.

In 1986, the mayor's liaison to the gay and lesbian community and gay activists pushed for passage of a gay rights bill. Opposed by many aldermen and influential groups (including the archdiocese of Chicago, which had issued a condemning position statement), the bill failed. However, sponsorship by the mayor, coordinated lobbying of aldermen by gay groups, and the broad coalition in support of this bill represented a benchmark for Chicago's lesbian and gay political activism (Pick 1993). In failure, the local movement leaders and activists found resolve.

A crucial development that led to the passage of the Chicago Human Rights Ordinance was the formation of the gay and lesbian town meeting. The town meeting, led by a core group of well-known activists, in an effort to attract additional support, developed a strategy that included drafting a new ordinance proposal with broader and more inclusive language (i.e., one that included disability, ancestry, and marital status; in all, thirteen categories of "human rights" were covered (Pick 1993: 14). During the fall of 1988, the revised ordinance produced passionate and fierce debates in the city council.

A detailed description of the dynamics around the passage of the ordinance is too complex to include here, but observers agree on three major points. First, the ordinance had gained added legitimacy by being introduced by the Chicago Commission on Human Relations. Second, interim Mayor Eugene Sawyer,[5] then preparing for the upcoming election, saw the gay vote as crucial to his electoral success and became a resolute advocate for the ordinance. This put pressure on allied council members. Third, Richard M. Daley, then Cook County state's attorney and, more important, the strongest contender in the upcoming election, lobbied aldermen to vote for the ordinance proposal.[6] Although some religious and conservative groups still staunchly opposed the measure, the human rights ordinance bill was passed on December 21, 1988, on a vote of twenty-eight to seventeen.

Human Rights Laws in Illinois

On April 21, 1993, a gay rights bill (House Bill 2182) passed the Illinois House of Representatives for the first time. The bill added sexual orientation to the groups protected under the State Human Rights Act in the areas of employment, real estate transactions, financial credit, and access to public accommodations. But a new Senate Republican majority opposed the bill and effectively stalled it in committee. The bill died in the Illinois Senate that same year.

The significance of this bill, though, is found in the broad coalition supporting it.[7] The coalition led by the Illinois Federation for Human Rights (IFHR) included other gay organizations such as the Illinois Gay and Lesbian Task Force and IMPACT but also groups such as the Leadership Council for Civil Rights, the American Civil Liberties Union, the National Organization for Women, the Illinois Federation of Teachers, the National Coalition of American Nuns, and the Chicago Urban League.

Important inroads were made during work on this bill. For example, Republican governor Jim Edgar attended a reception sponsored by IFHR and responded to a gay and lesbian (IMPACT) questionnaire prior to the 1994 election—the first time an Illinois governor had done so. Governor Edgar even stated that "[p]rivate and personal lifestyle decisions and sexual orientation are not a valid basis for denying someone housing or job opportunities" (Griffin 1994).

Passage of the bill in the Illinois House also revealed that gay SMOs were becoming very professional and more sophisticated in their strategies. During 1993–1994, IFHR hired two lobbyists to work in the Illinois capital, Springfield. The federation created its own political action committee and focused its attention on pro-gay state representatives who were being challenged as a result of their support for gay rights. As opposed to past efforts, a bipartisan approach was tried. IFHR and IMPACT formally solicited the Illinois Democratic party platform committee for continued commitment to passing a state antigay discrimination bill, but they also organized meetings with members of the Illinois Republican party during its state convention. During the 1994 primary and general elections, significant campaign contributions were made by IFHR to first-term Republicans regarded as especially vulnerable because of their support for the gay rights bill the previous year.[8] IFHR's petition drive to support a statewide gay and lesbian rights bill gathered twenty-five thousand signatures that were delivered to the state legislature during the 1994 fall session, while the voter registration campaign registered about six thousand new voters. Similar efforts were repeated during the 1995–96 election cycle.

As the recent efforts in Illinois show, gay political SMOs adopting a nonpartisan strategy in political campaigns, if helpful to broaden coalition support, does not necessarily lead to policy change. Regardless of organizational strategy, most gay and lesbian activists, especially in Chicago, are still strongly aligned with the Democratic party. This partisanship hindered the groups' efforts to gain support in regions of the state outside Chicago, such as the suburban counties and in southern Illinois—areas historically controlled by the Republican party. Importantly, the Illinois Human Rights Commission (IHRC) never took a clear position on sexual orientation and made no effort to intervene on behalf of its inclusion in the Human Rights Act.

So attempts to establish gay-inclusive antidiscrimination laws in Illinois have had mixed results. In spite of twenty years of lobbying by gay groups and their supporters, legislators have refused to include sexual orientation in the State Human Rights Act. Yet, access to policy makers was increased and gay SMOs were successful in putting the issue on the state political agenda. Importantly, many antigay bills were defeated thanks to the efforts of gay SMOs and their Springfield supporters to educate legislators.

Hate Crimes Statutes

During the late 1980s and early 1990s, while the debate over gay and lesbian civil rights issues continued, media attention and group activities turned to acts of violence committed against gays and lesbians. Human rights ordinances and laws providing statutory protection against acts of discrimination usually do not appropriately address criminal acts of violence perpetrated against "minority" groups or targeted at gays and lesbians.

Although federal law pertaining to hate crime violence was virtually nonexistent until 1990, public awareness of hate crimes grew during the 1980s. Work by various organizations such as the National Coalition of Anti-Violence Programs (NCAVP) helped the issue surface on the national government agenda, as crime and violence in general were becoming central themes in national politics. The magnitude of the problem was revealed by groups, the National Institute against Prejudice and Violence (NIAPV) and the Anti-Defamation League (ADL) among them, that collect data on crimes based on anti-Semitism, racism, gender, and religious bias. Antigay and lesbian hate crimes were documented by gay organizations such as the National Gay and Lesbian Task Force (NGLTF), which produced and disseminated reports on "Anti-Gay Violence, Victimization and Defamation," starting in 1985.

In 1990, the 101st Congress passed the Hate Crime Statistics Act, and Pres. George Bush signed it into law (Public Law 101-275). This law requires the FBI and the Department of Justice to collect statistics on crimes motivated by hate based on race, religion, sexual orientation, or ethnicity.

Importantly, this legislation marked the first time a gay-inclusive bill had ever become national law. The signature of the Hate Crime Statistics Act by a Republican president was also symbolically significant because it marked the first time a group of gay men and lesbians were invited to participate in a media event organized around a presidential signature ceremony.

By 1996, more than half of the states and many local jurisdictions had adopted hate crime laws, and many include sexual orientation as a category. Overall, these hate crime laws range in their application from simply re-questing that statistical records on the number of such incidents be kept by police departments and other state agencies to the stiffening of penalties for crimes.

After enactment of the federal hate crime statistics law, several measures pertaining to this issue were introduced in the Illinois legislature. Illinois already had a statewide hate crime law that, among other things, mandated additional penalties for crimes based on race, religion, or ethnic background but not sexual orientation. During its 1990 spring session, the Illinois state legislature approved a comprehensive hate crime legislation, and in September, Gov. James Thompson signed the Freedom from Violence Act, which amended Illinois's hate crime law, to add sexual orientation as well as ancestry and mental and physical disability to the categories of crimes covered by the law. With this law, Illinois became the tenth state to increase penalties for gay bashing and the second state to include sexual orientation in an existing hate crime law. The Freedom from Violence Act was also historically significant since it was the first legislation specifically including sexual orientation to pass the state legislature.

The Freedom from Violence Act can be interpreted as a response by the Illinois legislature and its governor to developments at the federal level (i.e., the mandate conveyed by the federal Hate Crime Statistics Act of 1990). But it also exemplified how gay and lesbian groups, led by the Illinois Gay and Lesbian Task Force (IGLTF), could organize an effective lobbying campaign with support from established politicians. Several gay SMOs and prominent Illinois politicians, including Mayor Daley of Chicago and Cook County State's Attorney Cecil Partee, pushed for passage of the Freedom from Violence Act and testified at hearings. When an amendment to exclude sexual orientation from the act was introduced in the Illinois Senate, they successfully lobbied against it.

Importantly, especially for those concerned with prevention of and prosecution of hate crimes, the Freedom from Violence Act had a pragmatic impact: it compelled police and judicial authorities to take antigay crimes seriously. Although some cases of gay bashing had received the attention of police, legal advocacy activists, and state agencies, there was now a legal obligation to apply the state's hate crime statute to antigay and antilesbian violence cases. This meant creation and funding of a mechanism to accomplish this mandate. The Illinois state's attorney allocated funds for a civil court advocate responsible for educating the population about hate crimes and publication of a 136-page guide to prosecuting hate crimes (Ellen Meyers, October 1994, personal communication).

Chicago Antiviolence Grassroots Mobilization

Between 1990 and 1994, antigay violence surfaced as a major issue in Chicago politics. Between 1989 and December 1990, a Hate Crimes Ordinance proposal was debated in the Chicago city council. A core group of gay activists called Action Network for Lesbian and Gay Issues (ANGLI) lobbied intensively for passage of this hate crime ordinance. Their work was facilitated by the fact that many aldermen had been educated on this issue during the debates over the Chicago Human Rights Ordinance (1987–1988), as well as during the debate over statewide measures concerning statistics on hate crimes and the Freedom from Violence Act of 1990. Also, the mayoral liaison to the lesbian and gay community had developed educational efforts, and the Chicago Police Department (CPD), through its neighborhood relations program and recruitment efforts, had outreached to the gay and lesbian community.

According to Chicago activists, though, the level of support for the ordinance at city hall was strongly influenced by the participation of two key alderman, Bernard Hansen (Forty-fourth) and Hellen Shiller (Forty-sixth). Both represented heavily gay lakefront wards, and they both cosponsored the ordinance. A lead activist of ANGLI explains that Hansen's and Shiller's support and leadership were crucial to passing the hate crime ordinance because they could influence a cross-section of interests in the city council:

> Each [alderman] has its own bloc in the City Council. Helen has the independent bloc. We know we have their support, but we need her to make sure it's solid. Bernie has the ability to work with a wide range of aldermen, including some who aren't identified with the independent block. We need people to work on both side of the Council to win. (Olson 1990:1).

The Hate Crimes Ordinance was approved unanimously on December 19, 1990. It increased penalties for crimes committed because of a victim's gender or minority status, including sexual orientation, and it initiated a coordinated strategy for combating such crimes, which included requiring the Chicago Police Department to expand a minority sensitivity program for police officers at all levels (by 1992, the CPD had appointed a full-time gay and lesbian liaison officer). In addition, the Ordinance mandated that the Chicago Police Department and Chicago Commission on Human Relations record hate crimes and inform the public about such crimes and how to report them.

Two years after passage of the hate crime legislation at both state and city level, activists and SMOs concerned about the increase in antigay violence and the lack of or lax enforcement of hate crime statutes formed a working coalition to ensure that these laws were appropriately implemented. The Chicago Antiviolence Alliance is a good example of a multiplicity of gay organizations working together with established advocacy groups to accomplish a common goal. They coordinated a wide range of activities including self-defense education, "take back the night" marches (night processions of antiviolence groups and political leaders through neighborhoods), participation in legislative hearings, and legal advocacy. Although no formal consultation between movement groups and authorities was activated (i.e., official Human Rights Commission inquiry and report), SMOs created alternative structures with the approval and participation of state and local agencies and elected officials.

Conclusion

This Chicago case study shows how the gay and lesbian rights movement mobilization and a tradition of activism has led to significant changes in policy and institutional behavior toward gays and lesbians. Abandonment of sodomy laws and of most severe sanctions against gays can be attributed partly to mobilization and application of resources by gay SMOs (e.g., litigation), but, importantly, policy change was associated with much broader "modernization" of public thinking and legal statutes brought about by a series of challenges from social movements and their SMOs. The development of the American gay and lesbian movement was greatly influenced by the rise of the civil rights movement and a collection of other "liberation" movements during the 1960s and 1970s. These precursory movements showed the way to gays and lesbians in combining confrontational strategies and protest tactics to more traditional participatory activities such as electoral and party politics.

Organizational mobilization of gays and lesbians included innovation in methods of participation in political processes, such as creating gay political clubs and election of openly gay candidates. It led to creating distinct civil functions for its SMOs, such as social service agencies and community street patrols. These were two ways the movement influenced political processes and institutions.

At the city level, gay activists benefited from leadership and electoral instabilities and the arrival of the more progressive administration of Harold Washington. As we saw, political leverage of gays and lesbians was increased partly because of the recognition of their electoral significance and partly because gay entrepreneurs active within the dominant political formation, the Democratic party, could press for change from within the political institutions. Thus, policy response on antidiscrimination (i.e., passage of human rights ordinances) proceeded from the city level where lobbying, coalition building, and electoral involvement influenced local political leaders to support the movement's demands. The role of government human rights agencies is crucial in adding legitimacy to those sponsoring the gay rights measures. At the state level, it appears that a tradition of strongly partisan politics, a diluted or thinly spread constituency of gays and lesbians, an increasingly conservative state legislature, and the lack of involvement from the state Human Rights Commission all contributed to delay in passing a gay-inclusive human rights law. However, access to institutions was increased, and agenda influence by gay SMOs was noticeable.

With regard to antiviolence, progress was influenced by the fact that this issue had become a national preoccupation. Hate crime legislation initiated at the federal level gave impetus to reform at the state and local levels. The necessity for antiviolence measures was effectively communicated by numerous SMOs, including local, state, and national gay and lesbian organizations. The impact of the movement activity on antigay violence was also demonstrated by the creation of alternative structures and mechanisms to oversee and help enforce these new hate crimes measures.

In summary, the movement has influenced institutions by quickening the pace with which modernization of attitudes takes place. What was punishable everywhere in the United States thirty years ago is now more or less overlooked by authorities. More significant, identities and behavior proscribed as sick and deviant are now tolerated and increasingly legally protected against discrimination. Finally, recognition of the deplorable effect of hate-based violence has forced authorities to shift policy one hundred eighty degrees, outlawing and punishing those who act violently on their prejudice against gays and lesbians.

Notes

1. More theoretical information and a comparative examination of the GLRM can be found in my manuscript "Comparative Analysis of Gay and Lesbian Rights Movements in Canada, the United States, and Australia," currently under revision for publication. For recent perspectives on gay and lesbian law reform struggles, see Michael Nava and Robert Dawidoff, *Why Gay Rights Matter in America* (New York: St. Martin's, 1994); and Didi Herman and Carl Stychin, *Legal Inversions: Lesbians, Gay Men and the Politics of the Law* (Philadelphia: Temple University Press, 1995).

2. Although prosecution under sodomy laws has almost completely been abandoned throughout the United States, with the notable exception of the U.S. military, a myriad of

other legal sanctions against gays remains. Selective prosecution of offenses such as "public indecency" and practices such as entrapment, raids, and police intimidation of gays continue to this day in Chicago and around the country.

3. Ironically, in Wisconsin and Massachusetts these antidiscrimination laws were passed even though these states still had sodomy laws on their books.

4. California, Connecticut, Hawaii, Massachusetts, Minnesota, New Jersey, Rhode Island, Vermont, and Wisconsin have antidiscrimination laws inclusive of sexual orientation.

5. Sawyer replaced Washington after his sudden death in the fall of 1987.

6. According to professor and ex-alderman Dick Simpson, the crucial element in passage of the ordinance was Daley persuading some aldermen to vote for it. Until that time, the split of the city council votes made it impossible to pass almost any measure, including this ordinance. The switch of a few "old guard" associates of Daley, such as Edward Burke (Fourteenth) made it possible (Dick Simpson, September 1991, personal communication).

7. According to IFHR cofounder Art Johnston, the gay rights bill to amend the Human Rights Act passed the Illinois House in 1993 with an unprecedented range of support. Votes came from rural, urban, suburban Republican, Democratic, Catholic, Protestant, Jewish, and prochoice and prolife state representatives. All African-American and Latino representatives voted yes as did all but one of the first-term Democrats. Significant in 1993 was the support of Republicans who were especially targeted by lobbyists. Seven Republicans voted yes and six more voted "present" (Art Johnson, July 1994, personal communication).

8. IFHR's PAC contributions for that year totaled $60,000 (*Now Is the Time!* IFHR pamphlet, 1994).

5

Mobilization at the Margins:
Organizing by the Homeless

Daniel M. Cress and David A. Snow

Nearly two decades after the flowering of the resource mobilization perspective on social movements, it has been observed that many of its assumptions have now been "assimilated as the routine and unstated grounds of much contemporary work" (Zald 1992: 327). One such taken-for-granted assumption is that resources are a *sine qua non* determinant of the course and character of social movement organizations and activity. Indeed, no other assumption is so fundamental to the resource mobilization perspective and a plethora of derivative work. Yet, there is little definitive understanding of a number of resource-related issues relevant to the dynamics of social movement organizations (SMOs). One such issue concerns the conceptualization and identification of resources; a second addresses the question of whether some types of resources are more important than others for mobilization and collective action; the third issue concerns resource derivation, particularly the relative importance of externally versus internally derived resources; and the fourth concerns the implications of external support for SMO viability and tactical actions. In this chapter, we address these issues with data derived from our research on fifteen homeless SMOs in eight U.S. cities, and we explore the implications of our findings for understanding movements of the poor more generally.

Unresolved Issues in the Study of Resource Mobilization

The central premise of resource mobilization theory, the dominant perspective on social movements since the mid-1970s, is that the principal antecedent task to collective action is resource aggregation and that fluctuation in the level of discretionary resources therefore accounts, in large part, for variation in social movement activity (Jenkins and Perrow 1977; McCarthy and Zald 1973, 1977; Oberschall 1973). Yet, despite all the research generated under the rubric of resource mobilization, our understanding of the presumed relationship between resources and social movement activity is surprisingly limited.[1] This gap is due largely to three oversights: the failure to clarify and empirically ground the resource concept, the failure to examine more concretely the linkage between types of resources and various mobilization processes or outcomes, and the failure to clarify empirically competing claims about the sources of resources and the consequences of whether they are externally or internally derived. Taken together, these three oversights give rise to the four issues we seek to illuminate.

Conceptualizing Resources

The resource concept is surprisingly slippery and vague given its ubiquity in the social movement literature. This ambiguity has been a source of concern among students of social movements for a number of years (Freeman 1979; Jenkins 1983; Marx and Wood 1975; Morris and Herring 1988; Piven and Cloward 1977; Zurcher and Snow 1981), but little headway has been made in anchoring resources conceptually or empirically. Conceptually, the tendency has been to include as resources anything that SMOs need to mobilize and deploy in pursuit of their goals (McAdam, McCarthy, and Zald 1988; McCarthy and Zald 1977; Oberschall 1973; Tilly 1978). Attempts have been made to add greater specificity to the concept by considering how resources are used (Gamson, Fireman, and Rytina 1982; Jenkins 1982; Rogers 1974), but this use strategy overlooks the plasticity of many resources (Jenkins 1983). Thus, most researchers merely list the resources used by the SMOs under study. The problem with this listing strategy as typically practiced is that it seldom goes beyond identifying the general categories of money, legitimacy, people, and occasionally expertise (Freeman 1979; Gamson et al. 1982; Lofland 1993; McCarthy and Zald 1977; Oliver and Marwell 1992; Tilly 1978); and, as a consequence, it is usually unclear whether the resources listed include all resources mobilized or only those deemed most critical by the researcher. The resource concept thus remains nearly as ambiguous as it did when it was introduced more than twenty years ago. Our intent is to identify empirically the range of resources mobilized by the fifteen homeless SMOs we studied and to assess their relevance for the viability of the SMOs.

Resources and Mobilization Outcomes

Given the assumption that resources are one of the necessary conditions for successful mobilization, one would expect detailed understanding of the link between specific types and combinations of resources and mobilization outcomes. This is not the case, however. Instead, understanding of the relationship between resources and mobilization remains mired at a very general level. For example, McCarthy and Zald (1973, 1977) argue that general levels of movement activity will be related to overall levels of discretionary resources within a society. Likewise, Jenkins and Perrow (1977) identify changes in the external sponsorship of the farm workers' movement that they contend accounted for the successful mobilization campaign of the late 1960s in contrast to the unsuccessful efforts to organize farm workers in the late 1940s.

More recently, Oliver and Marwell (1992) have attempted to concretize the consequences of mobilizing one category of resources rather than another (labor vs. money), arguing that the resources pursued constrain tactical action. This is clearly a step in the right direction inasmuch as attention is focused on the consequences of mobilizing particular types of resources. In this chapter, we extend this more concrete line of inquiry by examining the significance of a variety of resources and resource combinations for SMO viability.

Resource Derivation

A third unresolved issue concerns the derivation of resources. Two lines of argument emerge: One sees resources as emanating primarily from external sources—namely, "conscience constituents" (those who support movement activity without benefiting directly from attainment of its objectives) and extramovement organizations (McCarthy and Zald 1973, 1977); the second focuses attention on the indigenous character of resources, arguing that they are provided mainly by a SMO's constituency (McAdam 1982; Morris 1981).[2] Two questions follow that we explore: Are the resources mobilized by homeless SMOs externally or internally derived? And does their derivation make any difference for SMO viability?

External Support and Control

The fourth issue we examine flows from the resource derivation debate: does external support or patronage lead to cooptation or control? There are two overlapping hypotheses. One, dubbed the social control hypothesis, argues that external sponsorship moderates SMO goals and tactics, thus dampening the prospect of militant collective action (Haines 1984; McAdam 1982; Piven and Cloward 1977). The other hypothesis contends that external patronage does not automatically mute radical dissent but channels it into more professional and publicly palatable forms (Jenkins and Eckert 1986). Although these two propositions provide a useful point of departure in thinking about effects of external support, they focus exclusively on support from external elite organizations. Whether these hypothesized dynamics flow from nonelite sponsorship of SMOs remains an empirical question that we seek to illuminate.

Context, Data, Procedures

We examine the foregoing issues with data derived from qualitative fieldwork conducted among fifteen homeless SMOs and their organizational supporters and antagonists in eight U.S. cities between 1989 and 1991. Homeless activists and their SMOs constitute a particularly illuminating case for understanding the aforementioned issues. Given their overwhelming poverty, the homeless are unable to provide much other than their voices and physical presence to SMOs. Consequently, differences in the durability and accomplishments of homeless SMOs across the country must be partly the result of differential success in mobilizing resources, presumably from external organizational entities. Thus, a comparative study of homeless SMOs provides a unique opportunity to assess the importance of specifiable resources in relation to mobilization outcomes such as SMO viability.

The fifteen SMOs we studied were local variants of a larger social movement that emerged in the 1980s with the proliferation of homelessness throughout the United States. This issue generated a voluminous research literature and a great deal of public interest during the 1980s (Burt 1992; Rosenthal 1994; Rossi 1989; Snow and Anderson 1993; Wagner 1993; Wright 1989), but relatively little was done on the state or federal level to remedy the problem. In part because of this apparent indifference and policy initiatives that did little more than expand the nation's network of accommodative shelters, the homeless began to mobilize in one city after another in the 1980s. Although it is difficult to pinpoint the exact emergence of this movement, it first gained national visibility with Mitch Snyder's sixty-day fast in 1983 and the Community for Creative Non-Violence's (CCNV) embracement of homelessness as its focal concern. The pinnacle of the movement's mobilization in the 1980s occurred in October 1989 when an estimated 250,000 homeless and their supporters assembled at the foot of the nation's capitol under the banner of "Housing Now!"

While these events gained national visibility for the homeless movement, the vast majority of homeless collective actions—such as protest rallies and marches, housing takeovers, and encampments on government property—were local in organization and focus. Moreover, the scope of this activity was quite extensive, as indicated by the occurrence of homeless collective action in over fifty cities in the 1980s.[3] Although attempts were made to coordinate some of these local mobilizations by the National Union of the Homeless that surfaced in 1986 in Philadelphia, and although about fifteen local SMOs counted themselves as affiliates of the National Union, the movement was primarily a locality-based, city-level phenomenon.

Because of the local character of the movement, we focused our research on homeless SMOs in eight cities: Boston, Denver, Detroit, Houston, Minneapolis, Oakland, Philadelphia, and Tucson. Two factors influenced the selection of these cities. First, given our interest in the relationship between resource aggregation and mobilization outcomes, the cities needed to exhibit variation in level of mobilization. We determined this quality by content-analyzing newspaper accounts of homeless collective action in 18 U.S. cities that had a daily newspaper indexed throughout the 1980s.[4] Thus, the eight cities had to be selected from this population of eighteen cities. Additionally, we were constrained by time and access. Because of funding requirements, the fieldwork had to be conducted mainly during a three-year period. We also wanted to avoid having to gain access anew in each city because of the fieldwork's time-consuming nature. Consequently, we attempted to select cities where we had preestablished contacts with leaders of the local homeless SMOs. These contacts surfaced during the course of a year of pilot fieldwork in Minneapolis, Philadelphia, and Tucson.

The eight sampled cities and the broader population of eighteen cities from which they were selected are shown in Table 5.1 by size, region, and homeless rate. Both the sampled cities and the larger population are among the fifty largest cities in the United States, and they appear to be quite repre-

---

Table 5.1

Cities in Field Sample and in Larger Sampling Frame by Size, Region, and Homeless Rate

Population (1986)	Region			
	East	Midwest	South	West
>1,000,000	New York (1)[2] **Philadelphia** (5)[2]	Chicago (3)[4] **Detroit** (7)[4]	**Houston** (4)[4]	Los Angeles (2)[4]
500,000– 1 million	Washington, D.C. (17)[1] **Boston** (19)[1]	Cleveland (22)[4]	New Orleans (21)[4]	San Francisco (13)[2] **Denver** (25)[3]
<500,000		St. Louis (26)[2] **Minneapolis** (46)[2]	Atlanta (31)[1]	Honolulu (37)[3] **Tucson** (35)[3] **Oakland** (44)[4]

Note: Figures in parentheses indicate where the city ranks, as of 1988, among the fifty largest U.S. cities in terms of population size. Superscript numbers indicate homeless rate per 10,000 (figures derived from Burt 1992) app. A, 238–44): 1 = 45+, 2 = 30–45, 3 = 15–30, and 4 = <15. Cities in boldface are the ethnographic field sites.

sentative of these fifty cities by size, region, and homeless rate. Our primary concern, however, is not to generalize to the universe of homeless SMOs but to use our case findings to address the unresolved theoretical issues identified earlier.[5]

The principal objectives of our fieldwork were to map the organizational fields in which the SMOs were embedded in each city and to discern patterns of interaction, such as resource flows, within these fields.[6] Toward that end, we employed an "onion/snowball" strategy that began with a SMO and moved outward in a layered fashion contingent on the information and referrals received. The strategy involved a number of steps, each conditional on the preceding ones. Thus, we began in each city with a homeless SMO to which we had been referred and with which we had already established contact. We interviewed and listened to its leaders and cadre, and we attended meetings and participated in collective action events when they occurred. Based on these contacts, we then moved beyond the SMO to the facilitative organizations, such as service providers, churches, and activist organizations. They provided additional information regarding their ties to the homeless SMO and their resource contributions. Next, we gathered information on the targets of SMOs, such as mayors' offices, city councils, police departments, and HUD. In addition to allowing us to map the contours of the relevant organizational field, this onion/snowball strategy provided us with a number of interpretive validity checks on our various sources of information.

We also used this onion/snowball approach to gather information on homeless SMOs no longer in existence. In each case, former members were tracked down and interviewed. In addition, other significant organizations were interviewed for information on the SMO. Ultimately, data were gathered on fifteen homeless SMOs that had been active between 1984 and the end of 1992 in the eight cities. Nine of the SMOs were still active during the course of our fieldwork from 1989 through 1991.[7] The fifteen homeless SMOs varied in size, ranging from organizations with a half-dozen active homeless members to those with thirty or more active members. All claimed broader support among their local homeless constituents, but they differed in their abilities to mobilize the homeless for their collective actions. Some SMOs drew upward of five hundred homeless to their rallies and protests, while others managed to attract only a handful. Such differences were due in part to their differential success in mobilizing a range of other resources we will identify shortly.

Table 5.2 lists the homeless SMOs by city, and Table 5.3 provides a composite typology of the organizational field in which the SMOs were embedded. The typology classifies organizations that constitute the field in terms of a generalized response to homelessness and their more specific operating perspectives, which reflect what they actually do rather than their

Table 5.2
Social Movement Organizations and Locations

City	Social Movement Organizations	Abbreviation
Boston	Boston Union of the Homeless	BUH
	Homefront	HF
	Homeless Civil Rights Project	HCRP
Denver	Denver Union of the Homeless	DnUH
	Homeless People United	HPU
Detroit	Detroit Union of the Homeless	DtUH
Houston	Heads Up!	HU
	Houston Union of the Homeless	HUH
Minneapolis	Alliance of the Streets	AOS
	Minneapolis Union of the Homeless	MUH
	People United for Economic Justice	PUEJ
Oakland	Oakland Union of the Homeless	OUH
	Membership Caucus	MC
Philadelphia	Philadelphia Union of the Homeless	PUH
Tucson	Tucson Union of the Homeless	TUH

official objectives or proclamations. Theoretically, almost any of the organizations could be targets of homeless collective action, and they typically were, with the exception of the activists. In contrast to the targets of SMO attacks, the facilitative organizations were associated solely with the activist and caretaker modes of response. We will return to this observation later, but for now it will suffice to keep in mind that this composite typology describes the organizational fields in which homeless SMOs are embedded and in which homeless mobilizations occur.

The fieldwork roles we assumed were those that Snow and Anderson (1993) utilized in their research on the homeless in Austin, Texas: the role of the buddy/researcher when in contact with the homeless and their SMOs and the role of the credentialed expert when dealing with other relevant organizational actors.[8] In addition to the data gathered via these fieldwork roles, we examined documents from the homeless SMOs, facilitative organizations, and target organizations, as well as newspaper accounts of the SMOs and their collective actions within each of the cities. These additional data sources not only increased the informational yield but allowed us to cross-check claims of informants and documents against one another.

The observations and interviews yielded over 1,500 pages of field notes. The data were coded into master empirical and conceptual categories that

Table 5.3
Composite Organizational Fields of Homeless SMOs

Orientation	Operating Perspective	Organizational Carriers
Caretaker	Accommodative	Shelters, soup kitchens, clothes closets
	Restorative Medical	Detox, mental health, and health care facilities
	Salvationish	Skid Row missions, 12-step substance abuse programs
	Service provision	Transitional housing programs, job training and referral programs
Market	Exploitative	Plasma centers, day labor operations, liquor stores, SROs (single-room occupancy hotels)
Activist	Advocacy	Service provider coalitions (e.g., Community for Creative Nonviolence, National Coalition for the Homeless)
	Empowerment Humanist	Jobs with Peace, Welfare Rights, Urban League
	Social gospel	Catholic Workers, American Friends Service Committee
Social control	Expulsionist	Merchants, universities, residential neighborhoods
	Containment	Police departments
Apathy/indifference	Lip service and foot dragging	HUD, Department of Labor, Veterans Administration

dovetailed with issues in the study of social movements. For example, one category encompassed all information pertaining to the goals of the homeless SMOs, while another included all strips of data relevant to facilitative organizational relationships. The materials in the master categories were then coded further to elaborate the variation within each. This process helped to organize and make sense of the data and clarified the organizational dynamics and resource relationships within each city.

Findings

A Taxonomy of Resources

As noted earlier, previous discussions of resources suffer from the tendency to overlook their fungibility and to emphasize the broad generic categories of money, people, and legitimacy. We attempted to circumvent these problems first by identifying the range of resources mobilized by the fifteen SMOs and then by noting their specific uses or functions. Thus, we drew on aspects of both the resource type and resource use strategies while attempting to avoid their shortcomings. The result was the identification of a range of resources that we grouped into four categories: moral, material, informational, and human. These categories are exhaustive in the sense that they contain the range of specific resources that the homeless SMOs mobilized, and they are mutually exclusive inasmuch as the specific resources fit logically into only one category. Table 5.4 lists and describes the resource categories and the specific resources included within each.

The resource categories we have identified build upon and elaborate prior resource conceptualizations. For example, the category we call moral resources dovetails with the legitimacy concept used by others in that external legitimation is a possible consequence of both sympathetic and solidaristic support. But our conceptualization also emphasizes the internal validation and support that external endorsements provide for the homeless SMO. The sense that other organizations shared their concerns and supported their actions was an important morale boost for many of the homeless SMOs.

Likewise, material resources include the more mundane items that are typically overlooked or subsumed under the category of money. While money is one of the more frequently noted resources in the social movements literature (Lofland 1993; Jenkins and Eckert 1986; McCarthy and Zald 1977; Oliver and Marwell 1992), we were more concerned with the specific resources that money was used to acquire. Moreover, as we will see shortly, the homeless SMOs seldom received funds directly, and when they did, the funds were used to acquire the resources listed in this category.

Our category of informational resources builds upon other conceptualizations of "know-how" (Gamson et al. 1982; Oliver and Marwell 1992) by including knowledge relevant to conducting collective actions. But we also include knowledge about organization building and maintenance and knowledge about potential supporters in the homeless organizational field.[9] Finally, our category of human resources elaborates the general reference to peoplepower or labor by noting three specific types of human resources: leaders, cadre, and captive audiences.[10] Thus, the resource typology presented in Table 5.4 is empirically grounded in the homeless SMOs we studied but is linked to and extends previous resource conceptualizations.

Table 5.4
Types of Resources Mobilized by Homeless SMOs

Types of Resources	*Description of Resources*
Moral/legitimacy	Endorsements by external organizations (EOs) and both the aims and actions of homeless SMOs
A. Sympathetic support	Statements by EOs that are supportive of the aims and actions of homeless SMOs
B. Solidaristic support	Participation by an EO in the collective actions of the SMO
Material	Tangible goods and services mobilized by homeless SMOs
C. Supplies	Basic goods that facilitate the maintenance and action of the SMO (e.g., paper, poster boards, telephones)
D. Meeting space	Areas controlled by EOs used by homeless SMOs
E. Office space	Areas controlled by homeless SMOs to conduct organizational business
F. Transportation	Use of automobiles to take the homeless to organizational meetings and collective action events
G. Employment	Provision of jobs for members of SMOs
H. Money	Cash received by SMOs
Informational	Knowledge capital or know-how pertinent to organizational maintenance and mobilization
I. Strategic support	Knowledge that facilitates the organization of goal-attainment collective action, such as sit-ins and housing takeovers
J. Technical support	Knowledge that facilitates intraorganizational development and maintenance (e.g., knowing how to run a meeting and delegate tasks)
K. Referrals	Provision of connections to potential EOs for resources
Human	People who might or do donate resources, time, and energy to the SMO
L. Captive audiences	Constituency and bystander populations assembled for recruitment and resource appeals
M. Leaders	Individuals who provide relatively stable organizational guidance and function as spokespersons
N. Cadre	Individuals who function as lieutenants on a relatively permanent basis

Resources and Viability

We begin our examination of the relationship between the resources mobilized and viability by first conceptualizing viability. We do so by reference to three factors. The baseline barometer is survival, which is consistent with the emphasis in the organizational literature on survival as the primary goal of organizations (Dimaggio and Powell 1983; Hannan and Freeman 1989; Pfeffer and Salancik 1978; Stinchcomb 1965). We operationalize survival by whether an SMO existed for one year or more. The one-year criteria is used because it elicited the most reliable responses from our informants in assessing the longevity of SMOs that were not in existence while we were in the field.

Since it is possible to imagine organizations that persist without engaging in much activity, we also measured viability by considering the core activities of the SMOs: meetings and collective actions. First, we looked at how frequently an SMO typically met, categorizing them by whether they met at least twice a month. Second, we examined whether SMOs planned and conducted protest campaigns. By campaigns we refer to packages of collective actions organized around particular issues. All homeless SMOs protested, but much of this activity was reactive and short lived. Campaigns represent a higher order of viability in that they are proactive and more complex to execute because they involve a series of interrelated protest events.

Thus, we conceptualize SMO viability in terms of temporal survival, meeting frequency, and the capacity to sponsor collective action campaigns. Social movement organizations that met all three criteria are categorized as viable.

How did the homeless SMOs do in terms of resource acquisition and viability? Table 5.5 provides the answer by identifying the array of resources mobilized by the fifteen SMOs and by indicating whether they are viable. A homeless SMO was credited with a particular resource if it reported ongoing access to that resource.[11]

Looking at Table 5.5, we see that the SMOs demonstrate a wide range of success in securing different resources, with one-third having received five or fewer resource types, one-third securing eight to twelve resource types, and one-third acquiring thirteen to fourteen of the resource types. The general impression one gets is that SMOs with more resource types were more likely to be viable. But we are also interested in the question of whether some resources were more important than others to the viability of an SMO. What resources and resource combinations were necessary and sufficient for SMO viability?

To address these questions, we employ the technique of qualitative comparative analysis (Ragin 1987). This analytic framework, based on the logic

Table 5.5
Truth Table for Data on Resources and SMO Viability

SMO	Moral		Material						Informational			Human			Viable
	A	B	C	D	E	F	G	H	I	J	K	L	M	N	
AOS	1	1	1	1	1	1	1	1	1	1	1	1	1	1	1
OUH	1	1	1	1	1	1	1	1	1	1	1	1	1	1	1
PUH	1	1	1	1	1	1	1	1	1	1	1	1	1	1	1
DtUH	1	1	1	1	1	1	1	1	1	1	1	1	1	1	1
TUH	1	1	1	1	1	1	0	1	1	1	1	1	1	1	1
HCRP	1	1	1	1	1	1	1	1	1	1	1	0	1	0	1
PUEJ	1	1	1	1	1	0	0	0	1	1	1	0	1	0	1
BUH	1	1	1	1	0	0	0	1	1	1	1	1	1	0	0
HPU	1	1	1	1	1	0	0	0	1	1	1	0	0	1	0
DnUH	1	1	1	1	0	0	0	0	1	1	1	0	1	0	0
HF	1	1	0	0	0	0	0	1	1	1	0	0	0	0	0
HU	1	1	1	1	0	0	0	0	0	0	0	0	1	0	0
HUH	1	1	0	1	0	0	0	0	0	0	0	0	1	0	0
MUH	0	0	1	1	1	0	0	0	0	0	0	0	1	0	0
MC	1	0	1	1	0	0	0	0	0	1	0	0	0	0	0

Note: In columns with "causal" or outcome conditions, 1 indicates the presence of a condition; 0, its absence.

and techniques of Boolean algebra, allows for identification of the multiple and conjunctural causes of some event when comparing a relatively small number of cases. More specifically, it facilitates identification of the configuration of necessary and sufficient conditions for an event to occur, and it is especially well suited for situations with complex patterns of interaction among the specified conditions. In addition, the product of Boolean equations represents the conjunction or interaction of both present and absent conditions. Thus, qualitative comparative analysis allows us to identify the simplest combinations of resources that lead to viability from the many resource combinations that are possible.[12]

So what resources were most important for SMO viability? Using Boolean reduction, we can simplify the truth table for viable organizations (Table 5.5) to the following equation, with V standing for viability and the remaining letters corresponding to the specific resources listed in Table 5.4:

$$V = (ABCDEIJKM)(fghln + FGHln + FHLN)$$

In Boolean equations, capital letters indicate the presence of a condition, while lowercase letters indicate the absence of a condition. Letters not present in an equation are treated as irrelevant.[13] Indicators of multiplication are read as "and," while indicators of addition are read as "or." Thus, the nine resources in the left side of the equation are necessary resources for viability, as all viable SMOs acquired these resources, and they are sufficient in conjunction with one of the three other resource combinations in the right side of the equation. Table 5.6 lists the three pathways to viability and the SMOs associated with each. We illustrate each of these pathways and discuss how the resources contributed to the viability of the respective SMO(s).

A combination of nine resources was necessary for each of the viable SMOs. Each of the viable SMOs mobilized the moral backing of other organizations, in terms of both statements of support for the homeless SMOs (resource A) and participation with the homeless SMOs at their collective actions (resource B). The leader of the Oakland Union of the Homeless provided an example of this support in discussing a Christmas Day protest:

> We had a bunch of ministers from all over the Bay Area come, and their basic statement was, "I'm not here to say that our church can solve homelessness, I'm here to say our church can stand in solidarity with the homeless." And so they all stood there and pledged that night that even though their churches needed them on Christmas, they would commit civil disobedience with us.

Moral support facilitated viability in two ways. First, the backing of some organizations, such as churches or labor unions, provided legitimacy for the homeless SMOs among other entities in the organizational field. Second, moral support gave the SMO a sense that others were behind them, an important morale boost for a population that typically endures pariahlike status.

The viable SMOs also mobilized three of the six material resources: supplies (C), meeting space (D), and office space (E). Having a regular space to meet and adequate supplies constituted the nuts-and-bolts requisites for

Table 5.6
Resource Paths to Viability

Path	Necessary Resources	Additional Resource Combinations	SMO
1	(ABCDEIJKM)	(fghIn)	PUEJ
2	(ABCDEIJKM)	(FGHIn)	HCRP
3	(ABCDEIJKM)	(FHLN)	AOS, DtUH, OUH, PUH, TUH

doing regular organizational business. A supporter of the Detroit Union of the Homeless discussed the importance of these resources:

> Well, I think that giving people space makes life possible. You know, I mean what's the difference between a person who is homeless and a person who isn't homeless? The person who isn't homeless has a home. Well, the Homeless Union when it was homeless had a different character than when it had some place to be. There is a kind of franticness when you don't really have a place where you can invite anybody into. But when you do, people can find you. Strategies can be developed. You can get a sense of your own identity.

There are three reasons for the salience of these resources in relation to SMO viability. First, having a reliable place to meet not only centralizes an SMO's day-to-day operations but also lessens the prospect of the SMO being harassed for conducting its business in public spaces or facilities that were designed and intended for other activities. Second, a reliable meeting space is important symbolically in that it signifies the acquisition and control of a rare commodity for the homeless: physically bounded, private space. Third, the provision of office space by a facilitative organization more firmly anchors its commitment to the SMO and helps legitimate the SMO publicly.

All three of the informational resources—strategic support (I), technical support (J), and referrals (K)—were also necessary for viability. The importance of these resources to SMO viability is not difficult to understand given the generalized resource deprivation of the homeless. Not only do most come from a background of extreme poverty (Burt 1992; Rossi 1989; Shinn and Gillespie 1994), but they typically have lower educational levels than the general populace (Rossi 1989; Snow and Anderson 1993), and their employment experience and skills are usually associated with jobs at the bottom of the occupational structure (Rossi 1989; Snow and Anderson 1993). Additionally, the growing professionalization of the social movement arena (Jenkins and Eckert 1986; McCarthy and Zald 1973, 1977) has placed greater emphasis on managerial skills and organizational abilities that are in short supply among the homeless.

As a consequence of these overarching deficits, the survival of homeless SMOs is partly contingent on their abilities to mobilize the requisite informational resources. Thus, the Detroit Union of the Homeless established an advisory board of sympathetic organizations that could be called on to provide informational assistance. The director of the United Housing Coalition, a member of the board, explained how it works:

> If the president of the Detroit Union calls and needs something, we try to assist him. For example, right now they are working with HUD to obtain some houses. They wanted to put together the application form. The president called us last week to meet with the new head of the Union Business School that's

going to provide all the labor. So, you know, we help provide what is needed on an on-call basis.

Similarly, the director of the Women's Economic Agenda Project in Oakland explained how her organization assists poor people's movements, such as the Oakland Union of the Homeless:

> Well, we try to assist [them] from the standpoint of helping them with technical assistance. . . . it can be anything from sitting down with people and showing them how to make an agenda, to helping them with an outline for a speech for someone who knows how to raise hell but, you know, never intended to be involved politically but needs that confidence there. We also try helping them to do research, putting their issues into a broader topic.

And a lawyer for a Philadelphia law firm that specializes in civil rights and property law and does *pro bono* work for the Philadelphia Union of the Homeless described the nature of the strategic assistance he provides:

> My role is to assist them in how to use the law affirmatively, like in terms of lawsuits; how to force the city to comply with certain terms and agreements they've made. I also work on defense cases for their civil disobedience trials.

Taken together, these comments from facilitative organizational personnel in three cities not only illustrate concretely the character of informational assistance but further underscore its importance in relation to the viability of resource impoverished SMOs.

Finally, viable organizations all had relatively strong leaders (M), one of the three human resources. Leaders contributed to the viability of homeless SMOs in a number of ways. They often were the primary source for the critical informational resources mobilized by the organization, as illustrated by their absence. As an organizer with a local community center in Denver noted when discussing the failed Homeless People United:

> I'm convinced that had there been somebody who could have worked with that group full-time, some things could have happened differently. I was doing it as a part-time kind of thing, doing other stuff as well, and it was real clear to me that doesn't work. We had a core group of people who politically, at least, and ideologically had a sense of things that needed to be done. But I think they had to have more support there. I think they needed somebody who understood organizing well, who could spend the time working with them to do that. . . . They needed someone who had more time than an hour per day, [and then] Homeless People United could have developed.

In addition, leaders provided continuity for the organization and helped counter the persistent problem of population turnover among the ranks. Although all movements are confronted with this problem, it is particularly pressing among homeless SMOs, whose adherents are often likely to be tenuously committed because of the uncertainty of meeting basic survival needs and/or the necessity of being vigilant about looking for opportunities to get off the streets.

Taken together, these nine resources were the bare minimum necessary for viability, as six of the seven viable organizations needed to mobilize additional resources. The exception to this tendency was People United for Economic Justice (PUEJ) in Minneapolis, which illustrates the first pathway in the equation (see Table 5.6). PUEJ was somewhat distinctive from other SMOs in two ways. First, as a splinter SMO from another viable Minneapolis SMO, the Alliance of the Streets (AOS), PUEJ operated in a context of ongoing homeless activism. Second, and perhaps most important, it benefited from having an experienced and tenacious leadership. Its president had been active in the AOS, and he was sufficiently skilled and aggressive that he effected a coup that elevated him to the chairmanship of the local homeless social service provider coalition. Once this happened, the resource situation of the PUEJ improved. But before that, he and a few associates were able to steer the PUEJ through eight months without any external support—a period that included meeting in parks and libraries—because of their prior experience in homeless activism and leadership skills. Knowing some of the inherent difficulties in organizing the homeless enabled them to foresee and weather resource deficits that discouraged and sometimes doomed novice activists.

The two other pathways to viability required the mobilization of additional resources. One is illustrated by the Homeless Civil Rights Project (HCRP) in Boston, which acquired the other material resources of transportation (F), employment (G), and money (H). It was able to secure these additional material resources from a facilitative organization that was attempting to organize the homeless in Boston. A leader of a local activist group that helped form the HCRP explained their involvement with mobilizing the homeless:

> We thought that the best way we could organize the homeless was to essentially come up with the funding to back a homeless-run organization and, you know, allow for homeless people to build their own organization from the ground up, and that is what we wound up doing.

The activist organization provided transportation for HCRP members to organizational meetings and collective actions, which contributed to viability by increasing participation in both sets of activities. In addition, the provision of transportation enabled the HCRP to demonstrate in different locations across the Boston metropolitan area and the New England region.

This resource also increased their visibility and stature in the eyes of the local homeless.

Perhaps even more important was the facilitative organization's provision of employment to a homeless activist, which enabled him to devote his full attention to the HCRP. The leader of the activist organization elaborated:

> With Jack, we had the foundation for recruiting homeless people into the Homeless Civil Rights Project. He was able to do the outreach and be there to do the work to draw people into the organization. So after a couple of weeks, I hired him. And that was how Civil Rights Project started.[14]

The provision of employment for the homeless leader facilitated organizational viability by maintaining the involvement of a skilled homeless activist who might otherwise have been sidetracked by subsistence activities. It also provided leadership stability and continuity, which, as mentioned earlier, was a necessary resource for viability. Thus, for the HCRP, the additional material resources of transportation, employment, and money (which was used primarily for supplies), was sufficient in combination with the necessary resources for viability.

The third pathway to viability, like the second, also involved securing the additional material resources of transportation (F) and money (H). What distinguished pathway 3 from pathway 2, however, was the need for the two remaining human resources—captive audiences (L) and activist cadre (N), and the irrelevance of employment if both of these were secured. This was the most common pathway, with five of the viable SMOs following this track. Since we have already illustrated how money and transportation influence SMO viability with the case of the HCRP, we will focus on the contribution of human resources to viability, using the Tucson Union of the Homeless (TUH) as our illustrative case.

The Tucson Union of the Homeless was led by an activist from a local Catholic Worker community. While there was high turnover among the homeless rank and file, at any one time there was typically a cadre of half a dozen homeless who were the core active members in the organization. This cadre exercised strong influence on the issues that the TUH pursued, and they carried out the day-to-day work of the organization. They played key roles in executing collective action events, from developing and distributing fliers, mobilizing other homeless, and preparing food for demonstrations, to speaking and getting arrested. Thus, the cadre contributed to viability of the TUH by providing membership continuity as well as the muscle behind the work of the organization.

In addition to having a cadre of homeless activists, the TUH had access to a captive audience of homeless who ate the only noonday meal served in Tucson at a soup kitchen run by the Catholic Workers. This resource facilitated viability in two ways: it supplied the TUH with a guaranteed pool of homeless to offer feedback on the concerns and grievances of the homeless and the issues they wanted the union to pursue, and it provided a relatively large and concentrated number of homeless who could be targeted for mobilization whenever needed.

Having identified the three resource pathways of the viable homeless SMOs and suggested how the resources contributed to their respective viability, the question arises as to the causal ordering of the resource/viability relationship: Is viability a function of the mobilization of a pool of salient resources? Or do viable SMOs attract more salient resources? We suspect both processes occur, but we are certain about the first—that is, that the acquisition of a number of salient resources is a necessary condition for SMO viability. We say this not only because of the impoverished condition of the SMOs' homeless constituents but also because we consistently observed that SMOs with fewer resources held fewer meetings and engaged less frequently in protest actions. Both of these activities were essential to maintaining connections and a semblance of solidarity among the homeless, whose street relationships and agency ties tend to be highly tenuous and transient (Snow and Anderson 1993). Particular resources—such as meeting space, transportation, and strategic and technical support—clearly increased the probability that regular meetings and collective action would take place. In turn, SMOs that conducted these activities were more likely to survive. The case of the Denver Union of the Homeless (DUH) is illustrative. In the early days, it was barely able to survive because it had no regular place to meet. As its President explained when discussing this period:

> We were meeting in the shelter still, and we'd get other people to come in. We'd go and talk to them like on the street and tell them we're meeting at this place at a certain time, you know, and then we'd try to meet outside a few times. And a lot of things didn't work out. We'd try different things, and they didn't work out. It was exhausting sometimes, and sometimes we couldn't get anybody to meet.

But DUH's fate changed when a sympathetic supporter provided it with a house to be used as its organizational base. This enabled the SMO to enjoy a relatively stable period in which it engaged in a number of collective actions, the last being a highly publicized housing takeover. Because of the attention this takeover attracted, however, the previously generous supporter evicted the SMO and closed up the house. Returned to its initial state of not having a regular meeting place, the DUH soon dissolved.

In this case, like others, the failure to secure essential resources signaled the demise of the SMO. Thus, for the homeless SMOs we observed, organizational viability was contingent on the acquisition of the resource combinations discussed earlier. Viability was initially a function of successful resource mobilization, but once achieved it could facilitate the acquisition of subsequent support.

Resource Derivation, Organizational Benefactors, and Viability

Thus far we have examined the array of resources mobilized by homeless SMOs and identified the resource combinations linked to SMO viability, but we have said little about the seedbed of the mobilized resources. As noted earlier, there are two lines of argument regarding this issue: one focuses on external sources such as conscience constituents (McCarthy and Zald 1973, 1977); the other stresses the resource provision role of indigenous constituencies (McAdam 1982; Morris 1981). In this section, we address the questions of whether the resources mobilized by homeless SMOs were externally or internally derived and whether their external relationships made any difference with respect to SMO viability (see Table 5.7).

Although the homeless SMOs secured resources from both external and

Table 5.7
Source of SMO Resources and the Presence of Benefactor

SMOs	Resources														Bene-factor	Viable
	Moral		*Material*						*Informational*			*Human*				
	A	B	C	D	E	F	G	H	I	J	K	L	M	N		
AOS	E	E	E	E	E	E	E	I	E	E	E	E	E	I	1	1
TUH	E	E	E	E	E	E		E	E	E	E	E	E	I	1	1
OUH	E	E	E	E	E	E	E	E	E	E	E	E	E	I	1	1
PUH	E	E	E	E	E	I	E	E	I	I	I	I	I	I	0	1
DtUH	E	E	E	E	E	E	E	I	I	I	E	I	I	I	1	1
HCRP	E	E	E	E	E	E	E	E	E	E	E		I		1	1
PUEJ	E	E	I	I	E				I	I	E		I		0	1
BUH	E	E	E	E				I	I	I	E	E	I		0	0
HPU	E	E	E	E	E				E	E	E			I	0	0
DnUH	E	E	E	E					I	I	E		I		0	0
HF	E	E						E	I	I					0	0
HU	E	E	E	E									I		0	0
HUH	E	E		E									I		0	0
MUH			E	E	E								I		0	0
MC	E		E	E						E					0	0

Note: E = externally derived; I = indigenous or internally derived; 1 = present; and 0 = absent. Blank spaces indicate that the resource was not mobilized by the SMO.

internal sources, 75 percent of the resource types were derived from external sources. In addition, all but one of the viable SMOs mobilized the majority of their resource types from external supporters, which thus highlights the importance of facilitative organizational support in the case of homeless SMOs. The only exception to this pattern was again the PUEJ. It relied heavily on the meager resources of its members to remain viable, but this was not by choice. PUEJ competed with two other homeless SMOs, the Alliance of the Streets and the Minneapolis Union of the Homeless, for external support. PUEJ had a difficult time distinguishing itself from the better known Alliance when it sought resource support within the community, and it continually had to explain why it was not affiliated with the Alliance. Thus, the lack of external support was due more to competition with the other SMOs in the organizational field than lack of effort or need on the part of PUEJ.[15]

Our findings underscore the importance of external support to homeless activism in general. Almost all of the SMOs, viable or nonviable, mobilized the bulk of their support from external sources. What distinguishes viable from nonviable SMOs is the range of resource types provided by external supporters. Viable SMOs mobilized an average of 9.7 external resources, while nonviable SMOs were able to mobilize an average of only 4.5 external resources (significant at .08 using Levene's test for equality of variances).

Given this apparent pattern of external resource dependence, the crucial question becomes, What accounts for variation in the level of external support mobilized? One factor that stood out from our field observations is the type of relationship established with facilitative organizations: five of the seven viable SMOs were involved in relationships with one facilitative organization that supplied at least half of the resource types mobilized by the SMO, whereas none of the nonviable organizations had such a relationship. We refer to this type of relationship, summarized in Table 5.8, as a "benefactor relationship."

Table 5.8
SMO Viability by Benefactor Relationship

Benefactor	Viable	Nonviable
Yes	5	0
No	2	8

Note: chi-square = 8.58, df = 1, $p < .05$.

Although the relationship between organizational patronage and social movements has received considerable attention (Gamson 1990; Jenkins 1995; Jenkins and Eckert 1986), *patronage* is typically used as a cover term for any type of external support or sponsorship. We thus use the term *benefactor* to denote a variant of organizational patronage: the provision of 50 percent or more of the resource types to a single SMO.

Benefactors facilitated SMO viability by ensuring not only the provision of resources but particularly the ones necessary for viability. This finding was underscored in a conversation with the leader of the Boston HCRP:

> We've been trying to create a homeless empowerment organization, but it's tough to figure out—it's a really tough thing to do. So we looked at the successful models, and we found certain things that were in common. And what they were was that you had leadership development, ownership of the project by homeless people, and you had a sponsoring organization that was able to provide the sort of resources and financial backup that made the thing go. All the successful organizations had sort of like parent organizations that provided the resources.

Having a benefactor produced stable resource flows, which facilitated viability by allowing the SMO to devote more time to collective actions. SMOs were highly dependent upon sustained protest to maintain mobilization levels among the local homeless population. Because of the more tenuous ties that exist in this constituency, periods of inactivity usually resulted in membership attrition. SMOs that were less preoccupied with resource concerns could concentrate on organizing collective action campaigns that enhanced the prospect of viability. Taking these factors into consideration, it would appear that having a benefactor within its organizational field greatly increases the chances of an SMO's survival.[16]

The two viable SMOs that did not have benefactor relationships were the aforementioned PUEJ and the Philadelphia Union of the Homeless (PUH). The PUH was also an anomaly among the SMOs. Shortly after its formation by two homeless men, the PUH applied for and received a $21,000 grant from the city to open its own shelter—the first operated solely by the homeless in the nation—and to purchase necessary supplies. Thus, having its own base of operations early on in its career, the PUH was not as dependent on additional organizational support as most homeless SMOs. This initial financial support notwithstanding, we did not view the PUH as being involved in a benefactor relationship for two reasons. First, it did not meet our operational definition of the external provider supplying half or more of the resource types. Second, the city was often a target of PUH collective action, and, as a consequence, it is equally plausible to interpret this "support" as a collective action outcome. Either way, the PUH was not in the same kind of interactive relationship with the city as the other SMOs were with their benefactors.

These benefactors were not scattered at random throughout each SMO's respective organizational field but were concentrated among the activist, empowerment-oriented organizations identified in Table 5.3. We observed two types of empowerment organizations working with the homeless. One type was characterized by the overarching "humanist" objectives of securing dignity and equality for all people. Because of the breadth of this mandate, local organizational carriers (e.g., such as the Urban League, Jobs with Peace, and Welfare Rights) were committed to a range of issues in addition to empowering the homeless. The second type of empowerment organization working among the homeless we conceptualized as "social gospelites" because of their commitment to the Christian ethic to "stand with the poor." This ethic typically manifests itself through what the leader of the Catholic Worker house in Tucson called "acts of mercy" and "acts of justice." The former refer to charitable work conducted for the poor, while the latter encompass empowerment efforts. It is this latter focus that distinguishes the social gospelites from the religiously oriented caretaker agencies that service the homeless, such as the Salvation Army and the spate of Skid Row-like missions and soup kitchens.

Of the two types of empowerment organizations, the social gospelites were clearly more prominent, as they were involved in four of the six benefactor relationships. The reasons for the gospelites' establishment of benefactor relationships with homeless SMOs appear to be rooted in two factors. First, their calling to stand with the poor tends to locate them spatially more within the proximate orbit of the homeless and their SMOs than is the case with the humanist organizations. Second, commitment to this calling also provides the social gospelites with greater staying power, since assisting the homeless and other impoverished groups is an end in itself. In contrast, most humanist organizations, with their broader mandate, tend to work on behalf of a greater variety of causes and SMOs and thus are likely to be more diffuse in focus and action.

Patronage and SMO Control

The literature reminds us, as previously noted, that external support comes with a cost: a loss of SMO autonomy in general and, more particularly, a moderating influence with respect to SMO objectives and strategic actions (Jenkins and Eckert 1986; McAdam 1982; Piven and Cloward 1977). And if the general thrust of the literature is correct, these tempering influences should even be more pronounced the greater the resource dependency. Thus, in the case of homeless SMOs involved in benefactor relationships, we might expect to find less stridency or militancy.

Table 5.9 addresses this issue by assessing the relationship between the presence or absence of a benefactor relationship and the use of militant tactics. We define militant tactics as those actions that intentionally break laws and risk the arrest of participants, such as blockades, sit-ins, housing takeovers, and unauthorized encampments. In contrast, nonmilitant tactical action includes petitions and rallies and demonstrations that typically have been negotiated and sanctioned in advance.[17] Dividing the range of tactical actions engaged in by the fifteen SMOs into these two categories, we discern no significant relationship between the establishment of a benefactor relationship and a propensity to engage in either militant or nonmilitant action. Three of the five SMOs with a benefactor engaged in militant action, as did five of the ten SMOs without a benefactor. Thus, the benefactor relationship appears to enhance the viability of SMOs representing homeless constituents, but without necessarily moderating tactical action.

Conclusion

We argued at the outset that current understanding of the resource mobilization process in the study of social movements has been plagued by a lack of specification of the range of resources that SMOs commonly mobilize, by the absence of an empirically based understanding of the relationship between different types and combinations of resources and mobilization outcomes, by empirical and conceptual ambiguity regarding the relative importance of externally versus internally derived resources, and by the dearth of research on the consequences of different kinds of facilitative organizational relationships for SMO viability and tactical action. We have attempted to shed empirical and conceptual light on these ambiguities in the study of resource mobilization with data drawn from our research on fifteen homeless SMOs in eight U.S. cities.

Two general implications regarding the relationship between resources

Table 5.9
Militancy by Benefactor Relationship

Benefactor	Militant Tactics	Nonmilitant Tactics
Yes	3	2
No	5	5

Note: chi-square = .135 (not significant).

and social movements can be drawn from our findings. The first is that some varieties of SMOs clearly require a broader array of resources than generally has been discussed. As noted earlier, most of the literature has focused almost exclusively on money, labor, and legitimacy, and even here dimensions of these resources typically have been glossed. The underspecified conceptualization of resources is largely the result of schemes that are too narrow or too general. What we have done is to proceed inductively by attempting to identify the range of resources accumulated by the fifteen homeless SMOs and then categorize them around common functional dimensions. Although the resultant resource categories—moral, material, human, and informational—and their variants pertain directly to the homeless SMOs we studied, they are built on and extend prior resource conceptualizations. We therefore think our elaborated typology is sufficiently general to be applicable to other movements and contexts. Whether that conclusion is in fact true and whether the resources we identified would have the same categorical effects we observed are empirical questions. At the very least, however, our expanded taxonomy of resources underscores the utility of conducting more refined empirically grounded analyses of the resources that SMOs need and secure, in varying degrees, than has been customary in the research literature.

The second general implication of our findings is that they affirm the cornerstone assumption of the resource mobilization perspective: that the mobilization of resources profoundly affects the course and character of SMOs. This is a linkage that to date has been based more on theoretic assertion than empirical demonstration.

Notes

The research on which this chapter is based was supported in part by a grant from the National Science Foundation (SES 9008809). We thank Theron Quist and Kelly Smith for their assistance on the larger project in which this work is embedded, and Peter Adler, Andrew Jones, Doug McAdam, Fred Pampel, and Yvonne Zylan for their constructive comments on an earlier draft, as well as the other members of the Informal Social Movement Seminars at the University of Arizona and the University of Colorado at Boulder. We are also grateful for the constructive comments of the three anonymous reviewers, the editor, and one of the associate editors of the *American Sociological Review*. This is an abridged version of an earlier article, "Mobilization at the Margins: Benefactors and the Viability of Homeless Social Movement Organizations," *American Sociological Review* 61: 1089–1109 (1996).

    1. For a summary of this literature, see Buechler (1993), Jenkins (1983), and Pichardo (1988).

    2. For further discussion of these contrasting positions, see Pichardo (1988).

    3. This figure was derived from our inspection of newspaper reports assembled through the 1980s by the NewsBank Newspaper Index, which collects selected articles from 450 newspapers in the United States. To date, scant published research has appeared on these homeless protest events or on the homeless movement in general. But see the work of Rosen-

thal (1994), Wagner (1993), and Wright (1995) for descriptive accounts of homeless insurgency in several cities across the country.

4. We had originally hoped to conduct a random sample from among the fifty largest U.S. cities, and then use the New York Times Index and NewsBank Index to determine the incidence and intensity of homeless collective action across the sampled cities. However, prior fieldwork in Minneapolis, Philadelphia, and Tucson, including a summer working with the programs of the National Union of the Homeless in Philadelphia, made it clear that the incidence of homeless mobilization was dramatically underrepresented by these two services. In light of this observation, we were forced to turn to local dailies as the basis for information on homeless mobilization and collective action across U.S. cities. Our content analysis of the eighteen dailies yielded a count of nearly six hundred homeless protest events during the 1980s across the eighteen cities, ranging from a low of five to a high of seventy-four, with a mean of thirty-two.

5. The logic of using case materials to extend and refine existing theoretical positions is consistent with a growing literature exploring the rationale and uses of qualitative case studies. See Burawoy (1991), Feagin et al. (1991), Glaser and Strauss (1967), and Ragin (1987).

6. By *organizational fields*, we refer to a set of organizations that share overlapping constituencies and/or interests and that recognize one another's activities as being relevant to those concerns. This is an inclusive conceptualization that encompasses all organizations with which links might be established, be they facilitative or antagonistic. This conceptualization is consistent with the institutional perspective on organizations (DiMaggio and Powell 1983) and work on multiorganizational fields in the study of social movements (Klandermans 1992).

7. Since it is reasonable to wonder whether the founding and careers of each of the fifteen SMOs were affected by different period effects, it is important to note that all fifteen were founded between 1984 and 1989. This was the period in which homelessness escalated and become increasingly visible in the United States (Burt 1992; Jencks 1994; Rossi 1989). It was also then that public interest in the problem intensified, judging from media coverage of the problem (Bunis, Snow, and Yancik 1995). Since the end of the 1980s, there has been some speculation that the incidence of homelessness may have declined (Jencks 1994) and also that public interest in the problem has dwindled because of a combination of compassion fatigue and issue competition (Bunis et al. 1995). Taken together, these observations suggest that if there have been period effects with respect to homeless collective action, they do not appear to account for variation in the careers of the SMOs in our sample, since they were all founded during the same time period.

8. Whereas the buddy/researcher assumes a sympathetic but curious stance with respect to those being studied, the credentialed expert assumes a nonpartisan stance and embraces his or her professional identity as a means of legitimating the research inquiry. See Snow, Benford, and Anderson (1986) for a more detailed discussion of these and other fieldwork roles.

9. Oliver and Marwell (1992) identify mobilization technologies as intraorganizational know-how, but this is limited to knowledge about resource acquisition.

10. We did not include collective action turnout as a labor resource in part because we conceptualized it as an outcome of SMO mobilization activity. Most SMOs could not predict how many people an event might draw, so it was an unstable resource at best. We felt that leadership and cadre best captured the labor resources of the SMO.

11. We were unable to distinguish SMOs by volume of each resource mobilized. This is an admitted shortcoming, but it was unavoidable since the SMOs in question did not have systematic accounting procedures. Additionally, as Freeman (1979) notes, different resources have different utilities, making comparisons of resource levels between certain types (e.g. material vs. informational) inappropriate.

12. Research employing qualitative comparative analysis has typically used fewer independent conditions than we use in this chapter (Amenta and Poulsen 1994; Ragin 1987), because the greater the number of independent conditions, the greater the likelihood that the number of possible combinations will increase, which thus makes it more difficult to discern patterns among the cases. This approach would be problematic for our cases if each had a unique resource combination. As we will show, however, our cases cluster into a relatively few number of resource combinations.

13. Equations that are identical to one another in all but one aspect can be reduced by that aspect. For example, if two viable SMOs had the same pattern of resource acquisition except that one acquired employment and the other did not (e.g., FGHLN and FgHLN), employment could be dropped as necessary causal condition. Stated another way, in the presence of the other resources mobilized, it does not matter whether employment is present. This point is indicated by the absence of the appropriate symbol in the equation (e.g. FHLN). This quality is akin to experimental control in which only one aspect varies while others are held constant.

14. This is a striking example of the provision of employment as a selective incentive for participation, but it was not a commonplace occurrence across the fifteen SMOs. Moreover, it turned out to be a necessary condition only in the case of HCRP.

15. This finding, coupled with the fact that all but three of the fifteen SMOs were situated in cities with two or more homeless SMOs, raises two confounding propositions. One concerns the possibility that two or more homeless SMOs overtaxes the carrying capacity for such movements in the cities in which they are located and thus gives rise to intense competition for limited resources. We cannot assess this proposition directly, but our data do not appear to support it, as viable SMOs are found in cities with one (Detroit, Philadelphia, and Tucson), two (Oakland), and three (Boston and Minneapolis) SMOs. The second proposition raises the possibility of a "radical flank effect," which suggests that the presence of more radical or extremist SMOs within a movement industry encourages support for more moderate ones (Haines 1984). Here, too, we find little support for this proposition, as the more radical SMOs in some of the cities with multiple SMOs were the more viable ones. The Oakland Union of the Homeless and the Homeless Civil Rights Project in Boston are cases in point.

16. The high level of resource support that characterizes the benefactor relationship raises the issue of organizational boundaries. To what extent are the homeless SMOs involved in these relationships merely "front organizations" for their organizational benefactors? We would argue that the SMOs involved in these relationships were essentially autonomous organizations operating on their own initiatives. Even in the cases of AOS and HCRP, in which benefactors were responsible for the creation of the SMO, a deliberate attempt was made to maintain organizational separation on the part of both the SMO and the benefactor. In addition, there was no difference for viability between SMOs formed by their benefactors and those that were not.

17. Although there is no single, consensual scheme for distinguishing radical/militant tactics from negotiated and/or less institutionally threatening forms of protest, the distinctions we make here are consistent with other treatments of this issue. See, in particular, Lofland (1985: 260–9), Piven and Cloward (1992), Sharp (1973), and Tarrow (1994: 100–17).

6

Use of the Initiative Process by Woman Suffrage Movements

Lee Ann Banaszak

Eight years before the Nineteenth Amendment gave women the right to vote in the United States, the state of Oregon passed an equal suffrage amendment allowing women to vote in all state and local elections. Oregon was not the first state to give women the right to vote; in fact, the territory of Wyoming pioneered the cause of woman suffrage when it adopted women's voting rights in 1869. Indeed, woman suffrage activists procured the right to vote in some sort of local election in over thirty states by 1917 (Stapler 1917). What made Oregon unique was how women managed to keep the issue alive there. Using the newly gained right to initiate constitutional amendments, suffrage activists compelled voters to consider three constitutional amendments for women's voting rights—one each in 1908, 1910, and 1912. On their third initiative, voters granted women full voting rights.

The story of the Oregon suffrage movement supports the literature on political opportunity structure (Kriesi 1995; McAdam 1982; Tarrow 1988, 1989) which argues that movement success is constrained or facilitated by the characteristics of the political system. The initiative has been touted as providing groups with little access to political influence a means for raising issues and furnishing alternative pathways to acquire desired reforms (see, e.g., Schmidt 1989). In attempting to acquire voting rights, suffrage movements faced the problem of being challengers to the political system, attempting to change the distribution of political power but lacking "routine, low-cost access" to the decision-making process (Tilly 1978: 52; see also McAdam 1982). Compared with other challengers to the political system, woman suffrage movements were even more disadvantaged by their inability to use the threat of electoral mobilization to influence politicians.

In this chapter I examine whether the initiative helped American suffrage activists succeed. In so doing, I explore one strategy that woman suffrage movements utilized in their fight to be enfranchised, particularly when and why suffrage activists decided to use the initiative to acquire the vote. One way to examine initiative use is to compare the initiative experiences of U.S. suffrage activists with their counterparts elsewhere. Here I compare the American woman suffrage movement with its counterpart in Switzerland.

Why Switzerland?

The Swiss suffrage movement provides an interesting comparison with the American movement for a number of reasons. First, if some states in the United States were pioneers in adopting voting rights for women, some Swiss cantons[1] were laggards. Swiss women were enfranchised on the national level in a 1971 referendum, but the resulting national amendment permitted cantons to make their own voting laws for state and local elections. As a result, Appenzell Ausserrhoden, a small agricultural canton, only enfranchised women in 1989, and its neighbor—Appenzell Innerrhoden—did not adopt women's voting rights until 1990. A few cantons granted women voting rights in cantonal affairs before 1971, but even the earliest cantons to enfranchise women (Vaud and Neuchâtel) did so only in 1959, long after women had achieved full voting privileges in most other European countries. Thus, Switzerland serves as an excellent contrasting case with which to explore initiative use.

Second, although these two suffrage movements are separated in time and space, they share similar political contexts. Both countries have the federal structure that allowed local governments to enfranchise women independently of the national government. U.S. and Swiss federalism also has a cultural dimension (Elazar 1987; Duchacek 1987), with many citizens feeling more affinity for local governments, distrusting the federal government, and loathing federal interference into local affairs. Political parties in both Switzerland and the United States are decentralized and do not exercise discipline over party members. Instead, power was concentrated in local party organizations, each of which had its own character and platforms.

Finally, on the state and cantonal levels, both countries possessed a series of direct democratic institutions including referenda on constitutional amendments and in many cases the right to the initiative. Indeed, Swiss women had more opportunities to use the initiative than their American counterparts. While there are no direct democratic institutions on the national level in the United States, Swiss citizens may use initiatives to introduce constitutional amendments. If an initiative petition garners enough signatures, it is voted on in a national referendum. If a majority of the population and a majority of cantons vote in favor of the initiative, it is added to the constitution. Thus, it is possible to alter the Swiss constitution even if the initiative is opposed by the Federal Council and the Swiss parliament,[2] although this rarely happens. Remarkably, the Swiss suffrage movement never attempted to use this initiative right to acquire a woman suffrage amendment despite the fact that in 1928 they gathered the requisite number of signatures from male supporters in a national petition drive.

On the state or cantonal level, initiative rights were more widespread in Switzerland than in the United States. Some of the states in the United States permitted initiatives for constitutional amendments, and woman suffrage movements in the United States did, in fact, introduce initiatives for woman suffrage on the state level. However, during the period of the woman suffrage movement (1869–1920), the right to the initiative for constitutional amendments existed in only fifteen states (Ranney 1978: 70–72; Stapler 1917). Moreover, Table 6.1 shows that most states adopted the constitutional initiative only during the last decade of the suffrage movement (Price 1975; Ranney 1978). As a result, during the period under study, only very limited

Table 6.1
States that Permit Constitutional Initiatives and Their Use by the
Woman Suffrage Movement

State	Year Initiative Rights Introduced	Year Initiative Used
Arizona	1911	1912
Arkansas	1910	None
California	1911	None
Colorado	1910	None
Idaho	1912	None
Massachusetts	1918	None
Michigan	1913	None
Missouri	1908	1914
Nebraska	1912	1914
Nevada	1912	None
North Dakota	1914	None
Ohio	1912	1914
Oklahoma	1907	1910
Oregon	1902	1908, 1910*, 1912
Utah	1900	None

Sources: Book of the States 1964–1965, p. 14; Ranney (1978) for years initiative rights introduced. Woman suffrage initiative dates are the result of coding of state legislative histories. Information on coding is available from the author by request.
*This initiative was for white taxpayer suffrage only.

opportunities arose to utilize the initiative in the United States. In comparison, throughout the period of the woman suffrage movement (1920–1990), the laws in all Swiss cantons permitted popular initiatives for both constitutional and simple legislative questions (Delley and Auer 1986).[3] Because American and Swiss suffrage activists shared similar initiative rights at the state or cantonal level, I will concentrate on comparing the effect of the initiative on woman suffrage movements within the states and cantons of these two countries.

Thus, comparing the United States and Switzerland will help us analyze the significance of initiative rights to woman suffrage movements. Seeking the same goals in a similar political system, Swiss suffrage activists had more opportunities to use the initiative than their American counterparts. However, before I turn to a closer examination of the use of the initiative and its effect on the woman suffrage movements of both countries, let us examine how initiative rights affect the strategies and success of social movements.

The Initiative as a Political Opportunity Structure

Political opportunity structure theory argues that the political context of a movement affects the movement itself and the success of the movement (see, e.g., Eisinger 1973; Tarrow 1989, 1988; Kitschelt 1986; Kriesi 1995). The characteristics of government institutions, particularly the openness of state institutions (Tarrow 1989; Kitschelt 1986), influence the character and success of social movements. Openness of governmental institutions, which is only one dimension of the political opportunity structure, has been measured by the separation of powers between branches of governments (Kitschelt 1986), characteristics of political institutions such as mayor-council governments in cities (Eisinger 1973), and the characteristics of electoral politics (Eisinger 1973; Kitschelt 1986; and Kriesi 1995). Although this literature is not explicitly concerned with institutions of direct democracy, these institutions are also one component of greater openness of a political system, since initiatives help challenging movements by providing them with greater access to the political agenda.

Political opportunities affect a social movement by altering the strategic cost-benefit calculations (Kriesi 1995, Tilly 1978). On the cost side of the equation, the political opportunity structure may increase or decrease the costs associated with following certain strategies. For example, at one extreme some governments may arrest participants in a demonstration, thereby raising the costs associated with participating; at the other extreme, a government might lower the costs of collective action by helping groups organize. However, political opportunities also may increase or decrease the benefits accrued through collective action—either by making a positive outcome more likely or by altering the benefits of a particular outcome. For example, having allies in the government can increase the probability that demands for reform will succeed. Similarly, the political opportunity structure may influence the actual benefits that derive from a particular outcome. Thus, Kitschelt (1986) notes that even after a particular policy is adopted, the actual benefits a social movement derives from that policy depend on the effectiveness of the government in implementing it.

In all of these cases, political opportunity structure theorists assume that social movements always know what the political opportunity structure is and how it will affect the costs of various political actions (Kitschelt 1986; McAdam 1982; Tilly 1978).[4] McAdam (1982, 49), for example, states that "even when evolving political realities are of a less dramatic nature, they will invariably be made 'available' to insurgents through subtle cues communicated by other groups." Such an assumption implies that the movement will choose strategies that are most likely to succeed, since it has accurate and complete knowledge of the opportunities and constraints it faces. As we shall see later, this assumption is not always valid.

Advocates of initiative rights also view the initiative as empowering unorganized citizens and groups that lack access to political institutions. With initiative rights, all citizens (and not just government officials) may participate directly in the development of legislation, allowing greater citizen involvement in the creation of laws (Schmidt 1989). In addition, the right of initiative is perceived as permitting less powerful public interests to place their issues on the national agenda (Kerr 1987).[5] In this view, then, initiatives are the instruments that challengers to the political system can use to initiate reform. These instruments make it easier to gain access to the political system, decreasing the costs associated with acquiring such access.

The literature on direct democracy also finds that initiative rights change the potential benefits that movements achieve by action, even when the resulting legislation is rejected by the voters. In part, the potential benefits depend on the chances that the initiated legislation will be passed by the electorate. Since this may differ according to the group and legislation involved, in a later section I examine how initiatives affect the chances of success for suffrage movements in the United States and Switzerland. Initiatives may also increase the benefits to the organization by forcing the government to act even when they lose. Linder (1987) argues that the introduction of an initiative on atomic energy in Switzerland provoked the government into revising its energy policy. Even where governments themselves do not react, initiatives may bring issues onto the public agenda and provide the opportunity for groups to attempt to influence public opinion (Cronin 1989; Magleby 1988). Thus, the initiative is viewed as aiding opposition groups or challengers to the system because it grants them direct access to the public agenda. To examine the validity of this claim, I must first review the use of the initiative by American and Swiss suffrage activists.

The Use of the Initiative by Woman Suffrage Movements

The United States

In the United States only eight initiatives were introduced by woman suffrage activists (see Table 6.1). One of these initiatives, introduced in Oregon in 1910, would not have granted voting rights to all women; it called only for the enfranchisement of white taxpayers. The other seven asked for voting rights for all women in all state and local elections. With one exception all of these initiatives were introduced during the last ten years of the suffrage movement.

While eight initiatives may seem like a very small number, it represents quite extensive use of the initiative where it was available. Of the fifteen states that permitted initiatives, only four adopted the right to the initiative before 1910. Therefore, for forty of the fifty years that encompass the American woman suffrage movement, women had limited opportunities to initiate constitutional amendments. Moreover, four of fifteen states that permitted use of the initiative had already granted women full voting rights *before* they passed legislation creating the right of citizens to initiate legislation. Thus, woman suffrage activists in only eleven states had the right to the initiative available to them, and then only during the last decade of their struggle.

Of these eleven states, woman suffrage activists used initiatives in six of them. Woman suffrage organizations were among the groups that lobbied intensively for the right of the initiative (Cronin 1989), and, once it was in place, they were eager to use the newfound right of the initiative. In four states—Arizona, Nebraska, Ohio, and Oklahoma—woman suffrage organizations led initiative drives for the right to vote in the same year or the year following the creation of the initiative right. In fact, in Ohio the first initiative to be filed under the new legislation was for women's voting rights (Catt and Shuler 1926).

Woman suffrage activists tended to turn to the initiative when they could not achieve voting rights through traditional channels. In Arizona, the state legislature ignored numerous appeals from women to allow voters to decide the suffrage issue. In Missouri and Oklahoma, woman suffrage legislation repeatedly failed to come to a vote in the legislature. In Oregon and Ohio, woman suffrage activists were angry at unfair campaign practices by some business interests (particularly the liquor and beer industries) and determined to bring woman suffrage up for a second vote (Catt and Shuler 1926; Moynihan 1983). In all of these cases, activists perceived that the woman suffrage issue had not been given a fair chance to succeed through the normal channels of politics and that the right to the initiative could correct this problem.

On the other hand, those states where women did not use the initiative rights were states where woman suffrage activists were successful using existing legislative channels. In two of the states—Arkansas and Michigan—state legislatures had already granted significant voting rights to women by statute. Moreover, in all of these states, constitutional amendments granting full voting rights for women were presented to the voters at about the same time that initiative rights were introduced. Arkansas had a woman suffrage referendum in 1918, and Nevada successfully passed a constitutional amendment in a referendum in 1914. Two states had two referenda in the period immediately following the introduction of initiative rights: Michigan in 1913 and 1918, and North Dakota in 1914 and 1920. Massachusetts is the only exception; its woman suffrage referendum, held in 1915, preceded the introduction of initiative rights by three years. Consequently, woman suffrage activists had little reason to attempt initiatives because state legislatures already had presented woman suffrage referenda to the public.

Thus, woman suffrage activists in the United States used the initiative in the way that proponents expected. The initiative provided them, as challengers to the system, a means of putting their ideas on the public agenda. Woman suffrage supporters could use the initiative in those states where state legislatures or organized interest groups denied women the opportunity to introduce woman suffrage legislation. In this sense, the initiative does appear to permit greater access for challengers to the system. Thus, evidence from the United States indicates that this direct democratic institution does improve the political opportunity structure for social movements.

Switzerland

In Switzerland, twenty-two woman suffrage amendments were introduced by initiative, including eight initiatives in cantons where a single voter could initiate legislation.[6] Of those twenty-two initiatives, five of them called for only limited voting rights.[7] Even though initiatives were permitted throughout the nation, woman suffrage initiatives—whether for full or limited voting rights—were introduced in only thirteen cantons; initiatives for woman suffrage were never attempted in the other twelve cantons.

The lack of initiative drives in these cantons cannot be explained by overwhelming support for woman suffrage in the canton as it was in the United States. In fact, on a number of different dimensions, cantons where initiatives were introduced were very similar to the cantons where initiatives were never used. Of the twelve cantons that never used the initiative, only four granted women the right to vote prior to the passage of the national referendum in 1971. However, only five of the thirteen cantons with initiatives introduced woman suffrage before 1971.[8] Thus, cantons with initiatives were no more or less likely to have achieved woman suffrage prior to the national amendment in 1971.

While American suffrage activists did not use the initiative where woman suffrage referenda occurred through normal political channels, the use of initiative rights by Swiss suffrage activists was not related to cantonal woman suffrage referenda. A surprising number of cantons had no referenda on women's voting rights legislation before national suffrage was adopted in 1971. However, initiatives were no more or less likely to be utilized in these cantons. Of the thirteen cantons where initiatives were used, five of them had no referenda prior to 1971. Similarly, of the twelve cantons where no suffrage initiatives were introduced, five cantons held no cantonal woman suffrage referenda before 1971. Thus, while the American suffrage activists were moved to employ initiatives where governments did not respond to their demands, the use of the initiative in Switzerland was unrelated to the willingness of cantonal governments to consider woman suffrage.

Surprisingly, woman suffrage activists were not the sponsors of most women's voting rights initiatives. While in the United States suffrage activists were actively involved in all woman suffrage initiatives, only four of the twenty-two Swiss initiatives were run by woman suffrage organizations. Two initiative petitions were sponsored by the woman suffrage organization in Geneva in 1920 and 1940. The suffrage organization in Basel-stadt also initiated the constitutional amendment that gave them cantonal suffrage in 1966. And the woman suffrage organization in Bern sponsored an initiative in 1956 to allowed local communities to introduce their own suffrage legislation.

All of the other women's voting rights initiatives were introduced by political parties or by other political organizations. Of the fourteen initiatives launched by identifiable groups other than the woman suffrage organization, eleven were sponsored by opposition political parties or youth organizations. The most active opposition political party was the Communist Party (the Partei der Arbeit, or PdA), although both the Social Democrats (SP) and the Landesring der Unabhängige (LdU), a smaller, more centrist political party, also initiated legislation.[9] Both the LdU and the PdA were challenging parties; they had little representation in the cantonal legislatures and, with two exceptions, were not members of the governing coalition (Gruner 1984).[10] The other main impetus for suffrage came from the youth organizations of the various political parties, often acting without support from the party. Thus, most of the nonsuffrage organizations that initiated woman suffrage legislation were groups with little formal power in the cantonal governments.

Swiss woman suffrage activists were not always totally supportive of the woman suffrage initiatives introduced by these groups. In Zürich, for example, many activists were unhappy that the PdA launched the woman suffrage initiatives of 1947 and 1954. Women's groups that had previously supported woman suffrage withdrew their support on the PdA initiatives. Although the woman suffrage organization in Zürich officially endorsed the initiatives, it refused to campaign for the suffrage amendment because it was sponsored by the Communist party. Similarly, activists in Schaffhausen complained about the introduction of an initiative in 1969. As one activist recounted to me:

> It was a bit too much, naturally, to have it [a referendum on woman suffrage] again so soon, after only two years. . . . In 1969, we already had to begin to prepare for the national suffrage referendum in 1971. . . . So we said, stop, and that is also why the results are worse in 1969.[11]

Thus, not only did Swiss woman suffrage organizations sponsor few initiatives, they were not always appreciative allies when other groups championed the initiative.

While the evidence presented here concerning the American suffrage organization supports the argument that the initiative provides greater access to less organized groups, the results in Switzerland are mixed. Although there are many more initiatives introducing full or partial woman suffrage legislation than in the United States, few of these are sponsored by woman suffrage organizations. In fact, woman suffrage organizations in the United States introduced more initiatives than their Swiss counterparts although they had fewer opportunities to do so. All in all, the discussion of the Swiss suffrage movement paints a different picture of the relationship between social movements and the right to the initiative than we see in the American case. The literature on political opportunity structure suggests Swiss woman suffrage movements should avail themselves of the greater opportunities provided by the more open initiative laws. Yet the evidence shows that the existence and greater openness of this direct democratic institution does not necessarily imply its use by social movements.

If, however, the use of the initiative is not an effective means for social movements to institute social change, then the question of whether woman suffrage activists actually employed the initiative becomes moot. There is no reason to expect Swiss suffrage activists to utilize this tactic if it is not a useful means of achieving women's voting rights. Thus, before we can reassess political opportunity structure literature, we must consider the effectiveness of initiatives.

The Initiative and the Success of Woman Suffrage Movements

Initiatives might have affected the success of American and Swiss woman suffrage activists in two ways. First, most suffrage activists were firmly wedded to the idea that the enfranchisement of women required a great deal of public education and propaganda. Even if suffrage legislation lost, referenda campaigns afforded the opportunity to reach many individuals who would otherwise not be exposed to this propaganda. Thus, Mary R. de Vou, an activist in the Delaware Equal Suffrage Association, wrote, "the advocates of woman suffrage . . . suffer from the handicap peculiar to Delaware—no referendum to the voters possible on constitutional amendments [*sic*]—and therefore it never has had the advantage of a State-wide educational campaign" (cited in Harper 1992b: 86). To the extent that woman suffrage activists are able to initiate legislation earlier than if they had waited for state or cantonal legislatures to introduce referenda, initiatives may have provided important educational opportunities. Second, and most obvious, the initiative may have quickened the pace at which woman suffrage legislation was adopted.

The United States

The evidence on the usefulness of the initiative in the United States, as an educational tool and as a means of obtaining the vote for women, is mixed. If woman suffrage initiatives were a useful means for bringing the issue to the public agenda, we would expect that the average date of initiatives were the same as or earlier than the date of the first referenda. In fact, if we compare the six states where initiatives occurred with all of the other states where suffrage referenda were held, women's voting rights appeared on the ballot much earlier where suffrage activists utilized the initiative. The average year of the first referendum in the thirty-one noninitiative states is 1905. In states where suffrage organizations sponsored initiatives, the first referendum took place in 1900, on average. Thus, the sponsorship of initiatives allowed woman suffrage organizations in the United States to introduce the issue earlier.

Another way of measuring the utility of initiative rights is to explore whether voters accept suffrage when it is introduced as an initiative. Therefore, it also makes sense to examine the rate of passage of suffrage referenda, especially those proposed by initiative. In the United States, however, initiatives tended to be less successful than other suffrage referenda. In fact, 32 percent of the noninitiative referenda in the United States were adopted by the voters. In contrast, only two of the eight initiative referenda (25 percent) passed. Thus, woman suffrage initiatives were slightly less successful than other referenda.

Finally, states where suffrage organizations took advantage of their initiative rights did not achieve suffrage any sooner than other states. Of the eleven states that had not passed suffrage prior to adopting the right to the initiative, there was no difference in the timing of suffrage between those states where suffrage organizations used the initiative and those states where they did not. On average, both groups of states granted women the right to vote in 1917, two years before the federal amendment was passed. However, as I noted earlier, American woman suffrage activists sponsored initiatives only when state governments did not introduce woman suffrage referenda on their own accord. Thus, those states that did not use the initiative may not have needed it.

A second possibility is that the existence of the right to the initiative may force the government to act on the demands of challenging groups even before they initiate legislation. Legislators may have passed suffrage legislation in order to preempt initiative drives by suffragists once the right to the initiative existed. If this were true, states with the right to initiative should enfranchise women earlier than those where such rights did not exist. Again, however, the evidence is mixed. On the one hand, only one of the eleven states with initiative rights still denied women the right to vote when the Nineteenth Amendment was ratified. In contrast, seventeen of the thirty-seven states without initiative rights failed to enfranchise women before 1920. On the other hand, when one looks at the date when women's voting rights were adopted, there is almost no difference between states that permitted the initiative, where the average date of adoption is 1917, and those which did not (average passage 1916).[12] Thus, one cannot conclude with confidence that the existence of initiative rights increased the success of the American woman suffrage movement.

Switzerland

In Switzerland, on the other hand, a clearer connection exists between the use of the initiative and the success of the women's movement. For one thing, when suffrage organizations utilized the initiative, they accelerated public discussion of the woman suffrage issue. Most cantons did not consider woman suffrage referenda until rather late. In eleven of the twenty-five cantons, the first referendum on cantonal woman suffrage took place *during or after* the second national referendum on woman suffrage in 1971. The average date of the first referenda on the issue of full cantonal voting rights for women is 1958.[13] Although the average date of all initiative referenda is later (1962), much depends on which group sponsored the initiative. Political parties (outside of the PdA) and youth organizations did not initiate suffrage legislation, on average, until the 1970s. On the other hand, the PdA initiatives occurred in 1943, on average, and the average date of initiatives from the Schweizerisches Verband für Frauenstimmrecht, the Swiss suffrage organization, is 1948. Thus, when it exploited this opportunity, the suffrage organization initiated suffrage referenda considerably earlier than other groups or than cantonal parliaments or executives.

The second question is whether Swiss suffrage activists were discouraged from sponsoring initiatives because there was little chance that they would succeed. Again, this hypothesis seems to have little support. If one looks at all woman suffrage referenda, including those sponsored by cantonal governments, they had a very high chance of passing. Prior to 1970, the success rate of woman suffrage in all noninitiative referenda was 54 percent.[14] Referenda resulting from initiatives passed at a much lower rate; voters accepted only 27.2 percent of all initiatives. Yet, when this is broken down according to which group sponsored the initiative, legislation sponsored by suffrage organizations does quite well. Two out of four initiatives introduced by the suffrage organization passed. The low overall success rate of initiatives is a result of legislation sponsored by opposition groups; none of the PdA-sponsored initiatives were adopted, and only 14 percent of the referenda introduced by other political parties or youth groups passed. Thus, referenda initiated by women's suffrage organizations do almost as well as other Swiss referenda on woman suffrage.

Finally, initiatives are only useful in so far as cantons where initiatives occur enfranchise women earlier. However, the cantons where woman suffrage organizations employed initiatives were among the first cantons to achieve women's voting rights. On average, these cantons granted full voting rights to women three years before the cantons where no initiative was introduced (1966 vs. 1969). On the other hand, women were enfranchised last in those cantons where other groups introduced initiatives. The average year for the achievement of woman suffrage for these cantons is 1975, a full four years after the passage of the national woman suffrage amendment. Even after removing the two Appenzells from this calculation as outliers, the average year of introduction is still only 1971. Thus, although initiatives by other groups are associated with a delay in women's voting rights, where woman suffrage organizations instigated the initiative for success, women were enfranchised more quickly.

Understanding the Relationship between
Strategies and Political Opportunities

The evidence concerning the use of initiatives presents a puzzle. By every measure, Swiss woman suffrage activists were successful when they utilized initiatives. Yet few suffrage organizations chose to use this effective tactic. In contrast, American suffrage activists benefited less; yet, they sponsored a large number of initiatives despite their limited possibilities for doing so. The dearth of initiatives by Swiss suffrage activists even though such initiatives were successful calls into question the political opportunity structure literature. Contrary to the assumptions of many political opportunity structure theorists, the existence of political opportunities does not guarantee that movements will employ them.

One way of understanding why movements do not always utilize existing opportunities is to focus on the perceptions held by movement activists. Social movements may not always have complete and unbiased information about existing strategies and opportunities. Indeed, the U.S. and Swiss suffrage movements differ greatly in the amount of information they had about the use of initiatives. In the United States, suffrage activists had ties to the progressive direct democratic reformers who promoted the initiative. Such ties helped inform suffrage activists about the usefulness of the initiative. For example, soon after Oregon became the first state to adopt the initiative, the National American Woman Suffrage Association (NAWSA) held its annual convention there. William S. U'Ren, who spearheaded the addition of the initiative to the Oregon constitution, spoke at the convention "on the need and purpose of these political reforms" (Edwards 1990: 230) to suffrage activists from almost every state. As a result, the NAWSA passed a resolution supporting the initiative (Harper 1922a).

In contrast, my interviews with Swiss woman suffrage activists indicate that they did not perceive the right to the initiative as a useful means of acquiring voting rights. In interviews with sixty-one woman suffrage activists,[15] very few activists volunteered anything about the right to initiate constitutional amendments on either the national or the cantonal level. Few of the activists interviewed mentioned the initiative when talking about the tactics available to the organization, although many argued that the required referenda on constitutional amendments hurt the cause of woman suffrage in Switzerland. The use of the initiative was simply not part of the "repertoire" of tactics that the activists viewed as available to them. One suffrage activist even maintained that "we did not have the possibility to launch an initiative ourselves," incorrectly implying that women did not have the right or ability to do so.[16] Nor were the opinions of women suffrage activists in Switzerland changed in hindsight. Although the later women's movement used the initiative to pass the Equal Rights Amendment in 1981, only *one* activist argued that the woman suffrage movement should have utilized the initiative more:

> I would have started with initiatives instead of just petitions. Then the first initiative would have been lost, but we would have had a vote. That allows opportunity to explain, the petition disappeared . . . nothing. Then we could have done a second . . . and we would have had more propaganda opportunities.[17]

Yet, most suffrage activists did not think of the initiative when exploring possible tactics, and a small group of activists rejected the tactic on the basis of misinformation. This suggests that political opportunity structures alone are less important than the *perceptions* of them by suffrage movement actors.

How were those perceptions formed? In the United States, as I have already suggested, suffrage activists were closely connected to the prohibition and progressive movements. Even in states where the suffrage movement was weak, the prohibition and progressive movements encouraged women to use this tactic (Kraditor 1981). American suffrage activists knew of the initiative, even fought for initiative rights in some states, and had a sense of its potential utility as a strategy to gain the vote.

Swiss suffrage activists, on the other hand, lacked connections to other political actors who might have provided information about the initiative. While the workers' movement in the 1920s was one of the first groups to support woman suffrage, the support was mainly ideological and did not translate into concrete alliances between the two movements. A majority of the suffrage movement activists came from groups that opposed the worker's movement[18] and were unwilling to develop strong connections with it (Banaszak 1996: Chap. 8).

Most woman suffrage leaders felt ideologically close to or were members of liberal or Catholic political parties and women's organizations. However, these organizations were largely indifferent to the cause of women's voting rights, or they opposed it altogether and therefore were not strong allies of the woman suffrage movement. Moreover, a closer alliance with liberal and Catholic organizations would not necessarily have provided more information about initiatives. The liberal and Catholic political parties were the largest parties in the national government and in most cantons. Because they took a leading role in the governing Councils on both the national and the cantonal levels, these groups had little reason to utilize initiatives to bring issues to the political agenda. Thus, several studies (App 1987; Moser 1987; Hofer 1987) find that few initiatives are sponsored by these parties.

Conclusion

The use of initiative rights by American and Swiss suffrage activists suggests that the mere existence of structures of political opportunity does not ensure that social movement organizations will recognize those structures or follow strategies designed to optimize their chances under those political opportunities. Organizations and their leaders must first perceive those structures as opportunities. The current focus on political opportunity structures may be misleading since it slights the problem of perceptions. If perceptions of political opportunity structures differ from the objective reality, movements will choose strategies that reflect their perceptions.

If, as I have suggested, the perceptions of movement actors are influenced by their connections and alliances to other political actors, the mechanisms by which political opportunity structures affect movements may be very complex. Indeed, I have analyzed here only one small aspect of political opportunity structures—the openness of the political system through initiatives. Yet, other aspects of the political opportunity structure—specifically, the existence of allies (Kitschelt 1986; Kriesi 1995; Tarrow 1988, 1989)—affected Swiss and American suffrage activists' perceptions of the initiative. Thus, the political opportunity structure may do more than merely provide objective costs and benefits to which movements react; it may also affect the perceptions of movement actors.

Notes

This research was supported in part by a Swiss National Science Grant and by a research grant from the American Political Science Association. I would like to thank Andrew McFarland and Eric Plutzer for their comments on a previous draft.

1. A canton is the equivalent of a state.

2. The Federal Council is the executive decision-making body (i.e., government or cabinet) in Switzerland.

3. Initiative rights in both countries also vary in the legal requirements associated with using the initiative such as the number of signatures needed or the requirements associated with the passage of an initiative. A full comparison of these requirements can be found in Banaszak (1991). Here I simply note that the restrictions associated with the Swiss initiative were equal to or fewer than those associated with initiatives in the United States.

4. Recently scholars have begun to realize the problems with these assumptions. See, for example, Meyer (1995) and Sawyers and Meyer (1993).

5. Not all researchers agree that the initiative benefits challenging groups. For example, one study of California initiatives (Lee 1978) claims that the right to the initiative is most often used by those organizations that control more monetary resources or that also directly lobby the legislature. In Switzerland, App (1987) argues that groups that already have influence in the political system are one of the types of groups more likely to have their initiatives succeed.

6. Several Swiss cantons have yearly meetings of all voters in the canton to consider referenda and, in some, to elect cantonal officials. This particular institution is called the Landesgemeinde. For several of the cantons with a Landesgemeinde—Glarus, Appenzell Innerrhoden, and Appenzell Ausserrhoden—only one registered voter need raise an issue for it to be put on the agenda. Once on the agenda, a vote must be taken.

7. Three types of limited voting rights were requested: the right to vote for school boards, the right to elect the boards that govern churches, and a constitutional amendment that granted no voting rights but allowed local communities to introduce their own suffrage legislation.

8. Because women in the canton Jura gained the right to vote while Jura was still a part of the canton Bern, I do not include it as a separate canton in this analysis.

9. The SP was a member of the governing coalition in the national parliament and in many cantonal governments and so its position as an "opposition" party could be questioned. Nonetheless, the SP is often outnumbered in these coalitions by center and right parties. For

this reason, despite their position in the majority, the SP often emphasizes its oppositional role in elections.

10. The PdA has played a significant role in two cantons—Basel-stadt and Geneva. In Basel-stadt, there was a "red" government (a coalition between PdA and Social Democrats) between 1935 and 1949. In Geneva, the PdA received over 20 percent of the vote in several elections between 1950 and 1970.

11. Interview of March 21, 1988.

12. This difference is influenced by one exceptional state, Wyoming, which introduced woman suffrage while still a territory in 1869. When Wyoming is excluded from the analysis, the average year of introduction in noninitiative states is 1918, one year after states with the initiative.

13. Many cantons had earlier referenda considering only partial voting rights for women. The average date of the first suffrage referenda of any kind is 1954.

14. I limit the analysis to pre-1970 referenda since suffrage referenda had a very high chance of passing once the Federal Council announced the second national referendum in 1970. The success rate for suffrage referenda after 1969 was 77 percent. If the two Appenzell cantons are excluded, the post-1969 success rate jumps to 94 percent.

15. Interviews were conducted with sixty-two people (sixty-one women and 1 man) from twenty-five cantons (excluding Jura). For more information on the interview methodology, see Banaszak (1996).

16. Interview of December 15, 1987.

17. Interview of February 1, 1988.

18. For example, Ruckstuhl (1986) describes how the president of the Schweizerisches Verband für das Frauenstimmrecht sent a telegram to the Federal Council during the General Strike of 1918 supporting their actions against the strike; at the same time, the president noted that woman suffrage was among the workers' demands.

Part 3

Parties and Elections

7

Less than Conquerors:
The Christian Right in State Republican Parties

John C. Green, James L. Guth, and Clyde Wilcox

Perhaps no social movement in recent American history has experienced more deaths and resurrections than the Christian Right. Sociologists and journalists have been especially prone to chronicling the "rise" and "fall" of the movement (see, e.g., Bruce 1988). Death notices have often been followed closely by a new birth of Christian Right activism. In reality, however, the movement's growth has been much steadier than commonly depicted, although punctuated by several setbacks and some notable advances (Rozell and Wilcox 1996).

In this chapter, we go beyond the typical concerns of social movement theorists with the life cycle of the Christian Right and address instead the extent to which the movement has influenced established political institutions. In recent years, students of social movements have sought to explain why some movements penetrate the political establishment, while others do not (Tarrow 1996). Our focus here is on the Christian Right's interaction with the American party system, specifically, its efforts to control Republican party institutions (Oldfield 1996).

We proceed as follows. After a look at Christian Right inroads into state Republican party organizations, we draw on several strands of social movement theory and complementary facets of the party literature to explain the patterns of Christian Right success in grasping the levers of party power. We conclude that social movement theories stressing collective grievances, resource mobilization, and political opportunities all provide valuable insights: the Christian Right influences party institutions where it represents a large aggrieved population, mobilizes preexisting religious resources, and takes advantage of new political opportunities.

The Christian Right and State Republican Parties

In the fall of 1994, *Campaigns & Elections* magazine (*C&E*) assessed Christian Right influence in state Republican party organizations (Persinos

1994). Drawing on in-depth interviews with knowledgeable observers, *C&E* found that the Christian Right had *dominant influence* in eighteen states (i.e., the movement and allies had a working majority in the principal state party organ). In another thirteen it had *substantial influence,* with over one-quarter of the membership; and in the remaining nineteen, only *minor influence.* Despite the obvious limitations of these kinds of data, the results comport well with state-by-state accounts of Christian Right activities in the 1994 elections (Rozell and Wilcox 1995) and are corroborated by a 1993 study of Republican elites designed to assess Christian Right influence.[1] The latter survey asked respondents for an evaluation of Christian Right strength in their locality, scored on a seven-point scale. When averaged by state, these assessments correlate strongly with the *C&E* categories ($r = .74$). In fact, when state averages were divided into thirds ("strong," "mixed," and "weak") and cross-tabulated with the *C&E* measure, thirty-five states (70 percent) were in agreement. In no instance were the two measures strongly at odds.

Even the modest disagreements were instructive. In five states, the Republican elite survey found the Christian Right "strong," but *C&E* discovered only "substantial influence." Just the opposite pattern appeared in ten other states: the survey found "mixed" Christian Right strength where *C&E* saw "dominant influence." These inconsistencies are easily explained. In the first group of states, the Christian Right had not yet translated a strong political position into organizational influence, while in the second the movement had achieved organizational power despite its mixed strength and much opposition. In such areas, one might well expect heated intraparty conflict; a state-by-state review finds just such controversies.

To incorporate insights derived from comparison of the two measures, we combined them in a five-point "Index of Christian Right Influence," the dependent variable in our analysis. The first two index points include cases consistent on both measures: *weak influence* states ("weak" on the survey item and "minor influence" in *C&E*) and *modest influence* states ("mixed" on the survey item and "substantial influence" according to *C&E*). The next two categories, however, encapsulate instances in which the two measures differed modestly: *contested influence* ("mixed" on the survey item and "dominant influence" in *C&E*) and *strong influence* ("strong" on the survey item and "substantial influence" in *C&E*). The final category, *great influence* ("strong" on the survey item and "dominant influence" in *C&E*), again represents agreement between the studies. This combined index is strongly validated by other survey items, and the original, unrecoded Republican elite responses on Christian Right strength are more highly correlated with the new index ($r = .85$) than with the original *C&E* assessment ($r = .74$).

Where is the Christian Right influential in the GOP? Figure 7.1 illustrates the Index of Christian Right Influence, revealing that in 1994 the

Figure 7.1
Christian Right and State Republican Parties, 1993–94

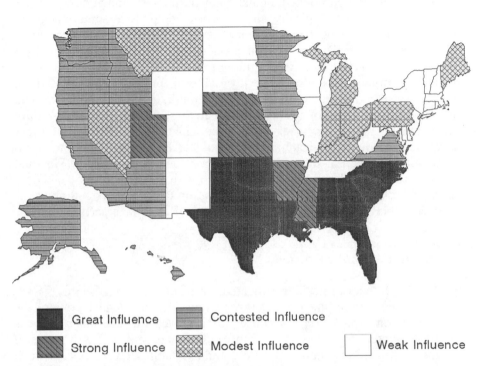

| | Great Influence | | Contested Influence |
| | Strong Influence | | Modest Influence | | Weak Influence |

movement had a great GOP organizational presence in eight southern states, ranging from North Carolina to Texas. Strong influence existed in two more southern states, Arkansas and Mississippi, and farther west in Kansas, Nebraska, and Utah.[2] On the other hand, the movement had contested influence in the far West, including all five states of the Pacific Rim, Idaho, and Arizona. This category also included Iowa, Minnesota, and Virginia. Next, the Christian Right enjoyed modest influence in some other midwestern states, centered on Ohio, as well as in Kentucky, Pennsylvania, Maine, Montana, and Nevada. Finally, the Christian Right was weak in the East, in several parts of Mississippi Valley, Northern Plains, Rocky Mountains, and in one southern (Tennessee) and one border (West Virginia) state.

Social Movement Theory and the Christian Right

What accounts for the varying success of the Christian Right? Over the past few decades a number of theories have been used to account for the appearance and behavior of social movements. Although these theories often overlap, they stress distinct aspects of movement activity. We will concentrate on three such approaches. What we will call *collective grievance* theory argues that unfulfilled political demands of particular populations give rise to social movements. Typically, these theories emphasize some change in traditional social arrangements, social class power, or economic disruption, often tied to modernization. Such approaches were later supplemented (or sometimes, replaced) by *resource mobilization* theories, which stress the preexisting organizational resources available to form a movement and the role of social movement entrepreneurs in mobilizing such resources, with the amount and types of resources critical to success or failure. A third model is *political process* theory, which recognizes the importance of grievances and existing organizational resources but highlights the political opportunities that permit the movement some prospect of success. We shall consider these theories in turn, evaluate each with appropriate data, and conclude with observations about their contribution to our understanding of the interaction between the Christian Right and the Republican party.

Collective Grievances Create a Demand for Christian Right Political Action

Although theories positing collective grievances as the stimulus for social movements have fallen out of favor among social scientists, one of the most common explanations for conservative movements continues to focus on the discontent of traditionalists confronting modernization. Advocates of "status politics," "symbolic politics," and related perspectives see such movements expressing a "demand" (to use a market analogy) for political action (Lienesch 1982). These demands typically involve official endorsement of traditional moral values, sexual mores, or religious practices in public life, often being eroded by the forces of modernity.

Despite the popularity of this approach, measuring traditionalist grievances has always been a difficult task. Many scholars locate such discontent indirectly, using sociological remoteness from modernity as a proxy: traditionalist concerns are often assumed to dominate among impoverished, poorly educated, white, older, and rural populations, often residents of the South and West (Lipset and Raab 1978). Despite frequent use, however, demographic proxies have not proven very useful in locating the Christian Right (Wilcox 1992). In fact, traditionalist demands are often most prevalent at the geographic intersections of tradition and modernity, not in locations far from modern life. Thus, the Christian Right prospers in rapidly growing metropolitan areas, with their burgeoning white-collar and professional classes, not in economically stagnant, rural, and blue-collar areas (Green, Guth, and Hill 1993). As a result, scholars have turned to more direct measures of grievances: assessments of political culture, traditionalism on social issues such as abortion and gay rights, and even general ideological conservatism (Hertzke 1993).

For our present case, then, collective grievance theories predict the greatest Christian Right impact where traditionalist demands are strong and voiced, providing incentives to participate in state GOP politics. Table 7.1 reports the bivariate correlations between a number of proxy and direct measures of such demands. Given the patterns in Figure 7.1, it should come as no surprise that region is powerfully associated with movement influence (r = .61), reflecting the Christian Right's southern strength and near absence in the Northeast. But region may really be a proxy for political culture, a point illustrated by the strong correlation of movement power with Elazar's (1984) popular typology: the Christian Right is most potent in "traditionalist" states, strong in "moralistic" ones, but weak in "individualistic" areas.[3]

Traditionalist political culture may indeed be associated with "tradition-

Table 7.1
Correlates of Christian Right Influence in State Republican Parties: Collective Grievance or Demand Factors

Variable	Correlation
Demographic proxies	
Region	.61*
Political culture	.58*
Income	−.35*
Education	−.29*
White population	−.35*
Age	.06
Rural	.03
Population increase	.29*
Attitudes	
Anti–gay rights	.44*
Family values	.33**
Antifeminist	.31*
Antiabortion	.31*
Mean "conservative"	.66*

Source: See text and notes.
Note: Figures are Pearson product moment correlations.
*p = .05 or better
**p = .01 or better

alist" demography, but we find only weak evidence connecting such factors to Christian Right influence.[4] True, Christian Right impact is negatively associated with income and education, but it is also negatively correlated with the size of the Caucasian population, unrelated to the size of rural or aged populations, and positively associated with population growth. No doubt these patterns are partly artifacts of region, but they also suggest that contact with modernization is as critical as distance from it in accounting for the Christian Right's appeal. Indeed, this finding resembles the "communal protest" approach in explaining traditionalist movements: such movements are reactions to major social transformations (see Wald, Button, and Rienzo 1996).

Such population traits, however, are usually surrogates for social attitudes, which we can tap directly by aggregating state-level survey data.[5] This operation reveals that the Christian Right is strongest where the public is most conservative on gay rights, traditional "family values," feminism, and abortion. Interestingly, the positive association grows for self-identified conservatism, surpassing even the correlations for region and political culture. Thus, public conservatism is clearly the best indicator of collective grievances, and the broadest measure of that conservatism is the most potent. In other words, the Christian Right is successful where its agenda resonates with popular attitudes, a finding that provides some support for a much criticized but classic perspective on social movements.

Resource Mobilization: "Supply-Side" Analysis of the Christian Right

An alternative view of social movements stresses organization over grievances. Resource mobilization theorists argue that movements appear when political entrepreneurs redirect existing social and organizational resources into politics (McCarthy and Zald 1977). From this perspective, the Christian Right will be most influential where religious resources are plentiful and already activated, thus providing the organizational means for participation in party politics.

Like grievances, mobilized resources are tricky to measure, and not surprisingly, scholars have often resorted to proxies here as well. Analysts usually employ data on membership in Evangelical Protestant churches, especially the more sectarian fundamentalist, Pentecostal, and charismatic communities, with their strong individual commitment and dense internal networks. As their hostility toward "the [modern] world" has been only imperfectly neutralized by an apolitical theology, these groups represent a cache of untapped resources already predisposed toward Christian Right goals (Bruce 1988). Additional resources may also be found in more mainstream Evangelical churches, such as the giant Southern Baptist Convention

(SBC), and from traditionalist Mormons, mainline Protestants, and Catholics. Other writers see Christian Right resources among those holding specific identities (such as "born again" Christians) or having strong faith commitments, regardless of religious tradition (Petrocik and Steeper 1987). Few scholars, however, have quantified the resources actually mobilized by the Christian Right, though such data might account for the movement more effectively than measures of potential resources can.

In any case, resource mobilization theory predicts that Christian Right influence arises from elite deployment of existing social resources in Republican politics. What do we find? Table 7.2 reports on several such potential and activated resources. The first is a crucial source of movement support: the proportion of the public belonging to conservative religious communities.[6] Not surprisingly, Christian Right power is highly correlated with the number of sectarian Protestants, including fundamentalists, Pentecostals, and charismatics, but their importance is matched by that of mainstream Evangelicals. (Data on the number of *churches*—i.e., organized affiliates of these traditions—show very similar results.) The number of black Protestants, "second cousins twice removed" of white Evangelicals, show nearly as strong a relationship with movement support, but these findings are largely an artifact of region: they are located in the same regions as their white religious kin. Membership in nontraditional conservative groups, such as the Mormons, shows a much weaker, but still positive, relationship to movement strength.

The size of other religious communities, however, is negatively associated with Christian Right influence, starting with modest correlations for small non-Christian groups, the secular population, and Jews. Negative correlations increase for the proportions of mainline Protestants (such as Episcopalians, Methodists, and United Church of Christ), liberal nontraditionalists (such as Unitarians), Eastern Orthodox, and Roman Catholics. Indeed, the strong negative correlation for the Catholic population matches the positive coefficients for Evangelicals. (Of course, these figures can be viewed in two ways, either as the absence of Christian Right resources or as indicators of the potential for opposition movements.) Not surprisingly, such measures of religious tradition can be combined into a single scale with Evangelicals at one end and Catholics at the other,[7] which is strongly correlated with Christian Right influence. In any event, these denominational variables outperform other religious measures, such as the proportion of "born again" citizens or those to whom religion is salient, although both are positively correlated with movement influence ($r = .36$ and $.22$, respectively). In addition, Christian Right influence is strongly associated with a measure of the Evangelical affiliation of state GOP elites, certainly another potential movement resource (Layman 1996).

"Potential" religious resources are important, but "activated" resources

Table 7.2
Correlates of Christian Right Influence in State Republican Parties: Resource
Mobilization or Supply Factors

Variable	Correlation
Religious measures	
Sectarian Protestant (percentage)	.55*
Evangelical Protestant	.56*
Black Protestant	.52*
Other traditionalist	.15
Non-Judeo-Christian	−.11
Secular	−.25*
Jewish	−.28*
Mainline Protestant	−.33*
Liberal nontraditional	−.35*
Orthodox	−.37*
Roman Catholic	−.52*
Index of Religious Affiliation	.62*
GOP elite religiosity	.53*
Movement characteristics	
Number of activists in state	.63*
Years of activism in state	.64*
Level of activism in state	.53*
Mass public support	
Belongs to "Religious Right" (percentage)	.52*
Religion influences own politics	.46*
Close to "Religious Right"	.39*
GOP elite assessments	
Christian Right is effective	.46*
Christian Right supports party	.45*
Christian Right cooperative	.34*

Source: See text and notes.
Note: Figures are Pearson product-moment correlations.
*$p = .05$ or better.

are even more vital. As Table 7.2 also reveals, Christian Right influence is very strongly linked to the number of Christian Right activists in a state, the duration of movement activity, and the extent of campaign involvement. Mass public identification with the Christian Right reveals a similar picture: party influence grows as more citizens claim to "belong to the religious right," say that their religion has an important impact on their politics, or that they feel close to the "religious right."[8] These findings also suggest that new theories of "identity politics" might be fruitfully employed in analysis of the Christian Right, as there is evidence here of the creation of a new, self-conscious political community (see Gamson 1992; Guth et al. 1996). These intuitively satisfying results are confirmed by assessments of the Christian Right mobilization by state GOP activists: influence is positively associated with their judgments that the Right has been effective, supportive, and cooperative in state politics. Thus, in summary, the Christian Right is most powerful where resources are not only available, but highly mobilized in politics. Taken together, these findings show that resource mobilization or supply factors also help account for Christian Right influence in the GOP. Indeed, at the bivariate level at least, the location of conservative religious communities and movement resources rivals the impact of region and public conservatism in explaining Christian Right power.

Political Process Theory: "Political Opportunities" and
the Christian Right

A third and increasingly influential kind of social movement theory is represented by political process perspectives. Students of "political opportunity structures" (McAdam 1982) argue that movement success hinges on the availability of opportunities to use resources to redress grievances, not on mere existence of either resources or grievances. From this perspective, the Christian Right should influence the GOP where opportunities abound. This simple formulation, of course, begs the question of what opportunities may exist in party politics. For insight into these, we turn to the party literature.

American political parties are notoriously permeable to outsiders (Epstein 1986). In the conventional party model (Aldrich 1995), such permeability has been understood as weakness in party control over candidates and constituencies. The more numerous the "weaknesses," the greater the opportunities to penetrate party structures (Gitelson, Conway, and Feigert 1984: 345–6). There are at least four ways of assessing the opportunities such weaknesses may offer social movements. First, party weakness may be *electoral*: the failure to attract voters, which is routinely measured by partisan identification in the mass public or by the electoral fortunes of party candidates (Bibby et al. 1990). Broader measures of party "competitiveness" combine votes cast, offices won, and government bodies controlled. A second notion of party weakness is *coalitional*, whether taking the form of elite factionalism or ideological division among party activists (Baer and Bositis 1988; Green and Guth 1988). Many scholars believe that both electoral and coalition weaknesses render parties more permeable: the former by making leaders more receptive to new constituencies to enhance prospects at the polls (Lowi 1963), the latter by leading rival factions to welcome—or even recruit—new allies (Schwartz 1995).

A third form of weakness is *institutional*, reflecting the debilitating effects of state law on organization (Advisory Commission on Intergovernmental Relations [ACIR] 1986). Legal regulation of parties' internal affairs and external activities reduces the autonomy of party leaders, whether by specifying central committee membership, prohibiting candidate endorsements, or requiring primaries to nominate candidates. A final kind of weakness might be dubbed *bureaucratic*, the absence of organizational capacity by party committee staffs, indicated by lack of funds, employees, or facilities (Cotter et al. 1984). Overregulation by state law reduces control by party leaders, making infiltration easier, while bureaucratic weakness may have the same effect (Lawson 1993; Yonish 1994).

Electoral, coalitional, institutional, and bureaucratic views of partisan opportunities obviously interact with collective grievance and resource mobilization theories as well. Those who see Christian Right power emanating from the demands of a previously unmobilized constituency might well stress the importance of electoral and coalitional weaknesses in providing opportunities to make good on followers' demands, while resource mobilization theorists should see institutional and bureaucratic weaknesses creating openings for Christian Right leaders to deploy their resources effectively. In any event, there is some evidence that the Christian Right has exploited each type of party weakness (Green, Guth, and Hill 1993; Oldfield 1996; Rozell and Wilcox 1996). Of course, if the conventional view of parties is in error, partisan opportunities may be occasioned not by party weakness but by strength—an alternative that we will consider later (Schwartz 1995).

Has the Christian Right benefited from such opportunities? In assessing the opportunity structure, we begin with electoral weakness, which reveals some initially unexpected patterns in Table 7.3. First, Christian Right influence is *positively* associated with the pre-1992 proportion of self-identified *Democrats* in the state electorate and negatively correlated with the number of independents; the positive relationship with self-identified Republicans is weak and statistically insignificant (Erikson, Wright, and McIver 1993). Thus, the Christian Right is strong where the Republican electorate was traditionally small. In contrast, movement influence is positively linked to recent *Republican* presidential voting: in 1996, for instance, Christian Right power was correlated negatively with votes for Clinton and Perot ($r = -.28$ and $-.20$, respectively) but positively with the size of the Dole tally ($r = .49$). These findings may at first seem contradictory, but they fit the regional patterns already identified: Christian Right strongholds in the South and many contested states in the West are traditionally Democratic, but have been trending Republican in recent federal elections. That the Christian Right is strong in these areas of partisan transition is illustrated by the mass

Table 7.3
Correlates of Christian Right Influence in State Republican Parties: Political
Opportunity Factors—Electoral and Coalitional Weaknesses

Variable	Correlation
Electoral weakness	
Mass party identification: Pre-1992	
Democratic	.48*
Independent	−.50*
Republican	.09
Mass party identification: 1996[a]	
Democratic	.03
Independent	−.30*
Republican	.27*
Party competitiveness	
State index 1988	.36*
State index 1992	.26*
Federal index 1988	−.34*
Federal index 1992	.40*
Index of Partisan Transition	.50*
Coalitional weakness	
State party factionalism	.50*
Elite conservatism	
GOP activists	.55*
GOP candidates	.42*
Net activist conservatism	.56*
Net candidate conservatism	.50*

Source: See text and notes.
Note: Figures are Pearson product-moment correlations.
*p = .05 or better.
[a]Data from Voter News Service Exit Polls.

party identification data for 1996, in which influence is now positively correlated with the proportion of self-identified *Republicans*.

This pattern can be seen more systematically using standard measures
of electoral competition. Table 7.3 presents two versions of the much-used
Ranney party competition index for 1988: a standard state office index and
a similar index for federal elections.[9] Christian Right influence is associated
with Democratic advantage in state elections (indicated by a positive correlation) and a Republican edge in federal contests (indicated by the negative
correlation). Parallel indices for 1992 (Bibby and Holbrook 1995) show the

same results, but with a decline in state Democratic bias and corresponding increase in the federal Republican advantage. We have captured this political transformation from Democratic to Republican by calculating an Index of Partisan Transition, which is strongly correlated with Christian Right influence.[10] Of course, such a partisan transition is as much evidence of contemporary GOP electoral strength as of the party's historic weakness. Interestingly, these data help explain one anomalous category in our Christian Right Index: four of five "strong influence" states have experienced a less dramatic disjunction between state and federal elections than have the Christian Right strongholds.

The relationship between Christian Right party gains and coalitional weakness is more mixed (Table 7.3). For example, Jewell and Olson's (1982: 58) measure of state party factionalism is indeed positively linked to Christian Right success. And if we combine their index of "cohesive," "bifactional," or "multifactional" state GOPs with Ranney's state party competitiveness scores, we find that the most multifactional and least competitive states have the strongest movement influence (data not shown). These patterns surely reflect region: the one-party South has been notorious for party factionalism and, until very recently, the absence of electoral competition. In contrast, another measure of coalitional strength, party elite ideology (Wright, Erikson, and McIver 1994), reveals unexpected results: Christian Right influence is strongly linked to conservative dominance among Republican activists and candidates rather than ideological diversity. These patterns suggest that the Christian Right benefits from ideological unity, arguably a party strength rather than a weakness.

What about the institutional strength of parties? First, we considered state regulation of electoral activities, internal party affairs (ACIR 1986: 123–62), and primary participation (Jewell and Olson 1988: 90). Contrary to our expectations, greater regulation (presumably a mark of weakness) is negatively associated with Christian Right influence, although only the internal affairs scale is statistically significant. The more the state restricts external and internal autonomy and participation in primaries, the less the influence of the Christian Right. This pattern is particularly strong for a subset of state rules, those governing membership in state and local committees. The more regulated the access to these committees, the weaker the Christian Right inroads. Because both primary and local/state committee rules are closely related, we constructed an Index of Committee Access, combining all three measures, which summarizes dramatically the effects of such regulation.[11] Basically, then, the more state regulation "closes" the process, the more difficulty the Christian Right has in penetrating party organs. This finding is confirmed by a separate measure of the autonomy parties enjoy in governing themselves, which is positively correlated with Christian Right strength (Appleton and Ward 1996: 372–6).

Apparently some state regulations that limit party autonomy also limit access by outside groups. Put another way, Christian Right inroads are facilitated by the openness of party rules. Of course, scholars have often noted that opening up party rules regarding primaries, caucuses, conventions, and reform has fostered participation by outsiders (Crotty 1983), and we observe yet another example. The data also provide insight into seeming anomalies: Tennessee and West Virginia, for example, have only weak movement influence despite a southern location; in both, the law sharply restricts access to party committees. On the other hand, some contested influence states, such as Virginia, Minnesota, and Washington, have unusually open party rules.

The bottom of Table 7.4 looks at bureaucratic weakness, using data from the Party Transformation Study (Cotter et al. 1984). Contrary to expectations, bureaucratic weakness in state Republican parties is *negatively* related to Christian Right influence, although the coefficient is not significant. Inspection of the raw data reveals why: state GOP organs are relatively strong everywhere, leaving only modest variance to explain.

Thus, we find only some of the hypothesized links between party weakness and partisan opportunities. But our findings do match two broader mea-

Table 7.4

Correlates of Christian Right Influence in State Republican Parties: Political Opportunity Factors—Institutional and Bureaucratic Weaknesses

Variable	Correlation
Institutional weakness: state regulation	
Election activities	−.15
Internal affairs	−.24*
Nomination rules	−.10
Local committee membership	−.26*
State committee membership	−.31*
Index of Committee Access	−.69*
State party autonomy	.42*
Bureaucratic weakness	
GOP state committee	−.17
GOP local committees	.51*
Traditional organization scale	−.41*
Interest group strength	.57*

Source: See text and notes.
Note: Figures are Pearson product-moment correlations.
*p = .05 or better.

sures of party institutions sometimes thought to assess party weakness. The first is Mayhew's (1986) "traditional party organization" scale, which taps the ability of parties to control candidacies; this measure shows a strong negative correlation with Christian Right influence. The second is Morehouse's (1981) measure of interest group strength. There is a strong positive relationship between the inability of parties to "control" constituency group pressures and Christian Right influence in state parties. In sum, the Christian Right is strong where parties do not exercise their traditional control over either candidates or interest groups. And taken in context with all our findings, they suggest that the Right is successful where a modern "service-vendor-broker" form of party (Frantzich 1989) is most common. Movement influence may be associated not so much with party weakness as with the emergence of a new kind of party (Schwartz 1990).

Thus, we find that Christian Right influence in state Republican politics is strongly associated with partisan opportunities, but not invariably in the expected form: electoral transition, ideological consistency, institutional weakness, and bureaucratic capacity all influence the movement's success.

Combining Perspectives: Multivariate Analysis of Christian Right Influence

So far we have found at least some support in our bivariate analysis for collective grievance, resource mobilization, and political process perspectives on Christian Right influence. Many variables in each model are strongly related to each other, of course; to produce the most parsimonious results, we conducted a series of multivariate analyses to arrive at the simple model in Table 7.5. Only five variables survived the regression, one each from the collective grievance and resource mobilization perspectives and three from among the political opportunity factors. Together, these five explain a very respectable 75 percent of the variance in Christian Right influence. The number of Christian Right activists in the state, a key resource mobilization variable, is the best predictor, followed closely by mass public conservatism, a critical grievance factor. The opportunity factors are less important: the Index of Committee Access has the third largest impact, followed by residual net activist conservatism,[12] and, last, the Index of Partisan Transition. All three reflect partisan opportunities but, as noted earlier, sometimes operate contrary to our initial expectations.

We should comment on one set of variables not making the final model: religious measures. As we might expect, the influence of conservative religion is massive but indirect, operating through other variables. A simple path model generates a total effects coefficient of .32.[13] Interestingly, there is no direct path between the size of conservative religious communities and

Table 7.5
Christian Right Influence in State Republican Parties: Regression Analysis (OLS)

Variable	Beta Coefficient
Collective grievance	
Mean public conservatism	.32*
Resource mobilization	
Number of movement activists	.34ˣ
Political opportunity	
Index of Committee Access	−.27*
Net party activist ideology	.21*
Index of Partisan Transition	.18*
R^2	.75

Source: See text and notes.
*p = .05 or better.

the number of Christian Right activists; instead, it is years of activity that link conservative religious affiliation to the size of the activist corps and hence to party influence. This finding points to a vital conclusion: movement resources, like popular grievances, may well originate in social conditions, but they must be activated to matter politically, and that often takes time.

Thus far we have explored the global differences between states where the Christian Right has great influence and where it is weak. But what about states with contested influence, located in the middle of our Index of Christian Right Influence? As we noted earlier, contested influence states are the most likely to experience intraparty conflict. Table 7.6 investigates the differences between these and other kinds of states by means of two discriminant analyses (using the same variables as in Table 7.5 plus the religion affiliation measure). The analysis in the first column differentiates the contested from the weak influence states, and that in the second, the contested from the great influence states.[14]

The results are quite revealing. Note first that the coefficients of three variables change signs between the two analyses: the number of movement activists, residual net GOP activist ideology, and conservative religion. Contested influence states have more activists than weak influence states do, but *fewer* than Christian Right strongholds. And contested influence states actually have a *more* liberal GOP activist corps and *fewer* conservative religious people than the weak influence states. A second set of variables does not change signs between analyses, but the coefficients change in size. On

Table 7.6
Discriminant Analysis of Contested Influence States

Variable	Weak vs.	Great Influence vs.
	Contested Influence States Structure Coefficients	
Number of movement activists	.81	−.12
Mean public conservatism	.17	.44
Index of Committee Access	−.38	−.20
Net party activist ideology	−.14	.33
Index of Partisan Transition	.14	.36
Religion Index	−.16	.50
Percentage cases correctly classified	96	94

Source: See text and notes.

the Index of Committee Access, contested states are more open than weak influence states but nearly match the great influence states. Public conservatism and partisan transition are more helpful in distinguishing the contested states from the Christian Right's bastions, as one might expect. Thus, the contested states have more Christian Right activists but also more liberal Republican activists and a smaller conservative religious public than one might expect on the basis of the regression analysis.

A clear interpretation is that in the contested states the strength of the Christian Right activist corps is disproportionate to the size of its mass base. Such "overmobilization" of activists is suggested by the 1993 Republican survey: GOP elites in these states saw the Christian Right to be far more "effective" than respondents in any other category of states. This insight also fits with the recent history of the Christian Right in Republican politics. Almost without exception, the initial appearance of the Christian Right produces intense conflict, and these early episodes represent at least a short-run over-mobilization of activists, sometimes followed by the activation of a large mass conservative constituency that solidifies the Right's position and reduces intraparty conflict.

Christian Right influence in the GOP stems in roughly equal measure from representation of conservative constituencies, based in conservative religious communities, and extensive mobilization of activists from the same communities, combined with easy access to potent and conservative party organizations enjoying the prospect of electoral gain. The movement has the greatest influence when the motivations, means, and opportunities for party politics converge.

Less than Conquerors

"The Religious Right," declared People for the American Way, "is committed to taking over the GOP. . . . It already controls many state parties and has plans to expand." Pat Robertson agreed, albeit with glee rather than alarm. Speaking at the 1995 national conference of the Christian Coalition, Robertson made reference to the same *C&E* assessments, remarking, "They say about 31 [states], but that leaves . . . a lot more. We've got more work to do. Because I like 100 percent, not 60 or 70" (Edsall 1995: A24).

Our evidence suggests that neither Robertson's hopes nor his enemies' fears will be realized. The Christian Right has indeed captured some state Republican parties, but this success arises from its mass constituency, aided and abetted by its own activities and favorable circumstances. But these same factors also limit the spread of its influence. In fact, the movement faces intense opposition and uncertain prospects among Republicans in as many states as it dominates and has only weak purchase in even more. Thus, the Right's influence is distributed about as one might expect if the collective grievance and resource mobilization perspectives are thought of as complementary hypotheses rather than contending theories. The collective grievance perspective is important because, contrary to much opposition hyperbole, the Christian Right actually has a mass following that can exploit opportunities presented by the GOP. But just as clearly, movement activists frequently operate beyond the "supply lines" from that mass constituency.

What do these data tell us about the Christian Right? First, this is a textbook example of a social movement: a set of activists dedicated to mobilizing an aggrieved but previously inactive group of citizens into mainstream politics by tapping slack resources and deploying them to best advantage. And like many other social movements, it has found one of the major political parties a valuable target, engaging in what Baer and Bositis (1988) have referred to as "partisan mobilization."[15] Second, the movement's success also reveals stern limitations to further growth. If the Christian Right's influence comes ultimately from Evangelical Protestantism, that large and geographically concentrated constituency falls far short of constituting a national majority. Gaining influence in additional states will require expanding its base beyond white Evangelicals to black Protestants, and especially to Catholics, something the movement has repeatedly attempted with little success. Likewise, the Christian Right has demonstrated an impressive capacity to arouse activists, but there are limits to their effectiveness, particularly in the absence of a mass base and in the presence of determined opponents. Finally, the movement can gain much from its influence in the state GOP: legitimacy, access to organizational resources, and a key role in nomination and platform politics. But none of this guarantees victory in primaries, general elections, or in policy making. Indeed, the Christian Right's more unpopular issue positions, if pressed, can be devastating to Republican campaigns; alternatively, winning as part of a broader coalition often carries its own disappointments (Wilcox 1994).

What do these data tell us about the Republican party? First, the Grand Old Party has made gains in the South and West in part because of its ability to absorb the Christian Right and related conservative movements. Part of this capacity is ideological, but there is an important organizational component as well. Republicans have built modern party organizations that can broker conservative interests and service the resulting candidacies effectively. The conventional model of parties that stresses control of candidates and constituencies may not adequately account for this situation. Ironically, Republicans may finally have become, in their own way, as representative of diverse social movements as the Democrats have been. Second, the GOP faces a major challenge in managing this emerging coalition, confronting problems not unlike those traditionally facing the Democrats. The Christian Right offers the GOP potent activist resources and access to a significant voting bloc, but it is a threat to many older Republican constituencies. Federalism allows the GOP to accommodate both the Christian Right and other interests in some places, but prolonged conflict is likely elsewhere. Party leadership is surely one key to managing these problems, but of equal importance is the Christian Right response to such leadership: will the movement follow a cooperative or confrontational strategy? Pragmatism may facilitate the institutionalization of the movement within the party, but purist demands from new activists and the mass constituency may have negative consequences for the party. Such possibilities reveal yet another example of the tension social movements have always generated in the American party system.

Notes

1. These data are from a survey of 1992 Republican national convention delegates conducted at the University of Akron in 1993, with a return rate of 52.6 percent for a total usable *N* of 998. The question read, "How would you evaluate the role of the Christian Right in 1992 . . . in your area?" with seven categories ranging from "very strong" to "very weak."

2. According to *C&E*, if the Mormon Church is considered part of the Christian Right, the movement dominates the Utah GOP as well.

3. This typology is often used as a nominal variable, but Elazar (1994) himself treats it as a scale. We assume an underlying dimension of cultural traditionalism, with individualistic

cultures being the least "traditional." Region is coded from northeast to south according to traditionalism.

4. All demographic variables come from the 1990 U.S. Census.

5. Mean self-identified conservatism is from Erikson et al. (1993). Social issue scores are aggregated state responses in 1992 (VRS) exit polls, the National Election Study, and the 1992 National Survey of Religion and Politics (Kellstedt et al. 1994).

6. Religious affiliation is derived from three sources: the 1980 and 1990 Glenmary Census of Churches (Quinn et al. 1982; Bradley et al. 1992) and national surveys by Kosmin and Lachman (1993) and Kellstedt et al. (1994). In each case, we picked the survey measure that performed best. The other religious measures were aggregated by state from the 1992 National Survey of Religion and Politics (Kellstedt et al. 1994).

7. The Index of Religious Affiliation is a factor score generated by principal components analysis using all the religious groups in Table 7.2. See Green and Guth (1991) for a justification for such a scale.

8. Activist estimates resulted from aggregating ZIP codes from mailing lists of movement activists and are calculated as the number of activists per thousand voters. The number of years the Right has been active in the state GOP was collected from news sources; electoral activism is the number of congressional races the movement was active in from 1978 to 1992, aggregated by state (Green, Guth, and Hill 1993). Elite assessments of the Christian Right came from the 1993 Akron survey. Popular support for the "religious right" is from 1994 VNS exit polls; proximity and religious relevance measures are from the 1992 National Survey of Religious and Politics (Kellstedt et al. 1994).

9. The authors calculated a Ranney index for the post-1988 era, following Bibby et al. (1990). An analogous federal elections index was generated using presidential and congressional votes, as well as the frequency of split-ticket outcomes.

10. The Index of Partisan Transition was calculated by dichotomizing state and federal Ranney indices and combining them into a four-point scale, with the states with Democratic state advantage and Republican federal advantage at one end, the reverse pattern at the other end, and consistent scores in the middle.

11. The Index of Committee Access results from cross-indexing three-point measures of regulation of membership in state and local party committees and then recoding the scale so that states with no regulations in either case were at one end, states with strong regulation of both at the other end, and various combinations in the middle. A few cases were reassigned based on the openness of state primaries. For example, Louisiana state law regulates membership in both state and local party committees, but its blanket primary renders these regulations moot.

12. As elite ideology, mass conservatism, and number of Christian Right activists in a state were highly intercorrelated, we regressed the elite ideology on the other two variables and used the residual in the regression analysis to avoid multicollearity problems.

13. As one can easily imagine, a path model using all the variables discussed earlier is quite complex and beyond the scope of this essay. However, there is a strong path between religious affiliation and mass conservatism, and a strong two-step path linking religion, the years of movement activity in state Republican politics, and the number of Christian Right activists in the state. Religion does not appear to operate through any of the other variables in the final regression.

14. A discriminant analysis of all five categories of the Christian Right Index generates four significant functions; the first essentially replicates the results of the regression analysis. The results presented here are consistent with the fourth function, which distinguishes contested influence states from others. We report these data as two analyses with dichotomous variables for ease of presentation.

15. Ironically, Baer and Bositis (1988: 75–81) dismiss the Christian Right as elitist, although it is an excellent example of their argument about mass-based social movements.

8

Citizen Groups, Political Parties, and Electoral Coalitions

Jeffrey M. Berry and Deborah Schildkraut

As inauguration day approached, President-elect Bill Clinton found himself under fire for his campaign promise to gay rights organizations to end the military's ban on homosexuals. Clinton searched for a way out of an issue that had become politically damaging. But a promise is a promise and a leader of the Lambda Legal Defense and Education Fund told the *New York Times*, "This issue must be dealt with swiftly, decisively and at the highest level" (Schmitt 1993: A1). As the issue exploded in Clinton's face, charges of pandering to interest groups began to surface. The idea that Clinton was some kind of "new Democrat," an image he actively tried to promote, became less credible. The only thing that seemed new was that gay and lesbian organizations had been added to a long list of liberal groups that could now make demands on Democratic presidents.

On one level, this is a story about an administration that was rather clumsy and naive as it began to take the reins of power. At another level, this story reflects the changing role of interest groups in presidential politics. Why was it that Clinton got in this position in the first place? Did he spontaneously announce early in the campaign that he was in favor of overturning the ban? Clearly not. Rather, Clinton was pushed by gay and lesbian groups to take a stand on an issue of central importance to these organizations, and he responded with an answer that pleased them.

The purpose of this essay is to explore the changing role of interest groups and social movements in party politics. Focusing primarily on presidential elections, we examine the relationship between candidates and interest groups as they pursue goals that only partially overlap. The argument here is that although there is some continuity in the way interest groups interact with the parties, citizen groups have fundamentally altered party politics. For both the Republicans and the Democrats, citizen groups have changed the way presidential candidates seek the nomination. Citizen groups have frustrated the eventual nominees by raising the price for party unity.

Finally, they have reconfigured the party coalitions in ways that pull both parties away from the ideological mainstream of American politics.

Parties, Groups, and Postmaterialism

Western democracies differ in the way interests are aggregated in the governmental process. The relative importance of political parties, interest groups, and social movements varies between countries and may vary over time within any single country. In the United States interest aggregation takes place largely within two dominant political parties and an extremely dense array of lobbying organizations.

Despite many practical and theoretical linkages between parties and interest groups, the study of these organizations in the United States has generally proceeded along two separate tracks. By and large separate communities of scholars study each, and research on the relationship between parties and interest groups is sparse. Most recent work on the connection between parties and groups has focused on political action committee (PAC) contributions, the mobilization of political activists, and platform writing.

The underlying reason for the continuing dichotomy between these two areas of research is the different theoretical concerns that guide each. A basic division in the scholarship is manifested in the way the goals of these two kinds of organizations are conceived. For party scholars, policy aggregation is instrumental to winning elections. Anthony Downs's (1957) conception of rational party behavior remains as the basis for contemporary theorizing about American political parties. Parties are *vote maximizers,* taking stands that have the broadest appeal to voters.

Interest group scholars generally view lobbying organizations as being relatively unconcerned about who wins elections. In our two-party system, having access to both parties is what is prized most. Interest groups are viewed as *policy maximizers,* concerned with furthering their policy goals regardless of who is in office (Berry 1997). Thus, it is common for an interest group to contribute money to candidates from both parties, hire some lobbyists with connections to Republicans and others with connections to Democrats, and easily adapt its lobbying strategies to whoever is in power at the time.

Some citizen groups and social movements diverge from this pattern, standing out because of their direct involvement in the electoral process. They are a source of ideological activists who work for candidates in the hopes of furthering their policy goals. Campaign contributions are guided by ideological preferences instead of pragmatism. What may be most important, however, is that these groups are the primary means of aggregating support within the parties for postmaterial issues. Unlike traditional lobbies, such as farm, labor, business, and professional associations, which try to improve the material well-being of their members, citizen groups focus more on quality of life issues, such as environmental protection, family values, women's rights, civil rights, good government, and education.

The material-postmaterial framework is a popular theoretical approach in the study of comparative politics. Most notably it has been used by Ronald Inglehart in *The Silent Revolution* (1977) to analyze the changing value structure of West European societies. Students of American politics have not made much use of this theory, which is unfortunate because it offers a useful perspective for analyzing interest groups. It is an especially promising tool to study citizen groups, organizations that fit poorly into the prevailing theoretical approaches used by interest group scholars.[1] The most influential contemporary theoretical approach in the interest group subfield emphasizes the collective action problem (Olson 1968). Despite its many virtues, public choice theory is of limited utility for understanding citizen groups because it suggests that most of these organizations now active in the United States should not exist.

The postmaterialist framework is useful not merely because of the vacuum of appropriate interest group theory but because it captures the central driving political force underlying most citizen movement politics. Most of these groups are actively pursuing policies designed to enhance rights, aesthetics, or morality. They endeavor to place quality-of-life concerns above those associated with expanding the material well-being of the nation. This theoretical approach is so appealing because it focuses on political change; traditional interest group scholarship emphasizes stability and even resistance to change (Lowi 1969; Lindblom 1977). A true theory of interest group politics, however, must incorporate a dynamic method of assessing political power rather than treating it as a static commodity. As interest groups' fortunes rise and fall, the collective power of political constituencies change. Finally, postmaterialism serves interest group scholarship well because it is a way of linking shifts in public opinion to interest group politics. Interest group scholarship generally ignores public opinion, concentrating instead on policymaking influenced by narrow constituencies rather than by the broader public. A core premise of postmaterialism is that broad shifts in values can empower new political movements, which in turn can influence a range of public policies.

Rising postmaterialism is common among Western democracies. As Seymour Martin Lipset (1981, 23) notes, "post-industrial politics is increasingly concerned with *noneconomic or social issues.*" Nevertheless, despite the relationship between the affluence of postindustrial societies and the rise of postmaterial goods, we ought not to assume that the prosperous Western democracies will all move to embrace such values. Inglehart (1977: 5–6) warns, "We cannot take it for granted that if increasing numbers of people hold given values, their political system will automatically adopt policies which reflect those values."

The reason that governments do not "automatically adopt" these policies is, of course, that there is typically strong opposition to them. For example, although everyone is in favor of protecting the environment in the abstract, the specifics usually generate considerable political conflict. Business interests are not demobilized by postindustrialism, and they will fight to protect themselves against the costs that would be imposed by consumer and environmental protection measures. The degree to which postmaterial values are embraced by a society will depend primarily on the effectiveness of the political organizations that advocate such policies and the effectiveness of those that oppose them.

There is reason to believe that postmaterialism is influencing American politics, though the degree of commonality with European politics is little understood. As citizen groups in this country have tried to influence the Democrats and Republicans, they have altered the identities of the parties. In a relatively short time, the Republican party has become strongly linked to the Christian Right. Church-based groups have given the party an avowedly pro-family values outlook; the party of business has become the party of church and business. For the Democrats, the changes have been more clearly linked to the broader patterns of postmaterialism in the other industrialized democracies. In Lipset's (1981: 24) words, "The reform elements concerned with postmaterialist or social issues largely derive their strength, not from the workers and the less privileged, the social base of the Left in industrial society, but from affluent segments of the well educated."

The analysis that follows examines the relationship among interest groups, movements, and political parties from 1948 to 1992. To provide some means of comparison for assessing the impact of citizen groups in influencing the parties, the data have been divided into three historical periods. The first, from Harry Truman's election to the end of the Kennedy years, is a time when only a modest amount of citizen group activity took place in the United States.[2] There was some lobbying by civil rights groups and a small amount of environmental activism. The second period, from Lyndon Johnson through Jimmy Carter, covers the time when the liberal citizen group movement was in full flower. The third, from the election of Ronald Reagan to the election of Bill Clinton, is a period when both liberal and conservative citizen groups were abundant and active in the political process.

Citizen groups are defined as organizations of like-minded individuals who pursue policies unconnected with their vocational concerns. They may pursue issues that involve the self-interest of their members—a women's group fighting for women's rights, for example—but any policies they pursue must benefit classes of people in ways unrelated to their vocations.[3] Many of these groups are part of larger social movements. For lack of a better term, we describe organizations that lobby for benefits for vocationally based members or constituents as "traditional" interest groups. This would include corporations, trade groups, professional associations, farm organizations, and labor unions. Schlozman and Tierney's (1986: 67) survey of Washington lobbies determined that roughly 14 percent of all interest groups with a Washington office are citizen groups. When all forms of representation are taken into account, citizen groups fall to just 7 percent of the interest group population.[4]

To conduct the research we report on here, we had to distinguish between material and postmaterial issues. Like Inglehart, we rely on Maslow's (1943) notion that needs and motivations can be hierarchically ordered. Concerns about quality-of-life issues reflect the desire for personal fulfillment rather than the motivation to satisfy basic human needs. Material concerns are those that focus on economic or physical security. Such issues are usually connected to the demands of organized labor, farmers, or business but relate to just about any constituency that wants some direct economic benefit. Material issues include such policies as pensions, Social Security, taxation, crime, agricultural subsidies, job training, trade restrictions and subsidies, economic regulation, and basic medical care. Postmaterial or quality of life concerns include such issues as the environment, equality and discrimination, abortion, various individual rights, consumer protection, education, and government reform. The postmaterial category also includes social service issues in which the advocates are not the ones who will receive the benefits.

The anlaysis that follows is organized around three phases of presidential campaigns. First, we offer a broad overview of the nomination process and examine the changing nature of candidate coalitions in the primaries. Second, drawing on data we have collected on elections from 1948 to 1992, we look at national party conventions, especially the platform writing process. Third, we consider the fall campaigns for the presidency, notably the content of the speeches that candidates make and the audiences they appear before. We also compare the presidential data to some data on Senate campaigns.

Assembling Primary Coalitions

The process of assembling a political coalition that will catapult one of the many who run for president into the White House begins long before the first votes are counted in Iowa and New Hampshire. Indeed, a politician's whole career can be viewed as an effort to build and maintain a viable political coalition. As prospective candidates begin the long drive toward the White House, they actively court groups and try to make them believe they will best represent their interests if elected.

Yet political scientists have generally ignored the mating game between presidential candidates and groups. There are a number of justifiable reasons for this. Most important, as organizations, interest groups are generally inactive during presidential primaries. Candidates may pursue people who have strong identities as environmentalists or businesspeople, but the political organizations that represent these interests are almost all idle in terms of the race for the nomination. As noted earlier, most interest groups want to appear to be nonpartisan, so activity on the presidential campaign level is counterproductive. Although they are more ideologically oriented than most interest groups, citizen lobbies will often find little unity within their organizations for any one candidate among the many competing for an open nomination. Even if there were strong consensus around a candidate, any individual group's scarce resources would still dictate a more prudent strategy than trying to predict which of six or seven candidates would win the nomination. For those interest groups who want to be involved in the electoral process, campaign activity is usually limited to PAC donations to congressional candidates.

Although there is little formal organizational involvement in primaries, interest group constituencies are passionately wooed by candidates. Moreover, group constituencies have become more important as parties have declined in American politics. The degree of party decline is often exaggerated by political scientists, who seemingly compare contemporary parties with a standard of unity, functionality, and rationality that American parties never had. Still, it is indisputable that in terms of presidential nominations, control has shifted decisively from party professionals to primary electorates.

Interest groups are also critical in the primary phase because they are a source of activists for campaign organizations. In 1994 Steve Largent, a Republican congressional candidate in Oklahoma, attracted somewhere between eight hundred and nine hundred volunteers, mostly Christian activists, and eventually sent some of them to work on another Republican campaign because he could not use them all (Bednar and Hertzke 1995). Citizen group activists are often very involved in political parties as well—they are not a distinct set of politicos who disdain party politics. Campaign organizations are full of citizen group activists, and party conventions at the state and local level are filled with delegates who are representatives of various interest groups (Baer and Dolan 1994; Pelletier 1995; Reiter 1993; Rochon 1990).

As candidates pursue campaign workers and primary voters, their goal is not to build a coalition to help them govern but to mobilize enough support to get at least a few more votes than their closest competitors (Polsby 1983). In the primary season it makes little difference to a candidate if the various interests he pursues—say, environmental groups and labor unions—have contradictory impulses, as long as he can make convincing pleas to both. Primaries are low turnout affairs, and mobilizing support among those constituencies that are sympathetic is critical. To gain those additional few thousand votes that are going to put them over the top, candidates try to distinguish themselves in ways that will give them an advantage with specific blocks of voters. At the broadest level, candidates will try to stake out an ideological position that will favor them. Following Downs (1957), political scientists conceive of the electorate as a bell curve or normal distribution. For primary electorates, we know that the distribution for each party is skewed away from the center of the entire electorate. The Democrats who vote in primaries are more liberal than the electorate as a whole, and Republican primary voters are more conservative than the general populace. Following Downs's logic, the primary candidate who can place himself at the center of his party's skewed electorate will have a distinct advantage in the primary process.

In a crowded primary field, a candidate's general ideological orientation may do little to distinguish him from many other candidates. Candidates can try to move to a less crowded part of the spectrum, but this strategy entails considerable risk. Because of ideological crowding, candidates are faced with the interest group imperative: win some interest group constituencies or increase the risks of being an also-ran. In short, it may do a candidate little good to be known as a dependable liberal if five other liberals are in the race, but being known as a longtime champion of environmental causes could give him an edge against the competition. All candidates turn to the constituencies they have worked hard for in their previous positions in government. When Senator Birch Bayh ran for the Democratic nomination in 1976, he could credibly claim to represent women because of his leadership role in the fight for the Equal Rights Amendment to the Constitution.

Mobilizing interest group constituencies presents its own set of problems. Some constituencies are so important to the party that everyone courts them. In 1988, for example, no one Democratic candidate emerged as the champion of feminists or environmentalists. All the candidates were in general sympathy with the views of these groups, and none was able to distinguish himself as substantially superior to the others as an advocate for feminist or environmental issues. Consequently, years of effort for a particular constituency may ultimately yield limited benefits when the moment of truth comes in Iowa or New Hampshire. Another problem is that members of an interest group constituency are pulled by other political forces. Even if a candidate has earned the gratitude of a constituency, those voters may not respond as anticipated. Despite Bayh's credentials with women, his campaign collapsed quickly with no evident support from any significant sector of the party.

Over time the interest group imperative has become an increasingly critical part of primary strategies. Compare the 1960 and 1976 Democratic nomination fights. In the 1960 campaign, three of the five Democratic candidates

(Lyndon Johnson, Stuart Symington, and Adlai Stevenson) did not even run in the primaries, and only one (Hubert Humphrey) counted heavily on appeals to interest groups. By 1976, however, the nomination process had clearly moved to "candidate centered politics" (Wattenberg 1991). All the eight major Democratic candidates ran in the primaries as party reforms and the increasing proportion of delegates selected through primaries made the Johnson-Symington strategy of relying on party leaders to deliver delegates a relic of the past. In the 1976 race, an avowed outsider, Jimmy Carter, had no visible party support but built a primary constituency by pursuing the support of blacks, Christians, farmers, and the United Auto Workers. In 1988 Michael Dukakis and his advisers decided early on in their planning to neutralize his weakness in the South by utilizing an interest group strategy. He knew that as a northern liberal he would do poorly with most white southerners, and that blacks who might otherwise consider him would most likely vote for Jesse Jackson. He targeted Hispanics in Texas and Jews in south Florida and devoted considerable resources to pursuing these two blocs of voters. Even though Dukakis lost badly everywhere else in the South, he was able to retain his credibility as a national candidate with victories in Texas and Florida on Super Tuesday.

The broad, diverse Democratic party provides candidates a range of constituencies to pursue. Traditionally, the more homogeneous Republican party has not offered the same opportunities for building interest group coalitions. Business, the Republicans' most important interest group constituency, is not effectively mobilized in any unified way during the primaries and almost all Republican aspirants are acceptable to this sector of the party. The Christian Right, however, is changing this process. Virtually all the conservative Republican candidates for the nomination in 1996 made a very public effort to associate themselves with the concerns of the Christian Coalition.

Since ideologues have always participated in disproportionate numbers in the primaries, the nomination process usually pulls the Democrats to the left and the Republicans to the right. Thus it may seem that there is nothing new or different in interest group constituencies pulling the parties away from the ideological center. As we shall see, however, the policies that many citizen groups draw attention to in the nomination fights are particularly salient and emotional issues. Some critics charge that the pursuit of interest group support during the primaries leads to serious problems of governance. Both Carter's and Clinton's travails as president have been blamed in part on their need to satisfy various liberal factions that supported their candidacies but whose policy preferences worked against these presidential leaders once they took office.

Yet even if this is true, there is no reason to assume that it is inevitable that the nature of a candidate's support in the primaries will dictate the course of his presidency. Newly elected presidents may finesse the divisions between the various groups they mobilized behind their candidacies in the primaries. Nor should we assume that presidential candidates prior to this postreform era led unified parties whose constituent parts were always willing to forgo their special interest demands for the good of the ticket or the administration in power. We need to look further to examine how parties try to come together after the primaries.

From Pluralism to Majoritarianism

The party conventions represent a transition between the race for the nomination and the general election campaign. Interest group leaders and party leaders enter the conventions with different goals in mind. For interest groups, the conventions are an opportunity to gain a commitment or a reaffirmation from the winning candidate to support their lobbying goals. To a certain extent, the winning candidate and the party hierarchy want to accommodate the groups they value with some reassurance about policy stands and priorities. The party may need to solidify the support of such groups so it can mobilize them for the upcoming campaign. A more important goal, however, is for the party to use the convention to project an image of unity around its most broadly appealing themes. The convention offers a chance for the party to communicate its majoritarian side and to argue that it is the party of the people and not the party of special interests. To effectively pursue these goals, the parties need organized groups to fade into the convention woodwork, demonstrating nothing but unbridled enthusiasm for the ticket and the platform.

In this section, we ask two questions about interest groups and the nominating conventions. First, how has interest group politics at nominating conventions changed since 1948? Second, after the primaries are over and the party tries to position itself firmly in the ideological center of the electorate, how do citizen groups react? Are they cooperative coalition partners, or are they ideologues who place policy above party?

The beginning point in the research was to document how the party nominees articulate a vision of their electoral coalition. Over time, have interest groups changed the way that the winning candidate projects a majoritarian or pluralistic image of the party? In this regard, the most significant part of the convention is the candidate's acceptance speech. Next to debates it is the most widely followed campaign appearance. In the acceptance speeches of all the nominees from 1948 to 1992, an unmistakable pattern emerges: candidate visions of the electoral coalition that will bring them victory in November are increasingly built around interest group constituencies. In each of these speeches, every reference to an organized constituency was recorded and then coded according to the type of lobbying organizations that represent the constituency.[5] For each of the three historical periods, the numbers in Table 8.1 are the averages for all of a party's acceptance speeches during that time. For example, in the 1948–1960 period the Democratic nominees appealed on average to four separate interest group constituencies. By 1980–1992, they appealed on average for the votes of 8.3 groups.

These figures must be viewed with some caution as they tell us little about the candidate's *commitment* to the causes of those groups. Some of these appeals surely fall into the category of symbolic politics—making a simple gesture toward a constituency that a candidate feels obligated to stroke. Still, as one reads these speeches, the changing nature of American politics is readily apparent. When Dwight Eisenhower accepted the Republican nomination in 1952, he made not a single reference to an interest group constituency. When George Bush made his acceptance speech at the 1992 GOP convention, he appealed to groups a total of fifteen times, including four separate references affirming his support for the Christian Right.

In sum, it is clear that appeals to both traditional groups and citizen groups have increased significantly. Traditional, vocationally related groups still receive more appeals than citizen groups, though the ratio has narrowed considerably. Both parties have shown similar trends. More broadly, as candidates step to the podium to give their most widely watched campaign speech, and they outline a vision of what their administration might look

---

Table 8.1
Interest Group Appeals: Averages, Candidate Acceptance Speeches, 1948–1992

	1948–60	1964–76	1980–92
Democrats/no. groups appealed to	4.0	5.0	8.3
GOP/no. groups appealed to	2.3	4.0	8.5
Democrats/no. appeals to all groups	6.8	7.3	14.5
GOP/no. appeals to all groups	2.5	4.3	11.8
Democrats/no. traditional groups appealed to	3.3	2.5	4.8
GOP/no. traditional groups appealed to	1.8	3.5	5.0
Democrats/no. citizen groups appealed to	0.8	2.5	3.5
GOP/no. citizen groups appealed to	0.5	0.5	3.5

Note: The number of groups appealed to represents the total number of separate interest group constituencies that a candidate appealed to during his acceptance speech. The number of appeals to all groups counts each appeal as one, regardless of whether that constituency had already been courted in the speech. The numbers are averages of all four acceptance speeches for each party during each period.

like, the nominees demonstrate an increasing tendency to define their goals in terms of what they can do for various interest groups.

The role of interest groups at the conventions can also be examined by looking at their participation in the platform writing process. For all its shortcomings as a guide to what an administration might actually look like, a platform is still a formal statement of what that party stands for. Interest groups actively try to influence the content of party platforms; indeed, a majority of those testifying before platform-writing committees are representatives from trade associations, citizen groups, corporations, unions, and other lobbies. At recent conventions a disproportionate number of these representatives were lobbyists from citizen groups (Fine 1994).

From election to election, platforms can tell us a great deal about the changing direction of a party (Janda, Edens, and Goff 1994). It is difficult, however, to attribute changes in the content of party platforms over time to interest group advocacy. The primary reason is that we lack the tools to distinguish interest group influence from the impact of public opinion. If a party alters its position on abortion from one campaign to the next, both interest group advocacy and the evolution of public opinion are likely causes. One strategy for trying to understand interest group influence on the platform is to closely examine the active lobbying of the platform committee. This approach was taken by Sandy Maisel (1993) in his study of the 1992 party conventions. Maisel's fieldwork was carefully done and he completed a painstaking paragraph-by-paragraph analysis of the platform drafts before and after the formal lobbying began. He found that little of substance in the platforms was changed by the advocacy of lobbies, intraparty factions, or any other groups that approached the committees.

Maisel's conclusion is that platform writing was controlled by the winning candidates; this was not only true in 1992 but at most other conventions as well. The reason is simple "[Platforms] are the ultimate indication that the parties exist to win the presidential election, not to push policy agendas" (Maisel 1993–1994, 697).

To better understand the conflict between the goals of groups and the goals of parties, we analyzed all significant platform fights for both parties for the period 1948–1992. These conflicts do not tell us all we need to know about the impact of interest groups on parties, but they do have the virtue of allowing us to focus on the efforts of interest groups to influence the parties' ideological orientation. All Democratic and Republican conventions had at least two platform fights, and most had three to five. Platform fights can be defined simply as the efforts of one or more groups to take the decision of the platform committee to the floor of the convention. The threat, which must be taken seriously, is that the challenging group will force a floor vote on a substitute plank, thereby exposing a rift in the party and producing a negative story line at a time the party is most conscious of projecting a unified image. One of the best-known examples of an interest group-based attack on the platform is the civil rights floor fight at the 1948 Democratic convention, led by the Americans for Democratic Action.

Table 8.2 documents the proportion of platform fights initiated by interest groups, first by traditional groups and then by citizen lobbies. The figures are averages for the Democratic and Republican conventions combined for each period. (When the figures are disaggregated, the patterns for the Democrats and Republicans look similar.) The data show a striking increase in the proportion of all platform fights generated by citizen groups. There has been a doubling of the percentage of platform fights with one or more citizen groups at the center. In the earliest period, the 29 percent figure for citizen groups reflects the perennial—quadrennial—fights over civil rights at both parties' conventions. In later years, fights over civil rights are joined by fights over the ERA, abortion, family values, and other staples of liberal and conservative citizen advocacy.

Over the same period, platform fights generated by traditional groups have dropped from a third of all such conflicts to virtually nothing in the last two periods. Although business interests have studiously avoided public fights over the platform (they surely do not have the same need to do this as other groups), farm and labor organizations did initiate fights in previous years. Today farm and labor lobbies may find such tactics counterproductive

Table 8.2
Platform Fights, Both Parties Combined

	1948–60	1964–76	1980–92
% platform fights, traditional group driven	36	0	3
% platform fights citizen group driven	29	62	59
% platform fights on postmaterial issues	29	45	53
% platform fights on postmaterial issues, citizen group driven	100	85	88
% of all platform fights with protests or floor battle	14	31	28
% of all platform fights with protests or floor battles that were citizen group driven	100	100	100

Note: The data were gathered from press coverage in the *New York Times*. Up to five platform fights meeting a minimal threshold of press coverage were included for each party. There were only a few conventions where there was sufficient coverage of more than five issues. In such cases the five receiving the most coverage were used.

or feel that they risk humiliating defeats if they force a public confrontation. It also seems likely that the protest-oriented style of citizen groups makes platform fights less appealing to traditional groups.

The citizen groups have focused primarily on postmaterial or quality of life concerns, though some have pushed national security issues. The data on line 3 in Table 8.2 indicate that the proportion of postmaterial issues has risen over the years to more than half of all platform conflicts. Although there is an occasional procedural issue that generates a platform fight, virtually all the remaining platform fights center around material issues, most commonly security matters. Clearly, citizen groups have been highly effective in gaining attention from the parties and from the media for their issues. Over time, their success at framing issues and gaining a disproportionate amount of media coverage devoted to the party platforms has reduced the attention paid to pocketbook issues.

Most platform fights end before they get to the floor, for two reasons. First, some fights are generated by small minorities within a party—for example, African Americans and feminists at recent GOP conventions. These efforts are easily quashed, as the groups knew they would be. The goal, of course, is to get some publicity for their issue and hope they will have some moderating influence on the party as the fall campaign begins. Second, when a conflict is generated by a group with more substantial representation in the party, both sides have strong incentives to settle. The nominee should have enough delegates to defeat alternative platform planks but wants to avoid press coverage of a debate on the issue. For their part, the interest groups want to go as far as they can in their threats of a floor vote to maximize their leverage, but they do not want their bluff called either.

One of the most interesting aspects of citizen group lobbying on the platforms is that this effort is almost always aimed at issues on which the two parties are already very far apart. Regardless of motive, citizen groups work to accentuate the differences between the parties, to drive the wedge in further so that the parties do not gravitate toward a more moderate position. Table 8.3 lists all the platform fights initiated by citizen groups for the most recent period studied, 1980–1992. The actions of these groups forced the parties to affirm their stance on the most emotional, hot-button issues of the day.

Twenty-four important platform fights were initiated by citizen groups in the eight conventions during this time. In the two columns on the right, a negative sign means that the party stood firmly against the initiating citizen group's position; a plus sign means they sided with the group. On twenty-three of the twenty-four issues, the two parties took opposite positions. These groups see platform writing as a chance to draw a line in the sand. Possibly the most extreme example of this took place at the 1996 Republican National Convention. Recognizing that he needed to move back toward the

Table 8.3
Outcomes of Platform Lobbying: Issues Where Citizen Groups
Initiated a Platform Fight

	Target Party	*Other Party*
1980:		
GOP:		
ERA	−	+
Abortion rights	−	+
Affirmative action	−	+
Democrats:		
Affirmative action	+	−
ERA	+	−
Abortion rights	+	−
1984:		
GOP:		
ERA	−	+
Nuclear freeze	−	+
Abortion rights	−	+
Affirmative action	−	+
Democrats:		
Affirmative action	+	−
Nuclear freeze/no first use	+	−
Simpson-Mazzoli immigration bill	+	−
Nonintervention in Central America	−	−
1988:		
GOP:		
Affirmative action	−	+
Abortion rights	−	+
ERA	−	+
Expanding child care	−	+
Democrats:		
Affirmative action	+	−
1992:		
GOP:		
Abortion ban	+	−
Family values	+	−
AIDS (Liberal approach)	−	+
Democrats:		
Abortion rights	+	−
Race relations	+	−

Note: With the exception of two issues before the 1992 GOP convention (a ban on abortions and a commitment to "family values"), all these conflicts were generated by liberal citizen groups. Conservative citizen groups generated the other two. For each convention, the issues are listed in order of their salience at the time, based on press coverage of the preconvention period and the week of the convention itself.

middle after showing his fealty to the Christian Right's concerns during the nomination fight, Bob Dole proposed a slight moderation of the previous platform's staunch antiabortion plank. The Christian Coalition and its sympathizers had firm control of the platform committee and publicly embarrassed Dole by rejecting his alternative wording.

A central, guiding belief of citizen groups seems to be that if the majority of the public does not support their position, so be it. Winning isn't everything; principle cannot be abandoned. In the last analysis, citizen groups see conventions not as a time of coalition building but as an opportunity to enhance their own influence within the party.

General Election Coalitions

As they face the fall campaign, the successful nominees must devise a strategy different from the one used to win in the primaries. As Aldrich (1992: 75) notes, "The trick in moving from nomination to general election is how to transform a successful campaign for building support within the party . . . into a campaign that faces a different opponent and must appeal to a larger part of the public, who previously could be ignored." As we have just demonstrated, however, citizen groups make life difficult for nominees as they move from their primary coalition to their general election coalition.

For the two major parties, the problem of broadening their appeal once the convention ends has emerged in different ways. For the Democrats the challenge has been the breadth of a coalition that now includes environmentalists, blacks, Hispanics, gays, Jews, feminists, organized labor, and senior citizens. As the coalition has expanded over the years, the difficulties of meeting the competing and sometimes conflicting demands of these groups has mounted. Holding together its less diverse coalition has not been much of a problem for the Republicans until fairly recently. For the contemporary GOP, the threat to party unity comes from the depth of feeling on abortion and other social issues held by the Christian Right.

To systematically assess how candidates balance the pressure from citizen groups with broader, majoritarian appeals, we looked at the campaigns that each major party candidate conducted during the period under study. From press coverage of the last two weeks in September and the last two weeks in October, we recorded what the candidates talked about and who they talked to. Table 8.4 divides what the candidate said on the campaign trail—essentially the story line of the day—into material and postmaterial issues. The analysis reveals that through 1992, Republican presidential candidates did not become appreciably more focused on postmaterial issues. The slight increase may be due to pressure for GOP candidates to say something about postmaterial issues such as civil rights and the environment,

Table 8.4
Presidential Candidate Speeches: Postmaterial versus Material Issues

	1948–60	*1964–76*	*1980–92*
Democrat/postmaterial (%)	12.5	23.6	21.0
Democrat/material (%)	87.5	76.4	79.0
(*n* = 213, n.s.)			
GOP/postmaterial (%)	7.8	13.3	12.5
GOP/material (%)	92.2	86.6	87.5
(*n* = 185, n.s.)			

Note: In calculating these figures the speeches for each party for each period were combined. If the candidate discussed more than one issue in an appearance, the issue coded was the one receiving the most coverage in the *New York Times.* Issues that fell into neither category (such as charging one's opponent with running a smear campaign or making a speech asking for party unity) were excluded. Such issues were emphasized in about 15 percent of all campaign appearances.

even if they were generally unsympathetic to those constituencies, and, in the past few elections, the need to make a gesture to the Christian Right. The tendency is stronger for the Democrats as their broader coalition leads their nominees to speak on a more diverse set of concerns. In the middle period between the 1964 and 1976 elections, Democratic candidates were devoting close to one out of four speeches to postmaterial issues. The trend is not strong enough, however, to achieve statistical significance.

We did two further tests to try to assess the balance between material and postmaterial concerns in political campaigns. First, using the same database, we determined what kind of audience the presidential candidates spoke before. It may be that one way presidential candidates finesse their pluralist and majoritarian imperatives is to appear before interest group audiences but to push their standard campaign themes. Alternatively, some interest group audiences have both material and postmaterial concerns. Democratic candidates, for example, could appear before an American organization and discuss jobs programs, a material issue.

The coding scheme used in Table 8.4 had to be altered because audiences do not come neatly labeled as material or postmaterial. Most campaign audiences are general audiences, composed of anyone who ventures to the city square, auditorium, or train station where the candidate is going to speak. In Table 8.5 such general audiences are combined with interest group audiences that are exclusively material in orientation, such as farm, labor, and business

Table 8.5
Presidential Candidate Campaign Audiences: Ethnic, Religious, and
Postmaterial Audiences

	1948–60	1964–76	1980–92
Democrat/ethnic, religious, postmaterial (%)	7.9	22.8	16.9
Democrat/general or material (%)	92.1	77.2	83.1
(n = 205, sig. .05)			
GOP/ethnic, religious, postmaterial (%)	2.5	4.5	6.0
GOP/general or material (%)	97.5	95.5	94.0
(n = 196, n.s.)			

Note: In calculating these figures, the appearances for each party for each period were combined.

organizations. (Material audiences are not disaggregated because relatively few appearances are made before such groups.) The second category includes religious audiences and ethnic groups along with organizations that are exclusively postmaterial in orientation, such as environmental groups. This coding scheme, while not as precise as we might like, has the virtue of separating out those groups that have been trying to expand the parties' traditional electoral bases.

The results show that over time Democrats have increased their appearances before religious, ethnic, and postmaterial groups. For the Republicans there is no significant increase. From 1964 to 1976, 22.8 percent of appearances by Democratic candidates were in front of such audiences. It dropped to 16.9 percent in the most recent period. It should also be noted that one or two appearances is all that it may take to reassure an interest group constituency of a candidate's fidelity to the cause. To go back to the example at the outset, although Clinton made his pledge to end the ban on homosexuals in the military many times, it was a single appearance before a gay group at the end of the campaign that was considered of symbolic importance in affirming that commitment.

The final test was to place the presidential campaigns into the broader sweep of party politics during this era. Presidential campaigns surely influence public perceptions of the parties in a disproportionate manner, but they are far from the whole story. To see whether congressional candidates mirrored the trends we have observed, data were collected on the Senate races in three states over the same time span. (Unfortunately, the press coverage of House races is too sparse to analyze in any meaningful way.) The three states could not be drawn at random because of the difficulty of finding newspaper collections that go back to the Truman years. In the end we were able to use the *Denver Post*, the *Chicago Tribune*, and the *New York Times*.[6] To better isolate the agenda of Senate campaigns independent of presidential politics, only off-year elections in those states were analyzed.

The results in Table 8.6 are quite revealing. There is a very sizable increase in the proportion of postmaterial issues emphasized by Democratic Senate candidates. In Colorado, where environmental issues became very important, postmaterial concerns rose from being invisible in the earliest period to being the focus of 46.4 percent of all Democratic campaign speeches. The figure for Colorado Republicans rose to 43.5 percent. Overall, however, the findings for the two parties are quite divergent. The Democrats show a sharp increase from the earliest period to the two later periods. There is no clear pattern for the Republicans.

In comparing the presidential campaigns to the Senate campaigns, it is clear that at least for the Democrats there is significantly more discussion of postmaterial issues by Senate candidates. What explains this? It is likely that the national focus of a presidential campaign pushes nominees toward the broadest, most all-encompassing issues. A related reason may be that the presidential candidates must try to appeal to the South, the most politically conservative section of the country. Since no southern newspaper was available far enough back, the three states included here are all from the north. For the Republicans it is important to note that the last data point for the Senate races is the 1990 off-year elections, which misses the Christian

---

Table 8.6

Proportion of Senate Campaign Appearances Emphasizing Postmaterial Issues

	1950–62	*1966–78*	*1982–90*	
Democrats:				
Colorado (%)	3.7	46.4	33.3	(n = 76, sig. .001)
Illinois (%)	12.5	33.3	*	(n = 105, sig. .01)
New York (%)	17.5	38.5	33.3	(n = 105, sig. .01)
Republicans:				
Colorado (%)	10.6	43.5	17.6	(n = 87, sig. .01)
Illinois (%)	0	14.6	*	(n = 76, sig. .05)
New York (%)	23.1	17.1	*	(n = 93, n.s.)

Sources: The *Denver Post*, the *Chicago Tribune*, and the *New York Times*.
* Insufficient press coverage.

Right's recent strength. In the 1994 off-year elections a number of hard-right Republicans won their Senate primaries with strong support from the Christian Right and emphasized family values during the fall campaign.

On the presidential campaign level, the differences between the two parties, while modest in size, are telling nevertheless. Since the Democrats have a much broader array of citizen group constituencies to contend with, it comes as no surprise that the party's presidential candidates speak more often on postmaterialist issues and appear more often before audiences concerned about such issues. Even if they want to downplay some of these issues, their effort to offer some symbolic reassurance to a number of different constituencies will add up over the course of the campaign. Beyond this, however, is at least one broadly appealing postmaterial issue, environmental protection, which Democrats like to trumpet. For the Republicans, beyond a few obligatory stops before African-American audiences and other ethnic groups, they have had every incentive to focus on traditional GOP issues such as taxes and the business climate. In the past two elections, after the Christian Right pulled the party away from the center on abortion, George Bush and Bob Dole struggled to distance themselves from their own party platform without actually repudiating their party's large contingent of postmaterialists. In the fall 1996 campaign, Dole first told the Christian Coalition that a scheduling conflict would prevent him from appearing at their well-publicized September convention. After Dole's refusal became public and after implicit threats by the Coalition, Dole made an unannounced visit to introduce a speech by his running mate, Jack Kemp (Gray 1996; Niebuhr 1996; Scales 1996). Dole understood only too well what the polls were showing: the Christian Coalition was an albatross around his neck.

Conclusion

In different ways, interest groups have always been involved in party politics. In recent years, however, citizen groups have become increasingly significant actors in primary and general election campaigns. For the two major parties, the same dynamic during the nominating process has enhanced the power of citizen groups. The decline of party organizations, the expanded number of primaries that came in the wake of the 1968 Democratic convention, and the rise of candidate-centered politics have all worked to make interest group support more crucial as aspirants try to forge a winning coalition.

The aggressive advocacy by citizen groups and the need of presidential primary candidates to seek their support have had profound consequences for the parties. Most importantly, these groups have the capacity to pull the parties away from the ideological center of the electorate. The rationality of positioning the party where the most votes are is confounded by the logic of citizen groups, who are not always ready to abandon principle in the hope of gaining victory in November. To citizen groups, conventions are opportunities to demand fidelity from the nominee and to ensure that the party takes positions that are distinctive and firm, even if such actions make the party more vulnerable in November.

The policy concerns these groups try to push to the top of the agenda in campaigns tend to be "wedge" issues—issues that are emotional and divisive. They promote issues that are about rights and morality, and citizen group constituencies tend to view compromise as a reflection of lack of principle rather than as a realistic necessity. Conflict is inherent in politics, and citizen groups should not be criticized for aggressively pursuing their interests the same way other lobbies or party factions pursue theirs. What is of concern, though, is that these groups make coalition formation within the parties more difficult—parties can become more collections of interests than partnerships with mutual goals. This amalgamation of differing interests may seem to broaden a party but can actually undermine it. Writing about the Carter agenda, for example, Walter Dean Burnham (1981, 383) condemns his presidency for policies that were "conflicting, crosspressured, incoherent even below any ideological horizon, and ultimately offering little or nothing positive to the lower half of the American population."

Citizen groups have altered what the parties stand for. Voters clearly perceive that the Democrats are the party of diversity and inclusiveness (Baumer and Gold 1995). This is, of course, a dilemma for the Democrats. On the one hand, many people are attracted to the party because it has been the party of civil rights, the environment, and women's issues. On the other hand, over the years liberal citizen groups advocating postmaterial issues have led many voters to believe that the Democrats have drifted away from the concerns of ordinary Americans. During a time when the American economy changed and made life more insecure for many, and at a time when people became increasingly antitax and increasingly antagonistic toward big government, the Democratic party became increasingly linked to groups advocating more governmental services and activism. Many of the postmaterial issues advocated by liberal citizen groups and Democratic candidates are peripheral to the lives of middle-class Americans struggling to make ends meet. The Democrats' preoccupation with civil rights, women's rights, environmentalism, and other causes has surely contributed to the Democrats' gender gap with white males. In the 1994 elections, fully 63 percent of white males voted Republican, and Southern whites continue to leave the party of the civil rights movement (Ladd 1995, 57).

Up until the 1992 election, the rest of the Republican party easily coexisted with its postmaterialists. The emergence of the Christian Coalition, however, has changed this. Unlike its predecessor, the Moral Majority, the

Christian Coalition has a strong grassroots base and has skillfully organized supporters to take over many statewide Republican party organizations. The Christian Right's social agenda, with its emphasis on abortion and its hostility to public education, has damaged the party's standing among women. Survey research shows that in 1992 the GOP's unflinching stand against abortion, which it was unable to move away from at the convention, hurt Bush in the general election (Abramowitz 1995). In 1996, women strongly favored Clinton while men were more evenly divided (Pomper 1997, 179).

Why has this happened? Why have the parties been so strongly influenced by advocacy organizations that do not always have the parties' best interests at heart? Parties are not rational bodies with one wise decision maker who accurately weighs costs and benefits. American political parties are disjointed, loosely organized, internally competitive bodies. No one decided that the Democratic party would be the party of postmaterial causes at the expense of working-class voters. Nor was there a referendum within the Republican party as to whether the Christian Coalition should control the most recent platform. The Democrats and Republicans became the party of these causes because they were effectively lobbied by groups engaged in old-fashioned political organizing.

Notes

1. Classic pluralist thought would certainly account for an active and vigorous citizen group sector in the lobbying universe. In its most idealistic form, commonly associated with Robert Dahl's *Who Governs?* (1961), all important interests are vigorously represented in the interest group system. However, since no interest group scholars today argue that we live in a pluralist democracy where all interests are adequately represented in public policy making, it is difficult to offer pluralism as a contemporary theory explaining citizen group politics.

2. In the two great works on interest groups during this time, citizen groups are barely acknowledged. See Truman (1951) and Key (1964).

3. "Citizen groups" is thus a broader category than "public interest groups," which are philanthropic in nature. See Berry (1977).

4. This figure combines Schlozman and Tierney's (1986) categories for citizen groups, civil rights/minority organizations, social welfare and the poor, and new entrants.

5. Nominees rarely mention a specific interest group organization. They appeal to blacks and not the NAACP or the Urban League; senior citizens and not the AARP. For that reason, it is an explicit appeal to an interest group *constituency* that is the unit of analysis.

6. The best collection in the Boston area is at Harvard University, which has a limited number of newspapers going all the way back to 1948. Some of these papers, however, had such limited coverage of Senate races that we could not use them. The only papers with sufficient coverage were the three we use here.

Part 4

The Presidency and Congress

9

American Social Movements and Presidential Administrations

Douglas R. Imig

In 1982, John Gardner, then director of the Sierra Club, credited President Ronald Reagan, Secretary of the Interior James Watt, and Assistant Secretary Anne Gorsuch for being the best fundraisers the Sierra Club could ask for: their pro-development rhetoric provided a visible and outspoken target for the Club. Today, Gardner is an undersecretary within the Interior Department, having successfully moved from vocal opponent of government inaction to an insider, with hands-on responsibility for the direction of government policy. This transition would seem to represent a major success in the environmental movement's efforts to shape federal environmental policy.

Championing a very different set of concerns, the Reverend Jerry Falwell led the Moral Majority to national prominence during the 1980 elections by helping fashion the Reagan landslide. At that time, Falwell and his seven million television viewers were seen as an emerging political force in American politics (Holsworth 1989: 3). Yet, not long after President Reagan coasted to reelection in 1984, the Moral Majority disbanded and Falwell turned his attention to running Liberty University. With the transition to the Clinton presidency, Falwell was once again featured in the national news, noting the "deep concern" the nation's pastors felt about a Clinton presidency and predicting a resurgence of profamily and Religious Right forces such as the Christian Coalition (Niebuhr 1992: 14).

These examples of the dynamic between the White House and American social and political movements present a puzzle. Social movements form and take action in response to a range of contextual factors, including the support or antagonism directed toward their cause by presidential administrations and through electoral campaigns. Often it appears that a political challenger's existence and support is predicated on being an outsider—fighting to defend a threatened cause or constituency. At the same time, the galvanizing capacity of oppositional politics can be tenuous, and weak challengers easily can be overpowered by intense institutional antagonism. Where they successfully fend off this challenge, they are aided by other sources of elite support, as well as by political acumen and strategic skill. Oppositional groups may also find that as the political pendulum swings, they gain the opportunity to contribute to policy deliberations and to earn long-sought concessions. Many groups have a difficult time making this transition. Social movements may dissipate in the absense of their principal antagonist, their opposition having become the cornerstone of their organizational identity and their most important recruiter. In these respects, presidential administrations—and the transitions between administrations—shape and reshape the context in which social movements operate and to which they respond.

Structures of Political Opportunity:
Understanding the Context of Mobilization

Social movements are becoming increasingly active in interest representation in the United States and globally (Imig and Tarrow 1996). Yet, the emergence of movements is by no means guaranteed and may have little to do with enduring social and political inequities (Gaventa 1981; Schattsneider 1960). Instead, the emergence of social movements—including both the shape of movement organizations and the venues for action available to activists—may follow more directly from contextual factors than from the causes and constituencies that political activists represent (Costain 1992; Jenkins and Perrow 1977; Walker 1983).

We can identify a range of influences that affect patterns of interest representation. Some of these factors are internal and others are external to political organizations. Influences internal to groups include the strategic actions and political acumen of their leaders. Charismatic leadership and managerial skill influence both the policy access and organizational longevity of individual social movement organizations (SMOs). However, more influences patterns of mobilization than simply political entrepreneurship. In fact, historically, social movement mobilization in this country has varied systematically both across time and across policy areas, with a range of SMOs concerned with an issue emerging and receding "in harness" (Meyer and Imig 1993: 262–4; Rosenstone and Hansen 1993).

The pattern of social movement mobilization has been described as a wave or cycle (Koopmans 1993; McAdam 1995; McFarland 1991; Tarrow 1994; Truman 1951: 59). As Salisbury (1989: 28) has noted, despite the enduring nature of many social concerns, "specific political movements tend to rise and fall within relatively brief spans of time." The episodic emergence, development, and decline of social movement sectors can be described in terms of a set of *political opportunity structures* that establish an operating context for group action. Political opportunity structures are systematic, though inherently unstable, facets of the social and political context that affect possibilities both of challengers taking action and of their achieving policy concessions. In Tarrow's words (1994: 85), political opportunity structures are:

> consistent—but not necessarily formal or permanent—dimensions of the political environment that provide incentives for people to undertake collective action by affecting their expectations for success or failure. Theorists of political opportunity structure emphasize the mobilization of resources *external* to the group. Although political opportunities are unequally distributed, unlike internal resources such as money, power or organization, even weak and disorganized challengers can sometimes take advantage of them.

From its inception, the political opportunity approach has linked mobilization of movements to relatively stable facets of institutional structure, such as governing coalitions. In attempting to explain patterns of urban protest in the late 1960s, Eisinger (1973) identified a set of structures of political opportunity that appeared to explain which city governments were most likely to encounter protest. He found a curvilinear relationship between levels of governmental accessibility and levels of protest, with protest most likely to occur where municipal governments were moderately accessible to citizen claims and participation. Intolerant city governments deterred protest, while accessible governments preempted it.

Tilly (1978) discovered a similar phenomenon at the national level, where governments have the capacity to repress protest or else to channel it into less volatile or disruptive venues. Through their reception of challengers, states can postpone or prevent the emergence of social protest. Tilly also found that national governments may preempt protest by assimilating challengers into the political process.

From the perspective of challenging groups, differences in structures of opportunity mean that seemingly similar movements are likely to meet different fates as a function of the responsiveness of the political institutions they challenge. Governments control not only the access groups seek but also the range of policy responses that will be offered to challengers. One consequence of this relationship is that, at the societal level, fewer social movements are likely to emerge under rigidly closed states. Those that do emerge under these conditions are likely to choose more confrontational strategies. By contrast, social movements in more receptive states are much more likely to choose assimilative strategies. In comparing Western European antinuclear movements Kitschelt (1986) found evidence of this pattern of differential responses.

Looking across shifting political landscapes, we can also identify more dynamic facets of political opportunity structure, which include the influence of emerging directions in public policy, political rhetoric, and waves of public, media, and foundation issue attention (see Jenkins and Perrow 1977; McAdam 1982; Gamson and Meyer 1996).

Presidential administrations and politics influence both relatively fixed and more dynamic facets of the opportunity structures confronting American social movements. White House support or antagonism can be particularly important for weak and marginalized movements.

In the United States, efforts to mobilize on behalf of the poor and homeless have historically been weak, short-lived, and of limited political efficacy (see Jennings 1994; Piven and Cloward 1979). The poor lack critical resources that would advance their tendency to act collectively, participate in electoral campaigns, or contribute to political organizations. With a few notable exceptions, few social movements have been directly concerned with social justice in this country, largely relegating these concerns to mobilizations "by proxy" (Jennings 1994; Piven and Cloward 1979; Imig 1996). Given the historical marginalization and disorganization of the poor, mobilizations for social justice are particularly sensitive to fluctuations in political opportunity structures.

The mobilization efforts of activists for the poor and homeless suggest a number of ways in which movements are bounded and shaped by available political opportunities, as well as a range of ways in which the White House contributes to structures of political opportunity, both directly and indirectly. The influence of the White House on social movements by and for the poor can be as direct as the Johnson administration's declaration of the War on Poverty, which legitimated vigorous government action on behalf of the poor, raised expectations for the success of antipoverty programs, and galvanized citizen demands for more government intervention on behalf of the poor and hungry (Katz 1989: 79–123). Conversely, the Reagan administration's repeated charges of "waste, fraud and abuse" in the welfare system, combined with the strongly antiwelfare budgets submitted by the president, bolstered conservative attempts both to cut spending on poverty programs and to defund advocacy groups that were accusing the administration of "mean spiritedness" and abdication of its responsibility to protect the poor and homeless (Melnick 1994).

Thirty Years of Mobilization for Social Justice

Social movement organizations for the poor are particularly susceptible to fluctuations in structures of political opportunity. Since the 1970s, advocates for social justice have reframed their agendas in response to shifting directions in domestic policy—usually led by the White House and generally marked by grudging support of New Deal initiatives. During the 1970s, activists took advantage of organizational opportunities extended through President Johnson's War on Poverty and its short-lived emphasis on encouraging the "maximum feasible participation" of poor people in politics (Moynihan 1969). Responding to the federal lead in welfare policy making, antipoverty forces rallied to focus their efforts on national politics (Jennings 1994).

That hunger became a rallying cry for activists during the 1970s reflected the confluence of public opinion and presidential politics. During this period, billions of dollars in surplus U.S. farm production led to federal agriculture subsidies for leaving land fallow, sales of surplus wheat to the Soviet Union, and massive stockpiles of excess agricultural commodities. In this climate, social justice advocates gained widespread support for their basic premise that hunger and malnutrition were unacceptable in such an affluent country. President Nixon declared that the continuing existence of hunger and malnutrition "in a land such as ours is embarrassing and intolerable" and, in 1976, 94 percent of Americans agreed with the statement that the United States must not let people who need welfare go hungry (Melnick 1994: 187).

Through the Nixon and Ford presidencies, poor people's SMOs increasingly came to focus on national politics and gained institutional funding from federal agencies, including the Community Services Administration and Legal Services Corporation (Davis 1993). As they increasingly became institutionalized, these groups maintained their organizational foothold in national politics despite receding public interest and periodic White House assaults on social welfare policy. Through this period, there were few examples of large-scale mobilizations for social justice, and the network of public interest groups fighting for the poor by and large maintained tenuous existences, subsisting on federal grants or else on income from the Campaign for Human Development or the Ford Foundation (Hall 1995; Imig 1992). Despite a pervasive low-level antagonism by the White House toward poor people's SMOs through this period, activist groups maintained steady, low-grade pressure on social policy making.

During the 1980s, in contrast, both social welfare spending and advocacy groups were attacked by the White House. The Reagan administration combined domestic budget cuts with a belligerent rhetorical position toward welfare recipients—at one and the same time providing a target for activists for the poor and undermining the presumption engrained in postwar welfare programs that social welfare was generally a worthy cause. In addition to the dramatic policy and rhetorical shifts brought by the new presidential administration, a deep recession between 1980 and 1982 increased the number of people in poverty to its highest levels since the early 1960s. The recovery from this recession, though robust in many respects, failed to boost the poorest members of society, exacerbating the class divide in the United States (Cutler and Katz 1992; Phillips 1990). Federal governmental policies contributed to this increasing marginalization of the poor (Committee on Ways and Means 1994).

Since the Great Society, welfare increasingly came to be seen as an entitlement. Not only was this understanding under siege during the 1980s, but the alternative offered by the Reagan White House—widespread economic well-being through decreased governmental parasitism—failed to materialize, as is evident in both the immediate recession and lopsided long-term recovery. Yet these factors failed to spark a widespread mobilization against Reaganomics. Why?

The poor are an easy target for budget cuts given both their political silence and the pervasive American ethos of self-reliance (Mendel-Reyes 1995). Yet public concern with poverty—as distinct from welfare—remained high throughout this period (Cook and Barrett 1992). Further, media attention to poverty, particularly to homelessness and child poverty, increased rapidly over the decade (Imig 1996: 98–103). In this respect, the Reagan administration's claims to having maintained the safety net for the truly needy increasingly came under public scrutiny (Katz 1989).

In a series of maneuvers, the White House effectively counterbalanced the potential for an expansion of political opportunity suggested by this set of circumstances. First, the administration's social welfare cuts spared the elderly—historically the only group of Americans likely to be *both* poor and politically active. From the 1970s on, poverty among the aged steadily dropped, even as the poverty rate for almost all other demographic groups grew. Sparing the elderly circumvented the potential opposition of the gray lobby.

Second, the administration's cuts in social welfare programs were concentrated in discretionary rather than entitlement programs. Since the late 1960s, discretionary programs had accounted for a growing share of the institutional support for advocacy organizations for the poor. Consequently, Reagan-era budget cuts undermined efforts to organize resistance by defunding the indigenous network of groups organized to battle hunger and poverty.

The policy changes championed by the Reagan administration had a profound and lasting effect on poor people and their supporters. Through budget cuts and rhetorical opposition to social support, the White House outmaneuvered domestic antipoverty groups on several fronts at once—in the rhetorical war of ideas over the meaning and functions of social services in the United States, by slashing federal subsidies to anti-poverty SMOs, and, most important, in the legislative arena where a Congress cowed by the Reagan landslide allowed the administration to hack away at Great Society programs (Gillon 1992: 302; Edsall 1984; Phillips 1990). The administration's frontal assault on domestic policy, backed by the electoral clout of a popular president, matched the rhetorical and policy-making clout of the White House against an increasingly marginalized sector of activists.

White House policy assaults on other interest sectors affected poverty groups as well by distancing advocates for the poor from potential allies. The administration's reorganization of the Departments of Interior and Justice, as well as increasing White House belligerence toward the Soviet Union, drew the attention of the environmental, civil rights, and peace movements—diverting these potential allies of the poor. Organized labor, long a supporter of advocacy for social welfare, meanwhile, was hamstrung through strikebreaking, legislative maneuvering, and antilabor judicial decisions (Goldfield 1989: 27; Sousa 1993).

In sum, the Reagan White House contributed to constricting the political opportunity structures bounding social justice movement organizations—directly through funding grants, rhetorical opposition, and policy assaults, and indirectly by increasing the competition among social movement organizations for dwindling foundation resources as well as by isolating this movement sector from its traditional allies.

The Response of Social Movement Organizations

How did social movement organizations for the poor respond to the shrinking opportunity structures that followed the Reagan inauguration? At the beginning of the 1980s, a range of political organizations—at the local, state, and national level—worked to provide advocacy for the poor. At the national level, a network of groups informally known as the "hunger lobby" included both public interest groups largely seeking institutional and incremental expansions in existing social support programs as well as a set of less institutionalized social movement organizations that were engaged in both direct action (e.g., seizing abandoned buildings and launching hunger fasts) as well as more institutional challenges to Reagan-era budget priorities.[1]

Among these groups, the early 1980s presented a period of organizational turmoil. Not only were social welfare policies under attack, but governmental and private grant money for advocacy groups was in short supply. Private foundations such as the Campaign for Human Development and the Ford Foundation were unable to offset federal cuts. The Ford Foundation's 1982 annual report explains:

> [D]emands for Foundation support have been increasing as national priorities and strategies have left many organizations and the social, cultural, and educational issues they address without adequate funding. We have tried to be re-

sponsive to this need. But when foundation and corporate philanthropic spending together amount to less than $6 billion per year, much of which is committed to important ongoing activities, it is impossible to compensate significantly for the withdrawal or reduction of federal support in amounts many times greater.

Many groups formed during the heyday of the Great Society as watchdogs over federal policy were severely undermined at this time. The Community Nutrition Institute (CNI), for example, found their budgets slashed by over 80 percent between 1981 and 1985 (Imig 1996: 50). With few options, CNI responded to devastating budget cuts by pruning back staff and services. The CNI lost most of its institutional base, scaled back its size and activities to operate on reduced revenue, and, in the process, was virtually forced out of national political action. With this major loss of income, CNI shifted to a more traditional relationship with funders, devoting its remaining resources to publishing a newsletter documenting the changes taking place in Washington. Other advocacy groups shifted their organizational focus to provide more direct services and less political advocacy. Most groups were forced to devote considerably more effort to fundraising, which also had the effect of diverting their time and attention from political advocacy to concentrate on organizational survival.

While national antipoverty groups were squeezed out of institutional channels, less well-established outsider groups increasingly gained agenda space by taking to the streets in support of the poor and homeless. Their actions reframed the politics of poverty in terms of an emerging homeless movement (Kessler 1988). Over the 1980s, both new and existing homelessness groups adopted an increasingly vocal and confrontational political posture, capturing media and public attention through their efforts. Reflecting expanding poverty rosters and emerging antipoverty activism from 1983 through 1987, the *New York Times* attention to poverty increased nearly fivefold over this same period (Imig 1996: 99). The dominant strain of actions recorded over this period were undertaken in support of the homeless. The number of homeless protests recorded in the national press rose from zero in 1980 to a handful in 1981 and then to more than ten in 1982. As avenues for institutional access were withdrawn, issue advocates sought other venues through which to press their grievances. Looking back over the decade, one of the leaders of the homeless movement explained:

We were interested in equalizing the dialogue. Other people have the power of voting . . . of political campaigns. The poor, however, . . . don't do the things that matter in capitalist society and therefore are ignored. This is where we come into the picture. We scare the crap out of people: putting our lives and freedom and health on the table in order to equalize the dialogue. (Imig 1996: 66)

In this case, that quest took them into abandoned buildings and the Capitol rotunda. In this way, attacks on social justice programs, coupled with constricting institutional access, constrained institutional action as well as heightened levels of noninstitutional participation by the poor and their supporters.

Homelessness activists seized the opportunity opened by the Reagan White House. Mitch Snyder and the Community for Creative Non-Violence (CCNV), for example, captured widespread media attention during the early 1980s with a string of protests blaming President Reagan for rising homelessness in America. Between the Reagan inauguration in 1981 and passage of the Stewart McKinney Homeless Assistance Act in 1987, CCNV launched two dozen protests that linked President Reagan directly and personally with the growing misery of the homeless. Many of these events also juxtaposed the grandeur of the White House with the mean conditions faced by the homeless on steam grates and park benches. CCNV activists doused the White House gates in blood and set cockroaches loose on the White House tour. Snyder and his colleagues also pledged to fast until the Reagan administration came to the aid of the homeless. Meanwhile, other homeless advocates—led by the Association of Community Organizations for Reform Now—raised shanty-town "Reaganvilles" for the homeless and staged "Nancy Reagan fashion shows for the Depression-minded."[2]

Mobilization of Weak Challengers: The Influence of the White House

A powerful and visible opponent in the White House can galvanize a movement and its supporters through a sense of urgency and injustice. Groups facing belligerent presidential administrations may be able to use this friction to raise funds and popular support for their cause. In this respect, opposition from the White House may provide a useful resource in the form of an identifiable antagonist. As Freeman (1983: 208) notes, "a solid opponent can do more to unify a group . . . than any other factor." The Reagan administration's welfare-bashing rhetoric and policy agenda gave activists for the poor and homeless a ready target.

On the other hand, the executive branch controls the flow of many of the resources on which social movement organizations rely. This is particularly true for weak groups with few financial supporters. As we have seen, among poor people's groups, sources of funding and tax status are key resources that easily can be manipulated by antagonistic administrations. More generally, the White House can close avenues to policy-making access and can make use of the rhetorical leverage offered by the "bully pulpit" of the presidency to marginalize particular issues and deligitimate their representatives.

The other half of the equation concerns the implications of supportive presidential administrations for social movements. Supportive administrations hold the potential to affect opportunity in a range of ways as well, both through the resources they extend and the opportunities for action they open.

Supportive administrations extend symbolic support to challengers, granting their positions legitimacy and their issues attention. Sympathetic administrations may extend both access and concessions to favored groups, giving them rhetorical support, contracts, grants, and favorable tax status. Looking at the rate and pattern of growth of citizen groups in the United States, Walker (1983: 404) notes:

> [I]nterest groups and their rate of growth are . . . heavily influenced by the incentives, supports, and opportunities created through public policies and legal provisions. Most governments choose to promote their allies, as the Johnson administration did through the War on Poverty, Model Cities, VISTA, the Older Americans Act, and many other programs of social reform.

Sympathetic presidential administrations can also open new venues for action by soliciting the input of particular advocates and activists. The Heritage Foundation gained access during the early Reagan years, for example, as Anna Kundratis left Heritage to join the White House as an undersecretary in the Department of Health and Human Services, where she maintained her vocal opposition to welfare and food assistance programs. Similarly, the Heritage Foundation's Robert Rector played a significant role in helping craft the welfare provisions in the House Republican's Contract With America.

Ironically, a supportive presidency may offer concessions that will actually placate and dissipate a movement and may even have the effect of energizing its opposition. Hall (1995) describes the relationship between community-based poor people's social movement organizations and supportive municipal officials—a situation with direct parallels to that between the White House and national social movements. "The perception of an ally in high places may induce quiescence among the members of an organization," who believe their concerns are in good hands and who are loathe to push someone they perceive to be an ally (81).

At the same time, supportive administrations diffuse the perception of policy crisis by appearing to address activist's concerns. This phenomenon can take two forms, as public concern with an issue is dissipated and as social movement organizations are drawn into institutional policy venues and drawn away from their mass base. A further concern for movement organizations facing sympathetic administrations follows from the tendency to become overreliant on a single patron who provides funding, prestige, recognition, and venues of access. Organizational vulnerability through overreliance on a single funder was evident among antipoverty groups in the 1980s. These groups suffered when they were cut off from federal funding.

The range of concessions offered by sympathetic administrations highlights one of the subtleties of the influence of the White House on political opportunity. Obviously, not all concessions are equally desirable. There is a danger that symbolic concessions without tangible policy change will coopt, mute, and defuse the oppositional spark underlying challengers' actions. This concern led Piven and Cloward (1979) to observe that those activist groups that survive the wave of mobilization that gives rise to them may well owe more to their elite supporters than they do to the cause they claim to represent. An activist for the homeless interviewed for this chapter commented that during the first two years of the Clinton presidency, poverty fighters were being "meeting-ed to death while rearranging the deck chairs on the *Titanic*." In other words, symbolic concessions can preempt and diffuse opposition, while tangible concessions are withheld.

Conclusion

This chapter has examined the influence of one facet of political context—the level of support or opposition extended by the White House—on social movement organizations for the poor and homeless. The case of the Reagan administration suggests a number of ways in which presidential administrations proscribe the political opportunity structures bounding mobilization efforts for social justice. The influence of the White House, in turn, helps explain patterns of social movement organization, mobilization, and decline.

In the confrontation between poor people's SMOs and the Reagan administration, we see how the White House can intimidate and subdue mobilization efforts by questioning their credibility, reducing their access and funding opportunities, and undermining their policy agenda. Unlike the contemporary environmental or antinuclear movements, activists for the poor were unable to capitalize on the potential advantages that being an outsider can offer (e.g., heightened perception of crisis and a visible antagonist). The failure of poor people's social movement organizations to mobilize largely followed from an institutional overreliance on a few grant-making institutions, including the federal government itself. Through the combination of federal policy shifts and increasing numbers of claimants for diminished foundation dollars, social movement organizations without a strong independent funding source spent much of the decade scrambling to find new sources of income to maintain their organizations.

At the same time, this case also highlights a number of efforts by challengers to skirt closed venues and seize opportunities where they emerged. This is evident in the long-term evolution of the master frames used by activists to present the issue of poverty in America—shifting from welfare rights to hunger, to homelessness, and to children in poverty. In each case, activists attempted to sidestep their limitations and opponents and to recapture public concern.

Similarly, through the 1980s the poor and their supporters took to the streets with increasing frequency, gaining media attention, celebrity participation, and agenda space in the process. Responding to shifts in political opportunity, activists pressed their demands in new ways. They gained allies, public attention, and media coverage in a much more public and larger political context defined by contemporary political trends, including the emergence of the New Right, the perception of a Republican electoral majority, and the Reagan revolution. Their claims took on a heightened urgency in the context of vocal White House opposition.

Activists for the homeless responded nimbly to the pressures and structures of opportunity they faced, importing well-known actions such as marches and sit-ins and innovating tactics such as protest soup kitchens and planting corn on the Capitol lawn. The Reagan administration provided a focal point for organizers. Activists blamed the administration for domestic poverty and called attention to the rough treatment given the poor by their own government.

On balance, the Reagan White House demonstrates a number of ways in which presidential administrations can constrict political opportunity structures confronting marginalized challengers. In response, social movement organizations either are left politically silenced or are forced to abandon accommodationist tactics in favor of more extreme confrontation.

Notes

An earlier version of this chapter was presented at the 1994 annual meeting of the Midwest Political Science Association, Chicago, April 14–17.

1. For a more complete account of the efforts of advocacy and activist groups to battle the Reagan initiatives, see Imig (1996).

2. Accounts of these events are drawn from *Nexis Omni File* records of *New York Times*, *Washington Post*, *Chicago Tribune*, and *Los Angeles Times* newspaper articles.

10

Women Lobby Congress

Anne N. Costain

In the United States organized groups of women have lobbied Congress on political concerns ranging from the right to vote, at the start of the century, to increased funding for medical treatment of breast cancer, in more recent years, with comparatively little notice. Scholars who study interest group politics are often more aware of lobbying by farmers, labor unions, and public interest groups than by women. Although women are a majority of the population and have been a presence in the Capitol since long before suffrage was granted in 1920, scholars have only sporadically examined what women have accomplished through pressuring Congress. The core of the current analysis will focus on the issues and tactics used by those seeking to advance women's interests and congressional response to them between 1958 and 1994. These years span the emergence of a new social movement representing women in the 1960s through the institutionalizing of that movement as a mainstream interest in the 1980s and 1990s. Yet, to evaluate the success of women's lobbying in recent times, it is necessary to provide some understanding of the historic role of lobbyists on behalf of women's concerns.

Historically, women have applied the most intense pressure on Congress when mobilized as a social movement. Early in the century, political scientist Pendleton Herring (1929: 194–5) wrote, "[T]he battle to remove sex as a qualification for voting was waged by two forces of organized women. . . . The suffrage fight served to develop the methods of the lobbyist of the present day and to impress upon women and upon the public generally the efficacy of organized agitation." Two aspects of this quotation deserve more notice than they have received in the sixty-eight years since they were first published, for they illuminate notable strengths and weaknesses of movement lobbying. This quote begins by acknowledging the split within the suffrage movement itself. The woman suffrage movement, like many other movements, experienced significant internal conflict as it tried to mix conventional political lobbying with protest politics. Historically, one wing of the movement blasted the major political parties of the day for inaction on suffrage, while it allied itself with the youthful labor movement. By contrast, the other branch of the movement intentionally avoided drawing attention to "social" evils and preferred to concentrate on what professional and educated women might contribute to the electorate as voters (Flexner 1973: 216–25).

The simple act of lobbying government successfully requires organization and planning, but this discipline and building of consensus itself frequently heightens stress within a social movement, forcing a choice of allies and issues. Parts of most active movements value their status as outsiders and may be reluctant to work with groups they oppose on other issues. Ferree and Martin (1995, 8) have observed, "A movement organization is not a contradiction in terms, but it is, by definition, in tension. It is always a compromise between the ideals by which it judges itself and the realities of its daily practices." Yet, as the Herring quote suggests, this duality itself adds a complexity to congressional lobbying that may bring the benefit of broadening access to the legislative body. When the goal to be achieved is both clear and shared, possessing a diverse range of supporters who will work to sway Congress through a variety of methods may be one way to prevail.

A second component of Herring's quotation is that women's suffrage served as a model for the methods of "organized agitation" used by the majority of lobbying groups in the period leading up to World War II. Women's organizations, according to Herring, were the second most numerous in the nation's capital during that time period, trailing only business associations. The contemporary parallel to this astonishing level of political presence may be the impact that the black civil rights movement has had on tactics and styles of lobbying in the 1960s and 1970s. Although the numbers of civil rights groups never rivaled those of big business or labor, their success in pioneering new techniques of political influence expanded their power beyond raw numbers (McAdam 1983). Women's groups were an analogous model of lobbying success in the early part of the century. This point, in and of itself, makes it interesting to consider why women's groups had such an impact on lobbying styles.

One may reasonably broaden the question further to ask why social movement-linked lobbies would wield so great an influence. As I have argued elsewhere (Costain 1980), despite the widely recognized advantages experienced by small, cohesive groups with a common political agenda, large and diffuse interests may also be powerful, if they have the motivation to work in concert. In eras in which party cohesion in Congress is weak, social movement strength may be magnified, since social movement-tied interests sometimes unite surprising factions in a common purpose (McAdam 1982). This development allows legislative majorities to form when they might not otherwise do so. Another advantage is their fluidity. Social movements, as noninstitutionalized political actors, may adapt to change much more quickly than either political parties or well-established interest groups such as the American Medical Association or the United Auto Workers. Movements can change more quickly because they must to survive.

Movements win adherents by providing explanations for the dissatisfaction that many in society have with existing conditions and proposing remedies. In the case of the women's movement, many studies of public opinion in the 1950s and 1960s showed that women were discontented with their lives (Keniston and Keniston 1964; Rossi 1964; Chafe 1972; Amundsen 1971). The women's movement gained support by affirming publicly that women should be discontented because of the narrow range of career and family options available to them. The movement urged women to remove the legal barriers to their exclusion from full participation in society both by passing an equal rights amendment to the U.S. Constitution and by overturning laws limiting women's social, economic, and political roles (Costain, Braunstein and Berggren 1996: 205–9). This strategy provided the women's movement with a shared agenda to advocate to Congress.

Another source of influence for interests linked to movements is their close tie to democratic politics. Because movements gain legitimacy, at least in part, through their support in public opinion, they are more closely attuned than many interest groups to their standing with the public. Similarly, Congress has been shown to respond to the issues advocated by movements most readily when public approval for them is rising steadily (Burstein 1985: 43–63; Costain and Majstorovic 1994).

In reviewing congressional response to women's issues since the turn of the century, then, it is evident that Congress pays most attention to women when a mobilized social movement is pressing for action. This accounts for the cluster of new "women's laws" in the early decades of the century as well as in the 1970s, 1980s, and 1990s. The only exception is found during World War II, when the necessity of mobilizing the population to fight a major war resulted in the passage of laws drawing women as well as men into nontraditional workplaces and the military (Costain 1988: 150–72). This overview suggests that to understand women's lobbying and its political impact, the lobby should be looked at over time and in a context of social movement politics.

Method

Women's groups organize to pressure Congress on such a wide variety of issues, ranging from funding school lunch programs to freezing the existing level of nuclear weapons, that on the surface most seem to have little to do with women as a group. Yet, the history of interest group politics in

America suggests that in examining group influence over time, it is reasonable to pay special attention to bills directed explicitly at the group as one way to assess the impact the group exerts on the political system. Particularly when analyzing group participation over a long period of time, this approach yields a common set of descriptors to trace its activitism and success. For that reason, Douglas Costain, a number of graduate students, and I have maintained a database consisting of bills introduced into Congress and laws passed by Congress that explicitly refer to women as a group. The index headings tracked include "woman," "women," "women's," and "civil rights (sex)."[1] We have used the indexes of *U.S. Statutes at Large* (1899–1994), the *Congressional Record* (1900–1994), and the *Commerce Clearing House* (1958–1994) to identify bills introduced and laws passed that refer to women as a group. These bills and laws vary from Defense Department appropriations to proposed amendments to the American Constitution to bans on government funding for abortions.

Early in this project, it seemed that we might be overwhelmed by the volume of laws addressing problems of over half of the population, but this has not proved to be the case. In fact, from 1958 to 1994, the highest proportion of U.S. laws that contain particular references to women in any single year is under 4 percent of all statutes passed in that year (see Figure 10.1). Of the bills introduced by Congress, no Congress had more than 2 percent of its total number of bills referring explicitly to women (Costain 1992: 11–13).

The bills and laws were coded by subject and then compared with coverage of women's issues in the *New York Times* and areas of women's movement activism as reported in the *Times*.[2] Finally, we regressed coverage and activism against the passage of laws by Congress.

Congressional Action

Congressional passage of laws directed at women as a group reached its high point in 1973, slightly before the peak of a mobilized women's movement in America, which is usually dated at 1974 or 1975 (Costain and Costain 1992). During the 1958–1994 period almost 40 percent of the women's laws passed by Congress focused on economic issues and jobs. The next most common type of legislation dealt with health (16.5 percent). Finally, civil rights laws, including passage of the Equal Rights Amendment (ERA) by the House and Senate in 1972, comprised almost 15 percent of the new legislative enactments (see Figure 10.2). In dividing these congressional laws into the time period prior to the final defeat of the ERA in 1982, it is clear that civil rights declined precipitously as an issue after the ERA was rejected (Figures 10.3 and 10.4). In the period when the ERA was moving

Figure 10.1
Women's Laws as a Percentage of All Laws, 1958–1994

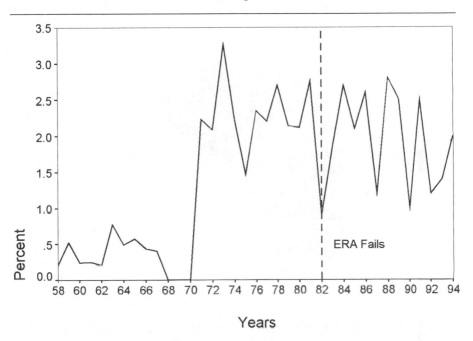

Years

toward ratification, 21 percent of the laws passed dealt with civil rights. By contrast, in the post-ERA period, legislation dealing with the economy and jobs, health policy, and education were all much more common than civil rights enactments. The agenda for women has broadened, so that the economy and civil rights, which in the earlier period made up more than 60 percent of all women's laws passed, have now shrunk to less than 40 percent, while legislation on crime, health policy, and education have all become more numerous.

This picture of civil rights enactments and economic legislation dominating the period as a whole, and particularly the first fifteen years, is underscored when one examines the types of bills introduced in Congress (Figure 10.5). From 1958 to 1994, over 60 percent of all bills dealing with women as a group fit the category of civil rights (see Figure 10.6). The next largest grouping deals with the economy and jobs. Together, these two comprise more than 80 percent of women's bills (Figure 10.6). Before the defeat of ERA, more than 85 percent of the legislation introduced looking at women as a group fit into these two areas (Figure 10.7). After 1982, like the laws

Figure 10.2
Proportion of Women's Laws by Subject Area, 1958–1994

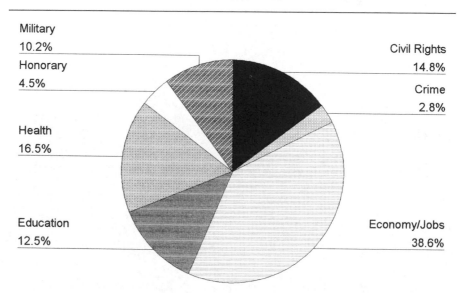

Military 10.2%

Honorary 4.5%

Health 16.5%

Education 12.5%

Civil Rights 14.8%

Crime 2.8%

Economy/Jobs 38.6%

passed, more bills were introduced on a wide range of subjects, with civil rights, economy/jobs, and health leading the list. To show the spread of concerns, civil rights and the economy now encompass just over half of all the bills, rather than 80 percent or more of women's legislation introduced.

The fact that many more civil rights and economic bills are introduced relative to the number of these laws that pass suggests that they are controversial in Congress. This linkage is underlined if we compare civil rights and economic bills with those dealing with education, health, the military, and crime, which have far greater chance for passage. When legislation on women in the military, women and crime, or women's health are introduced, their likelihood of passage seems quite high.

Pressure for Change

Since congressional action occurs in anything but a vacuum, where does this pressure for change in public policy toward women come from? It is evident in comparing the graphs of the percentage of women's laws passed and events related to women that are reported in the *New York Times* that there is a significant, although not overwhelming, correlation between these

Figure 10.3
Proportion of Women's Laws by Subject Area, 1958–1982

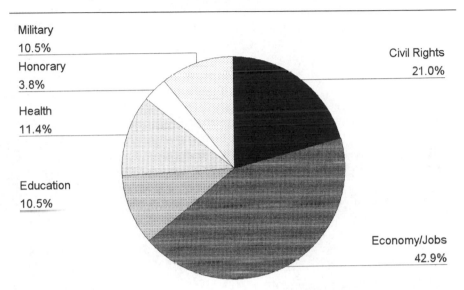

Military
10.5%

Honorary
3.8%

Health
11.4%

Education
10.5%

Civil Rights
21.0%

Economy/Jobs
42.9%

measures over time (r = .36, p < .03) (see Figures 10.1 and 10.9). As women's issues become increasingly newsworthy, the share of the legislative agenda devoted to women's laws also rises. Similarly, a positive relationship exists between women's groups pressuring Congress and the percentage of laws passed that address women as a group (r = .42, p < .01). One interesting aspect of the application of pressure by women's groups, as it is shown in Figure 10.10, is that lobbying began to increase in 1970, as the women's movement grew in size and became more vocal, that pressure continued into the early 1980s. Then, it drops rapidly in the late 1980s and 1990s. By contrast, the number of women's laws by Congress passed remains relatively high even as lobbying decreases. It may be that earlier pressure opened the congressional agenda for women's concerns. Despite the subsequent drop in women's activism, congressional responsiveness continues.

Initial analysis suggests that the level of conventional political pressure put on Congress by the women's movement, the introduction of bills related to women's economic and health concerns, and, rather unexpectedly, large numbers of women's events initiated by professional groups and educational institutions have some of the strongest positive correlations with passage of high proportions of women's laws by Congress. Together, these four vari-

Figure 10.4
Proportion of Women's Laws by Subject Area, 1983–1994

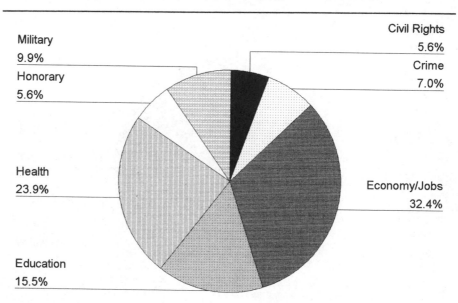

ables explain 40 percent of the variance in passing laws.[3] This seems to suggest that political support for women's concerns among educational and business elites, backed by women's movement activism and group lobbying results in successful congressional outcomes. This is particularly true for issues of economics and health.

Conclusion

The history of organized women applying political pressure is one of periodic success. Congress is most likely to respond favorably during times of mobilized women's movements. In the current period, Congress is more willing to pass laws dealing with the health, education, and employment needs of women than their civil rights concerns.

Notes

1. I owe particular thanks to Heather Fraizer and Heidi Berggren for adding and coding materials from 1987 to 1994 to the existing data set.

Figure 10.5
Women's Bills Introduced as a Proportion of All New Bills

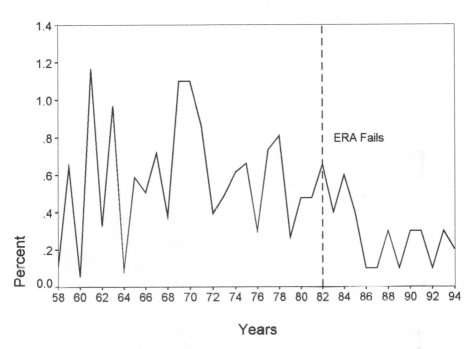

2. For a complete discussion of how the articles in the *Times* were selected and coded, see Appendix A from Costain (1992: 143–9).

3. The independent variables used are as follows:

Pressact = organized activities by women's movement groups to influence government through conventional methods, such as organizing new groups, registering voters, and writing letters to public officials

Ihealth = the number of bills introduced in Congress dealing with women's health concerns

Iecon = the number of bills introduced by members of Congress dealing with women's concerns about the economy and jobs

Edinit = women's events reported in the *New York Times* initiated by either educational institutions and groups or professional associations, such as the American Bar Association or the American Medical Association

The dependent variable is perlaw—women's laws as a percentage of all laws passed by Congress in that year. Statistical data are as follows: Multiple R, .683; R^2, .467; Adjusted R^2, .400; Significance of F, .0004, and beta and sig T, respectively, are Edinit, .36 and .055; Iecon, .28 and .058; Ihealth, .36 and .009; Pressact, .04 and .831.

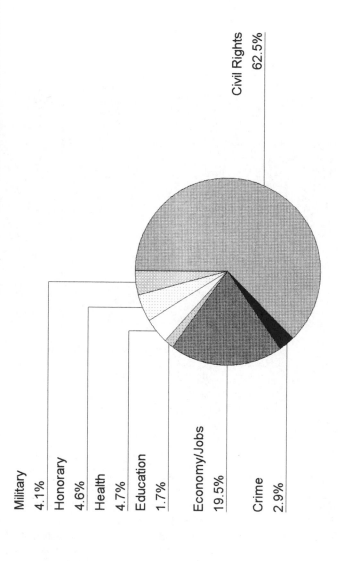

Figure 10.6 Proportion of Women's Bills by Subject Area, 1958–1994

Civil Rights
62.5%

Military
4.1%

Honorary
4.6%

Health
4.7%

Education
1.7%

Economy/Jobs
19.5%

Crime
2.9%

Figure 10.7 Proportion of Women's Bills by Subject Area, 1958–1982

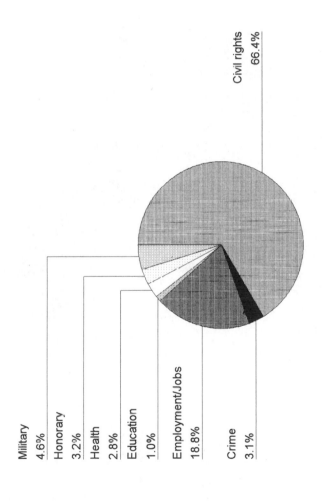

Military
4.6%

Honorary
3.2%

Health
2.8%

Education
1.0%

Employment/Jobs
18.8%

Crime
3.1%

Civil rights
66.4%

Anne N. Costain

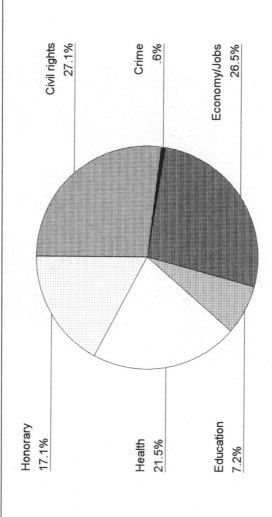

Figure 10.8 Proportion of Women's Laws by Subject Area, 1983–1994

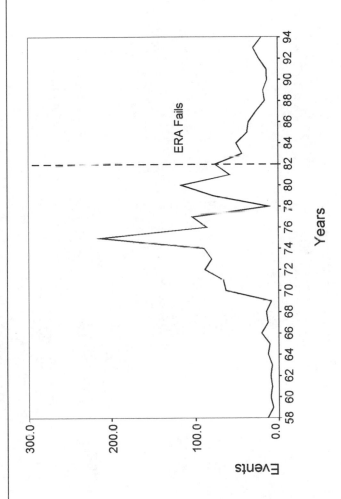

Figure 10.9 Women's Events Reported to the *New York Times*

Anne N. Costain

Figure 10.10 Laws Passed and Pressure from Women's Groups

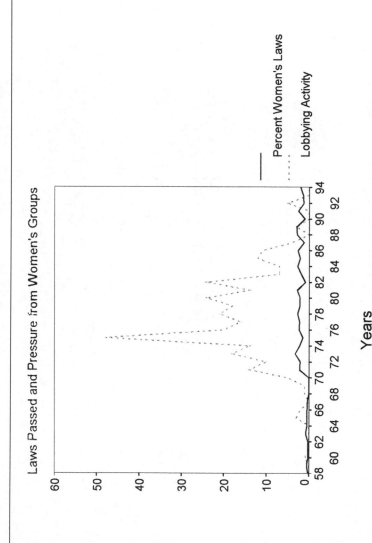

Laws Passed and Pressure from Women's Groups

Percent Women's Laws

Lobbying Activity

Years

11

The Environmental Movement and Congress

W. Douglas Costain and James P. Lester

The evolution of environmentalism over the past 100 years illustrates a number of important changes in the nature of the movement itself, the nature of policymaking, in the scope of the issues considered, the level of governmental responses, and in patterns of participation. Congress, as the most representative of the three branches of government, has been at the center of this evolution. From a concern over preservation of natural resources to a concern over "third-generation" environmental issues such as acid rain and global warming, the environmental agenda has been shaped by the interactions between the movement and the Congress. Policy changes, such as a shift from the "wise use" of natural resources to pollution prevention and waste minimization, have accompanied a move away from the elitist style of participation in the late 1890s to "participatory democracy" in the 1990s. Similarly, the emphasis in environmental policy making has evolved from a concern about adding environmental issues to the congressional agenda to environmental policy implementation and evaluation. Scholars also note that innovations in environmental policy making shifted from the national level to the state and local levels in the 1980s and 1990s (Lester and Lombard 1990; John 1994). Finally, scholars have noted the evolution from a concern over "environmental science" in the late 1800s to a concern over "environmental ethics" in the 1990s (Paehlke 1989; Young 1990).

All these changes, when taken together, suggest that the nature of environmentalism has greatly expanded over the past hundred years to include more issues, more diverse participants, and a greater public awareness of environmental issues. This evolving movement interacts with the dynamics within the institution of the Congress. The impact of the movement on Congress's agenda and the influence of the institution's operations on environmentalism shape this chapter.

The purposes of this chapter are threefold. First, we describe the evolution of environmentalism from the 1890s to the 1990s, paying particular attention to changes in the scope of issues considered, the patterns of participation, the nature of public policy in this area, and the dominant concerns within each period. Next, we discuss the growth and evolution of environmental interest groups within the broader movement over time. Finally, we discuss the impacts of this environmental interest group activity on congressional policy making and of Congress on the movement.

Evolution of the Environmental Movement

The history of environmental politics and policy may be roughly divided into four periods: (1) the "conservation-efficiency movement" from about 1890 to 1920, (2) the "conservation-preservation movement" from about 1920 to 1960, (3) the "environmental movement" from about 1960 to 1980, and (4) the contemporary period of "participatory environmentalism" starting in the 1980s (Hays 1959; Schnaiberg 1980; Caulfield 1989).[1] However, we can identify earlier attempts to protect the environment as well. For example, during the first part of the nineteenth century, the federal government took a number of actions to preserve good mast timber for ships, and President John Quincy Adams even went so far as to establish a program of sustained yield operations on some forest reservations in 1827 (Englebert 1961). However, there was not really much effort for environmental protection until after the Civil War. With the exception of the John Quincy Adams administration, no other presidential administration from Washington to Buchanan revealed any foresight in planning for the nation's future natural resource needs (Englebert 1961). Essentially, the years between 1865 and 1890 may be characterized as a period of resource exploitation by a rising industry, during which time natural resources were subordinated to the political objectives of industrial development, homestead settlement, and the promotion of free enterprise (Englebert 1961). During the Reconstruction era after the Civil War, the focus was on rebuilding the South and developing the American West, both of which required the use of resources rather than their conservation. Nevertheless, by the late 1800s, serious efforts began to protect the nation's natural resources.

The Conservation-Efficiency Movement, 1890–1920: Elitism in Policy Making

The years from 1890 until 1920 saw some of the nation's most bitter conservation battles as Republicans and Democrats began to take firm positions on the environment. The essence of the "conservation movement" was rational planning *by government* to promote efficient development and use of all natural resources (Hays 1959: 2). According to historian Samuel P. Hays (1959:5), "the modern American conservation movement grew out of the firsthand experience of federal administrators and political leaders with problems of Western economic growth, especially Western water development." Later, federal forestry officials joined hydrographers and campaigned for more rational and efficient use of timber resources. During the 1890s, the organized forestry movement in the United States shifted its emphasis from saving trees to promoting sustained-yield forest management (Hays 1961). By 1891, the executive branch took the lead to set aside "forest reserves" within the federal domain and to authorize selective cutting and marketing of timber in 1897 (Caulfield 1989).

A number of individuals, including W. J. McGee, Gifford Pinchot, John Wesley Powell, Frederick Newell, George Maxwell, and others, were concerned about the short-sighted commercial exploitation of the nation's natural resources. Many were employed by the federal government in the late 1800s, especially for the U.S. Geological Survey. Together, they formulated four basic doctrines for what later became the creed of the conservation movement: (1) conservation is not the locking up of resources—it is their development and wise use; (2) conservation is the greatest good for the greatest number, for the longest time; (3) the federal public lands belong to all the people; and (4) comprehensive, multiple-purpose river basin planning and development should be utilized with respect to the nation's water resources (Caulfield 1989).

Gifford Pinchot became an important link between the intellectual and scientific founders of the conservation movement and President Theodore Roosevelt, a Republican. Indeed, the Theodore Roosevelt administration is as noteworthy for the drive and support it gave the conservation movement as it is for the initiation of new policies or legislative enactments. A new spirit of law enforcement pervaded the once corrupt land management departments, dramatized to the country at large by the influence of Pinchot and his role as adviser to President Roosevelt (Englebert 1961). Under Pinchot's guidance, the Roosevelt administration greatly enlarged the area of the national forests and completely reorganized the Forest Service, infusing it with a new spirit of public responsibility (Hays 1959).

Numerous conflicts arose over conservation policy in the period of 1908–1920. For example, much of the Western livestock industry depended for its forage on the "open range" owned by the federal government but free for anyone to use. Soon the public domain became stocked with more animals than the range could support. Chaos, violence, and destruction of property were typical of the times as all struggled for control of the public grazing lands (Hays 1959).

Nevertheless, the deepest significance of the conservation movement, according to Hays (1959), "lay in its political implications: how should resource decisions be made and by whom?" Should conflicts be resolved through partisan politics, by compromise among various interest groups, or through the courts? To the conservationists, politics was an anathema; instead, scientific experts, using technical and scientific methods, should decide all matters of development and use of natural resources together with the allocation of public funds (Hays 1959). The crux of the gospel of efficiency, then, "lay in a rational and scientific method of making basic technological decisions through a single, central authority" (Hays 1959: 271). The inevitable tension that developed between those "grassroots" interests and the technocratic elites of this conservation-efficiency era raised a question that was to be addressed by future conservationists. How can large-scale government programs be effective and at the same time fulfill the desire for significant grassroots participation?

A parallel movement was active in urban industrial cities as some of the Progressives focused on public health issues such as pure foods, workplace safety, clean drinking water, and the construction of sewage facilities. This urban environmentalism would become the domain of local and state departments of health and federal agencies such as the Department of Labor and the Public Health Service, and it would come to the forefront again in the 1960s as public attention addressed air and water pollution.

The Conservation-Preservation Movement, 1920–1960:
The Growth of Subgovernments

The second form of conservationism, the preservationist movement, was very similar to the efficiency movement, except that this movement was more concerned with *habitat* than sustenance (Englebert 1961). That is, this preservationist movement developed largely under the pressures of increased leisure and affluence, and the growth of outdoor recreation. It drew its support from the upper middle class and also from hunting and fishing groups drawn from the working classes. Although there were conflicts over natural resource policy, they were largely confined to struggles between those who favored "multiple use" of public lands versus those who favored "pure preservation" (Schnaiberg 1980: 386). While the earlier movement was often characterized by conflicts between extractive industries in the West and manufacturing industries in the East, the preservationist movement often included capitalist sponsors, like Laurence Rockefeller, who facilitated the preservation of major tracts of land surrounding the hotels that he built (Schnaiberg 1980).

Beginning in 1920, water power, coal, flood control, and even wildlife were given special attention in the major party platforms. Much of the emphasis on natural resources was shifted from conservation of public lands to programs of conservation under private ownership (Englebert 1961). Another major difference between these two movements was that conservation-efficiency concerns resided with corporations and national and state agencies, while conservation-preservationist concerns resided in local and especially national interest groups, like the Sierra Club, the National Wildlife Federation, and the Wilderness Society.

The period from 1921 to 1950 took on a different look since much of the federal legislation for natural resources became associated with broad social and economic objectives like the Agricultural Adjustment Act of 1938, which was passed to control agricultural production. Similarly, the job-creating agencies of the New Deal often undertook major environmental protection responsibilities. The Civilian Conservation Corps planted millions of trees in the Dust Bowl states as well as upgrading many of the national parks. The legislative history of environmental and natural resource issues suggests that Democrats attained a much better voting record than their Republican counterparts during 1921–1950 (Englebert 1961). By the 1960s, however, the movement began to change dramatically as environmental concern was broadened to include many new issues involving groups that had previously been inactive.

The Environmental Movement, 1960–1980: Pluralism in Policy Making

One prominent scholar of environmental politics argues that the conservation movement was an effort on the part of leaders in science, technology, and government to bring about more efficient development of natural resources, while the environmental movement was a product of a fundamental change in public values in the United States that stressed the quality of the human environment (Hays 1959). The environmental movement, in contrast to the conservation movement, is best seen as a grassroots or "bottom-up" phenomenon in which environmental objectives arose out of deep-seated changes in values about the use of nature. Conservation, on the other hand, seems a "top-down" phenomenon in which technical and political leaders were stirred toward action. Essentially, the environmental movement integrated the habitat and sustainability concerns of the efficiency and preservation movements, but it also covered public health and a broader set of ecosystem concerns (Schnaiberg 1980). Renewed concerns were raised about the public health consequences of modern industrial society as well as who would decide on the distribution of risks and benefits within a capitalist democracy.

The environmental movement can also be characterized by the breadth of its constituency, as well as its strategies for political influence. For example, groups within the environmental movement used lobbying, litigation, the media, electoral politics, and even civil disobedience in contrast to the more conventional mechanisms used by the conservationists, such as technical negotiations, corporate sponsors, and small pressure groups (Schnaiberg 1980).

Finally, the base of support for the environmental movement was made up of a larger sector of the public, including the middle and working classes. Such broad support attracted the attention of entrepreneurial politicians seeking to attach themselves to popular causes. With the decline of strong programmatic national parties, ad hoc coalitions of opportunistic politicians advanced the issues of the movement. This transitory support became institutionalized in the laws and regulations that were administered by new agencies like the EPA. The media and the ambitious politicians would move on to newer topics, but the environmental groups and the civil servants were firmly rooted in "issue networks" and "policy communities."

The Contemporary Period, 1980s and 1990s: Toward
Strong Democracy and the Environmental Movement

Some of the recent literature describes a shift toward direct action and a turning away from "representative democracy" toward "participatory democracy" (Goldsteen and Schorr 1991). Others describe contemporary environmental politics in terms of "advocacy coalitions," in which groups from federal, state, and local levels form coalitions for the purpose of supporting or opposing major environmental issues (Sabatier and Jenkins-Smith 1988, 1993).

Still others argue that we are evolving toward "postenvironmentalism" in which we adopt environmentally sound methods of industrial production, solar technology, recycling, soft transport technology, and sustainable agriculture (Young 1990). Table 11.1 describes some of the more salient characteristics of each era of the environmental movement from 1890 to 1990.

The Growth of Environmental Interest Groups

As Ingram, Colnic, and Mann argue (1995: 115), "since the 1960s environmental interest groups have become permanent features in the landscape of American politics." Prior to the 1960s, environmental interest groups were visible participants in environmental policy making; however, the pattern of interest group politics in Congress during 1890–1960 was characterized by subgovernments or by an elite-dominated system of policy making (Costain and Lester 1995). This recent emergence and evolution of environmental interest groups attests to the dominance of interest group pluralism as an explanatory framework. Not only have environmental interest groups increased in Washington, but thousands of these groups have emerged at the local level as well. Basically, there have been "three waves" of environmental interest group activity. The first wave began with the roles played by such groups as the Sierra Club, the National Audubon Society, the National

Table 11.1
The Evolution of Environmentalism, 1890–1990

	1890–1920	*1920–1960*	*1960–1980*	*1980–1990*
Scope of the issues	Preservation issues	Conservation issues	2d-generation issues	3d-generation issues
Dominant policy	Public health and efficient use of resources	Multiple use of resources	Pollution abatement	Pollution prevention
Patterns of participation	Elite dominated	Subgovernments	Pluralism	Advocacy coalitions
Level of action	National government	National government	National government	State and local governments
Dominant concern	Environmental science	Technology development	Economics and politics	Philosophy and environmental ethics
Techniques of power	Technical negotiations	Corporate pressure	Middle-class politics	Participatory democracy

Wildlife Federation, and the Izaak Walton League, to name a few. These groups were concerned with the conservation of natural resources, with particular emphasis on land resources, protection against despoilation, and the preservation of wildlife species (Ingram et al. 1995).

Early on, both preservationist and hunting and fishing groups emerged and were visible participants in the policy debates of the period. However, a vast gulf is apparent between the two categories of groups. Audubon and Sierra were minuscule in contrast to the mass membership sportsmen's clubs, but their members were unusually well connected to the nation's political and economic elites, so they exercised an influence far out of proportion to their size.

In Table 11.2, we see an approximation of the eras when particular types of groups appear. It provides some further evidence of the evolution of interest groups in this issue area.

A "second wave" developed during the 1960s and 1970s that was devoted to lobbying around such issues as air, water, and land pollution. These groups (e.g., Natural Resources Defense Council [NRDC], Greenpeace, Friends of the Earth, etc.) were inspired by the writings of such scholars as Rachel Carson, Barry Commoner, and Paul Ehrlich. The groups that were founded during this era were deliberately focused on using the political sys-

Table 11.2
New National Environmental Organizations, 1890–1990

Decade	Examples
1890s	Sierra Club (1892)
	American Scenic and Historic Preservation Society (1895)
1900s	National Audubon Society (1905)
	National Conservation Association (1909)
1910s	American Game Protective and Propagation Association (1911)
	Save the Redwoods League (1918)
1920s	Izaak Walton League (1922)
1930s	Wilderness Society (1935)
	National Wildlife Federation (1936)
1940s	Soil Conservation Society (1944)
1950s	Nature Conservancy (1951)
1960s	Environmental Defense Fund (1967)
	Friends of the Earth (1969)
1970s	Natural Resources Defense Council (1970)
	League of Conservation Voters (1972)
1980s	Earth First! (1981)
	Bat Conservation International (1982)
1990s	People of Color Leadership Summit on the Environment
	(network of local groups) (1991)

Note: This table is illustrative of the emergence of groups during particular eras rather than a precise count of the number of groups.

tem to advance environmental protection. They were also membership groups, relying on a broad base of members and donors to fund their advocacy, as well as soliciting larger grants from foundations. The universe of environmental groups has grown to encompass a vast range of organizations, from the sedate real estate brokers in the Nature Conservancy to the theatrical rhetoric of Earth First!

The "third wave" of environmental interest group activity occurred during the 1980s and the 1990s, and it included the growth and expansion of grassroots groups that were organized at the local or regional levels (Bosso 1992; Ingram et al. 1995). The defining characteristic of these groups is their bottom-up, decentralized nature, as opposed to the centralized structure of the large mainstream groups (Ingram et al. 1995). According to Goldsteen and Schorr (1991), these grassroots groups constitute a "new paradigm" in which communities no longer accept the assurances of elite officials but instead demand a voice in decisions that impact their environment.

The sheer size and diversity of the groups make characterizations of the content of "environmentalism" today difficult since new participants often carve out new niches rather than directly compete with older groups. Moreover, this variety also suggests an expansion of the issue area with established issues and groups coexisting with emerging groups and subjects. While there are definitely eras when new groups form, like the late 1960s, and other periods of few births, like the 1950s, there is not a direct correspondence between the cycles of government initiative and the formation of new environmental groups.

Even the focus of new groups may not match the new agenda of the government as the anomalous appearance of the Wilderness Society during the peak of the New Deal suggests (Table 11.2). It is worth noting, however, that scholars examining the impact of the environmental movement on policy have pointed to the late 1960s and early 1970s as the time when old and new environmentalists were able to break into the closed circles of policy making (Culhane 1981). This was also the time when there was an influx of new groups and a revitalization of existing organizations.

In Table 11.2, we see an approximation of the eras when particular types of groups appear. It provides some further evidence of the evolution of interest groups in this issue area.

The Interactions of Congress and the Environmental Movement

At first glance, Table 11.3, with its simple matching of environmental laws by decades, demonstrates the tremendous expansion in environmental legislation in recent decades. However, in the decades before the 1960s, there is a good deal of variation in congressional activity on the environment. Table 11.4 helps explain some of this variation by summarizing media attention to environmental topics over the same time periods. Using the *New York Times Index* as a surrogate for both media coverage of the issues and the movement, we join the mainstream of congressional observers by pointing to the attentiveness of the legislative branch to issues raised in the media. The pattern of media coverage and movement activity is often parallel, as with the 1905–1915 peak in news coverage coinciding with the height of the Progressive initiatives (for annual data, see Costain and Lester 1995). Unfortunately, the next cycles are perversely the opposite of the prediction. Media attention to environmental topics booms during the 1920s, as well the 1930s, and it grows even more rapidly during the 1950s when few groups were active and few laws were being passed. In the late 1960s and early 1970s, during the Nixon and Ford presidencies, an overlap is evident, with the greatest period of laws passed with news coverage of environmental topics.

Table 11.3
New National Laws for the Environment, 1890–1990

Decade	Number of Laws	Examples
1890s	4	Forest Reserve Act (1891) River and Harbor Act (1899)
1900s	2	Lacey Act (enforcing state hunting laws) (1900) Reclamation Act/Newlands Act (1902)
1910s	3	National Park Service Act (1916) Migratory Bird Treaty (1918)
1920s	5	Mineral Leasing Act (1920) Oil Pollution Control Act (1924)
1930s	7	Civilian Conservation Corps (CCC) Act; Tennessee Valley Authority (TVA) Act (1933) Taylor Grazing Act (1934)
1940s	1	Federal Water Pollution Control Act (1948)
1950s	1	Water Pollution Control Act (1956)
1960s	7	Multiple Use Sustained Yield Act (1960) Wilderness Act (1964)
1970s	17	National Environmental Policy Act (NEPA) (1969) Clean Air Act and Amendments (1970, 1977)
1980s	12	CERCLA (Superfund) (1980, 1986) Clean Water Act Amendments (1987)
1990s	NA	Clean Air Act Amendments (1990) California Desert Protection Act (1994)

Source: Compiled from a variety of sources, especially Nash (1990: xi–xix).

Although we did not analyze the substance of the news stories in the *Index*, we did not find the disappearance of old subjects as new ones emerge. Instead, topics such as hunting and forestry continue to be covered, but other subjects such as air pollution get much more space.

The simple measure of space allotted to each subject also constrains our analysis. Certainly the increased complexity of the once narrow issue area and its scrutiny by the media are obvious. Since journalists often define news worth covering in terms of conflict and controversy, it is not surprising that the eras of policy change, such as the early 1970s, are also extensively fol-

Table 11.4
New York Times Index, Space on Environmental Topics, 1890–1990

Decade	Average Column Inches per Year*
1890s	3.1
1900s	13.5
1910s	12.6
1920s	36.5
1930s	42.9
1940s	40.1
1950s	110.3
1960s	284.5
1970s	944.7
1980s	688.9

*Inches are standardized to reflect varying type fonts and column widths.

lowed by the *Times.* Events external to the policy subsystem are key impetuses to policy change and media attention transmits, as well as creates, such external pressure. Increased media coverage in the otherwise tranquil 1950s may have been the harbinger of the policy innovations of the early 1970s. The longer time series allows us to see the gradual building of concern a decade *before* the explosion of activity in the late 1960s.

We do not find the parallel cycles of movement and government activity that some predict. The New Deal era does show an upsurge in new laws as expected, but even more legislative activity takes place in the supposedly quiet late 1970s and 1980s. Moreover, it is equally difficult to argue that the *substance* or content of recent laws are minor or less significant than those passed in times presided over by activist Congresses. Supporters and critics alike concur that the environmental laws passed in the 1970s and 1980s are of unprecedented scope and impact on the nation. (Whether these expensive actions are effective in addressing their problem area is another question.)

The early emphasis on laws regulating public lands and hunting and fishing has given way to a much broader array of antipollution and preservationist legislation in recent decades. At the same time, there is a historic continuity between the wilderness and endangered species laws of the 1970s and 1980s and the forest reserves and wildlife refuge laws ninety years earlier.

The "zigs and zags" of policy are obvious in the analysis of who benefits from the dominant thrust of the laws. The single unambiguous trend is away from unlimited private consumptive uses of "public goods," whether they are national forests or air. Debate persists as to which social groups benefit and lose from this redistribution, with conservatives arguing that upper-class environmental activists are winners and the poor are losers. Clearly the number and composition of the "advocacy coalitions" at work in this policy arena have grown over the decades. Evidence also indicates the impact of external events on the policies, namely, the arrival of two waves of social movements, the progressive and the environmental. In addition, the impact of the New Deal and its stimulus, the Depression, on these policies is evident.

Much more difficult to measure is the impact of Congress on the movement. Indeed, it is often radical critics of mainstream environmentalism who provide evidence of the changes within the interest groups at the center of the movement. Critics such as Dave Foreman (*Confessions of an Eco-Warrior*, 1991) and Mark Dowie (*Losing Ground*, 1995) catalog numerous examples of the largest ("Big 10") groups compromising with their industry opponents to get a bill out of committee or paying top salaries to lobbyists while neglecting their grassroots allies. Such co-optation may be seen as "selling out" by some or as signs of a maturing movement's becoming part of the mainstream of American politics. This type of internal debate and criticism may be evidence of the continuity of the vitality of the environmental movement. At the core of social movements is a demand for fundamental social change, and the continuity of this pressure from committed activists shows that environmentalism remains more than the sum of its interest groups. Radicals within the largest groups such as Greenpeace and the Sierra Club frequently challenge their leaders to live up to a set of values and goals that are not measured simply by laws passed or EPA appropriations. These critics and their more numerous grassroots colleagues provide a constant reminder of the movement that these groups represent.

Conclusions and Implications

From this brief overview of the environmental movement, we see how the environmental movement has steadily broadened its base of support over the past hundred years from 1890 to 1990. Specifically, it has moved from being largely an elitist concern, involving scientific and government experts, to one with broad-based support including middle-class and even working-class supporters. This broader base of public support has been joined by national environmental groups, ranging from the National Wildlife Federation to the Sierra Club, NRDC, Friends of the Earth, Greenpeace, and Earth First!

This tendency toward "opening up" this issue toward greater and more representative participation is also illustrated by the formulation or implementation of environmental policy. Initially, scholars stressed "subgovernments" as a major explanation for environmental policy making (Foss 1960). More recently, the literature suggests that "advocacy coalitions," composed of interests from all three levels of government and the private sector, are now involved in environmental policy making (Sabatier and Jenkins-Smith 1988; 1993). Clearly, this development suggests a change in the scope of citizen involvement over the past hundred years.

A number of other changes in the nature of environmental policy and politics have occurred over just the past thirty years. For example, how we evaluate the severity of the environmental problem has changed. Specifically, we have evolved from a primary concern over "natural resource issues" to "environmental issues"—or from first-generation problems (e.g., public lands, irrigation, water rights, park management), to second-generation problems (e.g., toxic waste, groundwater protection, air pollution), to third-generation problems (e.g., global warming, thinning of the ozone layer, tropical deforestation, acid rain). Along with this change, we have shifted our concern from purely localized issues involving air and water pollution in communities to the realization that an effective response to these second- and third-generation problems "requires diverse actions by individuals and institutions at all levels of society" (Vig and Kraft 1990: 4).

Moreover, the nature of public opinion on this topic has changed dramatically over the past thirty years. Initially, public opinion in the late 1960s and early 1970s reached a high level of support, but it was judged to be "soft support," meaning that it would dissolve in the face of concerns over economic development (or jobs over the environment). In the late 1980s, on the other hand, public opinion was said to be both strong and salient (Mitchell 1990; Dunlap 1989). The American public indicates in the 1990s that it wants stringent environmental protection regulations and is willing to pay for it in new taxes.

Finally, we have witnessed the growing involvement of states and cities and grassroots organizations in environmental management (John 1994; Lowry 1992; Ringquist 1993; Ingram, Colnic, and Mann 1995). With the advent of "New Federalism" in the 1970s and 1980s, states and communities are increasingly being asked to assume more of the environmental responsibilities that were previously handled by the federal government. Yet it is also clear that not all the states are able to muster the economic and institutional wherewithal to meet their new responsibilities (Lester 1986; Davis and Lester 1987; Lowry 1992; Ringquist 1993). Indeed, the states vary greatly in terms of their capacities to assume environmental management in the 1990s.

We may derive several implications from this discussion. First, if the present trend continues, then the next century should be characterized by significantly increased levels of citizen activism or "strong democracy" in the environmental movement. It is likely to be a new era in environmentalism in which we significantly change the nature of our approach to environmental protection by moving toward "postenvironmentalism," as described by John Young (1990) and others. Increasingly, localism will likely characterize environmentalism as salons, "study circles," neighborhood groups, and state- and citywide organizations become even more important in affecting the direction and scope of environmental protection (Dryzek 1989; Lester and Castensson 1990; John 1994).

The environmental movement is increasingly a global one as new local groups join the ranks of national and international organizations (Nagehaudhuri and Bhatt 1987; McCormick 1989; Caldwell 1984). Many domestic and global groups, such as Greenpeace, have begun to mobilize Third World natives *against* their own governments' development projects. Thus, we have witnessed the development of "cross-level and cross-national" grassroots environmental movements in the last twenty years.

Finally, our argument is that the patterns described here over the past hundred years suggest an expansion of the environmental movement from elitism to participatory democracy. While the contemporary situation does not embody all the elements of "strong democracy," as described by Barber (1984), it does nevertheless suggest an evolution over time toward that end.

It is within this larger context, then, that the interplay between Congress and the environmental movement is played out. As the movement's focus shifts away from Congress and toward state and local governments, it will become increasingly difficult to justify spending priorities that emphasize Washington lobbying. National groups may find themselves increasingly used as expert sources and as resources by local ad hoc citizen-activists. While this trend may suggest a diminution of the role currently played by Congress and national ecology groups, it seems that the globalization of environmental issues may actually counteract this result. The enhancement of the role of Congress in foreign affairs in the wake of the end of the Cold War is likely to intensify the debates in Congress over the export of U.S. environmental standards and values abroad. With the president no longer the predominant actor in setting U.S. global priorities, the investment made by environmental groups in lobbying Congress may yet be justified if they can be important in shaping a wide range of global policies.

Notes

1. Not all scholars are in agreement about the exact dates for these movements. These dates are acceptable as benchmarks for each movement.

Part 5

Social Movements in Court

12

Social Movements and the Mobilization of Law

Michael W. McCann

Much recent scholarship has contributed to our understanding of how law matters for social movements in U.S. history. Two rather different intellectual traditions have proved most directly relevant to the topic. Legal scholars have provided multiple insights about both the ways that prevailing legal norms tend to legitimate social hierarchies and the limited impacts of liberal judicial actions in challenging those hierarchies. Most such studies have focused on test case litigation in appellate courts, however, rather than on the wide variety of other legal claims, tactics, and practices of movement actors. Social movement scholars, by contrast, have documented many case studies in which legal advocacy figured prominently, but they have provided little direct conceptual analysis about how law did or did not matter for the struggles at stake. And, overall, little effort has been made to connect these two disparate traditions of analysis.

This essay will briefly outline such a synthetic approach to understanding how law matters for social movements. My general "legal mobilization" framework merges a dispute-oriented approach to understanding legal practice with insights from "political process"-based social movement theorizing about collective action.

A Legal Mobilization Framework[1]

Most fundamentally, the legal mobilization framework outlined here emphasizes the value of beginning analysis not with official legal texts or institutions, as does most conventional legal scholarship, but with the wide variety of legally oriented practices and understandings generated among movement participants engaged in social struggle. That is, my approach adopts a "decentered" view of how law becomes meaningful through the practical material activity of citizens struggling for social change (Harrington and Yngvesson 1991; Brigham 1988; McCann 1994).

Such an approach stresses that law is inherently plural in its practical manifestations and hence becomes meaningful in varying forms and ways. It is useful to recall in this regard the distinctions urged by E. P. Thompson (1975:260)—a pioneering movement scholar who wrote brilliantly about legal relations—between law as (1) *institutions* (courts, etc.), (2) *personnel* (lawyers, judges, etc.), and (3) *ideology*. While the first two manifestations of law emphasize the "official," often alien side of law, the emphasis on legal ideology (legal ideas and knowledge) identifies relatively autonomous modes of legal "power" that infuse and inform social interaction at multiple levels and in various degrees. The relative weight of specific legal norms *in* society is, of course, influenced by and loosely bound to official state practices (in courts, etc.). Yet, legal practices are more indeterminate, mutable, and pluralistic than recognized by formalist legal models (see Merry 1990; Ewick and Silbey 1992).

An important corollary of this point is that the indirect and "radiating" symbolic effects of official legal actions (e.g., by courts) often are far more important than their direct, command-oriented effects (see Handler 1978; Galanter 1983; McCann 1993, 1994). As Galanter (1983: 127) has argued, law should be understood broadly "as a system of cultural and symbolic meanings (more) than as a set of operative controls. It affects us primarily through communication of symbols—by providing threats, promises, models, persuasion, legitimacy, stigma, and so on." Evaluations of how reform litigation and other institutional activities matter thus require accounting for the variable ways that differently situated groups interpret and act on legal signals sent by officials over time (Brigham 1987; Galanter 1983).[2]

Just as the legal mobilization approach emphasizes the complex multiplicity of legal norms, it also highlights their contingency and interdependence with other social factors in shaping political struggle (Merry 1988). Both the content and relative power of legal meanings always vary among citizens as they are diversely and unequally located in specific institutional settings. It likewise follows that legal norms, conventions, and tactical practices also differ in significance over time. We might expect that particular legal strategies or institutional ploys become more significant at some points of struggle than at others.

This points to the further assumption that law (the aggregate of legal conventions) can at once *both* empower and disempower variously situated social groups in different types of relations. Legal "cultures provide symbols which can be manipulated by their members for strategic goals," notes sociologist Sally Engle Merry, "but they also establish constraints on that manipulation" (1985: 60). As such, legal norms, in general, may tend to sustain hegemonic hierarchies, as critical legal scholars contend, but they also can provide sources of challenge and change within particular institutional terrains (Hunt 1990; Scheingold 1989; McCann 1994). The key question is not *whether* legal conventions limit the potential for social resistance and transformation. Of course they do. The more important but difficult analytical task is to determine how and to what degree groups can work within and through these legal traditions to advance their causes. The social movement approach urged here specifies two levels at which legal power can be relevant to action—first, in shaping the overall "structure of opportunities" and constraints facing movements, and; second, in the various legal resources available to different parties struggling for position.

And this, finally, underlines the fact that law should not be considered as external to, or simply imposed on, citizens (Thompson 1975). The conflict-centered, political process approach assumes that movements, from the start, typically are embedded within a (more or less) legally constituted environment rather than developing outside law. It follows that activists themselves should be viewed as discrete (but unequally situated) legal *actors* rather than merely as consumers and recipients of law handed down from above (see Brigham 1987; McCann 1993). Scholars thus must be attuned to how legal norms play a role in shaping and expressing the terms of resistance, aspiration, and tactical struggle for institutional transformation. We must, in de Certeau's words, analyze law's "manipulation by users who are not its makers" (1984: xiii). As such, the dynamics of "legal consciousness" require attention in any assessment of how law matters for social movements (Ewick and Silbey 1992; Sarat 1990; McCann 1994).

All in all, the approach outlined here alerts us to the many ambiguous, shifting, complex ways in which legal norms and institutions can become manifest in social struggles. With these general premises in mind, we now turn to a more focused theoretical and empirical inquiry regarding actual social movement experiences with law. The following sections will be organized according to several levels or phases of social movement conflict at which law's power often is manifest.

Law and the Formation of Movements

Perhaps the most significant point at which law has mattered for social movements in the United States is during the earliest phases of organizational and agenda formation. Stuart Scheingold's well-known argument regarding the "politics of rights" provides a useful starting point for the discussion. As he puts it, it is possible for marginalized groups "to capitalize on the perceptions of entitlement associated with (legal) rights to initiate and to nurture political mobilization" (1974: 131; see also Handler 1978; Olson 1984; Milner 1986). This process can be understood to involve two separate, if often intimately related, dimensions of cognitive transformation in movement constituents.

The first of these entails the process of agenda building by which movement actors *draw on legal discourses to "name" and to challenge* existing
social wrongs or injustices. As such, legal norms can become important
elements in the process of forging a sense of collective aspiration and identity among diversely situated citizens. Elizabeth Schneider's provocative argument regarding the "Dialectic of Rights and Politics" in the evolving
women's movement provides some very useful insights into the logic of this
process. Schneider's (1986:550) primary argument is that the practice of
rights advocacy by feminist activists has been a self-generating process that
has "energized the women's movement" over time. Emphasizing that rights
advocacy is a dynamic, interactive process, she outlines how new rights
claims by women have developed from the tensions between past gains and
newly perceived challenges, and between the personal empowerment experienced by a politicized few and the still disempowered many available for
movement mobilization. As she describes it, "the assertion or 'experience'
of rights can express political vision, affirm a group's humanity, . . . and
assist in the collective political development of a social or political movement, particularly at its early stages" (590). Such movement building around
particular rights claims can emerge in a variety of ways, including: by exploiting the conflict between already settled rights claims and practices vio-
lating those rights, by identifying implicit contradictions within settled
discursive logics of rights, or by developing logical extensions or new practical applications of settled rights claims (Schneider 1986).

Social movement scholars likewise have provided much evidence for the
role of legal norms in framing movement demands, articulating a general
"causal story" about existing relations, developing a larger sense of purpose
over time, and hence forging a common group identity (see Stone 1989;
Snow and Benford 1988). Perhaps nowhere was this process more striking
than in the civil rights movement. Leading sociological interpreters have
explored at length how legal norms both framed movement demands and
shaped movement identity over time (McAdam 1982; Morris 1984; Tushnet
1987). Legal conventions shaped evolving demands in similar ways for the
early American labor movement (Forbath 1991; Tomlins 1985), the women's
movement (Costain 1992; McGlen and O'Connor 1983), the welfare rights
movement (Piven and Cloward 1979), the animal rights movement (Silverstein 1996), and the gay and lesbian rights movements. Although always a
matter of struggle, legal norms, discourses, and practices in each case were
an important constitutive element of evolving movement understandings,
aspirations, and strategic action.

A second related way in which legal practices can contribute to movement building is by *shaping the overall "opportunity structure"* within
which movements develop. As noted earlier, most scholars agree that movement formation and action is more likely in periods when dominant groups

and relationships are perceived as vulnerable to challenge (Piven and Cloward 1979; McAdam 1982). Advances through formal legal action—and especially by high-profile litigation—many times have contributed to this sense of vulnerability among both state and nonstate authorities. In particular, judicial victories can impart salience or "legitimacy" to general categories of claims (e.g., antidiscrimination rights) as well as to specific formulations of challenges within these broad legal traditions. Indeed, many scholars have noted a sort of "contagion effect" generated by rights litigation over the last forty years in the United States (see Tarrow 1983). As Epp (1990: 150) has argued, "rights consciousness develops in conjunction with the development and clarity of legally enforceable rights" sanctioned by officials.

The movement-centered approach urged here tends to interpret this latter aspect of legal "consciousness raising" somewhat differently than many characterizations by legal scholars. Judicial victories (or other legal actions) do not "reveal" injustice to oppressed groups so much as improve the chances that such injustices might be effectively challenged by movement action in and out of the courts (McCann 1994). Moreover, formal legal action alone rarely is likely to generate this "catalytic" or "triggering" effect on movement constituents (Rosenberg 1991). Only when concerted efforts are made by movement leaders and organizations to publicize such evolving opportunities and to use legal resources for movement-building purposes is successful organizing likely (McCann 1994).

It is important to emphasize, furthermore, that these two dimensions of legal catalysis are often interrelated in social movement development. For example, formal legal actions (litigation) can work initially to expose systemic vulnerabilities and to render legal claims more "sensible" or salient. As long as marginalized groups act on these opportunities, they often gain sophistication and confidence in their capacity to mobilize legal conventions to "name" wrongs, frame demands, and advance their cause. Piven and Cloward (1979) recognize this in their classic discussion of consciousness raising in protest politics. When citizens "begin to assert their 'rights' that imply demands for change," there often develops "a new sense of efficacy; people who ordinarily consider themselves helpless come to believe that they have some capacity to alter their lot" (see also McAdam 1982).

This complex process of legal catalysis was again well evidenced in the civil rights movement. As sociologist Aldon Morris (1984) analyzes it, the legacy of cases leading up to *Brown v. Board of Education* was vital to the evolving civil rights movement in two ways. First, it sparked southern blacks' hopes by "demonstrating that the Southern white power structure was vulnerable at some points" and providing scarce practical resources for defiant action (1984: 34, also at 30).

Second, the increasing "pressure on the Southern white power structure

to abolish racial domination" led to a massive, highly visible attack—
including legal assaults as well as physical violence—on the NAACP. These
reactions in turn forced a split between local, church-affiliated NAACP leaders urging more radical forms of protest action and the more bureaucratic,
legally oriented national organization. The result was a swell in both the
momentum of the grassroots protest campaign among southern blacks generally and their frustration about the efficacy of legal tactics alone. "The two
approaches—legal action and mass protest—entered into a turbulent but
workable marriage" (Morris 1984: 39, also at 26). Moreover, it was the
resulting escalation of conflicts between whites and blacks on both fronts
that "expanded the scope" of the dispute to include Washington officials,
federal courts, the northern media, and national public opinion (McAdam
1982). Court decisions thus did not unilaterally "cause," by moral inspira-
tion, defiant black grassroots action or, by coercion, federal support for the
civil rights agenda (see Rosenberg 1991). But legal tactics pioneered by the
NAACP figured prominently in elevating civil "rights" claims and intensify-
ing the initial terms of racial struggle in the South. As Morris (1984: 26, also
at 81) counsels, "It would be misleading to present the courtroom battles in
a narrowly legal light."[3]

Similar dynamics have been evident in the movements for the rights of
the disabled (Olson 1984), animal rights (Silverstein 1992), and gender-
based wage equity (McCann 1994). These examples are especially interesting because they demonstrate that conclusive, far-reaching judicial victories
are not necessary to achieve this legal catalyzing effect. The wage equity
issue, for example, largely developed in response to the limitations of traditional court-approved affirmative action policies for remedying discrimination against women workers locked into segregated jobs. After a string of
defeats in the 1970s, the wage equity movement won a small advance in
wage discrimination law at the Supreme Court level and one pathbreaking
lower court ruling, which later was overturned on appeal. But, in the five-
year interim between the first and the last of these three rulings, movement
leaders effectively used successful legal actions—despite their doctrinal limitations—to organize women workers in hundreds of workplaces around the
nation. A massive publicity campaign focusing on court victories initially
put the issue on the national agenda and alerted leaders that wage equity was
"the working women's issue of the 1980s." Lawsuits were then filed on
behalf of working women as the centerpiece of a successful union and movement organizing strategy in scores of public and private venues. Again, the
evidence suggests not that court decisions worked to "enlighten" working
women about their subordination, as sometimes is claimed. Rather, sustained
legal action over time worked to render employers vulnerable to challenge,
to expand the resources available to working women, to provide them a

unifying claim of egalitarian rights, and to increase both their confidence and sophistication in advancing those claims.

In the same way, of course, legal norms and official rulings can discourage action or narrow tactical options and opportunities. What law sometimes provides in terms of expanding opportunities also can be withdrawn. In this way, potential political challenges may be preempted and deterred before they are even taken seriously by aggrieved groups.

Legal Mobilization as Political Pressure

Law as a Symbolic Club

Another general way in which law and legal advocacy often matters to social reform movement activity is as a source of leverage against recalcitrant opponents. This leveraging role is closely related to—indeed, it is the flip side of—law's catalytic contributions to movement building. Just as legal rights advocacy can "pull" in strong affirmative support for reform goals from various groups, so can it be employed as a weapon to "push" otherwise uncooperative foes into making concessions or compromises. As in movement-building efforts, this second dimension of legal mobilization usually entails some measure of litigation or other formal legal action. Nevertheless, triumph in the courts is not necessarily pivotal to either short- or long-term successful legal leveraging. Again, this is because judicial actions typically are less significant in their singular, command-oriented aspects than in their indirect interaction with other political tactics such lobbying, negotiations, or mass demonstrations.

In some respects, this is hardly a pathbreaking insight. The uses of legal tactics and threats to compel informal resolution of everyday "private" disputes regarding divorce settlement, contractual obligations, liability for property damages, and the like are familiar and well documented (see Mnookin and Kornhauser 1979). However, the dialectical relationship of formal and informal legal action in social reform politics has generally received less scholarly attention (but see Handler 1978; Olson 1984; McCann 1994).

Litigation often offers formidable tactical leverage for social movements in several ways. For one thing, organizations targeted by reformers often are well aware that litigation can impose substantial transaction costs in terms of both direct expenditures and long-term financial burdens. Indeed, court costs in major public disputes—over race and gender discrimination, unsafe workplaces, or environmental damage, for example—often run in the millions of dollars and can tie up economically vital operations for years. More important, powerful public and private interests typically fear losing control of decision-making autonomy—whether concerning capital investment, wage policy, externalized costs, or the like—to outside parties such as judges, and they hence have a stake in cutting potential losses by negotiated settlements of conflicts with movements (see Handler 1978).

Finally, the symbolic normative power of rights claims themselves should not be discounted. This point links Scheingold's (1974) "myth of rights" and "politics of rights" analysis. Because citizens in our society are responsive to (legally sensible) rights claims, defiant groups often can mobilize legal norms, conventions, and demands to compel concessions even in the absence of clear judicial (or other official) support. This power of legal discourse has several related and indistinguishable dimensions, including: abstract appeals to the moral sensibilities of dominant groups; more concrete appeals to the interests of dominant organizations in maintaining cooperative relations with victimized groups, such as workers or consumers; and, perhaps, most important, indirect appeals for moral censure from the general public regarding the actions of specific powerful groups. The latter factor of stigmatizing publicity distinguishes somewhat the potential impact of legal action in high-visibility social struggles from that in everyday disputes. Formal legal actions by movements threaten to transform disputes by mobilizing not just judges as third-party intervenors but also a variety of social advocacy groups, nonjudicial state officials, and broader public sentiment or voting power through the catalytic dynamic discussed in the last section. In other words, litigation often provides a powerful means for, in Schattschneider's (1960) terms, "expanding the scope of conflict" in ways that enhance the bargaining power of disadvantaged groups and raise the perceived risks of hard line opposition from their foes.[4]

The implicit promise at stake here is that political struggles may advance more quickly, cheaply, and effectively when conducted in the "shadow" of favorable legal norms and threats of judicial intervention. Such legal gambits are hardly costless guarantees of success for social reformers, of course. Initiating legal action often does not generate concessions from powerful opponents and thus may commit movement supporters to long, costly, high-risk legal proceedings that they can afford far less than can their institutional foes. Even more important, eventual defeat in court can sap movement morale, undercut its bargaining power, and exhaust its resources. Consequently, legal leveraging is most successful when it works as an unfulfilled threat, but activists must be willing to follow through occasionally with action or lose considerable clout. In any case, the symbolic manifestations of law, as both a source of moral right and threat of potential outside intervention, imbue rights discourse with its most fundamental social power.

One final general point is relevant here. I have chosen to emphasize in this essay how the leveraging power of law sometimes can be deployed directly in efforts to "transform" existing relations (i.e., to amplify worker power, to challenge racial and gender hierarchies, to redistribute wealth, to compel environmentally responsible action, etc.). At the same time, however, we should not forget the important secondary ways that legal leveraging tactics often are employed to "defend" advocates of change from overt repression by dominant groups and state officials. On this front, I refer especially to the crucial battles for protection of both radical advocacy, including protest and acts of civil disobedience, as constitutionally privileged political speech and also for procedural rights of those radicals whose actions have been deemed "criminal" or otherwise punishable by authorities. While such protections have proved highly fragile in moments of dramatic social struggle, legal claims of basic rights surely have helped to expand some social space for radical challenge by workers, people of color, women, gays and lesbians, peace activists, and others (see Kairys 1990). Revolution in our own streets as well as those around the world surely have often been aided, although hardly secured, by claims of conventional liberal legal rights by dissident citizens.

The deployment of legal resources to pressure-dominant groups often takes place at several different, if often continuous, stages of movement struggles. Movement experiences with leveraging action at two of the general stages demarcated earlier will be briefly discussed.

Compelling Policy Concessions

One general affirmative use of legal leveraging by many movements has been to "get on the public agenda" recognized by dominant groups. That is, legal tactics often have proved useful in forcing attention to movement demands and compelling at least some general policy concessions from state officials or other powerful actors.

Silverstein (1996) has demonstrated how this tactic has generated some relatively important advances by the animal rights movement in recent years. In a variety of instances, she illustrates, litigation has been used to dramatize abuses of animals, embarrass particular institutional actors, and to win favorable media attention. When carefully coordinated with demonstrations, "pranks," and other media events, high-profile litigation worked as a double-barrelled threat—at once mobilizing public opinion against targeted "abusers" and threatening both costly legal proceedings and possible defeats in court. Overall, such legal tactics have proved to be one of the movement's most effective modes of forcing accommodation by state and nonstate authorities alike. My own study of gender-based pay equity revealed a similar dynamic (McCann 1994). Pay equity activists repeatedly used litigation not only to mobilize women workers but also to pressure employers indirectly by both branding them as "discriminators" in the public eye and by posing the risk that judges might impose new wage structures on them. In dozens of cases, legal tactics worked to draw attention to the issue, break collective bargaining or legislative deadlocks on wage policies, and secure wage advances for workers in female-intensive occupations.

Both of these studies confirm some often overlooked aspects of legal leveraging tactics. First, they illustrate again that repeated clear victories in court are not necessary to effective legal mobilization. In neither movement did lawsuits generate appellate decisions directly authorizing much of the new rights and remedies that activists sought. However, the ability at least to win some small advances on related issues and to win standing for major claims posed enough actual costs (bad publicity, legal fees) and potential risks (of judicially imposed policies) to pressure opponents into making significant concessions. Second, legal tactics again were useful primarily only in concert with other tactics, such as demonstrations, legislative lobbying, collective bargaining, and media mobilization. The fact that legal norms and institutional maneuvers constituted only one dimension of movement strategy complicates evaluation of their independent contributions, to be sure. However, in each movement, both activists and specific case histories confirmed the importance of such contingent, ancillary legal actions.

The legacy of the civil rights movement represents an even more complex example of such dynamics. On the one hand, Supreme Court rulings outlawing public segregation in the 1950s mostly generated hostility or apathy in the South. Direct compliance with the courts was very low (see Rosenberg 1991). On the other hand, much evidence suggests that *Brown* and other decisions helped to force growing federal intervention by escalating volatile confrontations, catalyzing northern public opinion, and bolstering the resolve needed for action among key federal officials. Judicial action alone did not determine these outcomes, of course; increasing demonstrations and white violence were probably even more important. Yet most social movement scholars have not discounted the importance of legal actions for the evolving struggle (see Morris 1984; McAdam 1982). Rather, the civil rights movement represents a classic case of how "law and disorder" can be joined in social movement strategies for change (Lowi 1971).

Important examples where legal tactics either failed to generate or even impeded progressive change are notable as well, however. The abortion case arguably offers a revealing example. While feminists won support for women's "right to choose" in *Roe v. Wade*, the provision of both medical services and financial aid to pay for exercising those rights did not materialize to any great degree. What is more, *Roe* generated a significant conservative countermovement bent on denying, or at least substantially restricting, the capacity of women to choose the abortion option (Rosenberg 1991). Finally, the "privacy" logic adopted to secure women's rights occluded key issues of power at stake and undercut prospects for winning state financial aid to low-income women (Copelon 1988). In short, legal tactics not only failed to leverage real change; they arguably undermined the potential for change that alternative tactics (legislation, grassroots organizing) might have produced.[5]

Backlashes against both race- and sex-based affirmative action policies authorized by the courts likewise have rendered mixed, at best, those efforts at leveraging social change in recent decades. Other cases are even more subtle. For example, litigation by Northwest Indian tribes seemingly won major policy victories over the predominantly white fishing industry in the 1970s. However, several studies demonstrate that Native Americans were forced to frame their claims in legal terms of property rights that both obscured the larger resource planning issues at the heart of the debate and ended up exacerbating inequalities of private wealth among the indigenous peoples themselves (Bruun 1982; Anderson 1987). The net result, so to speak, was hardly an improvement at all.

Finally, it is worth noting that legal leveraging tactics by opponents can significantly undermine and even destroy social movements. The successful mobilization of courts by business interests beginning in the late nineteenth century, for example, significantly throttled both the populist and radical labor movements. Court alliance with conservatives not only took away legal resources from "the common people," but it invited overt repression, sanctioned violence, and advantaged moderate wings of both movements that urged accepting the hierarchical terms of emerging corporate relations (Westin 1954; Forbath 1991; Goodwyn 1979). This history affirms the fact that legal leveraging tactics, like law generally, have been mobilized as resources by opponents more often and more effectively than by advocates of egalitarian change (Scheingold 1989). Not the least of the factors at stake in any particular historical moment are the reigning ideological propensities and partisan allegiances of judges on the bench. While judicial support hardly assures movement advances, hostility from the courts surely can, and often does, contain reformers on many fronts.

Policy Development and Implementation

Legal leveraging often figures prominently at the policy development and implementation stages as well. Somewhat surprisingly, however, both social movement scholars and legal scholars have provided only limited insights about these dynamics. In most scholarly portrayals, social movements—which usually are defined by disruptive tactics of mass organization, public protest, and the like—give way to more conventional hierarchical organizations and interest groups that then carry on bureaucratic battles for final policy formulation, execution, and enforcement (Piven and Cloward 1979; Tarrow 1983). By definition, implementation politics is nonradical, "nonmovement" activity. Such a romance with "mass action" strikes me as narrow and misguided, however, because it is precisely during these phases of struggle that the social ramifications of official policy changes often are most determined (Lowi 1979).

Legal scholars, by contrast, often do focus much attention on implementation politics, but only to show that legal tactics are relatively limited in impact. The most common explanation for this tendency is that courts lack the independence and resources to enforce their decisions on recalcitrant groups in government and society alike (Rosenberg 1991; Handler 1978). While largely valid in itself, such a focus once again ignores the degree to which legal norms and tactics can matter even in the absence of judicial enforcement action and simple citizen compliance (see Brigham 1987). Focusing on courts rather than on movement politics provides a truncated understanding of how the "shadow" of law and legal tactics matter at implementation as well as at other phases of struggle (McCann 1993).

Nevertheless, many studies in both traditions have provided some useful insights into how law matters for policy implementation battles. In particular, a host of empirical inquiries document how legal tactics—and especially actual or threatened litigation—can help movement activists to win voice, position, and influence in the process of reform policy implementation, whether sanctioned by state or nonstate authorities. These include policy areas regarding the environment (Sax 1971; Melnick 1983; McCann 1986), gender (Blum 1991; Gelb and Palley 1982), race discrimination (Burstein and Monaghan 1986), and the rights of the disabled (Olson 1984), among others (Lowi 1979; Handler 1978). Indeed, the continuing salience of such public policy issues itself stems in large part from their definition as legal "injuries" or "wrongs."

Legal advocacy can be especially important to one specific aim of many "outsider" groups—that of "formalizing" policy formulation and implementation processes. Formality, as understood here, refers to the degree to which relations are conducted according to procedures and standards that are public, general, positive, and uniform (Lowi 1979). The key supposition is that dominant groups tend to prefer relatively insular modes of highly discretionary policy implementation unhampered by standardized procedures, substantive guidelines, high visibility, and outside supervision. In such informal settings, established prerogatives of prevailing elites can more easily prevail to minimize costs, maintain control, and protect their own privileges, while granting empty symbolic gestures to challengers. By contrast, marginalized groups usually benefit from more formalized processes in which codified procedural rights and substantive standards can be employed to restrict the discretion of dominant interests that control the bulk of material and organizational resources (Lowi 1979; McCann 1994).

Social movement groups often use litigation specifically to create such institutional access as well as to apply pressure to make that access consequential. In this way, legal resources often provide a series of more refined tools—a template of procedures, standards, and practices—along with blunt leveraging tactics for shaping the "structure" of ongoing administrative relations at the "remedial" stage of struggles over policy (see Galanter 1983). For example, charges of unfair labor practices, reliance on arbitration and grievance mechanisms, and other related actions have constituted a routine strategy for labor radicals in the post-New Deal era (Fantasia 1988). This tactic also comprised the primary agenda of liberal public interest (environmental, consumer, good government) groups that, in the 1970s, tried to open up the administrative state to greater democratic participation (McCann 1986; McCann and Silverstein 1993). Similar efforts likewise defined one of the primary tactics of gender-based pay equity reformers seeking to prevent employer cooptation of wage restructuring implementation (McCann 1994).

One final example is noteworthy. Sociologist Lauren Edelman (1990) has demonstrated how employers routinely established in-house offices to avoid litigation and to maintain an appearance of good-faith compliance with race-based affirmative action principles in the 1970s. Though established for largely deceptive or defensive purposes, however, such offices (in alliance with minority groups) mobilized antidiscrimination norms and the specter of litigation to force "real" changes from within many corporate and state institutions.

Of course, as judicial impact studies suggest, legal leveraging often offers as little to reformers in policy implementation battles as at earlier stages of struggle (Handler 1978). The fact that judges shrink from cases requiring great technical knowledge and experience may make legal leveraging tactics less effective generally. Moreover, openly hostile courts often greatly undercut opportunities and deny resources in ways that actually disempower movement actors in the policy process. And, again, even where courts weigh in favorably for disadvantaged groups, injustice in most institutional settings will go unchallenged in the absence of well-organized constituencies willing to mobilize legal resources for change. Indeed, apparent advances in official law may even add insult to injury for marginalized citizens lacking organizational resources (Bumiller 1988). In short, law often does not help reformers and may constitute a considerable constraint on reform action. Understanding these variations requires analysis of law's workings within the larger web of social relations where struggle occurs.

The Legacy of Law in/for Struggle

Perhaps the least fully explored aspect of social movement politics concerns, finally, the *legacy* of particular struggles. Many movement scholars and legal scholars, we have seen, work from the assumption that movements tend to follow a linear pattern of development and have finite life histories (Tarrow 1983; McAdam 1982). That is, they rise, peak, and then fade into oblivion, leaving perhaps only a highly coopted residue of interest group representation in their place. But other scholars have challenged this scenario. Taylor's (1989) provocative analysis of the women's movement, for example, suggests that indigenous associations forming the core of social movements may recede from public struggle for periods of time, but they often continue quietly to thrive over time, only to resurface as opportunities arise for defiant action at later dates. In short, movement associations do not live and die so much as alternately howl and hibernate according to changes in the larger political climate.

This insight suggests the need for a complex assessment of social movement dynamics. Rather than focus merely on whether movements succeed or fail with regard to their primary short-term policy aims, we need also to assess how those struggles affect movement constituents and their relations with dominant groups over the long haul. Did a specific movement struggle pass quietly, leaving basic relations with dominant groups virtually intact? Or did struggles escalate, shift to new fronts, and fundamentally alter social relations in a variety of empowering ways for movement constituents? Or did the movement retreat, only to recharge and reemerge again in powerful form at a later date? In sum, has the movement been contained or expanded over time?

We need to assess the changing character of law's constitutive power in different social terrains. Social movement theory suggests three ways in which the legal dynamics of power relations can change through ongoing struggle. First, we might ask whether movement efforts altered the *legal (or rights) consciousness* of constituents and other publics. That is, have understandings, expectations, and ideological solidarity of disadvantaged groups and their allies been altered in ways that contribute to subsequent development of group struggle? Second, do specific movement struggles contribute to the development of new legal resources for disadvantaged groups? These might include new statutes, specific advances in judicial constructions, and broader ideological advances in prevailing legal norms signaled by such specific advances. Third, might both types of gains expand the opportunities for action by creating new vulnerabilities in institutional power? Such types of transformations again shape and reshape the context from which ongoing struggles—whether covert or overt—are waged by oppressed peoples. In sum, the focus on such changes underlines the complex ways in which legal conventions at once express, channel, and contain citizen efforts to achieve justice over time.

It is important to emphasize that legal conventions and institutions just as often contain or deter the expansion of struggles in our society. The populist, labor, and various poor people's movements clearly underline this fact.

Indeed, virtually all movements have left a legacy to some degree constrained by our limited and limiting legal inheritance. Sorting out this mix of potentially transformative and hegemony-affirming implications over time is one important dimension of assessing how law matters for specific movements.

Notes

This chapter is a reformulated version of "How Does Law Matter for Social Movements?" in Bryant Garth and Austin Sarat, eds., *How Does Law Matter?* (Chicago: Northwestern University Press, 1998).

1. I have worked out similar themes in my development of a "legal mobilization" framework in McCann (1991, 1994).

2. In this regard, the approach urged here challenges "realist" (both jurisprudential and empirical social scientific) perspectives assuming that legal indeterminacy robs legal norms of their intrinsic "power." See McCann (1994).

3. For a different, much more skeptical and critical viewpoint, see Rosenberg (1991).

4. "Going public" does not always benefit disadvantaged or exploited groups in the ways that Schattschneider suggests, of course. My point is simply that mobilization of public sentiment often *can* provide valuable leverage for resource-poor groups in many circumstances, especially when it involves appeals to widely accepted rights claims.

5. I am skeptical about this argument, but some scholars more knowledgeable about the political history of the issue have made compelling arguments along this line.

13

Litigation as Rebellion

Oneida Meranto

Although marginalized groups in the United States have historically used social movement activity as a strategy to generate power and push for social change, until recently the strategies observed by social scientists were limited to those defined as conventional and less conventional, with no overlap in or the merging of these categories. For relatively powerless groups, nonconventional or noninstitutional activities are often the only means available. What is different about the more contemporary social movements, however, are the strategies used to achieve a level of power within the given limitations of pluralism. For this reason, contemporary activists are examining the use of litigation as an instrument of social reform.

Challenging the actions of the government in the courts is not completely new. In the late 1950s and 1960s litigation was used by various protesting groups with some success to change society and social wrongs.[1] The most notable of these were the litigation activities of the early civil rights movement on issues of school desegregation. Federal courts became more willing to open their doors to the claims of the disenfranchised and certain minority groups in American society. The Warren Court, particularly, provided a period of judicial activism unforeseen in earlier periods. The apparent success of civil rights litigation and the receptivity of courts encouraged other groups to adopt litigation as a strategy.

Similar to activists in the civil rights movement, American Indian activists advocated law reform in their efforts to seek greater tribal self-determination.[2] Given Indians' relationship with federal and state governments and the administrative machinery created to control them, it has been difficult to increase the rights of Indians within typical mainstream politics.[3] Moreover, the very reason litigation may be effective for Indians is their special legal status that sets them apart from other protesting groups. Courts in particular have repeatedly recognized Indians' special status. Congress defined that relationship and has consistently used this definition to make judgements. As can be seen in the following quote, however, the status of Indians has been one that is often contradictory and ambiguous.

These decisions and many others, recognize: (1) Indian tribes are distinct, independent political communities," possessing all the rights, powers and privileges of any sovereign state; (2) their sovereignty is limited in that tribes have only internal power (e.g, they cannot make treaties with other powers); (3) and by treaty or legislation, Congress may at any time qualify the sovereignty of the tribes. (Warren 1972: 255–6)

Litigation, along with other noninstitutional means, increased the level of self-determination of tribes significantly in the 1970s. Indians were provided with a necessary means of representation and gained some ability to voice their discontent with past treaty violations and contemporary federal Indian legislation.[4]

This period of insurgency was short-lived, and declined significantly in 1973 soon after the occupation of Wounded Knee.[5] Similar to groups that were heavily suppressed before realizing their major goals, Indian activists, too, resurfaced, in the early 1990s with new leaders and new ideas on how to generate social change. Indian activism shifted from the cities and more directly to federally recognized reservations, and from the streets into the courtrooms. Indians once again are challenging their level of tribal sovereignty. Land and culture continue to be key issues, but Indians' sovereignty in economic development—specifically, their rights to establish gambling and gaming facilities—has become a major goal.

For most movements, as long as tactics remain nonviolent, society and public officials accord the movement a greater legality and legitimacy. Therefore, the use of courts for Indians has made their issues more salient and led to greater responses by the federal government than have other forms of collective behavior, certainly more than those tactics that encompass the use of violence.

In the 1990s the stage has been set for increased Indian judicial activism. Congressional leaders who originally initiated the Indian Gaming Regulatory Act (IGRA) of 1986 are now interpeting it as unfair to states. Powerful corporate casino owners continue to fuel the animosity toward Indians by suggesting that Indians receive preferential treatment. High-powered constituents voice their fear of organized crime, which often follows gambling. States assert the IGRA violates the Tenth and Eleventh Amendments, which protect the sovereignty of states. Indians confront and debate each other as to the consequences of this relatively new form of economic development. And among all of these various actors and diverse interests, tribes push ahead with their inherent rights of tribal sovereignty, historically limited but certainly not given by government. These constitute the preconditions for increased Indian political activity and increased use of litigation as a tool for social reform. It is within this context that Indians are increasingly becoming political actors.

Early Forms of Litigation

The historical Indian-government relationship and the extent to which Indians benefited from past activities correlate significantly with the types of strategies they now select. Put another way, their resistance is determined by their pattern of subjugation. The historical analysis of Indians reveals that the federal government was able to implement policy after policy to maintain the political, economic, and cultural domination of Indians. Consequently, the history of Native Americans is filled with policies of removal and isolation during the early 1800s, allotment in the late 1800s, a shift to quasi-self-governing fifty years later, and, finally, threats of termination in the 1950s. During the last thirty years, government has agreed on policies of self-determination, even though the level of self-determination has become the larger question (O'Brien 1989).

No matter what policies were implemented and no matter what strategies were used, American Indians could not as, Piven and Cloward (1977: 23) put it, "defy institutions to which they have no access, and to which they make no contribution." Indians understand that they are electorally impotent, economically powerless, have demands that often cannot or will not be met, and have a special legal status that is unique among challenging groups. These distinctions make the use of noninstitutional strategies often attractive and in many cases necessary. Consequently, Indians have been forced to play the political game outside the designated conventional arena of institutional politics.

That is precisely how the political game was played in the uprisings of the 1960s and 1970s; occupations, fish-ins, and prayer vigils (often accompanied by violence) occurred. These strategies were used in an attempt to minimize the dictatorial powers of Congress and effectively curtail federal agencies from orchestrating the future of Indians (see Mascarenas 1991).

Consequently, a movement of major proportions was created. There was upheaval in urban and rural areas, in the streets, and on many reservations. This period surpassed in scale, extent, and impact anything in Indian-European relations since the wars in the 1800s when the Creek Nation initiated the Red Stick Rebellion. Like the Red Sticks, the 1960s activists hoped to return to their traditional Indian languages, religions, cultures, and lifestyles, and natives made a monumental effort to achieve a level of self-determination not realized since the arrival of the Europeans (Weatherford 1988).

Indian activists shifted to more nonconventional strategies because the strategies used in previous years had made little progress toward changing federal policies or in alerting the federal government of their seriousness and commitment to change. Although there were small protests against stock reduction, methods of education, and other programs, these protests took place on individual reservations and had very little support from other tribes.

From 1955 to 1959 the protests initiated mainly arose in response to environmental policies and state civil and criminal jurisdiction. Litigation as a method of redress was also used, but with very little success (Mascarenas 1991).

Increased use of the courts came with the implementation of the Indian Claims Commission Act of 1946. The Indian Claims Act was ostensibly established to ensure that Indian tribes that historically suffered illegal expropriation of their lands would receive "justice" (DeLoria and Lyttle 1983). The commission, composed of non-Indians, selected certain Indian grievances to adjudicate. The grievances presented by tribes against the federal government often dealt with past treaties in which land had been taken away illegally or unjust policies were imposed on native people. Land, however, was never returned. Rather, the commission assigned Indians an award of monetary compensation. Tribes were encouraged to file court claims in hopes of ending long legal battles and of getting on with identifying Indians as citizens. The irony of the Indian Claims Act was that many government officials saw the act as providing a method whereby, within a few years, the slate would be clean of resentment, guilt, and frustration.

What did develop out of this policy was quite the opposite of the intended consequence of treating Indians identically with other citizens. When past government actions were brought to the forefront, they could no longer be swept under the bureaucratic carpet. Indians as well as non-Indians began to realize how unjustly the Native American population had been treated. In this respect, history did anything but absolve the federal government. Rather, the growing volume of cases heard by the commission set in motion rising expectations of Indians and provided a sense of optimism and political efficacy. Indians came to realize that they could change historical realities and put government in a more vulnerable position as they moved from hopeless submission into hopeful noncompliance.[6]

The political activism of Indians in the 1960s and 1970s was attributed to such political opportunities as urbanization, the termination policy, the Indian Reorganization Act, and clearly the Indian Claims Act, all of which structured Indian politics. In an earlier work (Mascarenas 1991) I demonstrated how these various policies were able to be defined as opportunities and later became the vehicle for a social movement.

The *New York Times* from 1963 to 1974 reveals a major increase in the number of recorded episodes and events that might be labeled Indian activism. It shows that litigation as a strategy was used more widely in 1972 than in any other period, still not overshadowing strategies such as large demonstrations and occupations.

By 1973 all levels of activism, courts included, dropped significantly. After the American Indian Movement (AIM) sponsored the occupation of Wounded Knee, which lasted for seventy-two days, Indian activism on a national level decreased substantially. Indian leadership was either delegitimized, put in jail, or killed, making the main militant organization, AIM, organizationally weak. Public support about Indian issues was at an all-time low.[7] Congress began funneling funds to police, providing them with the resources to abruptly curtail any type of Indian activism. As early as 1968, the U.S. Army had stockpiled riot control equipment in strategically located areas across the country, and more than fifteen thousand men had been especially trained for civil disorder service. Button (1989) regarded this increased spending in social control as preparation for a Second Civil War.

Conditions that had facilitated an Indian social movement, such as organizational strength, political opportunities, public support, and the willingness to challenge government, suddenly evaporated. It would be another fifteen years before the suitable factors would give rise to another useable and highly effective strategy.

The Indian Gaming Regulatory Act

The passage by Congress of the Indian Gaming Regulatory Act (IGRA) provided Indians with a new and different political opportunity. By itself, it significantly altered the political environment among states, casino owners, and tribes, thus necessitating the involvement of courts to resolve disputes between the various actors. In fact, there has been no other way to resolve the disputes arising out of the IGRA. A number of tribes have attempted to press their case through blockades and demonstrations, some with violence, as was the case of the Mohawks on the St. Regis Reservation (*The Economist* 1990). But, in almost all cases, tribes that started using traditionally noninstitutional strategies such as protest quickly shifted to include litigation as a method of redress.

For the first time, the battle over Indian gaming forced tribal governments to hire high-priced Washington lobbying firms that appeal to Congress to alter the adversary system Indians often confront. For example, the Viejas Tribe of Alpine, California, and the Cabazon Band of Mission Indians of Indio, California, have hired the Jefferson Group, a major Washington public affairs center that represents the tribes on a number of issues besides gaming. Still, compared with casino owners, tribes were marginally beginning to use bigger firms, while casino owners and developers have traditionally used Washington's most prestigious firms, this time to lobby for restrictions on Indian gaming (Moore 1995).

This use of sophisticated lobbying as a strategy points to the recognition by tribal governments that effective pressure now moves from protest in the streets to the hallways of Congress and later to the courts. In this way, the

IGRA has provided Indians with a level of judicial activism unforeseen in earlier periods of protest.

The implementation of the IGRA clearly is the structural factor that afforded the challenging Indians the opportunity to use litigation as a form of rebellion. Until the 1980s, gaming on tribal lands was nothing more than various games of bingo, nothing requiring any type of litigation. Tribes used these proceeds to fund tribal operations and services, and in some instances bingo proceeds worked effectively to reduce unemployment on reservations. Bingo was never a larger money-making venture for tribes; thus, it was never seen as a threat to the interests of non-Indians.

This all changed in 1987, when the Supreme Court "formally recognized the Indians' right to conduct gaming operations on their own land as long as [it] is not criminally prohibited by the state." In *California v. Cabazon and Morongo Bands of Mission Indian* (480 U.S. 202, 1987) the Supreme Court ruled that if states permit a form of gaming, tribes may operate such, without any state interference or restriction. Additionally, the Supreme Court held that a federal law that had given criminal jurisdiction over Indian country to states only gave states jurisdiction to enforce criminal prohibitory laws, not civil regulatory laws. Consequently, California's gambling laws are civil regulatory and thus could not be used to enforce or control gaming on reservations.

Following the Supreme Court's ruling, Congress passed the IGRA.[8] At this time the Reagan administration had significantly cut federal assistance to tribes, increasing the need to bolster tribal economic independence. Congress had hoped that tribes would become so rich from gaming enterprises that governmental funds to tribal programs would not be necessary (Hertzberg 1982). Tribal games, in several cases, were the sole source of revenue for tribes and were seen as an economic panacea by many tribes. In reality, tribal sovereignty and economic self-sufficiency have increased, but certainly not enough to substantially decrease funding to tribes (National Indian Gaming Association 1995).

Since the California ruling, nearly eighty-eight Indian tribes in nineteen states have agreements with their states known as "compacts" that permit them to operate gaming. The National Indian Gaming Commission (NIGC), an oversight commission appointed by the president and confirmed by the Senate, was established to review all gaming compacts with states and to prevent abuses, particularly by states.

Similar to other Indian legislation, gaming is not equally accepted by tribes and has led to increased tribal divisions. While some Indian nations suggest that casinos increase tribal sovereignty and view gaming as the ticket to increased economic autonomy and development and less dependency on federal funds, others see casinos as the ruin of tribal sovereignty and are heavily concerned about the consequences of gaming on traditional tribal values (Pasquaretta 1994).

The IGRA fuels debate among Indians, states, and tribes, in the same way Indian blood quantum as a criterion for tribal enrollment does. The blood quantum or "degree of Indian blood"—the standard of American Indian identification adopted by Congress in 1887 as a part of the General Allotment Act—has continued to plague Indian's identification (Jaimes 1992). In 1930 with the implementation of the Indian Reorganization Act, blood quantum again was seen as necessary for government to keep track of "its" Indians, since funding of programs was determined by tribal enrollment. The issue is, Who determines who is Indian? Should it be states, Congress, tribes, or some combination of the three? In recent Senate hearings, casino owners also want to have a shot at deciding who is Indian, recently suggesting that Indians running casinos are "not really Indian" (King 1993; Yoshihashi 1993).

The distinction of who is Indian is especially crucial since the IGRA is directed only at federally recognized tribes. This has spurred on some tribes that are not federally recognized to achieve that legal status, hoping to be given the opportunity to participate in gaming.

Like blood quantum, level of interference by states and other actors in the affairs of Indian gaming is largely determined by weighing the costs and benefits. It is only when states and other individuals have the potential to benefit that they pressure Congress to reexamine, redefine, and determine who is Indian. Suddenly what Indians do and if they indeed are Indian according to the blood quantum criterion becomes politicized. It has only been since states with vested interests and anti-Indian sentiments have been pressured by casino owners that Indian gaming suddenly entered the political limelight and the issue of "Indianness" resurfaced.

Under the index of "gaming" in the *New York Times*, a classic portrayal of Indian rights and gaming is painted. The earlier stories reported on the earnings of specific tribes and the millions of dollars they grossed from gaming. The second largest casino in the world, the Foxwood's Casino in Connecticut, ran by the tiny Mashantucket Pequot Tribe, grossed approximately $600 million dollars in 1993.[9] Immediately after the passage of the IGRA, other tribes wanted to implement gaming, hoping to experience similar economic benefits. Tribes were able to build schools, community centers, child development centers, and new housing, and provide college tuition for their young and health insurance for their elderly as a result of gaming proceeds. News stories focused on the change gaming brought about on reservations, suggesting that Indians are rolling in money as a result of this new form of economic development.

The tenor of the stories regarding gaming in the *New York Times* has changed in the last few years. Many of the later stories discuss conflict rather than peace or the positive aspects of gaming. In a short five years, since the passage of IGRA, non-Indian casino owners claim that Indians receive preferential treatment by not making them subject to the same regulations that govern other gambling establishments. State officials express concern over organized crime. Governors call for major reforms in Indian gaming laws. Tension has risen between Indians, while states and tribes continue to debate state legislation regarding gambling. An example can be seen in the recent uprising in Taos, New Mexico, after the New Mexico Supreme Court ruled that the state's Indian-run casinos were operating illegally (Johnson 1995).

Most recently, the Supreme Court ruling in *Seminole Tribe v. Florida* (11 F. 3d 1016, 1994) indicates the direction the high court has taken in deciding who has jurisdiction over gambling—tribes, states, or the federal government. The decision handed down in this volatile Indian gaming issue on March 27, 1996, held that the IGRA violates states' rights protected in the Constitution's Tenth and Eleventh Amendments, thus, giving a strong boost to states' rights advocates (Savage 1995: 42).[10]

The Eleventh Amendment reads, "The Judicial power of the United States shall not be construed to extend to any suit in law or equity, commenced or prosecuted against one of the United States by Citizens of another State, or by Citizens or Subjects of any Foreign State."[11] The amendment was created to protect state sovereign immunity. The Tenth Amendment, reserving to the states and people power not delegated to the federal government, has been used by Donald Trump, Atlantic City casino owner, in his suit against Secretary of the Interior Bruce Babbitt, claiming that IGRA gives Indians preferential treatment and thus discriminates against him (Greenberg and Zelio 1992).

The National Indian Gaming Association (NIGA), a lobbying group for Indian gaming, suggests the recent Seminole case should not be seen as a victory for states, since all this ruling does is return tribes to pre-IGRA status in which the interior secretary is responsible for completing gaming agreements with tribes, not states. States are not mandated to enter into "compacts" with tribes but merely given the opportunity to comment on tribal gaming. If a state refuses, tribes can negotiate with the Secretary of Interior, as they have before (*Moccasin Telegraph* 1996).

The introduction of the IGRA, much like the blood quantum or any number of other federal Indian policies, stimulated a rise in social movement activity. Indian gaming itself did not contribute to collective action, for large-scale tribal gaming predated IGRA by about ten years. The IGRA, in fact, limits and constrains the tribal rights recognized by California. Prior to the IGRA, tribes had a right to get involved in gaming that is identical to state ventures in gaming. Revenues from both state and tribal gaming are used for governmental purposes, not for individual profit. With the Cabazon hearing, states (specifically, Nevada and New Jersey) and organized commercial gaming interests pushed for legislation that would rein in Indian gaming and regulate it. The compacts are tribe-state agreements reviewed by the NIGC and approved by the secretary of interior. "The IGRA gives states some regulatory power over Indian gaming but not power to enforce or approve it," states Rick Hill, chairman of the NIGA. Despite the numerous efforts by the states to prohibit Indian gaming, until the *Seminole Tribe v. Florida* in 1996, the Supreme Court upheld the sovereign immunity defense of tribes.[12]

The historical relationship between the federal government and Indians has consistently bred conflict and tension among states. States want sovereignty, autonomy, and self-determination with little federal interference. Tribal governments desire the same. When states and tribes have clashed over whose sovereignty should be preferred, judicial activity has resulted.

The Reciprocal Congress

The evolutionary union between Congress and corporate interests on the issue of Indian gaming illustrates the importance of using litigation as a tool for change. Congress's recent decision to reexamine the IGRA demonstrates this point, along with its recent response to a petition signed by forty-nine governors asking it to correct selected sections of the law (Torricelli and Inouye 1994). While the immediate issues in Indian gaming concern regulatory control, the larger issues appear to be centered on federalism. In *Seminole v. Butterworth* (658 F. 2d, 1981, cert. denied, 455 U.S. 1020, 1983) the appeals court noted that the "state cannot have it both ways, gambling is either prohibited or regulated. If it is regulated, then it falls under federal, not state, jurisdiction" (McCulloch 1994).

Native insurgency can be seen as a result of two complementary processes—one generating from below within Indian organizations and one originating from above within the political center. The impetus from below flows from the nature and extent of Indian grievances and from the amount of organizational strength. The impetus from above is contained in the design of government policies and/or actions to control organizing. Put another way, the impetus from below determines whether mobilization will occur. The impetus from above often determines the shape mobilization will take (Nagel 1982).

A link between Congress and corporate interests is not new in American politics, nor is it new in American Indian politics. Congress has set numerous policies that restricted the power of tribal governments and essentially allocated power to corporations. A case in point was Congressional action in passing the Navajo Relocation Act in 1976. While the passage of this policy was touted by the media and decision makers as a necessary step to protect Navajo and Hopi tribes from each other, it has been well documented that the interests of Peabody Coal and other corporations became easier to secure with the relocation of those Indians unwilling to develop these resources (Kammer 1980).

Congress passes such legislation as the Navajo Act under the guise of protecting Indians. The Indian Relocation Act in 1830, for example, designated the federal government as the guardian of Indians while giving the state of Georgia access to gold on Cherokee land.[13] Ever since this period, Congress has passed numerous policies that claim to be working in the "interests" of Indians, while in reality many generate powerful political actors in the interests of corporations and/or states.

The behavior of congressional representatives is not likely to change. In May 1993 Representative Robert Torricelli from New Jersey and Senator Harry Reid of Nevada introduced a bill that would amend the IGRA, stipulating that states that offer one form of gaming such as lottery would not have to negotiate with tribes to set up full-scale casino gaming. The bill also would make state gambling laws applicable on Indian territory. The two congressmen said their bills were inspired by a number of public officials who were calling for major reforms in Indian gaming laws (Torricelli and Inouye 1994).

Whose interest is Congress to meet, especially when the rights of states and constituents are perceived to be at risk? Since Indian gambling has turned into a billion dollar industry (National Indian Gaming Association 1993), lawmakers are pressured to make gambling available to others. Small-scale casinos are run in resort towns in Colorado and South Dakota. Riverboat gambling is now legal in four Mississippi River states. A large casino complex is soon to be built in New Orleans, and more gaming developments are likely to occur (Rose 1991).

States are responding to the needs of their constituents by examining the potential role of gaming in resolving economic problems. And to reap the full benefits of gambling, states want to keep the option to initiate gaming in the future to themselves, rather than extending that option to tribal governments.

Public officials who oppose Indian gaming have handed Congress yet another problem: how to respond to a portion of the electorate who believe that with Indian gaming comes organized crime. The allegations seem to be totally unfounded. There does not appear to be any concrete evidence that public opinion is against Indian gaming. There is, however, much support to suggest the opposite. In the last decade several polls indicate that American people believe Indian tribes should be allowed to decide for themselves what types of gaming occur on their reservations. Sixty-eight percent of those surveyed believe Indians should have gaming on their reservations if they so desire (Harris 1992). The chairman of the NIGA, Rick Hill, stated that "what critics of Indian gaming are really afraid of is organized Indians."[14] The NIGA is a nonprofit group composed of Indian tribes and businesses engaged in tribal gaming and has become a powerful lobbying group.

Indian spokespeople such as Hill dubbed the bills of Torricelli and Reid "the Donald Trump Protection Acts," in reference to Trump, a private owner of three gambling establishments in Atlantic City. Trump's interests were ignited by the push of tribes such as the Ramapough Indians of New Jersey to get federal recognition so that they could create gaming. Trump saw the arrival of gaming on reservations as unfair competition and in April 1996 sued the federal government, maintaining that by allowing Indian tribes to open casinos he is discriminated against. Tribes have different legal standing vis-à-vis states than do private developers.

As can be seen, tribes, states, and Congress all claim the primary power to decide how Indian gaming will operate. The IGRA directed states and tribes to conduct "negotiations in good faith" to devise "tribal-state compacts." It also empowered federal courts to hear "any cause of action" stemming from the states' failure to enter into negotiations with tribes.

In *Seminole Tribe v. Florida* (11 F. 3d 1016, 1994) the Eleventh Circuit Court of Appeals ruled that Congress does not have the constitutional power to force states to negotiate with tribes. "The principles of federalism and sovereign immunity exemplified in the Eleventh Amendment prevent Congress from abrogating the states' immunity," ruled the court.

Under the Indian Commerce Clause, Congress has the power to abrogate a state's immunity from suit. Nonetheless the Supreme Court has been closely divided on when and whether or not Congress can waive state sovereign immunity. The tension that has developed out of the IGRA and the reciprocal relationship of Congress and states/corporations clearly necessitate action by the courts.

These recent examples demonstrate that when it comes to Indian gaming, Congress is more supportive of corporations and/or states than of Indian economic development. They also point to the willingness of Congress to defer to courts to settle the hotly debated controversy generated by the IGRA. In many cases Indian gaming has been a mixed blessing for the tribes. It has, on the one hand, restricted states from having complete control over tribal economies and thus allowed tribes to benefit from gaming. On the other hand, it still makes tribes dependent upon the discretionary will of Congress for the future of Indian gaming.

How, then, can the implementation of the IGRA be explained? Like the termination policies of the 1950s, the impetus for the IGRA was based purely on budgetary relief, not out of any real concern for increasing tribal sovereignty (Barsh 1994; McCulloch 1994). The only thing Congress was not prepared for was the litigation that followed. Responses by states, corporations, and constituents to Indian gaming has made Congress rethink its initiation of the IGRA.

Litigation as a Form of Protest

Litigation did not come to be used widely until the 1990s, specifically with the implementation of the Indian Gaming Regulatory Act. Like the Indian Claims Act, the IGRA provided tribal governments an opportunity to challenge any number of actors who opposed Indian gaming, this time with more litigation skills. Similar to the rebellion of the 1960s and 1970s, Indians have been forced to use a variety of tactics to challenge the various actors and interests within the gaming and gambling industry. Unlike the earlier period, Indians have increased the use of litigation as a strong tool and are better prepared to litigate. Indians have empowered themselves with knowledge and power of the law. They have become well versed on the U.S. Constitution, and its amendments and how they apply to Indian sovereign governments. And most important, Indians now have legal reformers who are willing to use the system to their clients' advantage as well as strong organizational strength. These last two characteristics give Indians an added advantage over the earlier periods to challenge government in its own arena (Dahl 1995: 86).[15]

The economic and social situation within the United States during the 1980s and early 1990s created a period of political flux. The belt-tightening policies of the Reagan/Bush years severely cut social services to the lower class and had a devastating impact on reservations. In 1983 alone aid was slashed by more than a third, from $3.5 billion to $2 billion (Hertzberg 1982). The increased encroachment of states in the affairs of Indians made them an entity difficult for Indians to reckon with, particularly regarding taxation. And the recent implementation of the IGRA of 1988, and Congressional response through the numerous "Donald Trump Protection Acts," has provided the conditions for increased Indian activism in the courts.

While strategies have changed, the main actors involved in Indian affairs have gone basically unchanged: the Bureau of Indian Affairs (BIA), the government's chief Indian agent, remains an unpopular agency among Indians; Congress with its plenary power maintains its partial supremacy over tribes; and states continue to declare themselves as the primary power in deciding what happens within their territories, on and off Indian land. Corporations interact with all three actors. Corporations are significant because of their increased interest in Indian gaming. The level of economic clout that corporations are able to wield versus the lack of economic clout of Indians, plus corporate ties to state interests, shifts the balance of power in favor of corporations. This demonstrates that using electoral politics and interest group lobbying as the only political strategy can be futile for Indians. Consequently, the types of activities Indians use have been and will continue to be a strange mixture of institutional and noninstitutional strategies.

Various tribal rights are at the heart of Indian sovereignty and continue to play a role in Indian activism. If we mix in the sovereignty issues of self-determination, tribal federal recognition, state jurisdiction, and intertribal conflict and then add the free market, notably corporate interests, and states seeking to increase their jurisdiction and protect their citizens from the corrupting influences of unregulated gambling, we have a volatile arena of increased conflict.

Indian mobilization to a great extent is shaped by the political and economic context in which Indians live. The mobilization of Indian activists is a response to a structure largely determined by federal Indian policies created by Congress. Indian gaming cuts directly at issues of Indian sovereignty, creating a strong negative reaction.

Like the earlier movement, the development of collective action in the 1990s can be directly linked to political factors that specifically structured political opportunities (McAdam 1982). For example, Jenkins and Perrow (1977: 263) attribute the success of the farm workers to "the altered political environment within which the challenge operated." No doubt the conditions were very different in the early 1960s compared with the 1950s when they made their initial challenge. In a similar fashion, Costain (1992) attributes the legislative victories for women to such opportunities as the sympathy of a presidential administration to women's rights. And McAdam (1982) demonstrates how the emergence of black protest activity is linked to several broad political trends.

Much like the above protests, the recent activism generated by tribal governments can be attributed to shifting political factors, both macro and micro. From the top down are such structural factors as the IGRA; a more sympathetic presidential administration, most notably under President Clinton; state rights advocacy; and litigation favoring Indians. From the bottom up, the activism can be attributed to microlevel factors such as strong lobbying groups; Indian lawyers, what Handler (1987) defines as law reformers; overwhelming support from the public; and Indian organizational strength.

Using litigation to challenge the government for past treaty grievances is a relatively new strategy to include as a form of protest. Indians' unique federal relationship gives them some advantages over other minorities in wielding both local and federal influences among the American majority. If this relationship is threatened or if Indians are not satisfied with federal policies regarding Native America or with federal actions, they can make appeals to the federal government for a reversal in policies. Either they are "distinct, independent political communities" giving them a status similar to sovereign nations, or they have power set by Congress, thus limiting their ability to control their economic well-being. How tribes are viewed often fluctuates according to the branch and level of government involved. As early as 1831, federal courts have been a formidable actor in Indian affairs. Since treaties, agreements, and acts ratified by the U.S. Senate have governed U.S.-Indian relations, the role of Congress has been important. Also the intrusion of state laws and regulations into the sovereignty of Native Americans has increased the role of states and has led to a crisis in federal-state-Indian relations, most recently with Indian gaming.

This increased role of state and federal government into issues of tribal sovereignty has necessitated the use of courts to determine the outcomes in such matters as fishing rights, water rights, the use of peyote in religious rites, and other significant matters.[16] Indian nations have and can challenge the power to regulate land and its resources, much like the powers of any sovereign nation. Subsequently, Indians have become very familiar with using the courts as a method to resolve almost every facet of their life.

An important difference between the earlier period of litigation and today is that during earlier uprisings much of the Indian litigation was in the hands of white lawyers. These individuals clearly did not see the cultural significance of negotiation for land rather than for money and certain tribal cultural goals. Since the 1970s, however, with the founding of the Native American Rights Fund (NARF), a national-interest law firm founded with a Ford Foundation Grant, the number of Indian lawyers has increased. As a result, land rather than money has become the issue at hand in many of the court cases. Indians have begun to eye the court's usefulness with new speculation, especially with the representation of Indians by Indians. It was only natural that litigation became a part of Indian protest and an effective method whereby Indians could increase their land base and civil rights.[17]

Conclusion

Litigation as a strategy could not have come to fruition during the uprising of the 1970s. Certain political factors had not surfaced, Indians had not acquired the level of required litigation skills, nor had they exhausted all other political strategies. It was only when the more militant activities had been suffficiently squashed that Indians began to eye the use of the white man's system to expose the gross injustices of the white man's past. Litigation was a less dangerous and less costly means than nonlegal struggles against formidable opponents, and it thus became the political opportunity that Indians—specifically, tribal governments—needed.

Furthermore, the debate over "Indianness" demonstrates how the due process clause, for example, has much potential to increase the use of litigation by Indians. Quite often debated has been the term *Indian*, which has been determined at law to be a political category, not a racial one. The NIGA, the watchdog of the IGRA and lobbyists for Indian gaming, requested that two Indians be members of any National Gaming Study Commission. The NIGA stated that this was not meant to be a racial category but that "Indian" is a political and legal description (*Moccasin Telegraph* 1996). The Federal Indian Self-Determination Act (1976) recognizes an Indian as a person who is a member of an Indian tribe that is federally recognized and is thus eligible for special programs and services. A Supreme Court decision during the Marshall court in 1830 made the federal government the protector of Indians. The preference was directed not toward a "racial" group consisting of Indians but toward members of "federally recognized" tribes (*Moccasin Telegraph* 1996). It was determined that in this sense, the preference is political rather than racial in nature.

The distinction of Indians being a political category rather than a racial one should eventually push any question or conflict over Indian gaming into the courtroom. As McCulloch (1994) states, Indians have pretty much run the full gamut of possible relations to the federal government. In the early period they started out being treated as sovereign nations where treaties were made. Then they were defined as "domestic dependent nations," later to be defined as wards of the federal government. In 1934 tribal governments were revived, albeit dressed up to be more modern with some increased tribal powers. Today Congress and courts equate tribal powers with states, giving tribes the power to use their status in the same ways as states do.

Clearly all of the attempts of tribes to use their powers as sovereign nations to initiate gaming and the challenges to that sovereignty by states or corporate casino owners will need to be decided through litigation. The most recent events suggest this. On December 15, 1995, the New Mexico Supreme Court ruled that the state's Indian-run casinos were operating in defiance of the law, since state law did not allow casino gambling. The lieutenant governor of Isleta Pueblo said, "We're not going to let anyone come onto our reservation and shut us down. If it comes to going to jail or prison or dying on the line, we have to make a stand. Otherwise, we might as well kiss sovereignty goodbye" (Johnson 1995: A18). In another case, four reservations in Arizona were raided by FBI agents who confiscated 750 electronic game machines. Indians responded by attempting to block the agents from leaving the reservation. The standoff lasted for five hours and was not resolved until the governor negotiated with the tribal chairman. Arizona interpreted the IGRA to mean that reservations could offer gambling only in those states that allow it. Subsequently, tribes in six states filed a suit against the regulations. In reaction to the suit, eight states filed suit, challenging the authority of the IGRA (Johnson 1992).

A number of instances like these demonstrate the progression of interactions between tribes and states regarding the IGRA and the evolution of litigation. Tribes point to the idea of self-rule on Indian country and ask why should sovereign nations need to get the permission of states. The states' rebuttal is that any Indian country within state territory must obey the laws of the state. All Indian country is within the confines of some state, suggest Indians, clearly forcing Indians to ask, "What Indian sovereignty?" What did Chief Justice Marshall mean by "domestic dependent nations" in 1830?[18]

If gambling were not such a profitable venture, it would be sidestepped by the state in much the same way as has tourism or bingo has. It is the potential profitability that makes gaming so volatile. For a population that refuses to consider the development of mineral resources (for those who have them) or a population that has no other means of survival, gaming has pushed the sovereignty buttons of both tribes and states, each party attempting to define its legitimate jurisdiction over gaming.

The diverse interests, therefore, will generate a new kind of Indian activism, one that will be fought in the courtroom. The shift to the courtroom should not suggest that the protest on reservations will cease, however. Like their counterparts in the 1970s, the activists of the 1990s realize that pressure must be maintained against certain corporate interests within the reservation, while their lawyers are battling it out in the halls of justice. Such increased pressure on reservations may ensure a quicker decision in the courts. It is in the best interest of Indians to use both: litigation and noninstitutional strategies. Given the confusion, ambiguity, and self-interest of Congress, litigation will undoubtedly be the preferred institutional strategy on issues of tribal sovereignty.

Notes

1. Handler (1978) examines the attempts of social movements to use court action to achieve concrete changes.

2. The terms *Indian*, *Native*, *Native American*, and *American Indian* are used interchangeably to refer to the indigenous peoples of the United States and their descendants.

3. Historically, Indians have been controlled first by the Department of War and then the Bureau of Indian Affairs. Nonetheless, Congress has enormous power over Indian affairs, so much so that in many cases even the courts have been reluctant to challenge the power of Congress. This point is important because, as will be shown, one of the most important strategies of Indians is litigation. See Vine and Lytle (1983).

4. Gamson (1990) points out that there are obvious problems in making connections between funds or other outcomes and movement activities, yet for Indians the mere increase in the number of activities challenging government was significantly higher than in any other period, which suggests that some benefit was garnished as a result of increased activism. In addition, in an interview with the author on July 11, 1991, Professor Charles Wilkenson, professor of law at University of Colorado, stated that since 1959 there has been a steady escalation in Indians using the courts as a form of strategy, and with some success.

5. Occupation of Wounded Knee, a town in South Dakota, occurred to bring attention

to the plight of Indians regarding tribal corruption, the failure of the BIA, and other concerns of Indians (Weyler 1984).

6. Cornell (1988) illustrates the evolution of what he defines as "indianization," which he states is the growth of a supratribal consciousness, the eventual emergence of "American Indians" as a politically self-conscious population.

7. Suppression was the most obvious choice for government since most of the movement's demands could not be met because they centered around land. If Indian demands had been met, that would have conflicted with the interest of the status quo.

8. Much of the information regarding the IGRA is from a booklet entitled "Speaking the Truth" by the National Indian Gaming Association (1995).

9. Statement by Rick Hill, chairman of the NIGA to the Senate Committee on Indian Affairs, May 9, 1996. See *Indian Gaming Insider*, August 1996, 33–38.

10. Savage states that tribal casino gambling is triggering federalism issues for the Supreme Court.

11. The amendment was ratified in 1795 as a result of *Chisolm v. Georgia* (2 Dallas 419, 1793).

12. Hill's statement appears in *Indian Gaming Insider*, the official magazine of the National Indian Gaming Association, issue 1, August 1996.

13. *Cherokee Nation v. Georgia*, 30 U.S. 1 (1831); see Wilkenson (1987).

14. Stated by Rick Hill in *CQ Researcher*, March 18, 1994, p. 256.

15. Dahl suggests that the casino boom is forging new relationships between Indians and the law.

16. 207 U.S. 564 (1908); *United States v. New Mexico*, 438 U.S. 696, 718 (1978); 108 S. Ct. 1319 (1988); *United States v. Washington*, 384 R. Supp. 312 (W.D. Wash. 1974).

17. Interview with John Echohawk, lawyer for the Native American Rights Fund, September 1988.

18. Interview with Lily Boyce, Lakota, September 19, 1996.

14

Social Movements and Abortion Law

Laura R. Woliver

Social movements have often used legal institutions to help achieve their ends (Kluger 1975; Walker 1990; Vose 1959). Social movement interest groups sometimes submit "friend of the court briefs" (amicus curiae) in attempts to persuade and educate members of the Supreme Court about their position on issues. Abortion movements (pro-choice and pro-life) center their legal debates, logic, passions, and activism on legal rights.[1] Past president of Planned Parenthood, Faye Wattleton (1996: 46), characterizes the abortion battles as "the debate over women's bodies." Past president of the National Right to Life Committee, John Willke (1994: 331), agrees abortion is indeed a "civil rights issue," but one for the unborn child killed in the womb.

Legalized abortion makes women's sexuality visible instead of hidden and documents the choices of defiant women claiming control over their bodies instead of passively accepting an unwanted, unplanned, or unhealthy pregnancy. Pro-life rhetoric erases women, doubts their ability to make choices for themselves (hence, twenty-four-hour waiting periods, mandatory counseling), and centers an image of the fetus (or baby, in pro-life terms) as the central topic of abortion law. Many in the pro-life movement are also concerned with "cultural fundamentalism" (Blanchard 1994: 40–50; see also Green 1995: 4).

The Pro-Choice Movement

Activists working to legalize abortion in the 1960s and 1970s had their first victories in state legislatures. Their efforts to affect abortion law grew to a national level, primarily after the *Roe v. Wade* (1973) decision. In the decades since *Roe*, the pro-choice movement has worked at the national level to hold its ground against the pro-life countermovement and to work once again with state level activists to protect abortion rights from state-by-state whittling away and larger erosions (Staggenborg 1991: 3).[2] After the *Roe* victory, the pro-choice movement's agenda was partially shaped by having to respond to the burgeoning pro-life countermovement (Tatalovich and Daynes 1981; O'Connor 1996). Abortion issues also became embroiled in battles over ratification of the proposed Equal Rights Amendment to the U.S. Constitution (Woliver 1989; O'Connor 1996, 96). Pro-choice weathered the backlash and grew over the years by "acquiring professional leadership and formalized organizational structures" (Staggenborg 1991: 5). Family planning and church activists were prominent early supporters (Staggenborg 1991: 17) and family planning, population, and women's movement groups assisted in the mobilization of an abortion movement by allowing their organizations and members to be absorbed into the movement (Staggenborg 1991: 18; see also O'Connor 1996). Mobilization was also facilitated by the cycles of protest of the 1960s and early 1970s.

The pro-choice movement knows that income limitations constrict people's choices. The Planned Parenthood Federation of America, for instance, decided to fight in court the Hyde Amendment prohibitions on using federal Medicaid funds to pay for abortions. Wattleton (1996: 48) believed "if we didn't secure a poor woman's right to abortion, the ability of all women to exercise their rights would be put in jeopardy."

The pro-choice movement cooperated not only in court battles, but in demonstrations, press conferences, and data gathering projects. The March for Women's Lives in April 1989, for instance, was mostly planned by Eleanor Smeal, president of the National Organization for Women (NOW). The march was timed deliberately for two weeks before the attorneys on both sides were scheduled to argue the *Webster* case. The Planned Parenthood Federation of America, among many others, participated enthusiastically in the march (Wattleton 1996, p. 53). Underscoring participants' identification with large feminist issues, both in the present and historically, pro-choice organization representatives and many of the hundreds of thousands of fellow marchers wore white with purple festoons, displaying symbolic alliance with the suffragists (Wattleton 1996: 53).

As Costain (1980: 478–9) found, lobbying through ad hoc issue coalitions won favor with women's rights supporters because "it brought together organizations with sufficient resources to lobby effectively" while allowing these groups to retain autonomy (see also Staggenborg 1991: 104–6). For the pro-choice movement, professionalization of staff and groups helped stabilize the coalitions, since "paid staff were available to coordinate coalition work around legislative lobbying" (Staggenborg 1991: 104). Pro-choice amicus brief coordination in the 1980s also benefitted from this professionalization (Woliver 1992; Samuels 1996; Behuniak-Long 1991). Groups only needed to agree on the desirability of legalized abortion to join the coalition.

Pro-choice coalitional work, though, tended to be oriented toward conventional interest group politics. Some groups within the movement became almost exclusively focused on legislative lobbying. The different specialties of groups within the movement, however, became an asset in helping to overcome a major problem in coalitional work. "When individual movement organizations work in the name of a coalition, they forego the recognition and visibility that they achieve with campaigns of their own," but this is balanced against the greater resources the coalition commands (Staggenborg 1991: 120).

The desire of reproductive rights/women's health groups to enlarge the focus to the contextual nature of "choice" and issues of women's health did not completely alter the tactics within the legislative and legal work of abortion rights groups to secure rights obtained in *Roe* against the insurgent pro-life movement, which was achieving visible gains (Staggenborg 1991: 120–1; Woliver interviews). Therefore, especially in the late 1970s and early 1980s, "[t]he multi-issue perspective of the reproductive rights movement was a luxury that other pro choice groups did not feel they could afford in the face of mounting threats from the anti-abortion movement" (Staggenborg 1991: 122).

When pro-life won its first major national victory, with passage of the Hyde Amendment in 1976 banning federal abortion funding, one result was to strengthen pro-choice forces. Over time, with the 1980 election of pro-life President Ronald Reagan and the pro-life platform of the Republican party, pro-choice interests increased their resources and developed an "insider" tactic emphasizing national policy making (Staggenborg 1991: 81). One example of this was the formalization and expansion of the Abortion Information Exchange. The original informal coalition grew with the Abortion Information Exchange to "include medical organizations, professional associations, labor unions, and environmental groups in addition to pro-choice movement organizations" (Staggenborg 1991: 83–84). Also joining the movement were reproductive rights organizations, including the Committee for Abortion Rights and against Sterilization Abuse and the Reproductive Rights National Network. Groups like these appealed to feminists who found some pro-choice groups too radical but worried about mounting threats to abortion rights (Staggenborg 1991: 84–85).

Pro-choice movement groups worked to keep the orientation on the women and girls facing unwanted and problem pregnancies. The direct action of antiabortion groups like Operation Rescue, ironically, helped refocus the abortion conflict back on women's experiences and pushed the revitalization of the grassroots pro-choice movement (Staggenborg 1991: 129).

Pro-life and pro-choice movement efforts have also included supporting or opposing presidential appointments to the federal judiciary. The 1987 defeat of President Reagan's appointment of Robert Bork to the U.S. Supreme Court was an important victory for the pro-choice movement coalition (Staggenborg 1991: 134–6; O'Connor 1996). Pro-choice movement activists used litigation, state and national lobbying, and a tactic of persuasion and education aimed at public opinion, especially at policy makers in legislatures and on the courts (Staggenborg 1991; Garrow 1994; Woliver 1996).

The Pro-Life Movement

The pro-life movement began organizing in earnest in the late 1960s, particularly in reaction to the state-level victories of pro-choice activists (Staggenborg 1991: 35; Garrow 1994; Tatalovich and Daynes 1981; Ginsburg 1989). In 1967, following passage of reform laws in three states, the National Conference of Catholic Bishops organized a Family Life Division (Blanchard 1994: 28; O'Connor 1996: 31, 59). The National Right to Life Committee, formed in 1973, grew from the Family Life Division, eventually becoming somewhat independent of the National Conference of Catholic Bishops (Blanchard 1994: 52; Woliver 1996b). Groups within the pro-life movement include single-issue abortion groups, antifeminist and pro-family groups, religious conservative groups, and the Catholic Church. In the late 1970s, pro-life groups joined neoconservatives to help defeat pro-choice political candidates, lobby at state and national levels for abortion restrictions, support legal challenges to pro-choice legislation, and defend in court their newly minted pro-life state-level policies (Himmelstein 1990; Sarat 1982).

Pro-life activists have passed national and state-level legislation to outlaw abortion, increase costs, and decrease access through myriad state regulations (Halva-Neubauer 1990), and they have reframed the issue to center on fetuses, and putting into the background, or rendering invisible, pregnant women. Their efforts to turn public opinion their way include pictures, billboards, and widely disseminated films such as *The Silent Scream*, which graphically depicts an abortion procedure. Another pro-life movement tactic is direct action, blocking access to abortion clinics, engaging in sidewalk counseling and acts of sabotage, and, for a zealous few, shooting pro-choice doctors and members of their staffs.

Rhetoric and Framing: Mobilization and *Webster*

Social movement rhetoric and metaphors provide important representations of the interests in abortion politics. The word choice or rhetoric in legal briefs give clues to the deeper ideological meaning activists wish to convey. The language used helps frame the issues. Issue frames often have serious implications for policy making. Ex-president of The National Right to Life

Committee John Willke emphasizes the value of every "successful semantic coup" for the pro-life movement. The term *pro-life* is an example.

Whether abortion is defined as murder or a health care option shapes the rest of the policy debate. For example, pro-life groups frequently label abortion clinics as abortion "industries." Although the differentiation between the two terms *clinic* and *industry* may appear slight and inconsequential, heavy ideological meanings are embedded in phrases chosen by pro-life groups as well as the pro-choice groups (Woliver and McDonald 1993; see also Condit 1990). The careful choice of frames in these amicus briefs displays the power of political language and issue framing (Edelman, 1964, 1977; Condit 1990; Iyengar 1991).

Both Presidents Reagan and Bush asked the Supreme Court, through Justice Department amicus briefs, to use the *Webster* case to overturn *Roe*. This strategy, along with increased direct action by groups like Operation Rescue and previous Supreme Court decisions maintaining *Roe* by a vote of five to four, galvanized an enlarged pro-choice coalition into large-scale mobilization. Many groups on both sides of the abortion debate saw *Webster* as the case that might overrule *Roe* and jeapardize legal abortion.

With such high stakes, many groups and professional associations joined in the amicus effort for *Webster*. More than 300 organizations, using more than 120 lawyers, drafted 31 friend-of-the-court briefs for the pro-choice position in the *Webster* case (Coyle 1989: 27; see also Craig and O'Brien 1993). The *Webster* pro-choice briefs were coordinated by attorneys at the ACLU Reproductive Rights Project, Planned Parenthood, and the National Abortion Rights Action League (NARAL) (Woliver interviews). The pro-life interests submitted forty-six amicus curiae briefs supporting the state of Missouri. For the first time, the U.S. solicitor general's brief called for an overturning of *Roe*.

Unique coalitions of interests worked together on several of the briefs. One pro-choice *Webster* brief signed by 281 historians attempted to refute the position of the U.S. Justice Department and pro-life amici that abortion had been outlawed throughout U.S. history, thereby making *Roe* an aberration (see also Mohr 1978). In answer to Justice Sandra Day O'Connor's questioning of viability criteria set up in *Roe*, given new medical advances, 167 scientists and physicians signed a brief maintaining that viability for a fetus still occurred at about twenty-four weeks gestation.

Centering Babies or Women

A big part of the debate for pro-life groups is the discussion of how the fetus is actually an "unborn" child or is merely momentarily "hidden." Such consistent use of terms identifying and personalizing the fetus as an individual rests on the premise that a person exists and is alive from the moment of conception. One of the most common images employed by the pro-life movement is substituting the term *fetus* with variations for the term the *unborn*.

Fetuses are never called fetuses, they are *always* "unborn children," "unborn life," "prenatal life," "children in the womb," "human life before birth," "unborn grandchildren," "viable unborn," "minor child," "unborn human life." In addition, pro-life forces hardly ever use the word *woman* but instead choose "mother." Discussions abound about "pregnancies" instead of "pregnant women." The U.S. Catholic Conference declares that the fetus and the woman are "separate patients" (*Webster* Brief 20).

In several places in the pro-life briefs, it is striking how the women actually involved in the debates disappear. The *Webster* brief by The Association for Public Justice et al. shows how pro-life groups incorporate medical advances in their logic: "Today an embryologist or fetologist can diagnose and treat an unborn child independently of treating the mother, including removing the child from its mother's womb for surgery, and then returning it to the womb to complete gestation." Hence, the brief asserts, "one can hardly consider the child a mere extension of its mother." From the second of fertilization, nevertheless, there are "children who happen to reside within their mothers' wombs" (*Webster* Brief 19). Missing in the pro-life briefs is recognition of what one scholar has called "the very geography of pregnancy" (Gallagher 1989: 187).

Pro-life groups deemphasize the social context of abortion decisions. Of the forty-seven pro-life *Webster* briefs, only three discuss social problems and women's plight. The *Webster* brief submitted by the Lutheran Church-Missouri Synod et al. states, "[A]s church organizations, we are fully aware, through our own agencies established to counsel and assist pregnant women currently facing the abortion decision, of the burden it places upon them and society in general to decide not to abort their pregnancies." Private and public funding could be expanded, they continue, "to meet the need for services and facilities for women facing unwanted pregnancies." Birthright, a pro-life group, notes how abandoned most women facing an unwanted pregnancy feel: "[A]bortion is a quick-fix cover-up" that "destroys and erodes the very fabric of values in our society" and actually harms women (*Webster* Brief 17; see also brief by Covenant House).

A difference between the pro-life and pro-choice briefs, therefore, is whether the context or rationale for the choice to abort the fetus is presented. While pro-life groups avoid discussion of women's reproductive lives, the social context of what brings women to consider the option of abortion is a key part of the argumentation in pro-choice amicus briefs.

No pro-life brief writer tries to answer directly the charge that reversing *Roe* would have devastating consequences on the lives of women. Indeed, the pro-life briefs do not speculate on what policies would be needed to implement an overturning of *Roe*.

Medical technology has a strong impact on the abortion debate in America (Gallagher 1989; Oakley 1987; Rothman 1986; Woliver 1989, Woliver 1991). New reproductive technologies have been used to strengthen the pro-life arguments that the fetus is an independent being. These technologies, particularly ultrasound, isolate the fetus and make it appear distinct and unconnected to the woman (Ginsburg 1989: 104–9; Woliver 1995). An extreme example of this seemingly distant relationship between the mother and fetus is seen in an analogy to the fetus being like "an astronaut" (*Webster* Brief 6). Images of the fetus used by pro-life activists usually do not encompass visualization of the woman the fetus is within (Condit 1990: 79–95; Gallagher 1989: 187–98; Gorney 1990: 38; Ginsburg 1989: 107–9; Petchesky 1984: 353, 1987; Woliver 1989, 1991, 1995). These carefully constructed fetal images are powerful aspects of the pro-life discourse (Condit 1990: 80). Technologies, therefore, that allow viewing, studying, and possibly medically treating fetuses prenatally "are likely to elevate the moral status of the fetus" (Blank 1988: 148; see also Field 1989: 118).

These technological advances add new elements to the politics of abortion. Many pro-life *Webster* briefs noted the contradictions, from their point of view, in medical technologies that allow and sometimes seem to require doctors to treat fetuses as patients yet that also let these "patients" be aborted.

A *Webster* brief by twenty-two international women's health centers, directly arguing against the brief by the United States, warns,

> [G]overnments can and will fashion abortion regimes that seek to coerce reproductive choice as official state policy. The nightmarish policies of criminalized abortion in Nazi Germany and the Soviet Union on the one hand and forced abortion in China on the other, are chilling reminders that women must be afforded the ability to make fundamental reproductive decisions free of governmental interference.

Many pro-choice briefs discuss this historical and comparative justification for legal abortion, some add Romania as a dire example of women having to sacrifice their physical integrity to serve the purpose of a state (*Webster* Briefs 65, 66, 84).

The rhetoric of democracy and rights is prominent in pro-choice briefs. They explain why access to safe and legal abortion is necessary for women to fully enjoy their constitutional rights. The Women's Equality Brief (56) signed by seventy-seven organizations including NOW, the American Association of University Women (AAUW), the League of Women Voters, and the National Federation of Business and Professional Women's Clubs, stresses the unequal burden "forced motherhood" would place on women. The women's rights organizations assert that "[i]t would do so for women alone; men are not required to endure comparable burdens in the service of the state's abstract interest in promoting life." Brief 65, signed by 885 law professors, holds, "For women to achieve the full promise of 'equal protection,' it is necessary for them to control the childbearing decision." Given the gender specific nature of abortion restrictions, Brief 75 by the National Coalition against Domestic Violence argues, in part, that abortion choice should be protected under the Fourteenth Amendment's Equal Protection Clause. Brief writers for NOW hold that the "forced pregnancy" would be akin to the involuntary servitude prohibited by the Thirteenth Amendment (Brief 59).

Framing Abortion: Murder or Health Care

Abortions are described by pro-life groups as murders. Abortion providers are painted by pro-life forces as greedy, money-hungry exploiters of vulnerable or selfish women. One position asks the Court why abortion providers, with a direct economic stake in the outcome, are left to decide when life begins (or when viability exists and an abortion may not proceed). "Such decisions of life and death are simply too important to be left to the technicians," one pro-life group alleges, "especially when the one who makes the actual decision has an economic stake in deciding against life" (*Webster* Brief 15).

Briefs attack the clinics and facilities where abortions are performed. Some question the medical training of the "technicians." In attempts to undermine the credibility of the establishments, pro-life groups describe the abortion clinics very negatively. The abortion clinics are repeatedly referred to as part of the "abortion industry" (*Webster* Briefs 15, 17, 24).

Willke (1994: 324) writes about the person who performs the abortion procedure:

> Never, never call him or her a "doctor" and certainly never a "surgeon." There is a certain dignity to these words and the person doing the abortion does not deserve that stature or dignity. We should always call this person an "abortionist." . . . The word "abortionist" is one of derision, of criminality, of killing, and is the label that they deserve. Use it always, use it consistently.

Always use the words "kill," "mother," "womb," "abortion mill," "abortorium," or "abortion chamber" (Willke 1994: 324–6). By referring to these people as technicians and the clinics as "factories" or "industries," pro-life groups try to make abortion distinct from legitimate health care and birth control.

Groups representing the medical profession are also drawn into abortion politics, not solely out of a concern about the rights of women but because the outcome of the abortion wars will profoundly affect medicine. Associations of hospitals, doctors, nurses, public health officials, bioethicists, and medical school faculty argued to the Court the medical nature of abortion, the infringement of government on the doctor-patient relationship, and the ethical obligations of medical professionals in reproductive health. The medical arguments, though, might highlight the science and technology of abortion procedures, with the unintentional result of overshadowing the social context in which women make their abortion decisions and reifying science as one of the arbiters of abortion jurisprudence (Woliver 1996).

Medicine's role in abortion politics will increase in importance as pro-life groups work to reframe abortion as the biological issue that human life begins at conception. *Webster* amici filed by medical associations voice concern about an eroding patient-doctor relationship and the ability of doctors to practice medicine without government control. Bioethicists for Privacy, in *Webster* Brief 74, mention new reproductive technologies and wonder whether, at some future time they would be outlawed, too (see also *Webster* Brief 81). These groups had mostly been silent on abortion politics before, letting the women's rights groups and the ACLU battle this messy fight for them (Woliver 1992a, 1992b; Staggenborg 1991: 30–31). By the late 1980s, though, there was much concern in the medical community about erosion of the doctor-patient relationship concerning proper reproductive health care.

One pro-choice *Webster* brief, that of the Association of Reproductive Health Professionals, discusses the problem of the overlap and merging of abortion with some forms of birth control (see also the *Webster* brief of the Planned Parenthood Federation of America). This brief was the one most often cited by the majority on the Court in the *Webster* decision itself.

In addition, several pro-choice *Webster* briefs argue that legalized abortion has improved women's health in various ways, especially for poor women who before *Roe* had no safe options. They argue further that restrictions on access to legal abortion in the United States will "disproportionately burden racial minority groups" and poor women. "The Women of Color Brief" for *Webster* reminds the Court of the poverty, inadequate access to health care, and dangerous restrictions on abortion choice posed for women of color in the United States (see also Nsiah-Jefferson 1989; Martin 1987; Davis 1990: 53–65; Fisher 1986). This brief lists 15 groups on the title page, an additional 115 groups and 17 concerned individuals in the appendix. The coalition includes African-American, Hispanic, Latina, American Indian,

American Asian, and Puerto Rican women's rights and women's health groups.

Webster's Aftermath

The 1989 *Webster* decision was a setback for the pro-choice movement, opening up opportunities for state-by-state erosion of *Roe* such as those approved in the Missouri law challenged in *Webster*. When the *Webster* decision was announced, Wattleton felt a sense of loss and dejection. "The Court has shielded women from those who would fully recriminalize abortion, but now it was allowing a wider opening . . . [T]his gap could be used to erode the protections guaranteed in *Roe*" (Wattleton 1996, p. 46).

All of these threats to *Roe*, however, also raised the stakes in the 1992 presidential election, making the pleas by pro-choice activists to vote to save legal abortion compelling to many voters. One of the first things newly elected President Clinton did was sign orders reversing pro-life rules such as the "gag order" on clinics receiving federal funds that prohibited health care workers from mentioning abortion as a legal option for patients. Clinton also appointed two pro-choice justices to the Supreme Court.

Abortion continues to be an issue in political party politics (Rozell and Wilcox 1995: 256–7). The Republican party maintained its strong pro-life platform at the 1996 convention in the face of opinion polls showing the strength of pro-choice sentiments, and a concerned faction within the Republican party, "Republicans for Choice," pushed for a more moderate platform statement. The Democratic party remains clearly pro-choice. The abortion issue is one of several creating a wide "gender gap" in the electorate favorable to the Democratic presidential candidates (see Costain 1996).

Convincing Justices: Movements and Framing

Women's rights groups worked to educate predominantly male judges about what unwanted pregnancies and illegal abortions mean to women. Women's rights litigants wanted to include the experiences of women with abortion and unwanted pregnancies as equally legitimate "expert testimony" in abortion cases in the early 1970s (Rubin 1987: 47–48).

Echoes of this same strategy are found in NARAL's *Webster* brief, written with the NOW Legal Defense Fund. In line with its "Silent No More" campaign, begun in 1985, NARAL solicited testimonials from over thirty-five hundred women and their friends who had had illegal abortions before *Roe* or legal abortions after. The letters listed in the appendix of the brief tell stories of frightened and desperate women who experienced their illegal abortions as nightmares contrasted with others who described legal ones as respectable choices. The women testify that abortion provided much relief to them and allowed them to get on with their lives, provide better care for their existing loved ones, and save their mental and physical health (see also the American Psychological Association's *Webster* Brief 80; Luker 1975). All stressed that this highly personal and private decision should be left to women to make. Several people describe friends who died from illegal abortions pre-*Roe*.

As the first (and for a long time the only) woman on the Supreme Court, Justice Sandra Day O'Connor has been a particular target of social movement lobbying on abortion cases (Woliver interviews; Estrich and Sullivan 1989). O'Connor's role as a vital swing vote on abortion cases is part of the reason for this attention. Another reason is that both pro-life and pro-choice groups attempt to push all the justices, but especially O'Connor, to visualize women, motherhood, babies, and children when casting votes and writing opinions on abortion. Sullivan and Goldzwig (1996: 29) argue, "In her role as a mediator on the Court, O'Connor's approach to moral decision-making, specifically abortion decision-making, is female-associated and foregrounds an approach that has been marginalized in patriarchal Western thought." They maintain that Justice O'Connor "has resisted reductionist reasoning concerning abortion cases; instead, her opinions reveal an appreciation of the complexities that must inform judgments in these cases. Her reliance on the 'undue burden' standard for judicial review in presenting opinions on abortion cases reveals her views concerning the balancing of rights and relations" (36).

Sullivan and Goldzwig's work concentrates on O'Connor's written abortion opinions. I believe that in O'Connor's construction of a middle ground on abortion based on the view that no undue burden should be imposed, she has been influenced by the pro-choice movement's decades-long campaign to educate the justices about what an unwanted or dangerous pregnancy means to real women, how women's lives are shaped by their reproductive histories, and the hopes many had that Justice O'Connor would visualize born women citizens, rather than center unborn fetuses, when making her decisions (Woliver interviews).

O'Connor pressed the attorney general of Pennsylvania during oral arguments in the *Casey* case to "contextualize the provision in terms of 'real women' " (Sullivan and Goldzwig, 1996: 44). The *Casey* joint majority opinion refused to treat women as chattel and "recognized that women making abortion decisions are 'different'; state restrictions that refuse to acknowledge the special circumstances of pregnant women are unconstitutional"; it also included the experiences of women who are abused (Sullivan and Goldzwig 1996: 47). I believe there is evidence here also of the effect of the concerted effort of the pro-choice movement to display the

contextual continuum in which women negotiate their reproductive
decisions.

Civil Disobedience or Criminal Violence

A majority of pro-life arguments indict *Roe's* logic. Pro-life groups
maintain that a *Webster* ruling upholding *Roe* would wreak havoc in the
judicial system. *Roe's* "crazy quilt interpretation of personhood" will lead
to such scenarios as "disorder in the streets" (Briefs 10, 6).[3] Some pro-life
briefs warn that "the civil disobedience in the streets will continue." Pro-
life U.S. Senators predict "legal instability" and "fermented social strife"
(Brief 16). Several briefs refer to the civil disobedience of "sidewalk counseling" or "rescues" to show the dissension *Roe* has caused (*Webster* Briefs
19, 30, 34, e.g.). This is a compelling example of how establishment interest
groups might publicly eschew disruptive or radical acts by other partisans
yet find their disorderly behavior useful for arguments in favor of policy
change (see also Blanchard 1994: 89–91). The Right to Life League of
Southern California asserts that outraged citizens "are engaged in what is
already by far the most widespread civil disobedience in U.S. history" (Brief
14).

The *Dred Scott* (1857) case is a dominant example in this argument (see
also Sernett 1994: 159–87). The same rationale of the *Roe* opinion, the
National Legal Foundation brief states, "was applied in the *Dred Scott* case
to arbitrarily deny the self evident humanity of the African-American"
(Brief 8 and many others; see also Sernett 1994).

"When such protection is denied to the unborn," the National Legal
Foundation brief asserts, "it opens the door for arbitrary withdrawal of such
guarantees to all men and women" (Brief 8; see also Brief 21). Many analo-
gies are made between Nazi policies against the "Untermenschen" and U.S.
abortion policies (Briefs 44, 45, 47).

A few pro-life briefs were aimed at proving that *Roe* was harmful to
women. Feminists for Life et al. (Brief 24) includes testimonies from the
book *Rachel Weeping* by women recounting their bad experiences with legal
abortion. Birthright views "abortion on demand not as an act of 'choice,'
but as an act of despair on the part of a woman" (Brief 17). "Abortion has
become an excuse for not offering real aid to pregnant women," it continues.
"[A]bortion is simply a financially cheap way for society to brush troubled
women out of the way while claiming to have done them a service. Abortion
is indeed a woman's issue, but it is an issue not of women's rights, but of
women's oppression." ? good arg.

Abortion has harmed women in many ways, pro-life amici argue, including increased infertility after abortion, postabortion depression and stress,

difficulty in bonding with subsequent children, and increases in divorce (Brief 20; also Brief 50). Therefore, the argument goes, *Roe's* desire to protect women's health is backfiring. Several pro-choice briefs seek to refute these points.

New Frames

New developments in reframing abortion debates might come about from recent scholarship that asks us to reconceptualize what abortion jurisprudence should focus on. Currently, the debates center on women's rights versus fetal rights, the extent of the state's interest and legitimate intrusion into privacy, and the meanings of viability and protecting women's health. Two new books provocatively challenge us to see abortion differently.

Eileen McDonagh (1996) bases her pro-choice stance on a morally based examination of "women's true consent to be pregnant." McDonagh's nuanced construction of a potentially transformative vision of abortion also shows how to restore government abortion funding. She grants pro-life movement arguments on the possible humanity of fetuses and shows that, nonetheless, no person (even a fetus) has the right to intrude into another's body without their explicit consent. As McDonagh puts it, "to the extent that the law protects the fetus as human life, the law must hold the fetus accountable for what it does" (7). The fetus causes the pregnancy, which has a profound impact on women's bodies; therefore, the pregnant women should have the right to choose to resist an unconsented to intrusion by a fetus and ask the state to help stop the intrusion (138). McDonagh's study "breaks the deadlock over abortion rights created by the clash of absolutes over the personhood of the fetus by recentering the abortion issue on a premise of self-defense, which is the common ground that can unite pro-life and pro-choice forces alike" (11).

Another reconceiving of the abortion debates is Mark Graber's (1996) research showing that criminalized abortion laws in the past were selectively enforced, with great freedom given private doctors to provide safe abortions to their private patients. These patients were overwhelmingly middle- to upper-class white women. Poorer women, young women with no connections to private doctors, and women of color, however, could not avail themselves of these safe options. The criminal statutes were applied to them. Therefore, an equal protection argument should be mounted to protect *Roe*. "Equal justice under law" would strongly defend legal abortion since it is a deeply valued principle in American law. If *Roe* is ever overturned, the flip side of this decision would likely be that abortion would be quickly relegalized if law enforcement uniformly applied the criminal abortion laws to all women (white, rich, poor, of color). One weakness in the pro-choice movement now, Graber explains, is that many people of privilege, given the history of abortion before *Roe*, do not believe they or their daughters would actually lose the choice of abortion, if abortion were recriminalized or severely restricted. Furthermore, abortion rights might be restored if people of privilege were faced with enforcement of "deadbeat dad" child support and maintenance statutes for the men and boys who contributed to the pregnancies of women and girls.

Conclusion

Groups have mixed results as amicis in federal court cases, not necessarily providing a winning advantage (Epstein and Rowland 1991; Songer and Sheehan 1993). Interest groups use these briefs to try and frame the legal reasoning on important Supreme Court cases. Research on recent abortion cases shows the shifting and shaping of abortion law jurisprudence based, in part, on important legal doctrines (Epstein and Kobylka 1992). Both sides also attempt to position themselves as reflecting public opinion, an influence recent scholars have shown plays a role in Supreme Court decisions (Franklin and Kosaki 1989; Mishler and Sheehan 1993). Precedents, supportive social movements, and societal socio-economic patterns play a powerful role in structuring abortion policy (Rosenberg 1991; Rubin 1987: 3; see also Epstein 1985; O'Connor 1980). Effective abortion amicus briefs attempt to highlight these social forces for the judges.

Interest groups and social movements play an important role in setting the Supreme Court's agenda (O'Connor and Epstein 1983, 1984; Caldeira and Wright 1988). It is unclear, though, what effect amicus briefs have on the Court. Both sides felt that their amicus brief efforts had been influential in the *Webster* case (Woliver 1992a, 1992b; also Kolbert 1989a; Grant 1989). Clearly, the high stakes of the *Webster* decision helped heighten mobilization of movements in lobbying the Supreme Court.

Abortion movements show the ebb and flow of organizational strengths given political opportunity structures (McAdam 1982; Banaszak 1996), the importance of issue framing, the fluid nature of social movements such as women's rights and religious conservatism (Woliver, 1993, Gusfield 1981; Himmelstein 1990; Blanchard 1994), and the impact of changing contexts (as with new reproductive technologies and changing court personnel) within an issue debate.

Notes

Research for this project was partially funded through a Research and Productive Scholarship Grant, The University of South Carolina—Columbia.

1. Throughout this chapter the terms *pro-choice* and *pro-life* are used. These are the terms that the activists employ to describe themselves. Although the accuracy of these terms can be debated, it is preferable to use the self-definition of the activists when describing their political behavior. This follows the decision rule Kristin Luker (1984) utilized in *Abortion and the Politics of Motherhood.*

2. See Costain (1992) for further examples of women's rights legislation and court decisions being achieved before the full strength of women's interest groups and the larger women's movement.

3. This seems almost prophetic given the murders and violence perpetrated by pro-life activists at abortion clinics. In addition, moderate pro-life groups did not completely distance themselves from more violent groups after bombings and other acts of mayhem. "The Catholic Bishops' Conference blamed bombings on the existence of the clinics, as did others perceived as moderates, such as John Willke, leader of the [National] Right to Life Committee" (Blanchard 1994: 76; see also 78). Willke (1994: 330) writes that the abortion providers are the violent ones, "We are a 'people of peace.' Our abortion chamber picketers are basically nonviolent. The violence occurs *inside* the doors of the abortion chamber, not outside."

Part 6

Conclusions

15

On the International Origins
of Domestic Political Opportunities

Doug McAdam

Over the past twenty years the study of social movements and revolutions has been something of a growth industry in American social science. Spurred, in part, by the turbulence of the 1960s and early 1970s, scholars in a variety of disciplines—principally sociology and political science—turned their attention to the study of "contentious politics" (McAdam, Tarrow, and Tilly 1996). This dramatic increase in research attention was accompanied by something of a paradigm shift in the field, with a new generation of scholars rejecting the individualist flavor of the older theories in favor of newer perspectives that emphasized the structural dimensions and dynamics of collective mobilization and action.

Among the most important of these "newer" perspectives was the *political process* model, whose proponents sought to explain the emergence of collective action as a response to broad structural changes that rendered existing regimes more vulnerable or receptive to challenge by previously powerless groups (Jenkins and Perrow 1977; McAdam 1982; Tarrow 1983, 1994; Tilly 1978). While the theory also emphasized the importance of organizational strength and the development of certain shared cognitions within the challenging group, at the analytic center of the model was the concept of "political opportunities." The "structure of political opportunities" refers to those features of institutional politics that simultaneously facilitate and constrain collective action. The concept has become a staple of social movement analysis, but, like all influential concepts, it has not been without problems. I want to take up what I see as a serious limitation in the way scholars have conceptualized the geographic and/or institutional focus of political opportunities. I am referring to the nearly universal tendency to think of political opportunities as an exclusive feature of *national* political systems. In this chapter, I will argue that the concept applies at all levels of institutional power and, further, that the pressure for shifts in national-level political opportunities often arise internationally. But taking up this issue, let me offer a brief review of the concept.

Origins and Limits of the Concept

Writing in 1970, Michael Lipsky (14) urged political analysts to direct their attention:

> away from system characterizations presumably true for all times and places. . . . We are accustomed to describing communist political systems as "experiencing a thaw" or "going through a process of retrenchment." Should it not at least be an open question as to whether the American political system experiences such stages and fluctuations? Similarly, is it not sensible to assume that the system will be more or less open to specific groups at different times and at different places?

Clearly, Lipsky felt the answer to both questions was yes. He assumed that the ebb and flow of protest activity was a function of changes that left the broader political system more vulnerable or receptive to the demands of particular groups. Three years later, Peter Eisinger (1973: 11) used the term "structure of political opportunities" to help account for variation in "riot behavior" in forty-three U.S. cities. Consistent with Lipsky's view, Eisinger (1973: 25) found that "the incidence of protest is . . . related to the nature of the city's political opportunity structure," which he defined as "the degree to which groups are likely to gain access to power and to manipulate the political system."

Within ten years, the key premise informing Lipsky's and Eisinger's work had been incorporated as the central tenet in a new political process model of social movements. Proponents of the model saw the timing and fate of movements as largely dependent on the opportunities afforded insurgents by the shifting institutional structure and ideological disposition of those in power. Since then, this central assumption and the concept of "political opportunities" has become a staple in social movement inquiry. The emergence and development of instances of collective action as diverse as the American women's movement (Costain 1992; Katzenstein and Mueller 1987), liberation theology (Smith 1991), peasant mobilization in Central America (Brockett 1991), the nuclear freeze movement (Meyer 1993), peace movements in Europe (Rochon 1988), mobilization among the homeless in Chile (Hipsher 1996), and the Italian "protest cycle" (Tarrow 1989) have been attributed to the expansion and contraction of political opportunities. Most contemporary theories of revolution start from much the same premise, arguing that revolutions owe less to the efforts of insurgents than to the work of systematic crises that render the existing regime weak and vulnerable to challenge from every quarter (Goldstone 1991; Parsa 1989; Skocpol 1979). Finally, this stress on the institutional facilitation of protest has spawned a comparative tradition among European movement analysts in which variation in the "political opportunity structure" of various national states has been used to explain the fate of the same movement in a number of countries (Joppke 1993; Kitscheit 1986; Kriesi et al. 1992, 1995; Rucht 1990).

The concept of political opportunities has thus proven to be a popular addition to the analytic arsenal of movement scholars. But the widespread adoption and general seductiveness of the concept carries with it its own set of dangers. As Gamson and Meyer (1996: 24) have argued:

> The concept of political opportunity structure is in trouble, in danger of becoming a sponge that soaks up virtually every aspect of the social movement environment—political institutions and culture, crises of various sorts, political alliances, and policy shifts. . . . Used to explain so much, it may ultimately explain nothing at all.

The dangers to which Gamson and Meyer point are real. In a recent article (McAdam 1996), I discussed three problems that owe to the widespread adoption of the political opportunity concept. The first two problems focused on the failure of movement scholars: (1) to distinguish distinctly *political* opportunities from other forms of environmental facilitation of collective action and (2) to more precisely define the features of systems of institutional power that comprise their "political opportunity structure." Failure to redress the conceptual vagueness reflected in these two issues leaves the concept open to the worst kinds of post hoc storytelling. That is, armed with such a loosely defined and malleable concept, any analyst committed to the "theory" could, after the fact, construct a "political opportunity" account to "explain" the rise of virtually any social movement or revolution. But, following Gamson and Meyer, such an explanation would explain nothing.

To prevent such post hoc abuses requires a much more limited and precise operational demarcation of the concept. Toward that end, a number of movement scholars have recently sought to specify what they see as the relevant dimensions of a given system's political opportunity structure. Among those who have offered such schema are: Charles Brockett (1991), Kriesi et al. (1992), Dieter Rucht (1996), and Sidney Tarrow (1994). In the article cited earlier (McAdam 1996), I surveyed these works and found that aside from minor terminological differences, there was actually considerable overlap in the dimensions noted by the four authors. Synthesizing across the four schemes yields the following largely consensual sketch of those dimensions of institutional politics that are held to shape the general prospects for collective action (McAdam 1996: 27):

1. the relative openness or closure of the institutionalized political system;
2. the stability or instability of that broad set of elite alignments that typically undergird a polity;
3. the presence or absence of elite allies;
4. the state's capacity and propensity for repression.

The first dimension merely emphasizes the importance attributed to the formal legal and institutional structure of a given polity by all of the authors. Similarly, items 2 and 3 speak to the significance attached, by all of the analysts, to the informal structure of power relations characteristic of a given system.[1]

But redressing the vagueness evident in previous operational definitions hardly exhausts the lacunae associated with the concept. In the remainder of the chapter, I want to address the problem touched on at the outset—that is, the nation-centric bias evident in the way movement analysts have sought to conceptualize the origin and locus of political opportunities.

The Multilevel Nature of Political Opportunities

In the nearly quarter century since Eisinger first used the term, the concept of "political opportunity structure" has come to be almost universally equated with the rules, institutional structure, and elite alliances characteristic of *national* political systems.[2] Since Eisinger himself used the concept to compare *municipal* political systems, this equation of political opportunity structure with nation states is ironic, to say the least. The fact is, the concept is inherently multilevel. This is true of both the institutional locus and geographic origin of political opportunities.

The Institutional Locus of Political Opportunities

Any system of institutional power can be simultaneously analyzed as a political opportunity structure. This point applies to nonstate systems—institutional governance in a firm, for instance—no less than state. I will, however, confine myself to the multilevel institutional structuring of *state* power. Even here though, things are very complicated. Most state systems nest power at more than one level. These hierarchically structured systems are apt to be more elaborate in nominally democratic systems, but even in less democratic regimes, power is typically institutionalized at levels other than the national. In China, for example, party officials at the village level retain considerable autonomy from their counterparts at the national level.

Accordingly, we can speak of a village political opportunity structure that shapes the prospects for collective action at the local level.

Within nominally democratic states, one tends to find even more variation in the organizational structure of state power. Certain highly centralized states such as France are characterized by fewer and, arguably, less significant levels of state authority than states that are decentralized or federal in their structure. The United States is a good example in this regard. And since this volume is primarily concerned with the relationship between movements and the state in the United States, it makes sense to take a closer look at the institutional structuring of state power in the American context.

Four primary levels of institutional power exist in the United States. These four are the institutions of municipal, county, state, and federal government. In addition, for certain purposes, there are also regional authorities that constitute separate political opportunity structures distinct from the cities and states that comprise them. These regional bodies normally involve the administration of large public works projects that span more than one state, county, or municipality. The Tennessee Valley Authority and the Bay Area Rapid Transit Commission are examples of this type of regional governance structure.

The practical implications of this kind of multilevel state system for the emergence, development, and fate of social movements has, for all intents and purposes, escaped the attention of movement researchers. They have been so preoccupied with developments at the national level that they have ignored a host of interesting and highly consequential dynamics taking place at other levels of the system. I will confine myself to a discussion of only two such phenomena.

Movement Action that Bypasses the National

One thing that movement analysts—and movement opponents, for that matter—can count on is a certain relentless opportunism on the part of insurgent groups. That is, activists can be expected to mobilize at whatever level(s) they interpret as most likely to bear fruit. The important implication of this is that the foreclosure of opportunities at the national level need not spell decline for movements in a multilevel system of governance. It may simply signal a period in which the movement concentrates its energies at those lower-level institutional sites that remain receptive or vulnerable to challenge.

The 1970s, for example, are generally regarded as a time of decline for left movements in the United States. With moderate Republicans in the White House for most of the decade and Democratic margins in both houses of Congress shrinking, the national level structure of political opportunities may have been less facilitative of left movements during the period than was

true for most of the 1960s. However, anyone who was attuned to left movement activity during this period would have reason to quarrel with this simple account of movement decline. It is simply hard to reconcile the image of
decline with the growing strength and activity levels of various left movements during the 1970s. Among the most vital of these movements were the
women's, environmental, and antinuclear struggles. What all these movements shared in common was a decided preference for mobilization and
action at the state and local levels. The organizational forms and general
New Left ideology of these movements, no doubt, encouraged local forms of
action as well. But, in the absence of other institutional levels, these internal
movement factors would have mattered little. That is, had these movements
only had recourse to a national political opportunity structure, they would
have foundered badly. The multiple state, and especially local, institutional
sites available to these movements meshed well with their forms of organization and ideological distrust of big, bureaucratic movements and allowed
these various struggles to thrive during a period of contraction in national-
level opportunities.

Social Movements as Multilevel Games

Besides mobilizing at those levels that they see as being most advanta-
geous to the movement, activists are relentlessly strategic in another sense
in their choices about when and where to act. Here I am referring to the
attempts by movements to play levels or branches of government against one
another in an effort to generate maximum leverage for the movement. As I
have noted elsewhere (McAdam 1982, 1983), the American civil rights
struggle affords a wonderful example of the kind of multilevel games that
successful social movements are often able to orchestrate. While it generally
mobilized at the local level in the South, the movement's real target during
the civil rights phase of the struggle was the federal government. However,
movement strategists such as Martin Luther King and Bob Moses understood
that their best chance of forcing a reluctant *federal* government to act was
by exploiting the tendency of *state and local* law enforcement personnel to
respond violently to civil rights demonstrators. Public support for the movement grew apace of these incidents and pushed federal officials into embrac-
ing broader and more favorable changes in civil rights policy.

It should be noted that state authorities and countermovement groups
have recourse to these multiple levels as well and are just as intent in seeking
to adjudicate issues at whichever of these levels they feel are most favorable
to their point of view. Much of the controversy over the 1996 welfare reform
process centered on the fact that the bill sought to shift control over welfare
programs from the federal to the state level. Convinced that there was greater
federal receptivity to the needs of the poor than was true in most states,

liberal opponents of the bill fought the transfer of welfare policy. Conservative proponents fought just as hard to secure the transfer, knowing that it would effectively shift adjudication of the issue to an institutional level that typically favored an established coalition of state officials and antiwelfare activists.

The International Origins of Domestic Political Opportunities

There is another and, for the purposes of this chapter, more important sense in which the concept of political opportunities is inherently multilevel. This concerns the geographic/institutional locus within which the pressures for change in the political opportunity structure (POS) develop. Once again, the tendency has been to conceptualize expansions or contractions in political opportunities as processes that unfold exclusively within the domestic sphere. So changes in access rules or shifts in political alignments have generally been explained in reference to developments occurring at the national level. But this presumption of domestic primacy in the generation of political opportunities is clearly unwarranted. The fact is, pressure for change in the national POS can emanate at many different levels. In the kind of decentralized, multilevel state system profiled earlier, significant changes or crises at lower levels can lead to institutional changes or elite realignments at the national level. But even this expansion in our geographic/institutional approach to locating the sources of change in domestic political opportunities omits another critically important arena within which significant pressures for change often arise. I am speaking of the international level and specifically the pressures for change that devolve from perturbations in international political economy.

The Role of International Allies in Movement Emergence

Foreign governments may be international allies for domestic movements. In his rich empirical analysis of the so-called "Four Eights Democracy Movement" in Burma, Kyaw Yin Hlaing (1996: 12) makes the following important point:

> Usually theorists of opportunity structure focus their attention solely on potential domestic allies . . . but the Burmese case suggests looking beyond domestic factors. History has shown that major Western countries, especially donor countries, have great influence on the governments of countries like Burma since the former have power to cut off foreign aid and impose economic embargoes on the latter. As a consequence, donor countries can serve as influential allies for . . . movement activists.

Hlaing goes on to document the critical role played by the United States, Japan, and Germany in pressuring the Burmese government to curb its repression of movement activists. The intervention of these governments into Burmese politics, however, was itself prompted by the actions of another pair of international allies: the British Broadcasting System (BBC) and the Voice of America (VOA). It was the publicity and favorable editorial stance taken by these two international media outlets that focused world attention on the situation in Burma and prompted the diplomatic actions taken by the United States, Germany, and Japan.

The international facilitation of domestic mobilization can take the form of a collapse of a previously stable and strategically important alliance between a foreign power and the target regime. In his analysis of the emergence of a broad-based opposition movement in Taiwan in the mid-1970s, Fu Chang Wang (1989) provides a clear-cut case of this phenomenon. In this period, the Taiwanese regime was still composed of aging, mainland Chinese who had fled China with the Communist ascension to power in 1949. The regime had long justified its autocratic rule on the basis of its claim to be the legitimate representatives of the Chinese people. The Taiwanese government was but a regime in exile awaiting its imminent return to the mainland. During the Cold War years, the United States had supported these claims with massive military and financial aid to the Taiwan regime. All of this changed with President Nixon's historic overture to the People's Republic in the early 1970s. Nixon's initiative simultaneously ended Red China's isolation in the international community and seriously undermined the strong U.S.-Taiwan alliance that had characterized the Cold War years. The result was a dramatic weakening of the Taiwanese regime and stepped-up mobilization by a coalition of opposition groups.

The emergence of popular rebellions throughout the former Soviet system affords a more recent and better-known example of this same phenomenon. Gorbachev's stated unwillingness to commit Soviet troops to the defense of Warsaw Pact regimes sent shock waves through the system, aggressively signaling (even as it was contributing to) a significant rupture in the previously inviolate relationship of the Soviet Union to its Eastern bloc allies. This break had, as a good many analysts have shown, a critical catalytic effect on the revolutions of 1988–89 (Bunce 1995; Meyer 1991; Oberschall 1996; Tarrow 1991).

International Influences on the Capacity for Domestic Repression

The international facilitation of domestic social movements may involve the diminution of the established regime's repressive capacity. The emergence of "new allies" and the collapse of previously stable elite alliances often have significant effects on the will or ability of the target regime to repress opposition movements. In the case of Burma's Four Eights Movement, international pressure from a host of "new allies" to the movement discouraged the socialist regime from exercising its full repressive capacity (Hlaing 1996: 12). In contrast, Gorbachev's decisive removal of the ultimate threat of Soviet military intervention in the domestic affairs of its Warsaw Pact allies greatly compromised the actual ability of the Eastern bloc regimes to repress the burgeoning democracy movements.

In still other cases, both the will and capacity to repress have been influenced by international developments. One need only think of the rise to power of the Sandinistas in Nicaragua to glimpse this dynamic in action. President Carter inadvertently aided the process by making human rights the cornerstone of his foreign policy. Specifically, by making continued economic and military support contingent on significant improvement in human rights and then effectively suspending support in the absence of sufficient progress, Carter compromised the Somoza regime's ability and propensity to repress the Sandinista movement. The suspension of military aid reduced the regime's capacity for repression; and Carter's "strings attached" foreign policy weakened its political will to repress (Parsa 1995).

New Points of Institutional Access in Response to International Pressures

Perhaps the dimension of political opportunity least likely to be influenced by international events is the creation of new institutional openings in domestic political systems. But even here, one can think of examples in which something of the sort appears to have occurred. The case of the Soviet Union under Gorbachev again comes to mind. While the etiology of the Soviet collapse remains a matter of intense scholarly debate, a good many analysts have interpreted Gorbachev's policy of *glasnost,* and the specific reforms that followed from it, as a response to the economic crisis occasioned or exacerbated by the renewed military buildup of the early 1980s. According to this view, the new forms of institutional access granted insurgents by the *glasnost* reforms were themselves by-products of the economic and military pressures attendant to renewed superpower competition. To the extent that these openings afforded insurgents a host of new opportunities to mobilize (Zdravomyslova 1996), we can speak of another instance of the international facilitation of domestic political unrest.

In the remainder of this chapter, I seek to sketch a single, telling example of the international facilitation of social movement activity within a core country, the United States after World War II, when the country was at the height of its international dominance. If one can show that the rise of a domestic movement within the United States during this period owed, in part, to the influence of international pressures, one will simultaneously have gone a long way toward demonstrating the more general importance of the international to an understanding of movements in *all* polities. The case in question—the American civil rights movement—involves perhaps the most widely studied social movement in history. The point is, the ignorance of the international in the rise of the movement cannot be explained by ignorance of the movement as a whole. Instead, the ignorance has to be attributed to the more general nation-centric bias that has long characterized the study of social movements.

The Role of International Pressures
in the Rise of the American Civil Rights Movement[3]

In 1936 Franklin Delano Roosevelt was elected to serve his second term as president of the United States. Indeed, his margin of victory—popular as well as electoral—was one of the largest in the history of presidential politics. The election also marked a significant shift in racial politics in the United States. For the first time since African Americans were granted the right to vote, black voters deserted the Republican party—the party of Lincoln—to cast the majority of their votes for the Democratic presidential candidate. The New Deal reforms had been accompanied by a general leftward swing in political attitudes and had conditioned the American people to countenance assertive government action on behalf of the "less fortunate" segments of American society. Finally, FDR was himself a liberal—socially no less than politically—as was his outspoken and influential wife, Eleanor. Yet, in spite of all of these factors, Roosevelt remained silent on racial matters throughout his four-term presidency, refusing even to come out in favor of antilynching legislation on the numerous occasions such bills were brought before Congress.

Just ten years later, FDR's successor, Harry Truman, inaugurated a period of active executive advocacy of civil rights when he appointed and charged his national Committee on Civil Rights with investigating the "current state of civil rights in the country and recommending appropriate legislative remedies for deficiencies uncovered" (quoted in McAdam 1982: 84). Two years later, in 1948, Truman issued two landmark executive orders, the first establishing a fair employment board within the Civil Service Commission, and the second calling for the gradual desegregation of the armed forces.

Why did Truman act when Roosevelt had not? Comparing the domestic political contexts in which FDR and Truman acted only deepens the puzzle. While Roosevelt's electoral margins left him politically very secure, Truman's status as a nonelected president (he assumed the presidency following Roosevelt's death in 1945) made him uniquely vulnerable to challenge as he pointed toward the 1948 election. Moreover, with black voters now returning solid majorities for his party, Truman had little to gain and everything to lose by alienating that silent, but critically important, partner to the New Deal coalition: southern Dixiecrats. And that, of course, is precisely what his advocacy of civil rights reform did. Angered by his active support for civil rights, the Dixiecrats broke away from the party in 1948 and ran their own candidate, Strom Thurmond, for president. The electoral votes of the once "solid South" were now in danger of being lost. Add to this Truman's own attitudinal qualms about race (McCullough 1992) and the "chilling effect" of the Cold War on the American Left, and one could hardly think of a less propitious time to be advocating for political and socially progressive causes.

The key to the mystery lies not in the domestic context but in the new pressures and considerations thrust upon the United States and the executive branch, in particular, in the postwar period. As I argued in an earlier analysis of the civil rights movement (McAdam 1982: 83), World War II and the onset of the Cold War effectively terminated "the isolationist foreign policy that had long defined America's relationship to the rest of the world. As a result, national political leaders found themselves exposed, in the postwar era, to international political pressures and considerations that their predecessors had been spared. Locked in an intense ideological struggle with the USSR for influence among the emerging Third World nations, American racism suddenly took on international significance as an effective propaganda weapon of the Communists." Writing in 1944, Gunnar Myrdal (1970: 35) showed great prescience in underscoring the significance of this postwar shift:

> The Negro problem . . . has also acquired tremendous international implications, and this is another and decisive reason why the white North is prevented from compromising with the white South regarding the Negro. . . . Statesmen will have to take the changed geopolitical situation of the nation and carry out important adaptations of the American way of life to new necessities. A main adaptation is bound to be a redefinition of the Negro's status in American democracy.

In short, the otherwise puzzling contrast between Truman's actions and FDR's inaction becomes entirely comprehensible when placed in the very different international contexts in which they occurred. However, here I am less interested in accounting for the difference than in explicating the facilitative effect that this policy shift had on the emerging civil rights movement. In the sections to follow, I will argue that all four of the dimensions of political opportunity were positively affected by the emerging political pressures and considerations attendant to the Cold War.

Elite Divisions: Cracks in the Racial Status Quo

In a successful effort to resolve the deadlocked presidential election of 1876, northern Republicans agreed to relax federal Reconstruction efforts in the South in exchange for southern congressional support for their candidate, Rutherford B. Hayes. The practical effect of the compromise was to, once again, render the "Negro question" a matter of local rather than federal purview. "In this sense, the compromise serves as a convenient historical referent marking the point in time at which the question of the sociopolitical status of black Americans was consciously 'organized out' of national politics" (McAdam 1982: 66). Though strained considerably by such domestic developments as the collapse of King Cotton, the mass migration of African Americans out of the South, and the growing electoral significance of the "black vote," the elite "understanding" on matters of race nonetheless held until the postwar period.[4] That is what makes Truman's actions so significant. They mark the first split in the elite alliance that had preserved the racial status quo for the previous seventy years. Reflecting the terms of the original compromise of 1876, the alliance turned on an implicit agreement between national leaders and the southern political and economic elite that on matters of race "local custom" would prevail. The ultimate effect of this agreement was, of course, the abrogation of the rights guaranteed under the thirteenth, fourteenth and fifteenth Amendments and the forceful reassertion of racial dominance within the South in the form of disenfranchisement, the Black Codes, widespread lynching, and the institution of Jim Crow more generally.

Truman's actions signaled an end to the federal/southern "understanding" on race and granted new leverage to civil rights activists. Indeed, perhaps the key strategic dynamic of the southern civil rights phase of the movement was the aggressive exploitation of the growing split between southern officials and the president (McAdam 1982: 174–9). The split owed to the increasingly different political considerations motivating the two parties to the conflict. Southern officials sought to maintain segregation as much to ensure their reelections as to preserve the "southern way of life." The challenge for the president was to minimize electoral defections while preventing the kinds of public crises that fueled Soviet propaganda campaigns.

The latter balancing act was much tougher for Democratic presidents than Republican. In reacting to events in the South, Kennedy and Johnson were inevitably forced to balance the interests of two key components of their electoral coalition: African Americans and Dixiecrats. This strategic dilemma made them reluctant to intervene in the South. But their Cold War-induced fear of crisis and public disorder gave the civil rights movement the tactical leverage it needed to compel the federal government to act. "Lacking sufficient power to defeat the supremacists in a local confrontation, insurgents sought to broaden the conflict by inducing their opponents to disrupt public order to the point where supportive federal intervention was required" (McAdam 1982: 174). In campaign after campaign, from the sit-ins through Selma, civil rights forces mastered the tactics of peaceful provocation and in so doing effectively exploited the federal/southern split on race characteristic of the Cold War years.

New Allies in the Racial Struggle

The Cold War years afforded civil rights forces new allies in their struggle for racial equality. These allies can be grouped into two general categories: foreign governments and domestic forces motivated by the strategic imperatives of the Cold War. I will take up each in turn.

Among foreign governments, it was the actions of the Soviet Union that exerted the most influence over the postwar shift in federal racial policy. In the race for international influence after the war, Soviet leaders recognized American racism for what it was: a propaganda weapon of enormous salience, especially among the host of Third World nations then emerging around the globe. That the Soviet exploitation of this issue was of concern to federal officials is clear from the mass of empirical evidence assembled by Azza Layton (1995) in her exhaustive treatment of the subject.

A single example will serve to underscore the point. In 1957 the newly created Civil Rights Commission requested a report from the State Department on the issue of U.S. racial policy and its effect on international affairs. In requesting the report, the commission asked the State Department to address two specific topics: the impact of American racial policies on U.S. relations with other governments and an appraisal of Soviet efforts to exploit U.S. vulnerability on the issue. Regarding the latter topic, the report acknowledged the effectiveness of Moscow's efforts, saying that "Soviet propaganda attacks on U.S. racism were geared into every political maneuver to 'expose' the 'American way of life' " (quoted in Layton 1995: 141). The report goes on to chronicle the Soviet Union's relentless exploitation of the issue. Layton's (1995: 141) summary captures the flavor of the report:

> The Little Rock crisis, for example, enabled Moscow to challenge the United States at UN debates over Hungary in 1957. The Soviets attempted to discredit the moral position of the United States on Hungary by pointing to the "unbelievable crimes and violations of the most elementary human rights taking place in the southern United States." The Soviets hit the United States repeatedly, not only for permitting the racists to abuse its only citizens but also for daring to reproach others while "its own hands were dirty." The Soviets, the report said, advised United Nations delegates from Asian and African na-

tions that in the country in which the United Nations was meeting, "people of their color are being persecuted."

But the Soviets were hardly alone in putting pressure on the United States for redress of its racial policies. As Layton's work makes clear, governments from every corner of the globe exerted diplomatic pressure on the American state. Not surprisingly, much of this pressure came from newly created Third World countries. The aforementioned report noted that sensitivity to U.S. racial policies was strongest in Africa and Asia "where a sense of self identification is involved, and where racial discrimination in the U.S. is inevitably linked with the presence or recent memory of white colonialism and domination" (quoted Layton 1995: 138–9). But criticism of U.S. racial policies was hardly confined to the Third World. Indeed, the report went on to note, some of the strongest criticism had come from Western Europe, from allies that were concerned about both the moral and strategic implications of U.S. practices.

In the context of the Cold War, this nearly universal condemnation of American-style racism had its effect on U.S. policy. Motivated by foreign policy concerns, new allies began to emerge within the federal government and to voice support for policy change. The pressures were felt first within the diplomatic corps and then spread quickly to high-placed State Department officials and on to the White House, charged, as it was, with the ultimate conduct of U.S. foreign policy. Besides the string of executive actions taken by Truman and his Cold War successors, the shift in federal civil rights policy was expressed in a series of important briefs filed by the U.S. attorney general in connection with several civil rights cases heard during the Cold War years by the Supreme Court.

Arguably the most important of these briefs was one filed in December 1952 in connection with a public school desegregation case—*Brown v. Topeka Board of Education*—then before the Court. The brief attests not only to the important substantive shift in U.S. racial policy but to the international considerations motivating it. In part the brief read, "[I]t is in the context of the present world struggle between freedom and tyranny that the problem of racial discrimination must be viewed. . . . Racial discrimination furnishes grist for the Communist propaganda mills, and it raises doubt even among friendly nations as to the intensity of our devotion to the democratic faith" (quoted in McAdam 1982: 83).

International Pressure and Segregationist Violence

An analysis of historical trends in supremacist violence also supports the idea that the onset of Cold War pressures led to a favorable shift in this last dimension of political opportunity. For all federal officials' reluctance to act as agents of southern law enforcement, the very real costs of inaction prompted them to intervene when segregationists threatened to produce the kind of *highly publicized* instances of racist violence that occasioned international outrage. Two telling contextual points are to be made here. The first is historical: despite the much higher levels and greater savagery of racist violence before World War II, one would have to go back to radical Reconstruction to find a single instance of federal intervention to prevent southern racist violence. The other point concerns the requirement that supremacist violence be "highly publicized" to prompt federal intervention. That is, even during the Cold War years, the federal government responded to only *some*—indeed, the great minority of—instances of racist violence. The conclusion is as obvious as it is depressing. Federal intervention was not motivated by the violence per se but the desire to defuse the international and domestic crises that threatened political interests.

Grudging and sporadic as it may have been, federal intervention did have an effect, as much for the indirect influence it exerted on southern segregationists as from the direct results it achieved. That is, faced with the threat of federal intervention, moderate southern segregationists began to weigh the benefits of violent social control against the costs of inviting the imposition of federal authority. Though violence continued to be—indeed, continues to be—a weapon of ardent segregationists, the civil rights years were marked by ever-increasing efforts to mobilize a wide range of legal, economic, and political obstacles to racial change. The net effect on the civil rights movement was to lower the costs of mobilization by curbing the most violent excesses of the white resistance movement.

Conclusion

This chapter was motivated by a simple premise: that social movement scholars, unlike their brethren who study revolutions, have truncated our understanding of the rise of social movements by ignoring the *international* forces that frequently shape the structure of *domestic* political opportunities available to challenging groups. I sought to demonstrate this contention in two ways: first, through a brief review of various cases in which international pressures appear to have encouraged the rise of domestic social movements; and second, through an account of the emergence of the American civil rights movement. The latter account focused primary attention on the facilitative influence that Cold War political pressures exerted on all four dimensions of political opportunity typically stressed by movement scholars.

This discussion represents, of course, little more than a sensitizing introduction to what I see as a critical "silence" in the social movement literature. Many daunting conceptual and, especially, methodological challenges await those who would take the chapter's implicit injunction seriously. If measuring changes in the domestic political opportunity structure is difficult, how can we ever hope to determine whether the origin of the changes are domestic or international? Who are the agents of such change? And what are the mechanisms that link international events and developments within domestic systems? These are only a few of the difficult issues that movement analysts will have to grapple with to move beyond the preliminary remarks advanced here. But difficult as they may be, I see little choice but to try to address these issues. To do otherwise would be to countenance the continued ignorance of what is clearly an important and consequential dynamic shaping many domestic social movements.

Notes

1. The only nonconsensual dimension I have incorporated into my list is state repression. Other than Brockett (1991), none of the other authors include this point in their schema. I find this omission puzzling. Considerable empirical evidence attests to the significance of this factor in shaping the level and nature of movement activity. Some observers (e.g., della Porta 1995) have speculated that state repression is really more an *expression* of the general receptivity or vulnerability of the political opportunity structure, rather than an independent dimension of same. I am not convinced that this is the case. To view repression as merely expressive of other features of a given system of institutional power is to blind us to the unpredictable nature of repression and the complex social processes that structure its operation. Anyone who doubts this point would do well to reflect for a moment on the fate of the 1989 Chinese student movement. On many key dimensions of political opportunity, the movement appears—even in retrospect—to have been in reasonably good shape. While the system remained formally closed to the students, they clearly were able to mobilize a number of key elite allies—most notably, the state-controlled media—during the conflict. Moreover, there were clear divisions within the ruling elite that granted an unprecedented opportunity to the students. Nonetheless, Communist party hard-liners were still able to mobilize the social control capacity and political will necessary to thoroughly repress the movement. The fact that in seemingly similar situations (e.g., Iran in 1979) the ruling elite was not able to do what the Chinese hard-liners did suggests the merit of considering state repression as a separate, though clearly related, dimension of the political opportunity structure.

2. Besides Eisinger, few analysts have applied the concept of POS at levels other than the national. Among those who have are Wisler, Barranco, and Tackenberg (1996), who compare police practices across several cities and cantons in Switzerland; and Marks and McAdam (1996), who seek to explain the fate of several broad categories of European social movements by reference, in part, to differences in the structure of political opportunities at the level of the European Union.

3. The argument that I develop in this section draws heavily on the groundbreaking work of Azza Layton (1995). While I asserted the importance of Cold War international pressures in my 1982 book on the emergence of the civil rights movement, I did so without providing any empirical evidence to buttress my claims. The significance of Layton's work stems from not only her sophisticated conceptual argument but also the thoroughness with which she has marshalled empirical evidence—drawn largely from government sources—to

document the weight and salience of these pressures within select government circles, especially the State and Justice Departments.

4. Even these nominally "domestic" factors received significant impetus from international developments. The decline of the cotton economy, for instance, resulted at least in part from the disruption of world trade during World War I and the opportunity this afforded other countries—principally Egypt and the Sudan—to develop competitive cotton economies of their own (Anderson-Sherman and McAdam 1983; McAdam 1982). After 1918, the United States never regained the unique trade monopoly it had enjoyed in cotton prior to the war.

16

Where Have All the Foils Gone?
Competing Theories of Contentious Politics
and the Civil Rights Movement

Mark I. Lichbach

Most books have a foil as well as a model. They are written to criticize some books and emulate others.

> Guenther Roth (cited in Weber [1924], 1968: lxvii)

Interesting philosophy is rarely an examination of the pros and cons of a thesis. Usually it is, implicitly or explicitly, a contest between an entrenched vocabulary which has become a nuisance and a half-formed new vocabulary which vaguely promises great things.

> Richard Rorty (1989: 9)

To understand protest in America, one must understand protest and one must understand America. More generally, the study of resistance against authority may adopt two foci: resistance and authority. One may therefore investigate those who challenge power and those who hold power (the rulers and the ruled); take the point of view of people who are oppressed and people who oppress (the victimizers and the victimizers); care about deviant actors and normal citizens (the majority and the marginalized); analyze insurgent politics and institutionalized politics (centrism and extremism); and explore social movements and political institutions (regimes and oppositions). Thomas Hobbes thus wrote two important books: *Behemoth* and *Leviathan*. The first monster is the symbol of lawlessness, chaos, disorder, anarchy, heterodoxy, and deviance; the second is the symbol of law, order, power, the state, domination, and social control.[1]

The study of protest in America thus involves two interrelated sets of empirical and moral concerns. First, are the disadvantaged represented in the system of mobilized groups? The suspicion is that intense interests and preferences are not enough and that some groups are more socially active and politically relevant than others. This cynicism leads to a set of empirical questions: Which groups successfully mobilize and which do not? Who gets included and who is excluded? Does the universe of politically active and effective groups mirror all the preferences and values in civil society? Or is the system of mobilized interests unjust, unfair, unequal, unbalanced, and hence undemocratic? Second, are America's institutions biased against the disadvantaged? This mistrust leads to another set of empirical questions: Which institutions are responsive to which preferences? Is the system as a whole accessible to some groups and closed to others?

These normative and empirical concerns can be put more concretely. The problem of protest in America is really an issue of the relative successes and failures of groups based on race, religion, ethnicity, gender, region, and class when they attempt to mobilize and confront capitalist democracy in America: its institutions of weak catch-all political parties, strong courts, a locally rooted Congress, a nationally elected president, federalism, nationally and internationally entrenched corporations, and its corresponding cultural ethos of "egalitarianism, individualism, populism, and laisssez-faire" (Lipset 1996: 31). For example, to understand black protest, one must therefore understand racist institutions; and to understand feminist activism, one must understand sexist institutions. The same homily holds for Jews, Indians, gays and lesbians, environmentalists, consumers, Italians, and Catholics. In short, a study of protest in America is a study of a historically concrete group-institution nexus. Specific institutions affect the mobilization of specific groups, and the mobilized groups in turn influence the institutions.

One important approach to the study of protest in America therefore focuses on America and its institutions. I call this macroscopic structuralist approach that has recently been consolidated by all of its leading members (Tarrow 1994; McAdam, McCarthy, and Zald 1996; McAdam, Tarrow, and Tilly 1996, 1997) Synthetic Political Opportunity Theory (SPOT). An important alternative approach to protest in American naturally concentrates on groups and their mobilization. I call this microscopic agential approach that has recently been systematized and analyzed in *The Rebel's Dilemma* (Lichbach 1995; also see Lichbach 1992, 1994a, Moore 1995) the Collective Action Research Program (CARP).

This chapter is designed to stimulate a dialogue between the two competing approaches—(rational) action-oriented CARP and structure-oriented SPOT—to social movements. My road map of the similarities and differences between the approaches is greatly enhanced by McAdam's (1982) seminal structuralist account and Chong's (1991) exemplary rationalist account of the civil rights movement. These will be contrasted to show differences between the two approaches, CARP and SPOT.

SPOT

This section develops an explanation sketch (Hempel 1965: 238) of SPOT. I then apply this sketch to the civil rights movement.

Theory

The structuralist's explanandum is "contentious politics": the "collective action" and "collective mobilization" of "contenders" for power. Structuralists also have a strong secondary concern, in practice often confounded with the first, with a group's success at achieving reformist change in policies and revolutionary change in governing institutions. The form of contention that has most occupied the structuralists' attention is therefore the social movement. Because they are not formally organized, with a well-defined leadership, goal hierarchy, and decision-making entity, movements are not interest groups (Tarrow 1994: 15–16). Nor are they mobs—unorganized and ephemeral collectivities. Rather, social movements are coordinated and sustained groups that engage in "contentious collective action" (Tarrow 1994: 2) with "elites, authorities and opponents" (Tarrow 1994: 1). Besides social movements, other highly structured phenomena that potentially fit under the broad explanandum of "contentious politics" include social revolutions, ethnic mobilizations, and cycles of protest.

SPOT skillfully weaves several strands of resource mobilization and political process arguments into a "broad framework" (Tarrow 1994: 2) that explains contentious politics. This new synthesis argues that social movements are "triggered by the incentives created by political opportunities, combining conventional and challenging forms of action and building on social networks and cultural frames" (Tarrow 1994: 1). To his (Tarrow 1994: 189) key question, "How movements become the focal points for collective action and sustain it against opponents and the state," Tarrow thus answers that three factors are crucial.

PO: Politics, Defined in Terms of Political Opportunities

The polity is structured by four features: "the relative openness or closure of the institutionalized political system," "the stability of that broad set of alignments that typically undergird a polity," "the presence of elite allies," and "the state's capacity and propensity for repression" (McAdam, McCarthy, and Zald 1996: 10). Political opportunities are therefore "consistent—but not necessarily formal or permanent—dimensions of the political environment that provide incentives for people to undertake collective action by affecting their expectations for success or failure" (Tarrow 1994: 85). Political processes, institutions, and alignments thus set the context for the strategic interaction of a movement with its allies and opponents in civil society and the state.

MS: Society, Defined in Terms of Mobilizing Structures

Civil society is structured along class, status, gender, ethnic, religious, and racial lines. These partially overlapping systems of stratification "link leaders with the organization of collective action—center with periphery—permitting movement coordination and allowing movements to persist over time" (Tarrow 1994: 136). Elite-mass linkages include "informal as well as formal [vehicles] through which people mobilize and engage in collective action" (McAdam et al. 1996: 3). Dissident mobilizing structures thus include community and association and are rooted in civil society.

CF: Culture, Defined in Terms of Cultural Frames

Culture is structured by shared meanings, symbols, and discourses. Social movements are thus constituted by the culture in which they operate. Structuralists also think of culture in another way (Lichbach 1995: 450, n. 5). Movements strategically frame meanings, symbols, and discourses so as to define grievances, pose solutions, and advance their "cognitive liberation" (McAdam 1982). Cultural framing therefore involves the "conscious strategic efforts by groups of people to fashion shared understandings of the world and of themselves that legitimate and motivate collective action" (McAdam et al. 1996: 6). For example, the American ethos of "egalitarianism, individualism, populism, and laisssez-faire" (Lipset 1996: 31) implies that protesters in America will be more successful if they hold a prayer vigil than if they burn the American flag. Culture, as much as politics and society, structures resistance to authority.

SPOT thus views social movements from a very attractive mix of Weberian structural and strategic perspectives: the historically rooted political, social, and cultural institutions of a social order define systems of stratification and set the contexts for the historically concrete struggles over power, wealth, and status. The polity, society, and culture structure who is mobilized and who demobilized and therefore who wins and who loses. Different structures institutionalize conflict, and hence bias politics, in different ways. PO, MS, and CF are therefore the windows through which groups understand and attack institutions. They are also the vehicles through which theorists understand and evaluate these conflicts: structuralists expect that these three nominalist (i.e., artificial and transhistorical) concepts will help them dissect real (i.e., historically concrete) groups and institutions.[2]

By placing contentious politics at the heart of the study of authority and resistance, structuralists can apply this explanatory framework to substantively specific explananda and raise big questions. For example, just as Tilly (1978) moved from mobilization to revolution, Tarrow (1994) shifts from movement to the larger world that movement turns upside down. He explores the emergence of the national social movement in the West over the last three centuries. He also studies the protest cycle, suggesting that the "early risers" in movements exploit and expose changes in PO and hence provide incentives for "late arrivers." In addition, he examines the political struggle to reform and produce policy outcomes. Finally, Tarrow speculates about the emergence of a "movement society" in which collective action (CA) is "disruptive" (i.e., permanent, transnational, and violent) rather than "conventional" (i.e., "absorbed and institutionalized into ordinary politics" (8), via "peaceful, orderly routines that break no laws and violate no spaces" (110). The issue here is whether contemporary political protest will go the way of the strike, sit-in, boycott, demonstration, petition, and political association.

Application

McAdam (1982) uses SPOT's three macrostructures to explain CA in the civil rights movement. First, he explores PO that influenced the movement and was ultimately shaped by it. He demonstrates how electoral politics, governing coalitions (e.g., the coalition of 1876, the New Deal alignment), white support and white backlash, segregation as a system of social control, and government repression and responsiveness to the movement affected the ebb and flow of black protest.

Second, McAdam analyzes MS, which he calls "indigenous organizational strength." Geographic mobility out of the South, the ending of cotton tenancy, and urbanization shaped the preexisting organizations in the black community—black churches, black colleges, and the southern wing of the NAACP—that directly influenced the surge and decline of black protest.

Finally, McAdam studies CF, which he calls "cognitive liberation." Black identity and consciousness, perceptions of racial injustice, expectations of powerlessness, feelings of fatalism and hope, and the prevailing liberal and democratic ideologies of American society affected the waning and waxing of black protest.

McAdam therefore offers a structurally oriented historical narrative of the black social movement cycle in America. The modernization of authority in America is linked to the modernization of black CA. PO, MS, and CF were thus individually necessary but not sufficient conditions for protest; the combination $PO \times MS \times CF$ was the necessary and sufficient condition for the civil rights movement.

CARP

This section develops an explanation sketch (Hempel 1965: 238) of CARP, the other contending approach to social movements. CARP focuses on groups, resistance, and protest rather than institutions, authority, and America. I again apply this sketch to the civil rights movement.

Theory

The fundamental assumption of CARP is that collective endeavors often involve public goods and Prisoner's Dilemma elements. The famous deduction and prediction of collective action (CA) thinking is therefore the Five Percent Rule: less than 5 percent of the supporters of a cause become actively involved in the cause, and activists outnumber nonactivists nineteen to one. Moreover, CA theorists expect that this rule will be correct 95 percent of the time—as a good a theory as we presently have in the social sciences (Lichbach 1996: sect. 1.2). Work on the Rebel's Dilemma, or the problem of free riding and nonparticipation in protest and rebellion, was sparked by economists (Tullock 1971) and sociologists (Gamson [1975] 1990) who drew upon Olson (1965). The idea that CA is the rare exception and not the general norm, because self-interest works against the collective good, has stimulated dozens of substantive contributions (Muller 1979; Muller, Dietz, and Finkel 1991; Muller and Opp 1986) and dozens of mathematical formalizations of the CA problem in protest and rebellion (Lichbach 1992, 1995; Moore 1995). Elsewhere I have outlined the four basic steps in this research program (Lichbach 1995: 292–3).

First, rationalists begin testing the Five Percent Rule[3] with a descriptive map of CA.[4] We try to observe collective action *and* inaction, what did *and* did not happen, positive *and* negative cases, or the dog that barked *and* the one that remained silent, in some particular context. Following Walker (1991: 1–3), we can consider the whole range of dissident groups that are and are not actively resisting some social order at one point in time, and then ask how so many groups came into being and why so many others did not. In short, we can compare the preference distribution of a population with a map of the constellation of dissident groups. Following McAdam (1982), we can also begin historically and follow the waning and waxing of CA in a single group in some social order. Or, following Katznelson and Zolberg (1986), we can follow one social group (e.g., class) across many different social contexts. Finally, following Kriesi et al. (1995), we can follow many different social groups (e.g., several new social movements) across many different social contexts. Whether we proceed with one social order and look at many groups cross-sectionally or one group longitudinally, or many different social orders and look at one group longitudinally or many groups cross-sectionally, CA theorists always begin with a group (or groups) rooted in a more or less well-defined historical tradition and linguistic community that define its long-run goals, ideals, meaning, and project (i.e., the public goods that it seeks). While a group's teleology will be important to assessing intended and unintended consequences in step 4, CA theorists recognize that groups always contain within-tradition conflicts that have major impacts on CA.

Second, rationalists produce an explanatory map of CA processes to solve the basic empirical puzzle of CA theory: how can we explain the 5 percent who did participate in CA? Certain CA processes are operative and others not. Which of the many plausible rival solutions to the CA problem did the work of mobilizing or demobilizing dissidents? In other words, which CA solutions, under which conditions, activated or deactivated most protest and rebellion?

Solutions to the CA problem vary on two dimensions (Lichbach 1995: 21). The first dimension is deliberative. The actors involved in a CA problem may or may not discuss their situation and ultimately devise an answer. Solutions to the CA problem may thus result in either unplanned or planned order. The second dimension is ontological. One might believe that the entities involved in a CA problem are individuals only, or one might believe that institutions, structures, and/or relationships preexist individuals and that they help impose order. Solutions to the CA problem may thus result in either spontaneous or contingent order.

Combining dimensions produces the classic distinctions of social thought. Market approaches to social order and CA assume only individuals who engage in no social planning. Market approaches thus feature unplanned and spontaneous order. Contract approaches also assume individuals, but individuals who collectively plan their society. Contract approaches thus feature planned but spontaneous order. Community approaches assume that institutions exist and that these communal structures are so effective that social planning is unnecessary. Community approaches thus feature unplanned but contingent order. Finally, Hierarchy approaches also assume that institutions exist, and in fact these institutions are created in order to plan society. Hierarchy approaches thus feature planned and contingent order. The result is that there are two approaches to unplanned order, Market and Community, and two approaches to planned order, Contract and Hierarchy. The result is also that there are two spontaneous approaches to social order, Market and Contract, and two contingent approaches to social order, Community and Hierarchy. The four possible solutions to the CA problem are displayed in Table 16.1.

Of these four sets of solutions, Market approaches to social order and CA may be thought of as the baseline. They operate by changing the parameters of the canonical model of CA. The other three sets of solutions are based on varying the context in which the baseline model is placed. Community solutions explore how common belief systems solve Olson's Problem, Contractual solutions study the ways in which mutual agreements produce CA, and Hierarchy solutions examine how hierarchies structure CA. Lichbach

Table 16.1
Solutions to the CA Problem: Deliberation Ontology

	Unplanned Order	Planned Order
Spontaneous order	Market	Contract
Contingent order	Community	Hierarchy

(1995) fits approximately two dozen sets of solutions to the CA problem into this typology of the organizational forms behind CA (see the appendix in Lichbach 1995). The practical idea, of course, is to pick a very small number of central or master CA solutions that define the character of a particular movement. CA theorists thus wager on a few driving variables, causal mechanisms, or CA models.

CARP therefore identifies a key issue ignored by SPOT: whether group mobilization occurs by Market, Community, Contract or Hierarchy. Mobilization by Market implies that individuals are driven by a variety of individual-level forces. The resulting forms of collective dissent are anomic and include, for example, rioting. Mobilization by Hierarchy, in contrast, involves preexisting dissident organizations that explicitly mobilize their followers. Leadership and organizational forms become important. The resulting forms of collective dissent include, for example, social democratic and Leninist types of protest. Mobilization by Contract and Community involves more self-organization by dissidents. Pure contract implies a single-function self-governing arrangement that is targeted only at protest. Pure Community implies a multifunctional self-governing arrangement that has been mobilized into protest. These are, of course, ideal types that may be used to investigate how actual cases of protest are structured. For example, covenant implies that an entire community has agreed to a contract. The resulting forms of collective dissent include, for instance, national liberation movements. Congregation, for another example, implies that a subset of a community has agreed on certain governing principles for protest. The resulting forms of collective dissent include, for example, sectarian forms of terrorism.

Third, rationalists trace the causes of the key operative and inoperative CA processes. This leads directly into politics: how did competing interests—the regime, dissident entrepreneurs, dissident followers, and the dissidents' allies and opponents—try to shape contexts, structures, and institutions so as to initiate, sustain, and terminate CA processes? This inquiry produces generalizations about the origins of the basic properties of collective dissent—for example, an etiology of the risk propensities of dissidents, dissident altruism, dissident self-government, and external patronage of dissent. These explanations ultimately help us understand group mobilization.

Finally, rationalists trace the effects of the key operative and inoperative CA processes. This leads to the intended consequences of group mobilization: new institutions, policies, and programs created by dissents that help relegitimize the social order. More important, it leads to the unintended consequences of group mobilization: the pathologies of dissent (e.g., Michels's Dilemma). In short, CA theorists are interested in determining how the goals and ideals of dissidents are fulfilled and frustrated. They look at the victories as well as the tragedies, comedies, and farces of collective dissent. In the case of social revolutions, for example, outcomes include bourgeoisie, fascist, or communist paths of development. Economic development, national development, state building, and nation building hold many intended and unintended consequences.

In sum, solutions to the CA problem are the basic building blocks of a rationalist theory of collective dissent and political quiescence. What is really useful about CA theories is that they lead to comparative and historical analyses of the causes and consequences of the basic properties of collective dissent: CA processes.[5] CARP is therefore an important approach to social movements because it is resolutely based on Olson's (1965) theory.[6] By elaborating his insights, CARP identifies many CA problems in conflict (e.g., among the rebel's organizations, within a rebel organization, among the state's supporters, or the State's Dilemma) and produces many new insights. CARP thus takes Olson's approach, runs with it, and sees where it goes.[7]

Application

Chong (1991) uses CARP's four steps to explain CA in the civil rights movement. First (chap. 1), he notes that the civil rights movement sought public goods. Some of the best examples of public-spirited CA include the attempts to remove Jim Crow Barriers, promote the passage of national legislation expanding civil rights, curtail racial prejudice, affirm the right to attend desegregated schools, and obtain the right to equal access to public accommodations. CA to achieve these goods varied among blacks, both over time and across geographic space.

Second, Chong (1991) explores many CA processes that both overcame and intensified the obstacles to CA by blacks on behalf of these worthy causes. The Market solutions that he argues mobilized and demobilized blacks include the probability of winning, costs (e.g., start-up costs, government repression), tactical innovations, and competitive mobilization. The Community solutions that he maintains helped and hurt blacks' CA include social incentives, means as ends (expressive or participatory benefits), group consciousness (community obligation), mutual expectations, and bandwagons. The Contract solutions that he believes affected the movement include tit-for-tat and self-government. Finally, the Hierarchy solutions that Chong thinks overcame and intensified blacks' CA problem include entrepreneurs, patrons (e.g., the federal government, labor, northern students, organized religion, traditional liberal organizations such as the ACLU), clubs (i.e., small size), effective groups (i.e., unanimity production functions), competition among allies, and material selective incentives.

Third, Chong explores the causes of various solutions to black's CA problem. The existence and strength of social incentives, reputational effects in tit-for-tat agreements, and feelings of group obligation and commitment, for example, were contingent upon strong preexisting black communities and such strong preexisting black organizations as churches (Chong 1991: chaps. 3–6). Government responsiveness and repression of the movement affected, for another example, the perceived costs of participation and estimates of the probability of success (Chong 1991: chap. 7).

Finally, Chong explores the consequences of adopting various solutions to blacks' CA problem. Government patronage of the movement, for instance, brought the movement high levels of mobilization and some successes. This patronage eventually became, however, a source of the movement's decline and failures because it fragmented the civil rights coalition just at the time the patronage itself was being withdrawn (Chong 1991: 228). The brutal white opposition to the movement, for another example, also brought the movement mobilization and success because it stimulated black solidarity and brought liberal allies and government assistance. The stimulation of more widespread white backlash, however, was responsible for the movement's eventual demise and defeats (Chong 1991: 200, 205).

Chong therefore offers a series of interrelated models of black CA. Each model has multiple test implications: the causes of CA solutions, the correlations of CA solutions with black CA, and the effects of CA solutions on the movement's successes and failures.

Civil Rights: Combining CARP and SPOT

We therefore have two competing stories of the civil rights movement. McAdam mostly tells us about America and its institutions: why PO, MS, and CF in America produced the movement. Chong mostly tells us about a group and its mobilization: how market, communal, contractual, and hierarchical CA processes mobilized blacks. Figure 16.1 joins the two explanations.

A CARP-SPOT explanation of the civil rights movement therefore con-

---

Table 16.2
Summary of CARP and SPOT

CARP	SPOT

1. Five Percent Rule
    Collective action and inaction
    PGs and identities
    Set of group traditions
	1. Political opportunities

2. CA processes
    Market
    Community
    Contract
    Hierarchy
	2. Mobilizing structures

3. Politics as causes
    State/authority
    State's Dilemma
	3. Cultural framings

4. Pathologies as consequences
    Intended
    Unintended	

---

siders macro- (institutions, PO, MS, CF, outcomes), meso- (Contract, Community, Hierarchy), and micro- (Market, action) factors. It is possible to fashion these factors into SPOT's top-down (macro to meso to micro) or CARP's bottom-up (micro to meso to macro) terms. I will start at the bottom with protest and work my way up to the top with authority, following the four-step approach to CARP indicated earlier.

1. *CA.* McAdam's (1982) methodology is exemplary. He produces a historical narrative of the movement cycle that is divided into four periods: dormancy (1876–1954), generation (1955–1960), flowering (1961–1965), and decline (1966–1970). He thus attempts to explain macro-level variations in group mobilization and group success. Variation in CA, however, is not limited to the macrohistorical level. Chong (1991) seeks to explain variation in CA among individuals (blacks, whites, leaders, followers) and collectivities (cities, regions, organizations, events). Within the framework of a historical narrative, many different domains of CA can therefore be explained.

2. *Micro- and meso-CA solutions.* The many CA solutions introduced by Chong (1991) are relevant here. These mobilization processes were discussed earlier.

Figure 16.1
A CARP-SPOT Consortium

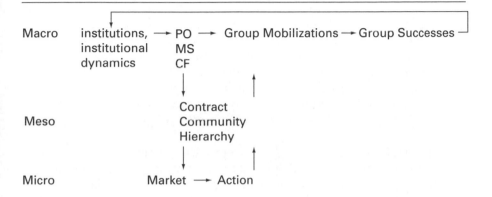

3a. *Causes*—Macrostructures. SPOT's PO, MS, and CF, as introduced by McAdam (1982), drive micro- and meso-CA processes. These structures were also discussed earlier.

3b. *Causes*—Concrete Institutions. It is interesting and significant that McAdam explores how historically concrete institutions drove PO, MS, and CF and that Chong explores how these institutions drove CA processes. Many institutions appear in either or both accounts. International factors and forces include immigration, foreign competition/trade, World War I, World War II, the Cold War, and Vietnam. State institutions include elections; enfranchisement/disenfranchisement; federalism; the division of powers among the president, Congress, and the Supreme Court; federal and local law enforcement agencies; and specific government policies of accommodation and repression. Societal institutions include churches, colleges, civil rights organizations, and the press. Economic institutions include markets that produced depression, urbanization, industrialization, and technical changes in production (e.g., mechanization and the introduction of synthetic fibers). State-society linkages include sociopolitical control systems (e.g., slavery, cotton tenancy, and segregation), institutions of democratic responsiveness (e.g., political parties and interest groups), dominant class-governing coalitions (e.g., Jeffersonian Republicans, Jacksonian Democrats, Compromise of 1876, populists, the New Deal coalition), and forms of social disorder (e.g., class conflict, civil war). Cultural changes include the growth of individualism and liberalism. Demographic changes include the change in age structure. Finally, there are a series of exogenous shocks, such as King's assassination, that also enter into the story. In sum, historically concrete institutions and institutional dynamics enter into a CARP-SPOT account of the Civil Rights Movement.

4. Macroconsequences. Many consequences of CA solutions, such as civil rights laws, were intended. Many consequences, however, were unintended. First, there was the loss of control of the movement. The 1960s witnessed the growth of black nationalism and separatism, the black power movement, and the strategic shift from nonviolence to anomic urban rioting. Second, there was white backlash. Many Northern white liberals eventually turned against the movement. Third, the civil rights movement spawned many other social movements: the student, antiwar, women's, environmental, gay and lesbian, Hispanic, and Native American movements of the late 1960s and 1970s can be traced to the civil rights struggles of the 1950s and early 1960s.

Any single account of the Civil Rights Movement would, of course, select among issues raised in this 4-step account to make theoretical and substantive points. Moreover, those who believe in the compatibility of the approaches would try to produce tight synergisms between structure and action. CA processes in different spheres would be expected to complement one another: they would be driven by the same structures and produce the same outcomes. Here, for example, are two interesting stories that could be developed. Story number one: Authority in America is characterized by federalism and the separation of powers. These two institutions create PO for blacks that activate certain CA processes: hierarchical black protest organizations will adopt a federal group solution and use tit-for-tat to coordinate among local chapters. The unintended result is that blacks will be more successful at mobilizing and achieving policy objectives at the local level than at the national levels. Marches on Washington will be rare; black mayors of major cities will not. Story number 2: Modernity might affect the CA problem in consistent ways. Blacks might develop modern consumer-oriented market relations and experience the rise of individualism and an ego-centered culture. These developments would mitigate black consciousness and induce the pursuit of material selective incentives. The unintended consequences could be the coexistence of two antithetical forms of dissent: anomic forms such as rioting and strongly hierarchical forms such as tightly knit extremist organizations.

In sum, one can develop a CARP-SPOT account of the civil rights movement that takes advantage of the synergisms between the approaches. Consider how it is therefore superior to either McAdam's or Chong's version of the events.

McAdam specializes in structure and context and does not actually study much action and protest. For example, his fascinating chapter 5, on "The Historical Context of Black Insurgency, 1876–1954" (McAdam 1982) is pure structure. Compared with this detailed account of such macroscopic changes as the decline of cotton tenancy, McAdam slights stories about civil rights organizations, the strategies and tactics of black protest, and the concrete struggles between supporters and opponents of black civil rights. However, these stories about protest itself are not completely ignored. The story of the struggle over civil rights appears as a series of subthemes that are not well integrated into McAdam's structuralist metanarrative. McAdam appears to recognize this theoretical disjuncture in his summary of "the political process model" in chapter 3. To account for the surge and decline of protest (i.e., explain variations in black CA over time), he says that he must add a "fourth" factor to his PO-MS-CF litany: "the shifting control response of other groups to the insurgent challenge posed by the movement" (53) that then directly affects black protest. "The level of social control" produces, in fact, most of the interesting dynamics of black insurgency. Hence, his chapters 6, 7, and 8 conclude with fascinating sections on "responses" to black protest during the 1955–60, 1961–65, and 1966–70 periods, respectively. It is here that McAdam introduces CA processes: the probability of winning, diffusion, movement-countermovement dynamics, movement-government dynamics (169), movement-ally dynamics (166), movement-movement dynamics or the problem of factions and issue consensus (153, 182, 187, 206), tactical variety (164, 221), and the concentration of movement forces (151, 190). To repeat: these mobilization processes are not well integrated into his structuralist perspective and do not neatly fit into the theoretical framework he initially introduced (51). McAdam, in short, tells us why blacks protested but offers no systematic account of how they did so. Moreover, McAdam is telling us that all the structural factors he identified conspired to produce failure before 1954, success between 1955 and 1965, and failure again thereafter. The struggle over the meaning and significance, as well as the use and implications, of these SPOT structures and CARP processes within each period is avoided. His account, put simply, is too theoretically tight and fits empirically too well.

Chong (1991) specializes in action and protest and therefore does not offer a systematic account of the context that is responsible for black insurgency. He specifically says that he does not wish to retell a narrative of the civil rights movement (231). While this is fair enough, Chong also does not offer a general theoretical account of the macrocontexts that drive the CA solutions he discusses. There are some speculations (described earlier), but they are never pulled together. This lacunae means that Chong never explores plausible rival theories and hypotheses about the civil rights movement, such as those available in SPOT. He thus offers examples from black protest to illustrate and elaborate a series of general models of CA.[8] Chong, in short, tells us how blacks protested but offers no systematic account of why they did so.

Conclusion

The structuralist approach is the hegemonic approach to social movements. SPOT, its major contemporary accomplishment, will continue to help define the field's agenda for years to come. However, the history of social science teaches us to be wary of its current dominance. Such a metatheory will face internal challenges from within its tradition and external challenges from competing traditions. A monopoly of ideas is, after all, the hardest monopoly of all to maintain.

Why? First, as the quotations cited at the beginning of this chapter make clear, social theories are not used just to study empirical reality. They contain critiques of competing views of the world that help us understand the intellectual, social, and political context of inquiry. We use theories as searchlights to illuminate other theories and theorists.

Structuralists have always used foils, to their great advantage, in this manner. During the 1970s Tilly's (1971) critique of Gurr (1970) raised our level of theoretical sophistication and paved the way to new and better theories. A second reason is methodological. Elementary statistics teaches us that one needs null hypotheses to test research hypotheses. Elementary research design, moreover, teaches us how to eliminate the threats that plausible rival hypotheses pose to our pet hypotheses. Hence, there is virtue to exploring a single case or a set of cases from two competing perspectives: a dialectical approach to theories, applying a battery of ideal type formulations, makes us aware of supporting and disconfirming evidence and contradictory clues and signals. During the 1970s the competitive testing of Gurr and Tilly also helped advance the field. The final reason to be skeptical of this new synthesis draws on Kant and Weber: theories are always probes of the world that offer partial perspectives on a reality that cannot be grasped all at once. Reality is everything, and no synthetic theory can ever capture it all.

The current synthetic structuralist attempt to subsume all possible approaches therefore needs to carefully identify its competitors (Tarrow 1994: 11–16). The field of social movements should not consist solely of a messy center of synthetic structuralism embodied in SPOT. There must be alternatives. In fact, much more will be learned from a dialogue than a synthesis and from constructive engagements than from grand coalitions. As partisans of CARP and SPOT argue that their approach is different and better than their opponents (Lichbach 1995: sect. 9.3), the sharpened conflict will improve both sets of ideas. To stimulate progress, the field thus needs creative confrontations, which can include well-defined syntheses among theoretical alternatives.

Notes

I wish to thank Anne Costain and Andrew McFarland for encouraging me to write this essay. An earlier version was presented to the 1996 Annual Meetings of the American Political

Science Association, San Francisco, California. Anne Costain, Dan Cress, and Chris Davenport provided invaluable feedback at a meeting of the University of Colorado's Social Movement Workshop.

1. McAdam (1982: 2, 36, 231) suggests that "all models of social movements imply adherence to a more general conception of institutionalized political power."

2. Since SPOT's practitioners are so interested in historically concete case and comparative studies, it is fair to wonder whether such nominalist concepts as PO, MS, and CF contribute to understanding a historically concrete group-institution nexus or whether they are stumbling blocks that lead to reification, obscurantism, and post hoc story telling. PO, MS and CF, after all, are merely tools to tell us about the interrelationship of historically concrete groups and institutions. They are tools to discover whether blacks, women, or workers are disadvantaged and whether institutions are racist, sexist, or exploitive in a capitalist sense. Do these nominalist concepts help solve age-old realist issues about the nature of the state and the significance of various systems of stratification? Three specific concerns may be raised.

First, one may wonder whether such transhistorical concepts really helped Tilly understand Old Regime France, Tarrow postwar Italy, or McAdam twentieth-century America. These structuralists dissected historically concrete institutions and groups, trying to understand real structures like elections, federalism, southern agriculture, and capitalist modernity; they were not interested, per se, in artificial structures like PO, MS, and CF (see my discussion of McAdam's focus on concrete institutions). Tilly, Tarrow, and McAdam also tried to understand peasants, workers, blacks, students, women, and so on in real terms. If SPOT had been developed thirty years earlier, would it have helped Tilly understand the Vendee, Tarrow student radicals in Italy, or McAdam the civil rights movement?

Second, it is not clear whether SPOT's proponents want to develop transhistorical generalizations. Are they suggesting that as PO (i.e., elite splits), increase, CA increases? If this is their goal, it is not clear that they can produce falsifiable hypotheses rather than a conceptual framework for telling stories about historical dynamics. Are PO, MS, and CF only known in hindsight? Do the proponents of SPOT have an empirically valuable theory, or have they merely constructed a set of flabby concepts and ideas that can redescribe any protest or rebellion in terms that their practitioners find intellectually pleasing but whose vocabulary ultimately lacks bite because of nonfalsifiability? Perhaps proponents of SPOT do case studies rather than group comparisons because comparative studies would force them to advance explicit hypotheses.

Finally, a focus on vague nominalist categories leads to an overemphasis on convergence among the categories and hence an integrative approach to social order and historical explanation. In McAdam (1982), for example, PO, MS, and CF move in the same direction, whereas the party system, urbanization, and liberalism in America have unique historical dynamics. A focus on historically concrete institutions leads to an emphasis on conflicts and tensions within and among institutions and hence a disjunctive approach to social disorder and historical explanation (which is very Weberian).

3. If the Five Percent Rule is interpreted from the authority's point of view, an interesting connection between CARP and SPOT is clarified. The Rule demonstrates that system-preserving apathy, depoliticization, and nonparticipation—which result from the uninformed, the indifferent, and the uninvolved—is voluntary and rational. Hence, nonparticipation by subordinate groups is related to nondecisions by authorities and the conservative institutions of churches, schools, political parties: all serve to reproduce the existing social order. Hence, structural forces and rational calculations combine so that classes are kept in place, the poor remain invisible, the propertied are protected from the propertyless, and acting on the basis of gender is delegitimized.

4. This is a bottom-up perspective, or what historians call history from below. The idea

is to discover how common or ordinary people experience and act as members of a social group.

5. This approach of starting with CA processes and locating their causes and consequences is a useful alternative to Coleman's (1987) and Boudon's (1987) approach of starting with structural propositions and locating their microfoundations. The search for such microfoundations is doomed to failure (Lichbach 1995: 292, chap. 9). Moreover, the search for microfoundations diverts attention from the more important question of looking for unintended consequences.

6. Hence, Lichbach (1996) develops the comparative statics of the PG/PD environment, or the comparative statics of the public good economy. This effort systematizes and extends many theoretical studies of the general CA problem as well as many empirical studies of CA in dissent.

7. Some of the rationalist literature in comparative politics ignores the CA problem and focuses on the game theoretic or strategic interaction among collectivities—groups, governments, parties, interest groups, organizations—that produce conflict and cooperation. For example, the political economy tradition explores the relationship among labor, capital, and the state (Przeworski and Wallerstein 1982; Golden 1988) and the formation and operation of state institutions (Bates 1989; Geddes 1994; Levi 1988). This approach can be applied to dissent (Lichbach 1984; 1989, 1990). However, it is ultimately unsatisfactory because a rationalist theory of protest and revolution that does not explain why rational people join protest and revolution is not much of a rationalist theory. It avoids the core issue in the approach and hence cannot deal with the most important and interesting contradiction and paradox produced by its theories.

8. Chong offers no systematic evidence on, for example, the Five Percent Rule.

17

Conclusion

Andrew S. McFarland and Anne N. Costain

The preceding chapters demonstrate a core argument about the role of social movements, American politics, and political institutions. That line of argument is in the mainstream of the study of American politics, proceeding from Dahl's pluralist theory of the 1960s, to Lowi's multiple-elite theory of the 1970s, to the postpluralist theory advocated since the 1980s by a variety of writers. Postpluralist theory is defined by its observation that countervailing power frequently exists in opposition to subgovernmental coalitions or iron triangles (McFarland, chap. 1). This argument is that social movements are a major source of countervailing power (although this does not imply that an equal balance results) and, as such, should be an important part of pluralistic discourse about the workings of American politics.

In the larger context of American politics, social movements are frequently integrated into a view of the American state that many scholars have derived from Tocqueville's writings. This perspective is that the existence of relatively strong state and local units of government, along with a particularly active interest group sector in the United States, stabilizes politics by scattering and transforming the activities of political movements, converting them into interest groups with incremental demands. But Tarrow (chapt. 2) argues that a reverse interpretation is more plausible: strong federal units provide an organizational base for social movements, thereby strengthening them. Over the course of history, these forces, along with the attachment of Americans to proselytizing religious movements, have led to movements such as those advocating an end to slavery, prohibition, and black civil rights that have exerted great influence on American politics.

If social movement organizations are becoming central to theories of the pluralistic political process, and if there is a strong argument that federalism and religious attachments magnify the impact of movements on the system, why should scholars of American politics hold to a distinction between social movement organizations and interest groups (Burstein, chap. 3)? Civil rights, environmental, and women's groups as well as religiously based moral concerns are normal in American interest group politics (Lichbach, chapt. 16; Costain and Lester, chapt. 11; Costain, chapt. 10; Green, Guth, and Wilcox, chapt. 7). An interest group theory in political science must also consider the movement aspects of group origins and development.

The research of Cress and Snow (chapt. 5), Banaszak (chapt. 6), and Dufour (chapt. 4) complement these observations. In America, the homeless, woman suffragists, and gays and lesbians have been particularly active in mobilizing at the local and state government levels of our federal system. Local level political success by these movements has led to political institutional support for their activities in other localities and at the national level as well. Similar observations probably hold true for many other movements in American politics.

The presidential nominating process is at the heart of the definition of our national political parties. Berry and Schildkraut (chapt. 8) show that citizen interest groups have played an increasing role in the presidential selection process. Such groups, which sociologists refer to as "social movement organizations," since they originated as parts of social movements, have provided still another avenue to affect political institutions. Similarly, Green, Guth, and Wilcox (chapt. 7) chart the course of the fundamentalist Christian movement in influencing Republican party organizations in the states, showing a range of movement strength between the different units of the federal system. Christian fundamentalists, while contenders for power in almost all states, are likely to dominate the Republican party in less than half of them. To a noticeable degree, social movement activity has permeated American institutional politics in the nineties.

Although movements and the U.S. government frequently battle one another, there are clear cases of government encouragement of social movement formation as well. Examples of each type of interaction are observable in Ronald Reagan's presidential administration. Reagan's self-proclaimed "conservative revolution" encouraged development of countermovements to civil rights, poor peoples', environmental, and women's movements, which had themselves been supported by liberal Democrat administrations. These actions shifted power balances by the addition of these new groups but also spurred mobilization among the very groups it challenged politically, as members poured into their organizations to try to halt Reagan-initiated policy shifts (Imig, chapt. 9). Similarly, the women's and environmental movements won places on the congressional agenda for their issues but then had to fight off opposition as they struggled to institutionalize their causes in an increasingly conservative political climate (Costain, chapt. 10; Costain and Lester, chapt. 11).

The courts, at first blush, may seem to be more sheltered and controlled venues for contention between movement and government. Yet, as McCann (chapt. 12) demonstrates across a range of cases, courts are not very different from other national institutions with respect to social movements. U.S. federal courts provide both a "bully pulpit," reminiscent of the pre-mass media presidency, and a similar intensely competitive arena to Congress. This judicial combination of authoritative pronouncements on weighty moral issues along with highly visible contention has allowed social movements to win new adherents to their causes even through very modest judicial victories. Woliver (chapt. 14) shows one way this might happen. Her analysis of legal language in amicus briefs shows how this language is used by each side to arouse followers and frame a struggle that attracts more people to the conflict. Finally, in the relatively recent struggle between Indian tribes and gaming/gambling interests, the Native American rights movement has shifted from past violent confrontations with national and state governments to a primarily legal fight for greater sovereignty. As Meranto (chapt. 13) points out, the courts balance the prerogatives of Indian tribes against those of states on relatively equal terms. Rather than Indians facing the armed power of the state, they confront the constitutional challenge of federalism. The courts, then, like the more political American institutions, provide ample scope for social movement influence.

The range of movements in this book, from those with few resources (poor people), to those with many (right-to-life and prochoice movements), demonstrate that large, mobilized movements can successfully influence government and win political recognition. This may occur even when they are relatively unsuccessful in their efforts to pressure national institutions directly. Attendant publicity may attract new followers, and even highly visible losses may result in additional resources, as the prospect of total defeat provides an incentive to sympathizers and followers to do more. This dynamic dance between movements and government creates much of the countervailing pressure within U.S. politics.

Doug McAdam (chapt. 15) points out that social movements are a recurrent point of access for international political issues entering the arena of U.S. politics. For instance, international concerns over racism, women's rights, and environmental pollution may spark social movements in this country as organizational costs are lowered by the global framing of issues. Lichbach (chapt. 16) also points to worldwide structural changes in economic markets along with the microlevel responses of individuals who fear loss of their jobs to foreign competition, as both feeding movement growth.

In advocating study of social movements by American institutionalists, we do not mean to neglect the value of the "new institutional" research, which has flourished in political science since the early 1980s. As Tarrow (chapt. 2) observes, it is not simply the weakness of American political institutions that makes space for movements to arise, but the U.S. federal structure itself that allows movements to build strength and raise resources in relatively sheltered spaces before they must compete with the broader range of interests active in national politics.

The new institutionalism has developed along two tracks, both of which deserve serious attention from social movement scholars. "Statist theory," associated with writers such as Skocpol (1992) and Skowronek (1982), uses historical and comparative approaches to ask macrotheoretical questions about institutional development. This work links institutions to changing professional and elite concepts of political rule. For instance, Skowronek showed how ideas of administrative rule were tied to the growth of a stable national civil service system in the United States and how German theories of the state and the military were related to the development of an institutionalized U.S. military command at the end of the nineteenth century. The other type of research on new institutionalism emphasizes the effects of institutional rules on political outcomes, often using models of rational human behavior and equations similar to those constructed by economists. Such an approach is stylistically similar to Lichbach's (chapt. 16) treatment of collective action theories. It can be related to scholarship on social movements by asking the question: whether institutional rules encourage or discourage collective action in social movements.

In linking the study of institutional politics and social movements, many research questions spring forth. How is the provision of opportunities for social movements affected by institutional rules? How do movements react when elites alter their concepts of the boundaries of institutional politics? Evidence indicates an important two-way interaction between institutions and movements that sculpts many of the more visible pathways to change in American politics.

Building on the cumulative research from this volume, we urge greater focus on boundary areas between political institutions and social movements. Formal political institutions are at once highlighted and challenged by the fluidity and indeterminant size of social movements. As examples, when civil rights shifts from an issue of state politics to one of national policy, or sexual harassment from a private to a public issue, new opportunities quickly open up for movements. Movements themselves may further extend these boundaries by using civil rights to expand the electorate and sexual harassment to contest elections (as in the wake of the congressional hearings on Supreme Court Justice Clarence Thomas). Research on these linkages might ask whether a newly elected president needs to appoint African Americans, gays, women, environmentalists, antiabortion activists, labor leaders, or farmers to cabinet positions in the administration. The answer may hinge on the level of mobilization or the degree of institutionalization of these varied social movements or the degree to which the presidential election raised issues relevant to these separable group interests. Flowing from this, the presumed life cycle of movements—from emergence, to a peak of mobilization, to decline—ignores the level of institutionalization in many movements. As an example, the American women's movement may be in decline, as measured by the drop in the number of activists, but electoral politics may increasingly be structured by "women's issues" such as educational policy and competition between the political parties for the "women's vote."

When social movements and institutions contend, both structural and individual antecedents are often blurred in the intellectual divide between sociology and political science. Structurally, sociologists often disregard the constitutional and legal factors undergirding institutional politics. Political scientists frequently give short shrift to the social understandings that shape how institutions are viewed and related to by citizens. On the individual level, political scientists will study the entrepreneurs and political patrons who organize and exert political power through institutions and social movement groups. Sociologists analyze the formal and informal networks that guide policy choice. The types of social movements to be expected in America depend a great deal on historic and constitutionally defined institutional structures. But the success of these movements is crucially set by the attitudes and organization of society during their period of emergence. The way political institutions function at a given time is closely tied to the coalition of support for their actions. Finally, movements and institutions are both major agents of change. Under the direction of skilled leaders, they will command necessary resources and tactical advantages to exploit opportunities. Without them change will be slow.

In conclusion, to make significant advances in understanding political institutions and social movements, their patterns of interaction must be analyzed and understood. To do this, it is necessary to bring together the primarily sociological literature on social movements with the largely political science literature on political institutions.

References

Abramowitz, Alan I. "It's Abortion, Stupid: Policy Voting in the 1992 Presidential Election." *Journal of Politics* 57 (1995): 176–86.

Abrams, Philip. *Historical Sociology*. Ithaca, NY: Cornell University Press, 1982.

Abramson, Paul, and Ronald Inglehart. *Value Change in Global Perspective*. Ann Arbor: University of Michigan Press, 1995.

Adam, Barry. "A Social History of Gay Politics." In *Gay Men: The Social History of Male Homosexuality*, ed. Martin P. Levine. New York: Harper & Row, 1979.

———. *The Rise of a Gay and Lesbian Movement*. Boston: Twayne, 1987.

Advisory Commission on Intergovernmental Relations. *The Transformation in American Politics: Implications for Federalism*. Washington, D.C.: Advisory Commission on Intergovernmental Relations, 1986.

Aho, James. "Popular Christianity and Political Extremism in the United States." In *Disruptive Religion: The Force of Faith in Social Movement Activism*, ed. C. Smith, 189–204. New York: Routledge, 1996.

Aldrich, John H. "Presidential Campaigns in Party- and Candidate-Centered Eras." In *Under the Watchful Eye*, ed. Mathew McCubbins, 59–82. Washington, D.C.: Congressional Quarterly Press, 1992.

———. *Why Parties? The Origin and Transformation of Political Parties in America*. Chicago: University of Chicago Press, 1995.

Amenta, Edwin, and Jane D. Poulsen. "Where to Begin: A Survey of Five Approaches to Selecting Independent Variables for Qualitative Comparative Analysis." *Sociological Methods and Research* 23 (1994): 22–53.

Aminzade, Ronald. "Between Movement and Party: The Transformation of Mid-Nineteenth Century French Republicanism." In *The Politics of Social Protest*, ed. J. Craig Jenkins and Bert Klandermans, 39–62. Minneapolis: University of Minnesota Press, 1995.

Amundsen, Kirsten. *The Silenced Majority*. Upper Saddle River, NJ: Prentice-Hall, 1971.

Anderson, Michael R. "Law and the Protection of Cultural Communities: The Case of Native American Fishing Rights." *Law & Policy* 9 (1987): 125–42.

Anderson-Sherman, Arnold, and Doug McAdam. "American Black Insurgency and the World Economy: A Political Process Model." In *Ascent and Decline in the World System*, ed. Edward Friedman, 165–88. Beverly Hills: Sage, 1982.

App, Rolf. "Initiativen und ihre Wirkungen auf Bundesebene seit 1974." *Schweizerisches Jahrbuch für Politische Wissenschaft*, 27 (1987): 180–206.

Appleton, Andrew M., and Daniel S. Ward. *State Party Profiles: A Fifty-State Guide to Development, Organization, and Resources*. Washington, D.C.: CQ Press, 1996.

Arnold, R. Douglas. *The Logic of Congressional Action*. New Haven, CT: Yale University Press, 1990.

Bachrach, Peter, and Morton Baratz. "Two Faces of Power." *American Political Science Review* 56 (1962): 947–52.

Baer, Denise, and David Bositis. *Elite Cadres and Party Coalitions*. Westport, CT: Greenwood, 1988.

Baer, Denise L., and Julie A. Dolan. "Intimate Connections: Political Interests and Group Activity in State and Local Parties." *American Review of Politics* 15 (1994): 257–289.

Banaszak, Lee Ann. *Why Movements Succeed or Fail: Opportunity, Culture, and the Struggle for Woman Suffrage*. Princeton, NJ: Princeton University Press, 1996.

———. "The Influence of the Initiative on the Swiss and American Women's Suffrage Movement." In *Schweizerisches Jahrbuch für Politische Wissenschaft* 31 (1991): 187–208.

Barber, Benjamin. *Strong Democracy: Participatory Politics for a New Age*. Berkeley: University of California Press, 1984.

Barsh, Russell Lawrence. "Indian Policy at the Beginning of the 1990s: The Trivialization of Struggle." In *American Indian Policy*, ed. Lyman Legters and Fremont Lyden, 55–60. Westport, CT: Greenwood, 1994.

Bates, Robert H. *Beyond the Miracle of the Market: The Political Economy of Agrarian Development in Kenya*. Cambridge: Cambridge University Press, 1989.

Baumer, Donald C., and Howard J. Gold. "Party Images and the American Electorate." *American Politics Quarterly* 23 (1995): 33–61.

Beck, Paul Allen, and Frank J. Sorauf. *Party Politics in America*, 7th ed. New York: HarperCollins, 1992.

Becker, Gary S. *The Economics of Discrimination*. Chicago: University of Chicago Press, 1971.

Bednar, Nancy L., and Allen D. Hertzke. "The Christian Fight and Republican Realignment in Oklahoma." *PS* 28 (1995): 11–15.

Behuniak-Long, Susan. "Friendly Fire: Amici Curiae and *Webster v. Reproductive Health Services*." *Judicature*, 74 (1991): 261–270.

Bernstein, Richard J. *Hannah Arendt and the Jewish Question*. Cambridge, MA: MIT Press, 1996.

Berry, Jeffrey M. *Lobbying for the People*. Princeton, NJ: Princeton University Press,1977.

———. *The Interest Group Society*, 3d ed. New York: Longman, 1997.

Berube, Allan. *Coming Out under Fire*. New York: Free Press, 1990.

Bibby, John F., Cornelius P. Cotter, James L. Gibson, and Robert J. Huckshorn. "Parties in State Politics." In *Politics in the American States,* 5th ed., ed. Virginia Gray, Herbert Jacob, and Robert B. Albritton. Glenview, IL: Scott, Foresman, 1990.

Bibby, John F., and Thomas H. Holbrook. "Parties and Elections." In *Politics in the American States,* 6th ed., ed. Virginia Gray and Herbert Jacob. Washington, D.C.: CQ Press, 1995.

Billington, Ray Allen. *The Protestant Crusade, 1800–1860. A Study of the Origins of American Nativism*. New York: Macmillan, 1938.

Birnbaum, Pierre. "Mouvements Sociaux et Types d'États: vers une Approche Comparative." In *Action Collective et Mouvements Sociaux*, ed. François Chazel, 163–76. Paris: Presses Universitaires de France, 1993.

Blanchard, Dallas A. *The Anti-Abortion Movement and the Rise of the Religious Right: From Polite to Fiery Protest*. New York: Twayne, 1994.

Blank, Robert H. *Rationing Medicine.* New York: Columbia University Press, 1988.

———. "Judicial Decision Making and Biological Fact: *Roe v. Wade* and the Unresolved Question of Fetal Viability." *Western Political Quarterly* 37 (1984): 584–602.

Blocker, Jack S., Jr. *American Temperance Movements: Cycles of Reform.* Boston: Twayne, 1989.

Bosso, Christopher J. *Pesticides and Politics: The Life Cycle of a Public Issue.* Pittsburgh, PA: University of Pittsburgh Press, 1987.

Boudon, Raymond. "The Individualistic Tradition in Sociology." In *The Micro-Macro Link*, ed. Jeffrey C. Alexander, Berhard Giesen, Richard Münch, and Neil J. Smelser, 153–73. Berkeley, CA: University of California Press, 1987.

Bowers v. Hardwick. 478 U.S. 186, 1986.

Bradley, Martin B., Norman M. Green, Dale E. Jones, Mac Lynn, and Lou McNeil. *Churches and Church Membership in the United States 1990.* Atlanta: Glenmary Research Center, 1992.

Brand, Karl-Werner. "Cyclical Aspects of New Social Movements: Waves of Cultural Criticism and Mobilization Cycles of New Middle-Class Radicalism." In *Challenging the Political Order*, ed. Russell Dalton and Manfred Kuechler, 23–42. New York: Oxford University Press, 1990.

Bridges, Amy. "Becoming American: The Working Class in the United States before the Civil War." In *Working-class Formation: Nineteenth-Century Patterns in Western Europe and the United States*, ed. Ira Katznelson and Aristide R. Zolberg, 157–96. Princeton, NJ: Princeton University Press, 1986.

Brigham, John. "Right, Rage, and Remedy: Forms of Law in Political Discourse." *Studies in American Political Development* 2 (1988): 303–16.

Brockett, Charles D. "The Structure of Political Opportunities and Peasant Mobilization in Central America." *Comparative Politics* 23 (1991): 253–74.

Bruce, Steve. *The Rise and Fall of the New Christian Right.* New York: Clarendon, 1988.

Bruun, Rita. "The Boldt Decision: Legal Victory, Political Defeat." *Law and Policy* 4 (1982): 271–98.

Brzezinski, Zbigniew, and Samuel P. Huntington. *Political Power: USA/USSR.* New York: Viking, 1963.

Buechler, Steven M. "Beyond Resource Mobilization: Emerging Trends in Social Movement Theory." *Sociological Quarterly* 34 (1993): 217–35.

Bunce, Valerie. "State Collapse after State Socialism: A Comparison of the Soviet Union, Yugoslavia and Czechoslovakia." Paper prepared for the Conference on Nationalism, Post-Communism and Ethnic Mobilization, Cornell University, April 21–22, 1995.

Bunis, William K., David A. Snow, and Angela Yancik. "The Cultural Patterning of Spans of Sympathy." Paper presented at the annual meeting of the American Sociological Association, Washington, D.C., 1995.

Burawoy, Michael. *Ethnography Unbound: Power and Resistance in the Modern Metropolis.* Berkeley: University of California Press, 1991.

Burke, Pamela. "The Politics of Transnational Collective Action: The Indigenous Rights Movement of Ecuador." Unpublished paper, Department of Government and Politics, University of Maryland, 1996.

Burnham, Walter Dean. *Critical Elections and the Mainsprings of American Politics.* New York: W. W. Norton, 1970.

———. "Toward Confrontation." In *Party Coalitions in the 1980s,* ed. Seymour Martin Lipset. San Francisco: Institute for Contemporary Studies, 1997.

Burstein, Paul. *Discrimination, Jobs, and Politics.* Chicago: University of Chicago Press, 1985.

———. "Legal Mobilization as a Social Movement Tactic: The Struggle for Equal Employment Opportunity." *American Journal of Sociology* 96 (1991): 1201–25.

Burstein, Paul, and Kathleen Monaghan. "Equal Employment Opportunity and the Mobilization of the Law." *Law & Society Review* 20 (1986): 355–88.

Burstein, Paul, Rachel L. Einwohner, and Jocelyn A. Hollander. "The Success of Political Movements." In *The Politics of Social Protest,* ed. J. Craig Jenkins and Bert Klandermans, 275–95. Minneapolis: University of Minnesota Press, 1995.

Burt, Martha R. *Over the Edge: The Growth of Homelessness in the 1980s.* New York: Russell Sage Foundation, 1992.

Button, James. "The Outcomes of Contemporary Black Protest and Violence." In *Violence in America,* ed. Ted Gurr. Newbury Park, CA: Sage, 1989.

Button, James, Barbara Rienzo, and Kenneth D. Wald. "The Politics of Gay Rights in American Communities." Presented at the annual meeting of the American Political Science Association, New York, 1994.

Cain, Petricia. "Litigating for Lesbians and Gay Rights: A Legal History." *Virginia Law Review* 79 (1993): 1551–642.

Caldeira, Gregory A., and John R. Wright. "Organized Interests and Agenda Setting in the U.S. Supreme Court." *American Political Science Review* 82 (December 1988): 1109–27.

Caldwell, Lynton K. *International Environmental Policy.* Durham, NC: Duke University Press, 1984.

California v. Cabazon and Morongo Bands of Mission Indians. 480 U.S. 202, 1987.

Carmines, Edward G., and James A. Stimson. *Issue Evolution.* Princeton, NJ: Princeton University Press, 1989.

Carroll, John. *Environmental Diplomacy: The Management and Resolution of Transfrontier Environmental Problems.* Cambridge: Cambridge University Press, 1988.

Castells, Manuel. *The City and the Grass Roots.* London: Edward Arnold, 1983.

Catt, Carrie Chapman, and Nettie Rogers Shuler. *Woman Suffrage and Politics: The Inner Story of the Suffrage Movement.* New York: Scribner's, 1926.

Caulfield, Henry P. "The Conservation and Environmental Movements: An Historical Analysis." In *Environmental Politics and Policy: Theories and Evidence,* In ed. James P. Lester, 13–56. Durham, NC: Duke University Press, 1989.

Chafe, William. *The American Woman: Her Changing Social, Economic, and Political Roles, 1920–1970.* New York: Oxford University Press, 1972.

Chauncey, George, Jr. *Urban Culture and the Making of the Gay Male World.* New York: Basic Books, 1994.

Cherokee Nation v. Georgia. 30 U.S. 1 (1831).

Chong, Dennis. *Collective Action and the Civil Rights Movement.* Chicago: University of Chicago Press, 1991.

Clemens, Elisabeth S. "Organizational Repertoires and Institutional Change: Women's

Groups and the Transformation of U.S. Politics, 1890–1920." *American Journal of Sociology* 98 (1993): 755–98.

Cloward, Richard A. and Francis Fox Piven. "Disruption and Organization: A Rejoinder." *Theory and Society* 13 (1984): 587–99.

Cohen, Jean L., and Andrew Arato. *Civil Society and Political Theory.* Cambridge: Cambridge University Press, 1992.

Cohen, Michael, James March, and Johan Olsen. "A Garbage Can Model of Organizational Choice." *Administrative Science Quarterly* 17 (1972): 1–25.

Coleman, James S. "Microfoundations and Macrosocial Behavior." In *The Micro-Macro Link,* ed. Jeffrey C. Alexander, Berhard Giesen, Richard Münch, and Neil J. Smelser, 153–73. Berkeley: University of California Press, 1987.

Colvin, D. Leigh. *Prohibition in the United States.* New York: Dolan, 1926.

Committee on Ways and Means. *Green Book: Background Material and Data on Programs within the Jurisdiction of the Committee on Ways and Means.* Washington, D.C.: Government Printing Office, 1994.

Condit, Celeste M. *Decoding Abortion Rhetoric: The Communication of Social Change.* Urbana: University of Illinois Press, 1990.

Congressional Record. Washington, D.C.: Government Printing Office, 1900–1994.

Cook, Faye Lomax, and Edith Barrett. *Support for the American Welfare State.* New York: Columbia University Press, 1992.

Copelon, Rhonda. "Beyond the Liberal Idea of Privacy: Toward a Positive Right of Autonomy." In *Judging the Constitution: Critical Essays on Judicial Lawmaking,* ed. Michael W. McCann and Gerald L. Houseman. Glenview, IL: Scott, Foresman, 1989.

Cornell, Stephen. *The Return of the Native.* New York: Oxford University Press, 1988.

Costain, Anne N. "The Struggle for a National Women's Lobby: Organizing a Diffuse Interest." *Western Political Quarterly* 33 (1980): 476–91.

———. "Women's Claims as a Special Interest." In *The Politics of the Gender Gap,* ed. Carol M. Mueller, 150–72. Newbury Park, CA: Sage, 1988.

———. *Inviting Women's Rebellion: A Political Process Interpretation of the Women's Movement.* Baltimore, MD: Johns Hopkins University Press, 1992.

———. "The Mobilization of a Women's Movement and the American Gender Gap in Voting." Paper presented at the American Political Science Convention, San Francisco, 1996.

Costain, Anne, Richard Braunstein, and Heidi Berggren. "Framing the Women's Movement." In *Women, Media, and Politics,* ed. Pippa Norris, 205–20. New York: Oxford University Press, 1996.

Costain, Anne and Steven Majstorovic. "Congress, Social Movements and Public Opinion: Multiple Origins of Women's Rights Legislation." *Political Research Quarterly* 47 (205–20): 111–36.

Costain, W. Douglas, and James Lester. "The Evolution of Environmentalism." In *Environmental Politics and Policy: Theories and Evidence,* 2d edition, ed. James P. Lester. Durham, NC: Duke University Press, 1995.

Cotter, Cornelius P., James L. Gibson, John F. Bibby, and Robert J. Huckshorn. *Party Organizations in American Politics.* Westport, CT: Praeger, 1984.

Coyle, Marcia. "Pro-Choice Forces Get It Together." *The National Law Journal,* May 1, 1989, 27.

Coyle, Marcia, and Marianne Lavelle. "Full Court Press." *National Law Journal*, May 1, 1989, 1.

Craig, Barbara Hinkson, and David M. O'Brien. *Abortion and American Politics*. Chatham, NJ: Chatham House, 1993.

Crenshaw, Kimberle Williams. "Race, Reform, and Retrenchment: Transformation and Legitimation in Antidiscrimination Law." *Harvard Law Review* 101 (1988): 1331–87.

Cress, Daniel M. and David A. Snow. "Mobilization at the Margins: Resources, Benefactors and the Viability of Homeless Social Movement Organizations." *American Sociological Review* 61 (1996): 1089–109.

Cronin, Thomas E. *Direct Democracy: The Politics of Initiative, Referendum, and Recall*. Cambridge, MA: Harvard University Press, 1989.

Cross, Whitney. *The Burned-Over District: The Social and Intellectual History of Enthusiastic Religion in Western New York, 1800–1850*. Ithaca, NY: Cornell University Press, 1982.

Crotty, William J. *Party Reform*. New York: Longman, 1983.

Cruikshank, Margaret. *The Gay and Lesbian Liberation Movement*. New York: Routledge, 1992.

Culhane, Paul. *Public Lands Politics*. Baltimore, MD: Johns Hopkins Press, 1981.

Culter, David M., and Lawrence F. Katz. "Untouched by the Rising Tide." *Brookings Review* 10 (1992): 41–45.

Dahl, Robert A. "A Critique of the Ruling Elite Model." *American Political Science Review* 52 (1958):463–69.

———. *Who Governs?* New Haven, CT: Yale University Press, 1961.

———. *Democracy and Its Critics*. New Haven, CT: Yale University Press, 1989.

Dalton, Russell J. *Citizen Politics in Western Democracies*, 2d ed. Chatham, NJ: Chatham House, 1996.

D'Anieri, Paul, Claire Ernst, and Elizabeth Kier. "New Social Movements in Historical Pespective." *Comparative Politics* 22 (1990): 445–58.

Davis, Angela Y. *Women, Culture, & Politics*. New York: Vintage, 1990.

Davis, Charles E., and James P. Lester. "Decentralizing Federal Environmental Policy: A Research Note." *Western Political Quarterly* 40 (1987): 555–65.

Davis, Martha. *Brutal Need: Lawyers and the Welfare Rights Movement, 1960–1973*. New Haven, CT: Yale University Press, 1993.

de Certeau, Michel. *The Practice of Everyday Life*. Berkeley: University of California Press, 1984.

Deloria, Vine, and Clifford Lytle. *American Indians, American Justice*. Austin: University of Texas Press, 1983.

della Porta, Donatella. *Social Movements, Political Violence, and the State. A Comparative Analysis of Italy and Germany*. New York: Cambridge University Press, 1995.

———. "Social Movements and the State: Thoughts on the Policing of Protest." In *Comparative Perspectives on Social Movements: Political Opportunities, Mobilizing Structures, and Cultural Framings*, ed. Doug McAdam, John D. McCarthy, and Mayer N. Zald, 62–92. New York: Cambridge University Press, 1996.

Delley, Jean-Daniel, and Andreas Auer. "Structures Politiques des Cantons." In *Handbuch Politisches System der Schweiz, Vol. 3: Föderalismus*. ed. Raimund Germann and Ernest Weibel. Bern: Haupt, 1986, 85–105.

D'Emilio, John. *Sexual Politics, Sexual Communities*. Chicago: University of Chicago Press, 1983.

DiMaggio, Paul J., and Walter W. Powell. "The Iron Cage Revisited: Institutional Isomorphism and Collective Rationality in Organizational Fields." *American Sociological Review* 48 (1983): 147–60.

Dodd, Lawrence C., and Calvin Jillson. "Conversations on the Study of American Politics: An Introduction." In *The Dynamics of American Politics: Approaches and Interpretations*, ed. Lawrence C. Dodd and Calvin Jillson, 1–122. Boulder, CO: Westview, 1994.

Dowie, Mark. *Losing Ground: American Environmentalism at the Close of the Twentieth Century*. Cambridge, MA: MIT Press, 1995.

Downs, Anthony. *An Economic Theory of Democracy*. New York: Harper & Row, 1957.

Dryzek, John. "Policy Sciences of Democracy." *Polity* 22 (1989): 97–118.

———. "Political Inclusion and the Dynamics of Democratization." *American Political Science Review* 90 (1996): 475–87.

Duberman, Martin, Martha Vicinus, and George Chauncey, Jr., eds. *Hidden from History: Reclaiming the Gay and Lesbian Past*. New York: New American Library, 1989.

Duchacek, Ivo D. *Comparative Federalism: The Territorial Dimension of Politics*. Lanham, MD: University Press of America, 1987.

Dufour, Claude. "Political Opportunity Structures and Movement Strategies: The Case of the Gay and Lesbian Rights Movements." Paper presented at the annual meeting of the Midwest Political Science Association, Chicago, 1994.

———. "Comparative Analysis of Gay and Lesbian Rights Movements in Canada, the United States and Australia." Ph.D. diss., University of Illinois, Chicago, 1995.

Dunlap, Riley. "Public Opinion and Environmental Policy." In *Environmental Politics and Policy: Theories and Evidence*, ed. James P. Lester. Durham, NC: Duke University Press, 1989.

Durkheim, Emile. *Suicide: A Study in Sociology*. Trans. John A. Spaulding and George Simpson. New York: Free Press, 1951.

Eckstein, Harry. "On the Etiology of Internal Wars." *History and Theory* 4 (1965): 133–65.

———. "Theoretical Approaches to Explaining Collective Political Violence." In *Handbook of Political Conflict: Theory and Research*, ed. Ted Robert Gurr, 135–66. New York: Free Press, 1980.

Economist. "War Gaming," May 5, 1990.

Edelman, Lauren. *Political Language: Words That Succeed and Policies That Fail*. New York: Academic Press, 1977.

———. "Legal Environments and Organizational Governance: The Expansion of Due Process in the American Workplace." *American J. of Sociology* 95 (1990): 1401–40.

Edelman, Murray. *The Symbolic Uses of Politics*. Urbana: University of Illinois Press, 1964.

Edsall, Thomas. *The New Politics of Inequality*. New York: Norton, 1984.

Edsall, Thomas B. "Robertson Urges Christian Activists to Take Over GOP." *Washington Post*, September 10, 1995: A24.

Edwards, G. Thomas. *Sowing Good Seeds: The Northwest Suffrage Campaigns of Susan B. Anthony*. Portland: Oregon Historical Society Press, 1990.

Eisinger, Peter K. "The Conditions of Protest Behavior in American Cities." In *American Political Science Review* 67 (1973): 11–28.

Elazar, Daniel J. *American Federalism: A View from the States*. 3d ed. New York: Harper & Row, 1984.

———. *Exploring Federalism*. Tuscaloosa: University of Alabama Press, 1987.

———. *The American Mosaic*. Boulder, CO: Westview, 1994.

Epp, Charles. "Connecting Litigation Levels and Legal Mobilization: Explaining Interstate Variation in Employment Civil Rights Litigation." *Law and Society Rev.* 24 (1990): 145–63.

Epstein, Lee. *Conservatives in Court*. Knoxville: University of Tennessee Press, 1985.

Epstein, Lee, and Joseph F. Kobylka. *The Supreme Court and Legal Change: Abortion and the Death Penalty*. Chapel Hill: University of North Carolina Press, 1992.

Epstein, Lee, and C. K. Rowland. "Debunking the Myth of Interest Group Invincibility in the Courts." *American Political Science Review* 85 (1991): 205–17.

Epstein, Leon. *Political Parties in the American Mold*. Madison: University of Wisconsin Press, 1986.

Erikson, Robert S., Gerald C. Wright, and John P. McIver. *Statehouse Democracy: Public Opinion and Policy in the American States*. New York: Cambridge University Press, 1993.

Estrich, Susan R., and Kathleen M. Sullivan. "Abortion Politics: Writing for an Audience of One." *University of Pennsylvania Law Review* 138 (1989): 119–55.

Ewick, Patricia, and Susan S. Silbey. "Conformity, Contestation, and Resistance: An Account of Legal Consciousness." *New England Law Review* 26 (1992): 731–49.

Faderman, Lilian. *Odd Girls and Twilight Lovers: A History of Lesbian Life in Twentieth Century America*. New York: Penguin, 1991.

Fantasia, Rick. *Cultures of Solidarity*. Berkeley: University of California Press, 1988.

Feagin, Joe R., Anthony M. Orum, and Gideon Sjoberg, ed. *A Case for the Case Study*. Chapel Hill: University of North Carolina Press, 1991.

Ferree, Myra Marx, and Patricia Yancey Martin. "Doing the Work of the Movement: Feminist Organizations." In *Feminist Organizations: Harvest of the New Women's Movement*, ed. Myra Marx Ferree and Patricia Yancey Martin. Philadelphia: Temple University Press, 1995.

Field, Martha A. "Controlling the Woman to Protect the Fetus." *Law, Medicine & Health Care* 17 (1989):114–29.

Fine, Terri Susan. "Interest Groups and the Framing of the 1988 Democratic and Republican Party Platforms." *Polity* 26 (1994): 517–30.

Flexner, Eleanor. *Century of Struggle*. Cambridge, MA: Harvard University Press, 1973.

Forbath, William E. *Law and the Shaping of the American Labor Movement*. Cambridge, MA: Harvard University Press, 1991.

Ford Foundation. *Annual Reports, 1970–1990*. New York: The Ford Foundation, 1990.

Frantzich, Stephen. *Political Parties in the Technological Age*. New York: Longman, 1989.

Freeman, Jo. "The Origins of the Women's Liberation Movement." *American Journal of Sociology* 78 (1973): 792–811.

————. *The Politics of Women's Liberation*. New York: McKay, 1975.

————. "Resource Mobilization and Strategy." In *The Dynamics of Social Movements*, ed. Mayer Zald and John McCarthy, 167–189. Cambridge, MA: Winthrop, 1979.

————. *Social Movements of the Sixties and Seventies*. New York: Longman, 1983.

Galanter, Marc. "The Radiating Effects of Courts." In *Empirical Theories of Courts*, ed. Keith D. Boyum and Lynn Mather, 117–42. New York: Longman, 1983.

Galbraith, John Kenneth. *American Capitalism*. Boston: Houghton Mifflin, 1952.

Gallagher, Janet. "Fetus as Patient." In *Reproductive Laws for the 1990s*, ed. Nadine Taub and Sherrill Cohen, 185–235. Clifton, NJ: Humana, 1989.

————. "Prenatal Invasions and Interventions: What's Wrong with Fetal Rights." *Harvard Women's Law Journal* 10 (1987): 9–58.

Gamson, William. "Political Discourse and Collective Action." In *From Structure to Action: Comparing Movement Participation Across Cultures*, ed. P. G. Klandermans, H. Kriesi, and S. Tarrow, 219–44. Greenwich, CT: JAI, 1988.

————. *The Strategy of Social Protest*. Belmont, CA: Wadsworth Publishing, [1975] 1990.

————. "The Social Psychology of Collective Action." In *Frontiers in Social Movement Theory*, ed. Aldon D. Morris and Carol McClurg Mueller. New Haven, CT: Yale University Press, 1992.

————. *Talking Politics*. New York: Cambridge University Press, 1993.

Gamson, William A., Bruce Fireman, and Steven Rytina. *Encounters with Unjust Authority*. Homewood, IL: Dorsey, 1982.

Gamson, William A., and David S. Meyer. "The Framing of Political Opportunity." In *Opportunities, Mobilizing Structures and Framing: Comparative Applications of Contemporary Movement Theory*, ed. John McCarthy, Doug McAdam, and Mayer N. Zald, 275–290. New York: Cambridge University Press, 1995.

Gamson, William A., and Emile Schmeidler. "Organizing the Poor." In *Theory and Society* 13 (1984): 567–85.

Gaventa, John. *Power and Powerlessness: Quiescence and Rebellion in an Appalachian Valley*. Urbana: University of Illinois, 1981.

Geddes, Barbara. *Politician's Dilemma: Building State Capacity in Latin America*. Berkeley: University of California Press, 1994.

Gelb, Joyce, and Marian Lief Palley. *Women and Public Policies*. Princeton, NJ: Princeton University Press, 1982.

Gillon, Steve. *The Democrat's Dilemma: Walter F. Mondale and the Liberal Legacy*. New York: Columbia University Press, 1992.

Ginsburg, Faye D. *Contested Lives: The Abortion Debate in an American Community*. Berkeley: University of California Press, 1989.

Gitelson, Alan R., M. Margaret Conway, and Frank B. Feigert. *American Political Parties: Stability and Change*. Boston: Houghton Mifflin, 1984.

Glaser, Barney G., and Anselm L. Strauss. *The Discovery of Grounded Theory*. Chicago: Aldine, 1967.

Golden, Miriam. *Labor Divided: Austerity and Working-Class Politics in Contemporary Italy*. Ithaca, NY: Cornell University Press, 1988.

Goldfield, Michael. "Worker Insurgency, Radical Organization, and New Deal Labor Legislation." *American Political Science Review* 83 (1989): 1257–82.

Goldstone, Jack A. "Theories of Revolution: The Third Generation." *World Politics* 32 (1980): 425–53.

———. *Revolution and Rebellion in the Early Modern World.* Berkeley: University of California Press, 1991.

Gorney, Cynthia. "The Dispassion of John C. Willke." *The Washington Post Magazine,* April 22, 1990, 21–25, 38–42.

Gould, Roger. "The Whiskey Rebellion." Paper presented at the conference on the "Past and Future of Collective Action," Amsterdam, June 1995.

Graber, Mark A. *Rethinking Abortion: Equal Choice, the Constitution, and Reproductive Politics.* Princeton, NJ: Princeton University Press, 1996.

Grant, Edward R. "Conclusion: The Future of Abortion as a 'Private Choice.' " *American Journal of Law & Medicine* 15 (1989): 233–43.

Gray, Jerry. "Christian Coalition Offers Dole Both Cheers and Sharp Prodding." *New York Times,* September 15, 1996, 1:38, 1.

Green, Donald P., and Ian Shapiro. *Pathologies of Rational Choice Theory: A Critique of Applications in Political Science.* New Haven, CT: Yale University Press, 1994.

Green, John C. "The Christian Right and the 1994 Elections: An Overview." In *God at the Grass Roots: The Christian Right in the 1994 Elections,* ed. Mark J. Rozell and Clyde Wilcox, 1–18. Lanham, MD: Rowman & Littlefield, 1995.

Green, John C. and James L. Guth. "The Christian Right in the Republican Party: The Case of Pat Robertson's Supporters." *Journal of Politics* 50 (1988): 150–65.

———. "Religion, Representatives, and Roll Calls: A Research Note." *Legislative Studies Quarterly* 16 (1991): 571–84.

Green, John C., James L. Guth, and Kevin Hill. "Faith and Election: The Christian Right in Congressional Campaigns 1978–1988." *Journal of Politics* 55 (1993): 80–91.

Greenberg, Edward S., and Benjamin I. Page. *The Struggle for Democracy,* 2d ed. New York: HarperCollins, 1995.

Greenberg, Pam, and Judy Zelio. "States and the Indian Gaming Regulatory Act." *State Legislative Report,* July 1992.

Griffin, Kimberly. "Impact Endorses Netsch." In *Windy City Times,* September 15, 1994, 6.

Gruner, Erich. "Parteie." In *Handbuch Politisches System der Schweiz, Vol. 2: Strukturen und Prozesse.* Bern: Haupt, 1984.

Gurr, Ted Robert. *Why Men Rebel.* Princeton, NJ: Princeton University Press, 1970.

———. "The Revolution-Social Change Nexus: Some Old Theories and New Hypotheses." *Comparative Politics* 5 (1973): 359–92.

Gusfield, Joseph R. "Social Movements and Social Change: Perspectives of Linearity and Fluidity." In *Research in Social Movements, Conflicts, and Change,* ed. Louis Kriesberg, 317–39. Greenwich, CT: JAI, 1981.

Guth, James L., John C. Green, Lyman A. Kellstedt, and Corwin A. Smidt. "The Political Relevance of Religion: The Correlates of Mobilization." In *Religion and the Culture Wars: Dispatches from the Front,* ed. John C. Green, James L. Guth, Corwin E. Smidt, and Lyman A. Kellstedt. Lanham, MD: Rowman & Littlefield, 1996.

Haines, Herbert H. "Black Radicalization and the Funding of Civil Rights: 1957–1970." *Social Problems* 32 (1984): 331–72.

———. *Black Radicals and the Civil Rights Mainstream.* Knoxville: University of Tennessee Press, 1988.

Hall, Melvin. *Poor People's Social Movement Organizations: The Goal Is to Win.* Westport, CT: Praeger, 1995.

Halva-Neubauer, Glen. "Abortion Policy in the Post-WEBSTER Age." *Publius* 20 (Summer 1990): 27–44.

Handler, Joel F. *Social Movements and the Legal System: A Theory of Law Reform and Social Change.* New York: Academic Press, 1978.

Hannan, Michael T., and John Freeman. *Organizational Ecology.* Cambridge, MA: Harvard University Press, 1989.

Hansen, John Mark. *Gaining Access: Congress and the Farm Lobby, 1919–1981.* Chicago: University of Chicago Press, 1991.

Harper, Ida Husted, ed. *History of Woman Suffrage: Vol. 5. 1900–1920.* Salem, NH: Ayer, 1922a.

———. ed. *History of Woman Suffrage: Vol. 6. 1900–1920.* Salem, NH: Ayer, 1922b.

Harrington, Christine and Barbara Yngvesson. "Interpretive Sociolegal Research." *Law & Social Inquiry* 15 (1990): 135–48.

Harris Poll. "Public Ambivalent About Casino Gambling in General, but Opposed Allowing It in Nearest City." October 4, 1992.

Harry, Joseph, and William B. DeVall. *The Social Organization of Gay Males.* New York: Praeger, 1978.

Hartz, Louis. *The Liberal Tradition in America.* New York: Harcourt, Brace, 1955.

Heclo, Hugh. *Modern Social Politics in Britain and Sweden.* New Haven, CT: Yale University Press, 1972.

———. "Issue Networks and the Executive Establishment." *The New American Political System,* ed. Anthony King. Washington, D.C.: American Enterprise Institute, 1978.

Heinz, John P., Edward Laumann, Robert L. Nelson, and Robert H. Salisbury. *The Hollow Core: Private Interests in National Policy Making.* Cambridge, MA: Harvard University Press, 1993.

Hempel, Carl G. *Aspects of Scientific Explanation and Other Essays in the Philosophy of Science.* New York: Free Press, 1965.

Herring, E. Pendleton. *Group Representation Before Congress.* Baltimore: Johns Hopkins University Press, 1929.

Hertzberg, Hazel. "Reaganomics on the Reservations." *New Republic,* November 22, 1982: 15–17.

Hertzke, Allen D. *Echoes of Discontent.* Washington, D.C.: CQ Press, 1993.

Hilgartner, Stephen, and Charles Bosk. "The Rise and Fall of Social Problems." *American Journal of Sociology* 94 (1988): 53–78.

Himmelstein, Jerome. *To the Right: The Transformation of American Conservatism.* Berkeley: University of California Press, 1990.

Hipsher, Patricia. "Is Movement Demobilization Good for Democratization? Some Evidence from the Shantytown Dwellers' Movement in Chile." *Politics and Society* (Spring 1996).

Hlaing, Kyaw Yin. "The Mobilization Process in the Four Eights Democratic Movement in Burma." Paper presented at the Annual Meetings of the Asian Studies Association in Honolulu, Hawaii, April 1996.

Hobsbawm, Eric. "Should Poor People Organize." In *Workers: Worlds of Labor,* ed. E. Hobsbawm, 282–96. New York: Pantheon, 1984.

Hofer, Bruno. "Die Volksinitiative als Verhandlungspfand." *Schweizerisches Jahrbuch für Politische Wissenschaft* 27 (1987): 207–36.

Holsworth, Robert D. *Let Your Life Speak: A Study of Politics, Religion and Antinuclear Weapons Activism.* Madison: University of Wisconsin Press, 1989.

Hunt, Alan. "Rights and Social Movements: Counter-Hegemonic Strategies." *Law and Society* 17:3 (1990): 309–328.

Hunter, Floyd. *Community Power Structure.* Chapel Hill: University of North Carolina Press, 1953.

Hunter, James Davison. *Culture Wars.* New York: Basic Books, 1991.

Hunter, Nan, Sherryl E. Michaelson, and Thomas B. Stoddard. *The Rights of Lesbians and Gay Men*, 3d ed. Carbondale: Southern Illinois University Press, 1993.

Imig, Douglas R. *Poverty and Power: The Political Representation of Poor Americans.* Lincoln: University of Nebraska, 1996.

———. "Resource Mobilization and Survival Tactics of Poverty Advocacy Groups." *Western Political Quarterly.* 2 (1992): 501–20.

Imig, Douglas R., and Sidney Tarrow. "The Europeanization of Movements? Contentious Politics and the European Union, October 1983–March 1995," Working Paper #96.3. Institute for European Studies, Cornell University, Ithaca, NY, 1995.

Inglehart, Ronald. *The Silent Revolution.* Princeton, NJ: Princeton University Press, 1977.

———. *Culture Shift in Advanced Industrial Societies.* Princeton, NJ: Princeton University Press, 1990.

Iyengar, Shanto. *Is Anyone Responsible? How Television Frames Political Issues.* Chicago: University of Chicago Press, 1991.

Jaimes, M. Annette. "Federal Indian Identification Policy." In *The State of Native America*, ed. M. Annette Jaimes. Boston: South End Press, 1992.

Janda, Kenneth, Christine Edens, and Patricia Goff. "Why Parties Change: Some New Evidence Using Party Manifestos." Paper presented at the XII World Congress of Sociology, Bielfeld, Germany, 1994.

Jeffery-Poulter, Stephen. *Peers, Queers and Commons: The Struggle for Gay Law Reform from 1950 to the Present.* New York: Routledge, 1991.

Jencks, Christopher. *The Homeless.* Cambridge, MA: Harvard University Press, 1995.

Jenkins, J. Craig. "The Transformation of a Constituency into a Movement." In *The Social Movements of the 1960s and 1970s*, ed. J. Freeman. New York: Longman, 1982.

———. "Resource Mobilization Theory and the Study of Social Movements." *Annual Review of Sociology* 10 (1983): 527–53.

———. "Social Movements, Political Representation, and the State." In *The Politics of Social Protest*, ed. J. Craig Jenkins and Bert Klandermans, 14–35. Minneapolis: University of Minnesota Press, 1995.

———. "Channeling Social Protest: Foundation Patronage of Contemporary Social Movements." In *Private Action and the Public Good*, ed. Walter Powell and Elisabeth Clemens. New Haven, CT: Yale University Press, 1995.

Jenkins, Craig, and Craig Eckert. "Insurgency of the Powerless: Farm Worker Movements, 1946–1972." *American Sociological Review* 42 (1977): 249–68.

———. "Channeling Black Insurgency: Elite Patronage and Professional Social Movement Organizations in the Development of the Black Movement." *American Sociological Review* 51 (1986): 812–29.

Jenkins, J. Craig, and Bert Klandermans, ed. *The Politics of Social Protest: Comparative Perspectives on States and Social Movements.* Minneapolis: University of Minnesota Press, 1995.

———. "The Politics of Social Protest." In *The Politics of Social Protest: Comparative Perspectives on States and Social Movements,* ed. Craig Jenkins and Bert Klandermans, 3–13. Minneapolis: University of Minnesota Press, 1995.

Jenkins, J. Craig, and Charles Perrow. "Insurgency of the Powerless." *American Sociological Review* 42: 249–68.

Jennings, James. *Understanding the Nature of Poverty in Urban America.* Westport, CT: Praeger, 1994.

Jewell, Malcolm E., and David M. Olson. *Political Parties and Elections in American States,* rev. ed. Homewood, IL: Dorsey, 1982.

———. *Political Parties and Elections in American States,* 3d ed. Chicago: Dorsey, 1988.

Johnson, Dirk. "Raid on Indian Casino Inflames Issue of Self-Rule." *New York Times,* May 17, 1992, 18L.

Johnson, George. "New Mexico's Indian Tribes Vow to Defy Move to Close Casinos." December 21, 1995, A18.

Johnson, Paul E. *A Shopkeeper's Millennium: Society and Revivals in Rochester, New York, 1815–1837.* New York: Hill & Wang, 1978.

Jones, Bryan D. *Reconceiving Decision-Making in Democratic Politics.* Chicago: University of Chicago Press, 1994.

Joppke, Christian. *Mobilizing against Nuclear Energy: A Comparison of West Germany and the United States.* Berkeley: University of California Press, 1993.

Kairys, David. "Freedom of Speech." In *The Politics of Law: A Progressive Critique,* 2d ed., ed. David Kairys, 237–72. New York: Pantheon, 1990.

Kammer, Jerry. *The Second Walk: The Navajo-Hopi Land Dispute.* Albuquerque: University of New Mexico Press, 1980.

Katz, Jonathan Ned. *Gay American History.* New York: Crowell, 1992.

Katz, Michael. *The Undeserving Poor: From the War on Poverty to the War on Welfare.* New York: Pantheon, 1989.

Katzenstein, Mary Fainsod, and Carol McClurg Mueller, eds. *The Women's Movements of the United States and Western Europe: Conciousness, Political Opportunity, and Public Policy.* Philadelphia: Temple University Press, 1987.

Katznelson, Ira. *City Trenches: Urban Politics and the Patterning of Class in the United States.* New York: Pantheon, 1981.

Katznelson, Ira, and Aristide R. Zolberg, ed. *Working Class Formation: Nineteenth-Century Patterns in Western Europe and the United States.* Princeton, NJ: Princeton University Press, 1986.

Keech, William R., Robert H. Bates, and Peter Lang. "Political Economy within Nations." In *Political Science: Looking to the Future; Comparative Politics, Policy, and International Relations,* ed. William Crotty. Vol. 2, 219–63. Evanston, IL: Northwestern University Press, 1991.

Kellstedt, Lyman A., John C. Green, James L. Guth, and Corwin E. Smidt. "Religious

Voting Blocs in the 1992 Election: The Year of the Evangelical?" *Sociology of Religion* 55 (1994): 307–26.

Keniston, Ellen, and Kenneth Keniston. "An American Anachronism: The Image of Women and Work." *American Scholar* 33 (1964): 355–75.

Kerr, Henry. "The Swiss Party System: Steadfast and Changing." In *Party Systems in Denmark, Austria, Switzerland, the Netherlands and Belgium*, ed. Hans Daalder. New York: St. Martin's Press, 1987.

Kessler, Brad. "The Homeless Movement: After Charity, Start Organizing." *The Nation*, 16 (1988): 528–30.

Kimmel, Michael S. *Revolution: A Sociological Interpretation*. Philadelphia: Temple University Press, 1990.

King, Wayne. "Trump in Federal Lawsuit, Seeks to Block Indian Casinos." *New York Times*, May 4, 1993: B6.

Kingdon, John W. *Agendas, Alternatives, and Public Policies*. Boston: Little, Brown, 1984.

Kitschelt, Herbert P. "Political Opportunity Structures and Political Protest: Anti-Nuclear Movements in Four Democracies." *British Journal of Political Science* 16 (1986): 57–85.

Klandermans, Bert. "The Social Construction of Protest and Multiorganizational Fields." In *Frontiers in Social Movement Theory*, ed. Aldon D. Morris and Carol M. Mueller, 77–103. New Haven, CT: Yale University Press, 1992.

———. *The Social Psychology of Protest*. Oxford: Blackwell, 1997.

Klandermans, Bert, Hanspeter Kriesi, and Sidney Tarrow, ed. *From Structure to Action: Comparing Social Movement Research Across Cultures. International Social Movement Research I*. Greenwich, CT: JAI, 1988.

Kluger, Richard. *Simple Justice: The History of Brown v. Board of Education and Black America's Struggle for Equality*. New York: Vintage, 1975.

Koopmans, Ruud. "The Dynamics of Protest Waves: Germany, 1965–1989." *American Sociological Review* 58 (1993): 637–58.

Kosmin, Barry A., and Seymour P. Lachman. *One Nation under God*. New York: Harmony, 1993.

Kraditor, Aileen S. *The Ideas of the Woman Suffrage Movement: 1890–1920*. New York: Norton, 1981.

Krehbiel, Kenneth. *Information and Legislative Organization*. Ann Arbor: University of Michigan Press, 1991.

Kriesi, Hanspeter. "The Political Opportunity Structure of the Dutch Peace Movement." In *West European Politics* 12 (1990): 295–312.

———. "The Political Opportunity Structure of New Social Movements: Its Impact on Their Mobilization." In *The Politics of Social Protest*, ed. J. Craig Jenkins and Bert Klandermans, 167–198. Minneapolis: University of Minnesota Press, 1995.

Kriesi, Hanspeter, Ruud Koopmans, Jan Willem Duyvendak, and Marco G. Giugni. "New Social Movements and Political Opportunities in Western Europe." *European Journal of Political Research* 22 (1992): 219–44.

———. *New Social Movements in Western Europe: A Comparative Analysis*. Minneapolis: University of Minnesota Press, 1995.

Ladd, Everett Carll. *America at the Polls 1994*. Storrs, CT: Roper Center for Public Opinion Research, 1995.

Lawson, Kay. "Questions Raised by Recent Attempts at Local Party Reform." In *Machine Politics, Sound Bites and Nostalgia,* ed. Michael Margolis and John C. Green, 38–45. Lanham, MD: University Press of America, 1993.

Layman, Geoffrey C. "The 'Culture Wars' in the States: Religious Polarization Among State Party Elites and State Electorates." Paper presented at the annual meeting of the American Political Science Association, Chicago, 1996.

Layton, Azza Salama. "The International Context of the U.S. Civil Rights Movement: The Dynamics between Racial Policies and International Politics, 1941–1960." Ph.D. diss., University of Texas, Austin, 1995.

Lee, Eugene C. "California." In *Referendums,* ed. David Butler and Austin Ranney, 81–122. Washington D.C.: American Enterprise Institute, 1978.

Levi, Margaret. *Of Rule and Revenue.* Berkeley: University of California Press, 1988.

———. *Contingencies of Consent.* Cambridge: Cambridge University Press, 1997.

Lichbach, Mark Irving. "An Economic Theory of Governability: Choosing Policy and Optimizing Performance." *Public Choice* 44 (1984): 307–37.

———. "Deterrence or Escalation? The Puzzle of Aggregate Studies of Repression and Dissent." *Journal of Conflict Resolution* 31 (1987): 266–97.

———. "An Evaluation of 'Does Economic Inequality Breed Political Conflict Studies.' " *World Politics* 41 (1989): 431–70.

———. "Will Rational People Rebel against Inequality? Samson's Choice." *American Journal of Political Science* 34 (1990): 1049–76.

———. "Nobody Cites Nobody Else: Mathematical Models of Domestic Political Conflict." *Defense Economics* 3 (1992): 341–57.

———. "Rethinking Rationality and Rebellion: Theories of Collective Action and Problems of Collective Dissent." *Rationality and Society* 6 (1994a): 8–39.

———. "What Makes Rational Peasants Revolutionary? Dilemma, Paradox and Irony in Peasant Collective Action." *World Politics* 46 (1994b): 382–417.

———. *The Rebel's Dilemma.* Ann Arbor: University of Michigan Press, 1995.

———. *The Cooperator's Dilemma.* Ann Arbor: University of Michigan Press, 1996.

———. "Social Theory and Comparative Politics." In *Comparative Politics: Rationality, Culture, and Structure,* ed. Mark I. Lichbach and Alan S. Zuckerman. Cambridge: Cambridge University Press, 1997.

Lichbach, Mark, and Adam Seligman. "Theories of Revolution and the Structure-Action Problem in the Social Sciences." Unpublished manuscript, University of Colorado at Boulder, 1996.

Lienesch, Michael. "Right-Wing Religion: Christian Conservatism as a Political Movement." *Political Science Quarterly* 97 (1982):403–25.

Lindblom, Charles E. *Politics and Markets.* New York: Basic Books, 1977.

Linder, Wolf. *Politische Entscheidung und Gesetzesvollzug in der Schweiz.* Bern: Haupt, 1987.

Lipset, S. M. *The First New Nation.* New York: Norton, 1979.

———. "Party Coalitions and the 1980 Election." In *Party Coalitions in the 1980s,* ed. Seymour Martin Lipset, 15–46. San Francisco: Institute for Contemporary Studies, 1981.

———. *American Exceptionalism: A Double-Edged Sword.* New York: Norton, 1996.

Lipset, Seymour Martin, and Earl Raab. *The Politics of Unreason,* 2d ed. New York: Harper & Row, 1978.

Lipsky, Michael. *Protest in City Politics*. Chicago: Rand McNally, 1970.

Lofland, John. *Protest: Studies of Collective Behavior and Social Movements*. New Brunswick, NJ: Transaction, 1985.

——. *Polite Protesters: The American Peace Movement of the 1980s*. Syracuse, NY: Syracuse University Press, 1993.

Lohmann, Susanne. "A Signaling Model of Informative and Manipulative Political Action." *American Political Science Review* 87 (1993): 319–33.

Lowi, Theodore J. "Toward Functionalism in Political Science: The Case of Innovation in Party Systems." *American Political Science Review* 57 (1963): 570–83.

——. *The End of Liberalism*. New York: Norton, 1969.

——. *The Politics of Disorder*. New York: Basic Books, 1971.

——. *The End of Liberalism: The Second Republic of the United States*. New York: Norton, 1979.

Luker, Kristin. *Abortion and the Politics of Motherhood*. Berkeley: University of California Press, 1984.

——. *Taking Chances: Abortion and the Decision Not to Contracept*. Berkeley: University of California Press, 1975.

MacIntyre, Alasdair. *After Virtue*, 2d ed. Notre Dame, IN: University of Notre Dame Press, 1984.

Magleby, David B. "Taking the Initiative: Direct Legislation and Direct Democracy in the 1980s." *PS* 21 (1988): 600–11.

Maguire, Diarmuid. "Opposition Movements and Opposition Parties: Equal Partners or Dependent Relations in the Struggle for Power and Reform?" In *The Politics of Social Protest*, ed. J. Craig Jenkins and Bert Klandermans, 199–228. Minneapolis: University of Minnesota Press, 1995.

Maier, Pauline. *From Resistance to Rebellion: Colonial Radicals and the Development of American Opposition to Britain, 1765–1776*. New York: Knopf, 1972.

Maisel, L. Sandy. "The Platform-Writing Process: Candidate-Centered Platforms in 1992." *Political Science Quarterly* 108 (1993): 671–98.

Mann, Michael. *The Sources of Social Power*, vol. 1. Cambridge: Cambridge University Press, 1986.

Marks, Gary, and Doug McAdam. "Social Movements and the Changing Structure of Political Opportunity in the European Union." *West European Politics* 19 (1996): 249–78.

Martin, E. *The Woman in the Body: A Cultural Analysis of Reproduction*. Boston: Beacon, 1987.

Marx, Gary and James Wood. "Strands of Theory and Research in Collective Behavior." *Annual Review of Sociology* 1 (1975): 363–428.

Mascarenas, Oneida S. "Indigenous Movement Behavior: The Rise and Expansion of the Native American Movement." Ph.D. diss., University of Colorado, Boulder 1991.

Maslow, Abraham. "A Theory of Human Motivation." *Psychological Review* 50 (1943): 370–39.

Mayhew, David R. *Placing Parties in American Politics*. Princeton, NJ: Princeton University Press, 1986.

McAdam, Doug. *Political Process and the Development of Black Insurgency, 1930–1970*. Chicago: University of Chicago Press, 1982.

———. "Tactical Innovation and the Pace of Insurgency." In *American Sociological Review* 48 (1983):735–54.

———. " 'Initiator' and 'Spin-Off' Movements: Diffusion Processes in Protest Cycles." Paper presented at the Conference on Cross-National Movement Diffusion, Vevey, Switzerland, June 1995.

———. "Conceptual Origins, Current Problems, Future Direction." In *Comparative Perspectives on Social Movements*, ed. Doug McAdam, John McCarthy, and Mayer Zald, 23–40. London: Cambridge University Press, 1996.

McAdam, Doug, John D. McCarthy, and Mayer Zald. "Social Movements." In *Handbook of Sociology*, ed. Neil Smelser, 695–737. Beverly Hills, CA: Sage, 1988.

———. "Introduction: Opportunities, Mobilizing Structures, and Framing Processes— Toward a Synthetic, Comparative Perspective on Social Movements." In *Comparative Perspectives on Social Movements: Political Opportunities, Mobilizing Structures, and Cultural Framings*, ed. Doug McAdam, John D. McCarthy, and Mayer N. Zald, 1–20. Cambridge: Cambridge University Press, 1996.

———. *Comparative Perspectives on Social Movements. Political Opportunities, Mobilizing Structures, and Cultural Framings*. New York: Cambridge University Press, 1996.

McAdam, Doug, and Dieter Rucht. "The Cross-National Diffusion of Movement Ideas." In *Annals of the American Academy of Political and Social Science* 528 (1993): 56–74.

McAdam, Doug, Sidney Tarrow, and Charles Tilly. "To Map Contentious Politics." *Mobilization* 1 (1996): 17–34.

———. "Toward an Integrated Perspective on Social Movements and Revolutions." In *Comparative Politics: Rationality, Culture, and Structure*, ed. Mark Lichbach and Alan Zuckerman, 142–73. New York: Cambridge University Press, 1997.

McCann, Michael W. *Taking Reform Seriously: Perspectives on Public Interest Liberalism.* Ithaca, NY: Cornell University Press, 1986.

———. *Rights at Work: Pay Equity Reform and the Politics of Legal Mobilization.* Chicago: University of Chicago Press, 1994.

McCann, Michael W., and Helena Silverstein. "The 'Lure of Litigation' and Other Myths about Cause Lawyers." In *The Politics and Practice of Cause Lawyering*, ed. Austin Sarat and Stuart Scheingold. New York: Oxford University Press, 1997.

McCarthy, John, Clark McPhail, and Jackie Smith. "Images of Protest: Dimensions of Selection Bias in Media Coverage of Washington Demonstrations 1982 and 1991." In *American Sociological Review* 6 (1996): 478–99.

McCarthy, John D., and Mayer N. Zald. *The Trend of Social Movements in America: Professionalization and Resource Mobilization.* Morristown, NJ: General Learning Press, 1973.

———. "Resource Mobilization and Social Movements: A Partial Theory." *American Journal of Sociology* 82 (1977): 1212–41.

McCulloch, Anne Merline. "The Politics of Indian Gaming: Tribe/State Relations and American Federalism." *Publius* 24 (Summer 1994): 99–112.

McCullough, David. *Truman.* New York: Simon & Schuster, 1992.

McDonagh, Eileen L. *Breaking the Abortion Deadlock: From Choice to Consent.* New York: Oxford University Press, 1996.

McFarland, Andrew S. "Interest Groups and Theories of Power in America." *British Journal of Political Science* 17 (1987): 257–84.

———. "Interest Groups and Political Time: Cycles in America." *British Journal of Political Science* 21 (1991): 257–84.

———. "Interest Groups and the Policymaking Process: Sources of Countervailing Power in America." In *The Politics of Interests*, ed. Mark P. Petracca, 58–79. Boulder, CO: Westview, 1992.

McGlen, Nancy, and Karen O'Connor. *Women's Rights.* New York: Praeger, 1983.

Melnick, R. Shep. *Regulation and the Courts: The Case of Clean Air.* Washington D.C.: Brookings, 1983.

———. *Between the Lines: Interpreting Welfare Rights.* Washington, D.C.: Brookings, 1994.

Mendel-Reyes, Meta. *Reclaiming Democracy: The Sixties in Politics and Memory.* New York: Routledge, 1995.

Merry, Sally Engle. "Concepts of Law and Justice among Working-Class Americans: Ideology as Culture." *Legal Studies Forum* 9 (1985): 59–69.

———. *Getting Justice and Getting Even: Legal Consciousness among Working Class Americans.* Chicago: University of Chicago Press, 1990.

Meyer, David. "Protest Cycles and Political Process: American Peace Movements in the Nuclear Age." *Political Research Quarterly* 47 (1993): 451–79.

———. "How the Cold War Was Really Won: A View From Below." Paper prepared for presentation at the International Studies Association annual meeting, Vancouver, British Columbia, 1991.

———. "Policy Reform and Political Protest: The Paradox of Open Windows." Paper presented at the annual meetings of the Eastern Sociological Society, Philadelphia, 1995.

Meyer, David S., and Douglas Imig. "Political Opportunity and the Rise and Decline of Interest Group Sectors." *Social Science Journal* 30 (1993): 253–70.

Meyer, David, and Sidney Tarrow, eds. *The Social Movement Society.* Boulder, CO: Rowman & Littlefield, 1998.

Mills, C. Wright. *The Power Elite.* New York: Oxford University Press, 1956.

Mishler, William, and Reginald S. Sheehan. "The Supreme Court as a Countermajoritarian Institution? The Impact of Public Opinion on Supreme Court Decisions." *American Political Science Review* 87 (1993): 87–101.

The Moccasin Telegraph. "The Definition of Indians." 1 (April 1996): 11, 16.

Moen, Matthew C. "The Evolving Politics of the Christian Right." In *PS* 29 (1996): 461–4.

Mohr, J. C. *Abortion in America: The Origins and Evolution of National Policy.* New York: Oxford University Press, 1978.

Moore, John. "When It Comes to Congress, Why Gamble?" *National Journal*, June 24, 1995, n. 25.

Moore, R. Laurence. *Selling God: American Religion in the Marketplace of Culture.* New York: Oxford University Press, 1994.

Moore, Will H. "Rational Rebels: Overcoming the Free-Rider Problem." *Political Research Quarterly* 48 (1995): 417–54.

Morehouse, Sarah. *State Politics, Parties, and Policy.* New York: Holt, Rinehart & Winston, 1981.

Morris, Aldon. *The Origins of the Civil Rights Movement.* New York: The Free Press, 1984.

———. "Black Southern Student Sit-in Movement: An Analysis of Internal Organization." *American Sociological Review* 46 (1981): 755–67.

Morris, Aldon D., and Cedric Herring. "Theory and Research in Social Movements: A Critical Review." In *Annual Review of Political Behavior,* ed. Samuel Long, vol. 2, 137–98. Boulder, CO: Westview, 1988.

Moser, Christian. "Erfolge Kantonaler Volksinitiativen Nach Formalen und Inhaltlichen Gesichtspunkten." *Schweizerisches Jahrbuch für Politische Wissenschaft* 27 (1987): 159–188.

Mouriaux, René, and Françoise Subileau. "Les Grèves Françaises de l'Automne 1995: Défense des Acquis ou Mouvement Social." *Modern and Contemporary France* NS3 (1996): 299–306.

Moynihan, Daniel Patrick. *Maximum Feasible Misunderstanding.* New York: Free Press, 1969.

Moynihan, Ruth Barnes. *Rebel for Rights: Abigail Scott Duniway.* New Haven, CT: Yale University Press, 1983.

Muller, Edward N. *Aggressive Political Participation.* Princeton, NJ: Princeton University Press, 1979.

Muller, Edward N., Henry A. Dietz, and Steven E. Finkel. "Discontent and the Expected Utility of Rebellion: The Case of Peru." *American Political Science Review* 85 (1991): 1261–82.

Muller, Edward N., and Karl-Dieter Opp. "Rational Choice and Rebellious Collective Action." *American Political Science Review* 80 (1986): 471–87.

Murray, Stephen O. "Components of Gay Community in San Francisco." In *Gay Culture in America,* ed. Gilbert Herdt. Boston: Beacon, 1992.

Myrdal, Gunner. "America Again at the Crossroads." In *Roots of Rebellion: The Evolution of Black Politics and Protest Since World War II,* ed. Richard P. Young, 13–46. New York: Harper & Row, 1970.

Nagel, Joane. "The Political Mobilization of Native Americans." *Social Science Journal* 19 (1982): 37–45.

National Indian Gaming Association. *Annual Report,* 1995.

———. *Speaking the Truth.* Pamphlet, 1995.

Niebuhr, Gustav. "The Religious Right, Finding Victory in Defeat." *The Washington Post National Weekly Edition,* November 16–22, 1992: 14.

Niebuhr, Gustav. "Dole Gets Christian Coalition's Trust and Prodding." *New York Times,* September 16, 1996, A1, 3.

Neustadtl, Alan. "Interest-Group PACsmanship: An Analysis of Campaign Contributions, Issue Visibility, and Legislative Impact." *Social Forces* 69 (1990): 549–64.

Nsiah-Jefferson, Laurie. "Reproductive Laws, Women of Color, and Low-Income Women." In *Reproductive Laws for the 1990s,* ed., Nadine Taub and Sherrill Cohen, 23–67. Clifton, NJ: Humana, 1989.

Oakley, Ann. "From Walking Wombs to Test-Tube Babies." In *Reproductive Technologies: Gender, Motherhood, and Medicine,* ed. Michelle Stanworth, 36–56. Minneapolis: University of Minnesota Press, 1987.

Oberschall, Anthony. *Social Conflict and Social Movements.* Upper Saddle River, NJ: Prentice Hall, 1973.

————. "Opportunities and Framing in the Eastern European Revolts of 1989." In *Comparative Perspectives on Social Movements,* ed. Doug McAdam, John McCarthy, and Mayer Zald, 93–121. London: Cambridge University Press, 1996.

O'Brien, Sharon. *American Indian Tribal Governments.* Norman: University of Oklahoma Press, 1989.

O'Connor, Karen. *Women's Organizations' Use of the Courts.* Lexington, MA: Lexington Books, 1980.

————. *No Neutral Ground? Abortion Politics in an Age of Absolutes.* Boulder, CO: Westview, 1996.

O'Connor, Karen, and Lee Epstein. "Court Rules and Workload: A Case Study of Rules Governing Amicus Curiae Participation." *Justice System Journal* 8 (1983): 35–45.

————. "The Role of Interest Groups in Supreme Court Policy Formation." In *Public Policy Formation,* ed. Robert Eyestone, 63–81. Greenwich, CT: JAI, 1984.

Offe, Claus. "New Social Movements: Challenging Boundaries of Institutional Politics." *Social Research* 52 (1985): 817–68.

Oldfield, Duane M. *The Right and the Righteous.* Lanham, MD: Rowman & Littlefield, 1996.

Oliver, Pamela E., and Gerald Marwell. "Mobilizing Technologies for Collective Action." In *Frontiers in Social Movement Theory,* ed. Aldon D. Morris and Carol M. Mueller, 251–72. New Haven, CT: Yale University Press, 1992.

Olson, David. "City Council Unanimously Votes for Hate Crimes Bill." *Windy City Times,* December 27, 1990, 1, 5.

Olson, Mancur, Jr. *The Logic of Collective Action: Public Goods and the Theory of Groups.* Cambridge, MA: Harvard University Press, 1965.

Olson, Susan M. *Clients and Lawyers: Securing the Rights of Disabled Persons.* Westport, CT: Greenwood, 1984.

Page, Benjamin I., and Robert Y. Shapiro. *The Rational Public.* Chicago: University of Chicago Press, 1992.

Parsa, Misagh. *Social Origins of the Iranian Revolution.* New Brunswick, NJ: Rutgers University Press, 1989.

————. "States, Entrepreneurs and Revolution: A Comparative Analysis of Iran, Nicaragua and, the Philippines." Paper prepared for the Conference on Structure, Identity, and Action in Honor of Charles Tilly, Amsterdam, June 2–4, 1995.

Pasquaretta, Paul. "On the 'Indianness' of Bingo: Gambling and the Native American Community." *Critical Inquiry* 20 (1994): 694–714.

Pelletier, Réjean. "Are Political Parties in Decline? A Comparison of Political Parties and the New Social Movements from a Standpoint of Materialist and Postmaterialist Values." Paper presented at the Conference on Political Parties in the Year 2000, Manchester, England, 1995.

People for the American Way. Press release, November 7, 1994.

Persinos, John F. "Has the Christian Right Taken Over the Republican Party?" In *Campaigns and Elections* 15 (1994): 20–24.

Petchesky, Rosalind Pollack. *Abortion and Woman's Choice: The State, Sexuality, and Reproductive Freedom.* New York: Longman, 1984. [Rev. ed. published by Northeastern University Press, 1990.]

————. "Fetal Images: The Power of Visual Culture in the Politics of Reproduction."

In *Reproductive Technologies: Gender, Motherhood, and Medicine*, ed. Michelle Stanworth, 57–80. Minneapolis: University of Minnesota Press, 1987.

Petrocik, John R., and Frederick T. Steeper. "The Political Landscape in 1988." *Public Opinion* 10 (1987): 41–44.

Pfeffer, Jeffrey, and Gerald R. Salancik. *The External Control of Organizations: A Resource-Dependence Perspective*. New York: Harper & Row, 1978.

Phillips, Kevin. *The Politics of the Rich and Poor*. New York: Random House, 1990.

Pichardo, Nelson A. "Resource Mobilization: An Analysis of Conflicting Theoretical Variations." *Sociological Quarterly* 29 (1988): 97–110.

Pick, Grant. "Gays and Lesbians in Chicago: Into the Mainstream." *Chicago Tribune*, February 7 (1993): 14–16, 18.

Piven, Frances F., and Richard A. Cloward. *Poor People's Movements: Why They Succeed, How They Fail*. New York: Vintage, 1977.

———. "Normalizing Collective Protest." In *Frontiers in Social Movement Theory*, ed. Aldon M. Morris and Carol M. Mueller, 301–25. New Haven, CT: Yale University Press, 1992.

Ploski, Harry A., and Warren Marr II, eds. *The Afro American*. New York: Bellweather, 1976.

Polsby, Nelson W. *Community Power and Political Theory*. New Haven, CT: Yale University Press, 1963.

———. *Consequences of Party Reform*. New York: Oxford University Press, 1983.

Pomper, Gerald M. "The Presidential Election." In *The Election of 1996*, ed. Gerald M. Pomper. Chatham, NJ: Chatham House.

Price, Charles M. "The Initiative: A Comparative State Analysis and Reassessment of a Western Phenomenon." *Western Political Quarterly* 28 (1975): 243–62.

Przeworski, Adam, and Michael Wallerstein. "The Structure of Class Conflict in Democrataic Capitalist Societies." *American Political Science Review* 76 (1982): 215–38.

Putnam, Robert. "Diplomacy and Domestic Politics: The Logic of Two Level Games." *International Organization* 42 (1988): 427–60.

Quinn, Bernard, Herman Anderson, Martin Bradley, Paul Goetting, and Peggy Shriver. *Churches and Church Membership in the United States 1980*. Atlanta: Glenmary Research Center, 1982.

Ragin, Charles C. *The Comparative Method: Moving beyond Qualitative and Quantitative Strategies*. Berkeley: University of California Press, 1987.

Ranney, Austin. "The United States of America." In *Referendums: A Comparative Study of Practice and Theory*, ed. David Butler and Austin Ranney, 67–86. Washington D.C.: American Enterprise Institute, 1978.

Reiter, Howard L. "The Rise of the 'New Agenda' and the Decline of Partisanship." *West European Politics* 16 (1993): 89–104.

Riker, William H. *Liberalism against Populism: A Confrontation between the Theory of Democracy and the Theory of Social Choice*. San Francisco: Freeman, 1982.

———. *The Art of Political Manipulation*. New Haven, CT: Yale University Press, 1986.

Rochon, Thomas R. *Mobilizing for Peace: The Antinuclear Movements in Western Europe*. Princeton, NJ: Princeton University Press, 1988.

———. "The West European Peace Movement and the Theory of New Social Movements." In *Challenging the Political Order*, ed. Russell J. Dalton and Manfred Küchler, 105–121. New York: Oxford University Press, 1990.

Rogers, M. "Instrumental and Infrastructural Resources." *American Journal of Sociology* 79 (1974): 1418–33.

Rogowski, Ronald. *Commerce and Coalitions: How Trade Affects Domestic Political Alignments*. Princeton, NJ: Princeton University Press, 1989.

Rorty, Richard. *Contingency, Irony, and Solidarity*. Cambridge: Cambridge University Press, 1989.

Rose, Nelson I. "The Rise and Fall of the Third Wave: Gambling Will Be Outlawed in Forty Years." In *Gambling and Public Policy: International Perspectives*, ed. William R. Easington and Judy A. Cornelius. Reno: Institute for the Study of Gambling and Commercial Gaming, University of Nevada, 1991.

Rosenberg, Gerald. *The Hollow Hope: Can Courts Bring about Social Change?* Chicago: University of Chicago Press, 1991.

Rosenstone, Stephen J., and John Mark Hansen. *Mobilization, Participation, and Democracy in America*. New York: Macmillan, 1993.

Rosenthal, Rob. *Homeless in Paradise: A Map of the Terrain*. Philadelphia: Temple University Press, 1994.

Rossi, Alice. "Equality between the Sexes: An Immodest Proposal." *Daedalus* 93 (1964): 607–52.

Rossi, Peter H. *Down and Out in America: The Origins of Homelessness*. Chicago: University of Chicago Press, 1989.

Rothman, Barbara Katz. *The Tentative Pregnancy: Prenatal Diagnosis and the Future of Motherhood*. New York: Viking, 1986.

Rozell, Mark, and Clyde Wilcox, eds. *The Christian Right in the 1994 Elections: Reports from the Grassroots*. Lanham, MD: Rowman & Littlefield, 1995.

———. "The Past as Prologue: The Christian Right in the 1996 Elections." In *God at the Grass Roots: The Christian Right in the 1994 Elections*, ed. Mark J. Rozell and Clyde Wilcox, 253–263. Lanham, MA: Rowman & Littlefield, 1995.

———. *Second Coming: The New Christian Right in Virginia Politics*. Baltimore: Johns Hopkins University Press, 1996.

Rubenstein, William B., ed. *Lesbians, Gay Men and the Law*. New York: New Press, 1993.

Rubin, Alissa. "Interest Groups and Abortion Politics in the Post-Webster Era." In *Interest Group Politics*, 3d ed., ed. Allan J. Cigler and Burdett A. Loomis, 239–255. Washington, D.C.: Congressional Quarterly Press, 1991.

Rubin, Eva R. *Abortion, Politics and the Courts:* Roe v. Wade *and Its Aftermath*, rev. ed. New York: Greenwood, 1987.

Rucht, Dieter. "Campaigns, Skirmishes, and Battles: Anti-Nuclear Movements in the USA, France, and West Germany." *Industrial Crisis Quarterly* 4 (1990): 193–222.

———. *Modernisierung und Neue Soziale Bewegungen: Deutschland, Frankreich und USA im Vergleich*. Frankfurt: Campus, 1994.

———. "The Impact of National Contexts on Social Movement Structures: A Cross-movement and Cross-national Comparison." In *Comparative Perspectives on Social Movements,* ed. Doug McAdam, John McCarthy, and Mayer Zald, 185–204. London: Cambridge University Press, 1996.

Ruckstuhl, Lotti. *Frauen Sprengen Fesseln, Hindernislauf zum Frauenstimmrecht in der Schweiz.* Bonstetten: Interfeminas Verlag, 1986.

Russel, Ina, ed. *Jeb and Dash: A Diary of Gay Life 1918–1945.* Boston: Faber & Faber, 1993.

Salisbury, Robert. "An Exchange Theory of Interest Groups." *Midwest Journal of Political Science* 13 (1969): 1–32.

———. "Political Movements in American Politics: An Essay on Concept and Analysis." In *New Perspectives in American Politics,* ed. Lucius Barker. New Brunswick, NJ: Transaction, 1989.

Samuels, Suzanne U. "The U.S. Supreme Court and Abortion Politics: An Examination of the Amicus Briefs Filed in the Abortion Cases." Paper presented at the Midwest Political Science Convention, Chicago, 1996.

Sarat, Austin. "Abortion and the Courts: Uncertain Boundaries of Law and Politics." In *American Politics and Public Policy,* ed. Allan P. Sindler, 113–153. Washington, D.C.: Congressional Quarterly Press, 1982.

———. "Legal Effectiveness and Social Studies of Law." *Legal Studies Forum* 9 (1985): 23–31.

——— " '. . . The Law Is All Over': Power, Resistance and the Legal Consciousness of the Welfare Poor." *Yale Journal of Law and the Humanities* 2 (1990): 343–79.

Savage, David G. "States Rights Gamble." *ABA Journal* 81 (1995): 42.

Sawyers, Traci M., and David S. Meyer. "Missed Opportunities: Social Movement Abeyance and Public Policy." Paper presented at the 1994 Midwest Political Science Association annual meetings, Chicago, 1993.

Sax, Joseph L. *Defending the Environment: A Strategy for Citizen Action.* New York: Knopf, 1971.

Scales, Ann. "Dole Woos Christian Coalition at Forum." *Boston Globe,* September 15, 1996.

Schama, Simon. *Citizens.* New York: Knopf, 1989.

Schattsneider, E. E. *The Semi-Sovereign People: A Realist's View of Democracy.* New York: Holt, Rinehart & Winston, 1960.

Scheingold, Stuart A. *The Politics of Rights: Lawyers, Public Policy, and Political Change.* New Haven, CT: Yale University Press, 1974.

———. "Constitutional Rights and Social Change." In *Judging the Constitution,* ed. Michael W. McCann and Gerald L. Houseman, 73–91. Glenview, IL: Scott, Foresman/Little, Brown, 1989.

Schlesinger, Arthur F., Jr. *The Cycles of American History.* Boston: Houghton Mifflin, 1986.

Schlozman, Kay Lehman, and John T. Tierney. *Organized Interests and American Democracy.* New York: Harper & Row, 1986.

Schmidt, David D. *Citizen Lawmakers: The Ballot Initiative Revolution.* Philadelphia: Temple University Press, 1989.

Schmitt, Eric. "Clinton Aides Study Indirect End to Military Ban on Homosexuals." *New York Times,* January 13, 1993, A1, 2.

Schmitt, Richard. *Beyond Separateness: The Social Nature of Human Beings—Their Autonomy, Knowledge, and Power.* Boulder, CO: Westview, 1995.

Schneider, Elizabeth M. "The Dialectic of Rights and Politics: Perspectives from the Women's Movement." *New York University Law Review* 61 (1986): 589–652.

Schwartz, Mildred A. *The Party Network*. Madison: University of Wisconsin Press, 1990.

———. "Penetrating the Democratic and Republican Parties: Entry from the Extremes." Paper presented at Conference on Party Politics in the Year 2000, Manchester, England, 1995.

Scott, James C. "Exploitation in Rural Class Relations." *Comparative Politics* 7 (1975): 489–532.

Sernett, Milton C. "Widening the Circle: The Pro-life Appeal to the Abolitionist Legacy." In *When Life and Choice Collide: Essays on Rhetoric and Abortion*, ed. David Mall, 159–187. Libertyville, IL: Kairos, 1994.

Sewell, William H., Jr. *Work and Revolution in France. The Language of Labor from the Old Regime to 1848*. New York: Cambridge University Press, 1980.

———. "Artisans, Factory Workers, and the Formation of the French Working Class." In *Working-class Formation: Nineteenth-Century Patterns in Western Europe and the United States,* ed. Ira Katznelson and Aristide R. Zolberg, 45–70. Princeton, NJ: Princeton University Press, 1986.

Sharp, Gene. *The Politics of Nonviolent Action*. Boston: Sargent, 1973.

Shinn, Marybeth, and Colleen Gillespie. "The Roles of Housing and Poverty in the Origins of Homelessness." *American Behavioral Scientist* 37 (1994): 505–21.

Silverstein, Helen. *Unleashing Rights: Law, Meaning, and the Animal Rights Movement*. Ann Arbor: University of Michigan Press, 1996.

Skocpol, Theda. *States and Social Revolutions: A Comparative Analysis of France, Russia and China*. Cambridge: Cambridge University Press, 1979.

———. "Rentier State and Shi'a Islam in the Iranian Revolution." *Theory and Society* 11 (1982): 265–83.

———. *Protecting Soldiers and Mothers: The Political Origins of Social Policy in the United States*. Cambridge, MA: Harvard University Press, 1992.

———. Contribution to "The Role of Theory in Comparative Politics: A Symposium." *World Politics* 48 (1995): 37–46.

Skowronek, Stephen. *Building a New American State*. Cambridge: Cambridge University Press, 1982.

———. *The Politics Presidents Make*. Cambridge, MA: The Belknap Press of Harvard University Press, 1993.

Smelser, Neil J. *Theory of Collective Behavior*. New York: Free Press, 1962.

Smith, Christian. *The Emergence of Liberation Theology: Radical Religion and Social Movement Activism*. Chicago: University of Chicago Press, 1991.

———. *Resisting Reagan: The U.S. Central American Peace Movement*. Chicago: University of Chicago Press, 1996.

——— ed. *Disruptive Religion: The Force of Faith in Social Movement Activism*. New York: Routledge, 1996.

Snow, David A., and Leon Anderson. *Down on Their Luck: A Study of Homeless Street People*. Berkeley: University of California Press, 1993.

Snow, David A., and Robert D. Benford. "Ideology, Frame Resonance, and Participant Mobilization." In *From Structure to Action: Comparing Movement Participation across Cultures*, ed. P. G. Klandermans, H. Kriesi, and S. Tarrow. Greenwich, CT: JAI, 1988.

Snow, David A., Robert D. Benford, and Leon Anderson. "Fieldwork Roles and Informational Yield: A Comparison of Alternative Settings and Roles." *Urban Life* 15 (1986): 377–408.

Snow, David. A., E. B. Rochford, Jr., S. K. Worden, and R. Benford. "Frame Alignment Processes, Micromobilization, and Movement Participation." *American Sociological Review* 51 (1986): 464–81.

Songer, Donald R., and Reginald S. Sheehan. "Interest Group Success in the Courts: Amicus Participation in the Supreme Court." *Political Research Quarterly* 46 (1993): 339–54.

Sousa, David. "Union Decline and American Politics." Paper presented at the American Political Science Convention, Washington, D.C., 1993.

Staggenborg, Suzanne. *The Pro-Choice Movement: Organization and Activism in the Abortion Conflict.* New York: Oxford University Press, 1991.

Stapler, Martha, ed. *The Woman Suffrage Year Book, 1917.* New York: National Woman Suffrage Publishing, 1917.

Starr, Paul. *The Social Transformation of American Medicine.* New York: Basic Books, 1982.

Stimson, James A., Michael B. MacKuen, and Robert S. Erikson. "Dynamic Representation." *American Political Science Review* 89 (1995): 543–65.

Stinchcomb, Arthur. "Social Structure and Social Organizations." In *Handbook of Organizations,* ed. James March, 142–193. Chicago: Rand McNally, 1965.

Stone, Deborah. "Causal Stories and the Formation of Policy Agendas." *Political Science Quarterly* 104 (1989): 281–300.

Stout, Harry S. *The Divine Dramatist: George Whitefield and the Rise of Modern Evangelicalism.* Grand Rapids, MI: Ecrdmans, 1991.

Sullivan, Patricia A., and Steven R. Goldzwig. "Abortion and Undue Burdens: Justice Sandra Day O'Connor and Judicial Decision-Making." *Women & Politics* 16(3) (1996): 27–54.

Szymanski, Ann-Marie. "Think Locally, Act Gradually: Political Strategy and the American Prohibition Movement in the Nineteenth and Twentieth Centuries." Ph.D. diss., Cornell University, Ithaca, NY, 1996.

Tarrow, Sidney. *Struggling to Reform: Social Movements and Policy Change During Cycles of Protest.* Occasional Paper 15, Center for International Studies, Cornell University, Ithaca, NY, 1983.

———. "National Politics and Collective Action: Recent Theory and Research in Western Europe and the United States." *Annual Review of Sociology* 14 (1988): 421–40.

———. *Struggle, Politics, and Reform: Collective Action, Social Movements, and Cycles of Protest.* Western Societies Program, Occasional Paper 21, Ithaca, NY, Cornell University, 1989.

———. *Democracy and Disorder: Protest and Politics in Italy, 1965–1975.* New York: Oxford University Press, 1989.

———. " 'Aiming at a Moving Target': Social Science and the Recent Rebellions in Eastern Europe." *PS: Political Science and Politics* 24 (1991): 12–20.

———. *Power in Movement: Social Movements, Collective Action and Politics.* New York: Cambridge University Press, 1994.

———. "Linking Politics and Collective Action." Paper presented at the annual meeting of the American Sociological Association, Washington, D.C., 1995.

———. "States and Opportunities." In *Comparative Perspectives on Social Movements: Political Opportunities, Mobilizing Structures, and Cultural Framings,* ed. Doug McAdam, John McCarthy, and Mayer N. Zald, 41–61. New York: Cambridge University Press, 1996.

———. "Social Movements in Contentious Politics: A Review Article." *American Political Science Review* 90 (1996): 874–83.

Tatalovich, Raymond, and Byron W. Daynes. *The Politics of Abortion: A Study of Community Conflict in Public Policy-Making.* New York: Praeger, 1981.

Taylor, Verta. "Social Movement Continuity: The Women's Movement in Abeyance." *American Sociological Review* 54 (1989): 761–75.

Taylor, Verta, and Nancy E. Whittier. "Collective Identity in Social Movement Communities: Lesbian Feminist Mobilization." In *Frontiers in Social Movement Theory,* ed. Aldon D. Morris and Carol McClurg Mueller, 104–129. New Haven, CT: Yale University Press, 1992.

Thompson, E. P. *Whigs and Hunters: The Origin of the Black Act.* New York: Pantheon, 1975.

Tilly, Charles. "Review of *Why Men Rebel.*" *Journal of Social History* 4 (1971): 416–20.

———. *From Mobilization to Revolution.* Reading, MA: Addison-Wesley, 1978.

———. "Social Movements and National Politics." In *Statemaking and Social Movements,* ed. Charles Bright and Susan Harding, 297–317. Ann Arbor: University of Michigan Press, 1984.

———. *The Contentious French.* Cambridge, MA: Harvard University Press, 1986.

———. *Popular Contention in Great Britain, 1758–1834.* Cambridge, MA: Harvard University Press, 1995.

———. "To Explain Political Processes." *American Journal of Sociology* 100 (1995): 1594–1610.

Tocqueville, Alexis de. *Democracy in America,* trans. Henry Reve, ed. Phillips Brady. 2 vols. New York: Vintage, 1954.

———. *The Old Regime and the French Revolution,* trans. Stuart Gilbert. Garden City, NJ: Doubleday, 1955.

———. *Journey to America,* ed. J. P. Mayer, trans. George Lawrence. New Haven, CT: Yale University Press, 1960.

———. *Recollections: The French Revolution of 1848.* New Brunswick, NJ: Transaction, 1992.

Tomlins, Christopher L. *The State and the Unions: Labor Relations, Law, and the Organized Labor Movement in America, 1880–1960.* New York: Cambridge University Press, 1985.

Torricelli, Robert and Daniel Inouye. "Is the Indian Gaming Regulatory Act (IGRA) Unfair to the States?" *CQ Researcher* 18 (March 1994): 257.

Tribe, Laurence H. *Abortion: The Clash of Absolutes.* New York: Norton, 1990.

Truman, David B. *The Governmental Process.* New York: Knopf, 1951.

Tullock, Gordon. "The Paradox of Revolution." *Public Choice* 11 (1971): 89–99.

Tushnet, Mark. *The NAACP's Legal Strategy against Segregated Education, 1925–1952.* Chapel Hill: University of North Carolina Press, 1987.

U.S. Statutes at Large. Washington, D.C.: Government Printing Office, 1899–1994.

Usher, Douglas. "Republican Rules and Religious Right Takeovers: A Study of GOP Convention Delegate Selection Rules and Outcomes, 1984–1992." Paper presented at the Annual Meeting of the Midwest Political Science Association, 1995.

Vig, Norman, and Michael E. Kraft. *Environmental Policy in the 1990s.* Washington, D.C.: Congressional Quarterly Press, 1990.

Vose, Clement E. *Caucasians Only: The Supreme Court, the NAACP, and the Restrictive Covenant Cases.* Berkeley: University of California Press, 1959.

Wagner, David. *Checkerboard Square: Culture and Resistance in a Homeless Community.* Boulder, CO: Westview, 1993.

Wald, Kenneth D., James W. Button, and Barbara A. Rienzo. "The Politics of Gay Rights in American Communities." *American Journal of Political Science* 40 (1996): 1152–78.

Walker, Jack L. "The Origin and Maintenance of Interest Groups in America." *American Political Science Review* 72 (1983): 390–406.

———. *Mobilizing Interest Groups in America: Patrons, Professions, and Social Movements.* Ann Arbor: University of Michigan Press, 1991.

Walker, Samuel. *In Defense of American Liberties: A History of the ACLU.* New York: Oxford University Press, 1990.

Walters, Ronald G. *The Antislavery Appeal: American Abolitionism after 1830.* Baltimore, MD: Johns Hopkins University Press, 1976.

Wang, Fu-chang. *The Unexpected Resurgence: Ethnic Assimilation and Competition in Taiwan.* Ph.D. diss., University of Arizona, Tucson, 1989.

Wapner, Paul. "Politics beyond the State: Environmental Activism and World Civic Politics." In *World Politics* 47 (1995): 311–40.

Warren, John. "An Analysis of the Indian Bill of Rights." *Montana Law Review* 33 (1972): 255–265.

Wattenberg, Martin. *The Rise of Candidate-Centered Politics.* Cambridge, MA: Harvard University Press, 1991.

Wattleton, Faye. "A Champion for Choice: Adapted from *Life on the Line.*" *MS* 7 (1996): 45–53.

Weatherford, Jack. *Indian Givers.* New York: Ballantine, 1988.

Weber, Max. [1924]. *Economy and Society.* 2 vols. Berkeley: University of California Press, 1968.

———. [1903–17]. *The Methodology of the Social Sciences*, trans. and ed. Edward A. Shils and Henry A. Finch. New York: Free Press, 1949.

Webster v. Reproductive Health Services. 57 L.W. 5023, June 27, 1989.

Westin, Alan Furman. "The Supreme Court, the Populist Movement, and the Campaign of 1896." *Journal of Politics* 15 (1953): 3–41.

Weyler, Rex. *Blood of the Land.* New York: Vintage, 1984.

Wilcox, Clyde. *God's Warriors.* Baltimore, MD: Johns Hopkins University Press, 1992.

———. "Premillennialists at the Millennium: Some Reflections on the Christian Right in the Twenty-first Century." *Sociology of Religion* 55 (1994): 243–62.

Wilcox, Clyde, John C. Green, and Mark Rozell. "Faith, Hope, and Conflict: The Christian Right in State Republican Politics." Presented at the annual meeting of the American Sociological Association, Washington, D.C., 1995.

Wilkenson, Charles. *American Indians, Time, and the Law: Native Societies in a Modern Constitutional Democracy.* New Haven, CT: Yale University Press.

Wilentz, Sean. *Chants Democratic: New York City and the Rise of the American Working Class, 1788–1850*. New York: Oxford University Press, 1984.

Willke, John C. "The Battleground of Semantics." In *When Life and Choice Collide: Essays on Rhetoric and Abortion*, ed. David Mall, 321–331. Libertyville, IL: Kairos, 1994.

Wilson, Frank L. "Neo-Corporatism and the Rise of New Social Movements." *In Challenging the Political Order: New Social and Political Movements in Western Democracies*, ed. Russel J. Dalton and Manfred Küchler, 67–83. Cambridge: Cambridge Policy Press, 1990.

Wilson, Graham K. *Interest Groups*. Oxford: Blackwell, 1990.

Wilson, James Q. *The Politics of Regulation*. New York: Basic Books, 1980.

Wisler, Dominique, Jose Barranco, and Marco Tackenberg. "Police, Mass Demonstrations and Politics." Paper prepared for presentation at the Second European Conference on Social Movements, Vittoria, Spain, October 1996.

Wolfinger, Raymond E. "Reputation and Reality in the Study of 'Community Power.' " *American Sociological Review* 25 (1960): 636–44.

Woliver, Laura R. "Review Essay: The Equal Rights Amendment and the Limits of Liberal Legal Reform." *Polity* 21 (1988): 183–200.

———. "The Deflective Power of Reproductive Technologies: The Impact on Women." *Women and Politics* 9 (1989a): 17–47.

———. "New Reproductive Technologies: Challenges to Women's Control of Gestation and Birth." In *Biomedical Technology and Public Policy*, ed. Robert Blank and Miriam K. Mills, 43–56. Westport, CT: Greenwood, 1989b.

———. "Reproductive Technologies and Surrogacy: Policy Concerns for Women." *Politics and the Life Sciences* 8 (February 1990): 185–193.

———. "The Influence of Technology on the Politics of Motherhood: An Overview of the United States." *Women's Studies International Forum* 14 (1991a): 479–490.

———. "Lobbying the Supreme Court: Coalitions of Abortion Interests and the *Webster* Decision." Paper presented at the Southern Political Science Convention, Tampa, FL, 1991b.

———. "Rhetoric and Symbols in the Pro-Life Amicus Briefs to the *Webster* Case." Paper presented at the 1992 American Political Science Convention, Chicago, September 3–6, 1992a.

———. "Symbols and Rhetoric in the Pro-Choice Amicus Briefs to the *Webster* Case." Paper presented at the 1992 Southern Political Science Convention, Atlanta, GA, November 5–7, 1992b.

———. *From Outrage to Action: The Politics of Grass-Roots Dissent*. Urbana: University of Illinois Press, 1993.

———. "Reproductive Technologies, Surrogacy Arrangements, and the Politics of Motherhood." In *Mothers in Law: Feminist Theory and the Legal Regulation of Motherhood*, ed. Martha Albertson Fineman and Isabel Karpin, 346–359. New York: Columbia University Press, 1995.

———. "National Right to Life Committee." In *U.S. Women's Interest Groups: Institutional Profiles*, ed. Sarah Slavin, 417–421. Westport, CT: Greenwood, 1995.

———. "Rhetoric and Symbols in American Abortion Politics." In *Abortion Politics: Public Policy in Cross Cultural Perspective*, ed. Dorothy McBride Stetson and Marianne Githens, 5–28. New York: Routledge, 1996.

Woliver, Laura R., and Tracy McDonald. "Amicus Curiae Rhetoric in Abortion Litigation." Paper presented at the 1993 South Carolina Political Science Convention, Presbyterian College, Clinton, SC, 1993.

Wotherspoon, Garry. *City of the Plain: History of a Gay Sub-Culture.* Sydney: Hale & Iremonger, 1991.

Wright, Gerald C., Robert S. Erikson, and John P. McIver. "The Impact of State Party Elite Ideology." *American Review of Politics* 15 (1994): 305–27.

Wright, James D. *Address Unknown: The Homeless in America.* New York: Aldine de Gruyter, 1989.

Wright, Talmadge. "Tranquility City: Self-Organization, Protest, and Collective Gains within a Chicago Homeless Encampment. In *Marginal Spaces*, ed. Michael Peter Smith, 37–68. New Brunswick, NJ: Transaction, 1995.

Yishai, Yael. "Interest Parties: The Thin Line Between Groups and Parties in the Israeli Electoral Process." In *How Political Parties Work: Perspectives from Within*, ed. Kay Lawson, 197–225. Westport, CT: Praeger, 1994.

Yonish, Steven. "Local Parties and Interest Groups: Group Representation at National Convention." Paper presented at the annual meeting of the American Political Science Association, New York, 1994.

Yoshihashi, Pauline. "As Indian Casinos Spread, Politicians and Rivals Maneuver to Right the Trend." *Wall Street Journal*, May 4, 1993, B1, B5.

Young, John. *Post-Environmentalism.* London: Belhaven, 1990.

Zald, Mayer. "Looking Backward and Forward: Reflections on the Past and Future of the Resource Mobilization Program." In *Frontiers in Social Movement Theory*, ed. Aldon D. Morris and Carol M. Mueller, 326–348. New Haven, CT: Yale University Press, 1992.

Zdravomyslova, Elena. "Opportunities and Framing in the Transition to Democracy: The Case of Russia." In *Comparative Perspectives on Social Movements*, ed. Doug McAdam, John McCarthy, and Mayer Zald, 122–137. London: Cambridge University Press, 1996.

Zurcher, Louis A. and David A. Snow. "Collective Behavior: Social Movements." In *Social Psychology: Sociological Perspectives*, ed. Morris Rosenberg and Ralph H. Turner, 447–482. New York: Basic Books, 1981.

Index

abolitionism, 26, 29–30. *See also* slavery
abortion, 4, 19; education of judges re, 242–43;
    effect on medical practices, 241; effect on
    women, 243, 244–45; federal funding for, 234,
    235, 242, 245; language and issue framing,
    236–42, 245–46; law and jurisprudence re,
    233–34, 236, 245, 246; litigation's effect on,
    210; medical technology and, 237, 238, 239,
    241; Republican party stance on, 150, 154,
    156, 235, 242; self-defense and, 245; social
    context of, 238–44. *See also* pro-choice move-
    ment; pro-life movement
Abortion Information Exchange, 235
access to institutions, 62, 212–13, 218; Congress,
    172; environmentalists, 193; international in-
    fluences on, 259; local, 65, 67, 71; political
    parties, 125–30; relationship to protest levels,
    161; restriction of, 166–67; traditional chan-
    nels for, 104–5; woman suffrage activists, 99
action, collective. *See* collective action; interest
    groups; social movements
activism, 3; amount of, 24; professionalization of,
    59, 66
activists: ideological, 137; as legal actors, 203;
    number of, 124, 130, 132; sources of, 141
Adams, John Quincy, 16, 186
advocacy: coalitions, 190, 196, 197; focus shifts
    in, 166; protection of, 209
affirmative action, 206, 211, 213
agenda formation, 8, 10–12, 59, 67, 71, 162, 209,
    286; education and, 108; environmental issues,
    185; through initiatives, 103, 105, 108; wom-
    en's movement, 173. *See also* issues
Agricultural Adjustment Act of 1938, 189
AIM. *See* American Indian Movement
Aldrich, John H., 46, 48, 49, 150
Alliance of the Streets, 88, 92
American Indian Movement (AIM), 219–20
American Indians. *See* Native Americans
amicus curiae (friend of the court) briefs, 4, 233–
    44, 246, 287
Aminzade, Ronald, 46
Anderson, Leon, 79
animal rights movement, 204, 206, 209

anti-abortion movement. *See* pro-life movement
anti-Catholicism, 21, 25, 27, 38n16
antinuclear movements, 161
arbitration, 213
association: forms of, 30; private, 22; social move-
    ment building through, 30, 32
Association of Community Organizations for Re-
    form Now, 167
autonomy, 22; in decision making, 207–8; local,
    24; political parties, 126, 128

Babbitt, Bruce, 223
Bachrach, Peter, 8
backlash, 211, 277, 280
Baer, Denise, 133
Banaszak, Lee Ann, 3, 286
Baratz, Morton, 8
Barber, Benjamin, 198
Bayh, Birch, 142
Beck, Paul Allen, 46, 54
behavior, 33
belief systems, 274
benefactor relationships, 92–94, 95
Bensel, Richard, 36n2, 37n12
Berry, Jeffrey, 3, 286
Berube, Allan, 60
BIA. *See* Bureau of Indian Affairs
Birnbaum, Pierre, 37n6
birth control, 241
Bork, Robert, 235
Bositis, David, 133
Bowers v. Hardwick, 62
Bridges, Amy, 25
Brockett, Charles, 253
Brown v. Board of Education, 205, 210, 264
Bureau of Indian Affairs (BIA), 227
Burma, 257, 258, 259
Burnham, Walter Dean, 155
Burstein, Paul, 2
Bush, George, 67, 145, 154, 237
business coalitions, 9, 10
business interests, 13, 139, 143; interaction with
    federal government, 224–27; party platform
    fights, 147
Byrne, Jane, 64

About the Editors

Anne N. Costain is Professor of Political Science, Director of the Keller Center for Study of the First Amendment, and Associate Dean for the Social Sciences at the University of Colorado, Boulder. Her research areas include: the politics of social movements and interest groups, gender politics, and civil rights and liberties. She is author of *Inviting Women's Rebellion: A Political Process Interpretation of the Women's Movement* (Johns Hopkins University Press, 1992).

Andrew S. McFarland is Professor and Acting Head of the Political Science Department of the University of Illinois at Chicago. His major research interests are interest groups, social movements, and American public policy. Among his publications are *Common Cause: Lobbying in the Public Interest* (Chatham House, 1984) and *Cooperative Pluralism: The National Coal Policy Experiment* (University of Kansas, 1993).

About the Contributors

Lee Ann Banaszak is Associate Professor of Political Science at the Pennsylvania State University. She is the author of *Why Movements Succeed or Fail: Opportunity, Culture and the Struggle for Woman Suffrage* (Princeton University Press, 1996), and has written articles on women's movements and attitudes toward feminism in the United States and Western Europe.

Jeffrey M. Berry is Professor of Political Science at Tufts University. His books include *The Rebirth of Urban Democracy* (co-author, Brookings, 1993) and *The Interest Group Society* (Longman, 1997).

Paul Burstein is Professor of Sociology and Adjunct Professor of Political Science at the University of Washington. He is the author of *Discrimination, Jobs, and Politics* (University of Chicago Press, reissued, Spring, 1998). His current work focuses on how public policy is affected by the interplay among public opinion, interest organizations, and political parties.

W. Douglas Costain is Senior Instructor in Political Science at the University of Colorado, Boulder. His research and publications focus on lobbying, interest groups and the environmental movement.

Daniel M. Cress is Assistant Professor in the Department of Sociology at the University of Colorado at Boulder. His research examines political action by marginalized groups. He has published work on protest by homeless people in the U.S. and is currently engaged in a historical study of Native American political action and a contemporary study of student rioting behavior.

Claude Dufour is a lecturer in the Political Science Department at the University of Illinois at Chicago. His doctoral dissertation, now being revised for publication, compares gay political movements in local politics in Australia, Canada, and the United States. He is also a specialist in Canadian politics.

John C. Green is the director of the Ray C. Bliss Institute and Professor of Political Science at the University of Akron. He has written extensively on religion and politics; he is co-author of *The Bully Pulpit: The Politics of*

Protestant Clergy (University of Kansas, 1997) and *Religion and the Culture Wars* (Rowman and Littlefield, 1996).

James Guth is professor of Political Science at Furman University. He is the co-author of *The Bully Pulpit: The Politics of Protestant Clergy* (University Press of Kansas, 1997) and *Religion and the Culture Wars* (Rowman and Littlefield, 1996).

Douglas Imig is an Associate Professor of Public Administration at UNLV and a Research Fellow at the Program on Nonviolent Sanctions and Cultural Survival at Harvard University. His work concerns social movement and public interest group responses to shifting national and international political opportunity structures. He is author of *Poverty and Power: The Political Representation of Poor Americans* (University of Nebraska Press, 1996).

James P. Lester is Professor of Political Science at Colorado State University and Director of The Policy Studies Institute. His books include: *Public Policy: An Evolutionary Approach* (West/Wadsworth, 1996), which he co-authored, and *Environmental Politics and Policy: Theories and Evidence* (Duke University Press, 1995), which he edited. His research interests include American politics and public policy (with a focus on U.S. environmental and space policies).

Mark Irving Lichbach is Professor of Political Science and Chair of the department at the University of Colorado, Boulder. A theorist and a comparativist, his published books include *The Rebel's Dilemma* (University of Michigan, 1995) and *The Cooperator's Dilemma* (University of Michigan, 1996).

Doug McAdam is Professor of Sociology at the University of Arizona and the author of numerous books and articles on the relationship between social movements and institutionalized politics, especially in the American context. His books include: *Political Process and the Development of Black Insurgency, 1930–1970* (University of Chicago Press, 1982) and, with John McCarthy and Mayer Zald, *Social Movements in Comparative Perspective* (Cambridge University Press, 1996).

Michael McCann is Professor of Political Science at the University of Washington. He is author of several books, including *Rights at Work: Pay Equity Reform and the Politics of Legal Mobilization* (Chicago: 1994), and numerous articles on law and social reform, the politics of rights, cause lawyering, judicial impact, legal culture, and issues related to civil liberties.

His most recent research concerns media coverage of civil litigation and the politics of tort reform in the United States.

Oneida Meranto is Assistant Professor in the Department of Political Science at Metropolitan State College. Her research interests include social movements and the politics of Native American and indigenous peoples.

Deborah Schildkraut is a doctoral candidate in Political Science at Princeton University, where she specializes in American politics.

David A. Snow is Professor in the Department of Sociology at the University of Arizona. His books include: *Down on Their Luck: A Study of Homeless Street People* (University of California Press, 1993), *Broadening Perspectives on Homelessness* (Sage, 1994) and *Social Movements: Readings on Their Emergence, Mobilization, and Dynamics* (Roxbury, 1997), which he co-edited.

Sidney Tarrow is Maxwell Upson Professor of Government at Cornell, where he teaches comparative politics and social movements. Author of *Peasant Communism in Southern Italy* and *Democracy and Disorder: Protest and Politics in Italy, 1965–1975* (Oxford University Press, 1989), he has recently completed a new edition of his *Power in Movement: Social Movements and Contentious Politics* (Cambridge University Press, 1998) and edited (with David Meyer) *Towards a Movement Society?* for Rowman and Littlefield, 1998.

Clyde Wilcox is professor of government at Georgetown University. He is the author of *Onward Christian Soldiers: The Christian Right in American Politics* (Westview, 1996), coauthor of *Second Coming: The New Christian Right in Virginia Politics* (Johns Hopkins University Press, 1996), and coeditor of *God at the Grassroots 1996: The Christian Right in the 1996 Elections* (Rowman and Littlefield, 1997). His other research areas are gender politics and campaign finance.

Laura R. Woliver is an associate professor of political science at the University of South Carolina in Columbia. She is the author of *From Outrage to Action: The Politics of Grass-Roots Dissent* (University of Illinois Press, 1993), and numerous articles and book chapters dealing with women's rights, civil rights, grass-roots dissent, and reproductive politics.